On the Genre and Message of Revelation:
Star Visions and Sky Journeys

ON THE GENRE AND MESSAGE OF REVELATION

Star Visions and Sky Journeys

BRUCE J. MALINA

Copyright © 1995 by Hendrickson Publishers, Inc.
P. O. Box 3473
Peabody, Massachusetts 01961–3473
All rights reserved
Printed in the United States of America

ISBN 1–56563–040–8

First Printing — August 1995

Library of Congress Cataloging-in-Publication Data

Malina, Bruce J.
    On the genre and message of Revelation : star visions and sky
journeys / Bruce J. Malina.
    Includes bibliographical references and indexes.
    ISBN 1–56563–040–8
    1. Bible. N.T. Revelation—Criticism, interpretation, etc.
    2. Stars—Observations. 3. Bible and astrology. I. Title.
    BS2825.2.M36   1995
    228'.06—dc20   95-6226
                                                                 CIP

Selections from *The Old Testament Pseudepigrapha* by James H. Charlesworth. Copyright (c) 1983, 1985, by James H. Charlesworth. Used by
permission of Doubleday, a division of Bantam Doubleday Dell Pub-
lishing Group, Inc.

Selections from *The Greek Magical Papyri In Translation Including
Demonic Spells* by Hans Dieter Betz (ed.). Copyright (c) 1986. Used by
permission of the University of Chicago Press.

Selections from *The Loeb Classical Library*, reprinted by permission of
the publishers, Harvard University Press.

Except for the author's translation of the book of Revelation, the Scripture quotations in this publication are from the Revised Standard Version of the Bible, copyrighted 1946, 1952, © 1971, 1973 by the Division
of Christian Education of the National Council of the Churches of
Christ in the USA, and are used by permission.

Figure 2, pages 86–87, the zodiac's movement across the sky, appears
courtesy of the Biblical Archaeology Society and is used with permission.

For My Wife
Diane Jacobs Malina

TABLE OF CONTENTS

LIST OF FIGURES AND IMAGES

PREFACE

___

This book is intended to be an introductory guide through the biblical book of Revelation, also known as the Apocalypse. Nearly ten years ago I began a study that compared the ways in which people perceived time in peasant and industrial societies. The purpose of that study was to develop a model for what people said about time in the Mediterranean world of the New Testament period as compared with how Americans deal with time (see Malina 1989). Among other things, I found it truly surprising that people in peasant societies were unconcerned with the future. Ordinary peasants were totally focused on the present, and if the present proved difficult, they harkened back to the past to find solutions to their problems. Elite peasants used stories of past events and of illustrious ancestors to guide their present concerns. Peasants simply did not bother with what might possibly occur or with what human beings could think of as possibly happening. Such possibility based conception of what might be is what we call "the future." Peasants were rather exclusively concerned with probabilities rooted in the actual present, with what might better be called "the forthcoming." In other words, the peasants' "future" was a "forthcoming" rooted in some present condition. For example a pregnant mother looked forward to her coming baby; the baby was forthcoming. A farmer whose wheat was bearding looked forward to the harvest; the harvest was forthcoming. In such processes, the forthcoming is not some abstract future, but some process rooted in the present and soon to be realized. The forthcoming was organically bound up with the present. Even for us, once a football game begins with the kick-off, we can expect a last quarter and the end of the game. Or once a symphony begins, we hear the various movements unfold up to the grand finale. We would not think of dropping the second and third quarters of a football game to save time; nor would we drop several symphonic movements so as to get done sooner. The forthcoming has to do with the soon-to-be-realized phases of a process that unfolds in due course, once set under way.

The point is that peasants were not at all concerned with the future the way we who live in an industrialized, abstract, clock-oriented world are. If this is so, then perhaps the persons who populate the pages of the New Testament were not concerned about the future at all. Perhaps they had no eschatology (concern about the end of things); perhaps they never were apocalyptically minded (expecting a cosmic cataclysm soon). It was with doubts about what my professional colleagues had to say about the future orientation of the Book of Revelation that I began to consider that book. If that book derived from the first-century Mediterranean, one would have to presume that it dealt with its author's present, with a look to the past (not the future) to explain the present.

This present volume, then, considers Revelation as a document in which a Christian prophet deals with his present and looks to the past to clarify the present situation of the Christians he addresses. The perspective adopted in the writing of this book is a historical one. Specifically, it seeks to contribute to answering the question: what did the original author say and mean to his original audience in the first-century Mediterranean? It is not directly concerned with the author's ideas apart from their cultural context (history of ideas analysis), nor with how the author said what he said (aesthetic or literary analysis), nor with the literary sources presumably used by the author (source analysis), nor with how the book might be appropriated by modern Christians (hermeneutics). Surely all these other concerns merit attention, and I recommend modern commentaries to those readers who would like to learn more about them. Rather, in this book I will focus on the meaning of what the author told his audience that he saw and heard. Surely most modern biblical scholars do have something to say about this sort of historical information in Revelation. Then what is distinctive about this book?

Consider the following instance. Most modern Christians know the medieval conception of Christian living as a very temporary arrangement in "this vale of tears," through which we pass as exiles, as aliens and strangers, on our way to our true home in heaven. Of course this way of conceiving Christian life has its New Testament roots in Ephesians (2:19) and 1 Peter (1:1; 2:11) where Christians are in fact called sojourners, strangers, exiles, and the like. Now in a very perceptive book about early Christians in Asia Minor, John H. Elliott asks his readers to take 1 Peter's references to Christians as "exiles and aliens" (1:1; 2:11) quite literally. The result is a new point of view with a new perception and a new vision of actually displaced and homeless persons. Elliott rightly suggests that the author of 1 Peter was writing to a group of Christians who were in fact resident aliens, much like those foreigners in our midst who lack the "green" (actually red, white and blue) card issued by the Immigration and Naturalization Service. What happens if we, with Elliott, take these designations as factual — that the problem of the recipients of 1 Peter was that they had to live like resident aliens, outside their own ethnic lands. What meanings does the letter now bear (see Elliott 1981; 1991)?

I wish to do much the same with the book of Revelation as Elliott has done with 1 Peter. In Revelation, I will take Babylon, "the Great Harlot," to mean Babylon (not Rome or Washington or any other place). And I will take "the great city, called spiritually Sodom and Egypt, where too their Lord was crucified" to be Jerusalem (not Rome or Washington or any other place). The Pregnant Woman in the sky, like the Dragon and the Beasts, is a sky being, just as the author says it is. In other words, I will believe the author when he speaks of looking up into the sky, of seeing celestial visions, of mounting up into the sky; but I will also ask: what was there to see in the first-century sky? If one recalls high school or college biology and one's first view through a microscope, the focused blobs on the other end of the eyepiece were all but indecipherable. We needed the help of another person to show us what to see! The same holds for the sky. What persons taught us to view the sky? What was a first-century Mediterranean taught to see in the sky? What if one were taught that the lights in the sky were really living beings or marked off the area of living beings? What if one learned that comets, depending on their shape, were called: trumpets, bowls, horses, spears and the like? What if everybody knew that every comet's appearance meant bad news for the region over which it appeared? What if one were told that along with sunburn, one could be moonstruck because the beings on, in, or around the moon proved sometimes negative, sometimes positive?

Unlike most persons in industrialized society, the ancients could clearly see the sky in all its starry fullness. For them, the sky was an interactive part of their daily living. It offered direct indication of when the day began or ended, when to plant or harvest, when the new month and year began, and the like. Persons in the past identified the sky personages who exercised influences on the earth, either for good (Rev 1:20) or evil (e.g., moonstruck: Matt 4:24; 17:25; and Wormwood in Rev 8:11). God's sky servants, the angels, were part and parcel of the social environment. God's powerful and controlling sky wind, God's spirit, produced magnificent and significant effects on God's friends and enemies alike. And certain stars might exercise particular power over mortals on earth (such as Jesus the Morning Star in Rev 22:16).

Similarly, the time perspective in Revelation will be seen to be essentially about the past and the author's present. After all, God rules the world now, Jerusalem was about to be destroyed (perhaps even as the author wrote), the Dragon called Satan was thrown down from the sky before the Garden of Eden was set up, Babylon/Babel was destroyed in the past, and the descending Jerusalem is presently descending. Even the urgency that Jesus Messiah come soon is forthcoming rather than future. And he surely will come "on time," for in the Mediterranean world, significant people are never considered late. Rather, whenever they arrive is on time, and that is when things properly begin.

This book presents a tour through the Revelation of John to show and tell about the major concrete, actual items that the author was talking about. What did the scenes described by the author mean to his contemporaries? How would people imagine the development of those scenes? The purpose of this book is to return to that alien yet familiar first-century world depicted in the New Testament's final book. With our modern sense of history, we believe that things once were not the way they are today; hence things need not remain the way they are. Well, how exactly were things in the first-century Mediterranean world? What did people see in the sky?

The book develops a tour through Revelation as follows. After an introductory chapter essentially about how first-century persons assessed the sky, the second chapter considers how persons obtained revelations in the ancient Mediterranean, while the third chapter presents two tourist maps of the book of Revelation. The first map is a rather brief overview for orientation's sake, while the second is more fully developed; but both are basically to familiarize the reader with the book of Revelation. The subsequent chapters deal with touring through the five sectors of Revelation. Each chapter begins with John, the prophet, describing his experience (with a passage or segment of the text of Revelation), and then proceeds with explanations of what John has just said, most often by calling upon ancient Mediterranean informants who had similar experiences or noted similar things. The work concludes with a description of the problems of the seven churches of Asia Minor mentioned at the outset of Revelation and with some theological conclusions as well.

Before closing this preface, I should like to mention those who contributed to the book in so many ways. To these persons, I would now like to express my gratitude, notably the members of the international Context Group, Dr. Ernst J. Brehm of Omaha and my wife Diane Jacobs Malina. Special thanks to a number of colleagues around the world for their making library resources accessible to me: Prof. Dr. Marcello del Verme and the library of the University of Naples and the National Museum in Naples, Dr. Carlos Del Valle and the collections of the Consejo Superior de Investigacciones Cientificas in Madrid, Dr. Marianne Hovorka-Baumgart and Dr. Gerd Baumgart and University of Vienna, Prof. Dr. Halvor Moxnes and the University of Oslo, and especially Dr. K. C. Hanson of Claremont for a range of library resources and for closely reading the penultimate draft.

Bruce J. Malina

1

INTRODUCTION:
JOHN THE SEER, REVELATION, AND THE SKY

The present book is based upon the premise that the author of the book of Revelation, the prophet John, has his initial, ecstatic vision while considering the vault of the sky. His subsequent ecstatic visions take place after he mounts up into the sky, is displaced to an unnamed wilderness, or is transferred to an unnamed high mountain. As he considers the sky, he observes various phenomena and interacts with various sky entities. What he reports, then, derives from his perceptions of the vault of the sky and beyond. Modern historians ascribe the experience of John and other prophets like him to imagination (Collins 1984) or literary fiction (Boll 1914, Festugière 1950). Interpreters are often at pains to tell the modern reader to consider John's visions as symbolic and to translate those symbols into ideas in order to get to the message of the book:

> When the seer describes a vision, he translates into symbols the ideas suggested by God; he goes on then, by accumulating colors, symbolic numbers, etc., without giving a thought to the resulting plastic effect. His purpose is, above all, to translate the ideas received from God, not to describe a coherent vision, an *imaginable* vision. To follow him to the end on the way he has chosen, one must play his game and convert into ideas the symbols he describes without troubling oneself about their incoherence. Thus, it would be a mistake to try to represent visually the Lamb with seven horns and seven eyes (5:6); or the Beast with seven heads and ten horns (13:1), and to wonder how ten horns can be distributed among the seven heads; it would be an error to take offense at the complete lack of plastic effect of such descriptions. One must content oneself with an *intellectual* translation of the symbols without pausing upon their more or

less disconcerting peculiarities: the Lamb possesses knowledge and power
in fullness; the Beast represents the Roman Empire with its emperors (the
heads) and the vassal kings (the horns). If we do not take into account
these disconcerting forms of expression, it is impossible to understand
anything at all in the Apocalypse (Boismard 1965: 697).

While there is a good deal of symbolism in the book of Revelation, as
indeed there is in every New Testament book, I submit that this is not
the distinctive feature of this work. Further, nearly all commentators
spend endless pages making sure the author's presumed sources are
clearly spelled out, thus making the book of Revelation "little more
than a midrash of the Old Testament via the Apocrypha and Pseudepigrapha" (Moore 1982: 91; see e.g., Charles 1920; Ford 1975). All too
many authors concerned with the seer's presumed sources rely exclusively on Israelite literary sources, as though the author were an academic with the traditions of Israel solely on his mind.

In this work I suggest that John's visions derived from experiences
generally unavailable to human perception in a culture such as ours. In
other words, during the centuries before and after John of Patmos, a
number of persons reported a range of visions involving celestial entities and celestial phenomena, just as he did. Many report having ascended into the sky and having observed a range of events. I intend to
take these persons seriously, at their word, and interpret what they have
to say within the framework of their culture—not ours. Mainstream U.S.
culture frowns upon and even denies the human capacity for ecstasy and
experiences of alternate realities (see the anthropologist, Goodman
1988; 1990; and especially Pilch 1993). Pilch cites the work of Erika
Bourguignon, who compiled a sample of 488 societies in all parts of the
world, at various levels of technological complexity, and found that
ninety percent of these societies evidence "alternate states of consciousness." Her conclusion: "Societies which do not utilize these states
clearly are historical exceptions which need to be explained, rather than
the vast majority of societies that do use these states" (cited by Pilch
1993). Thus it would be quite anachronistic and ethnocentric to take our
post-Enlightenment, post-Industrial Revolution, technologically ob-
sessed society as normative for judging anyone other than ourselves.
Hence I presume that for most of the world, even today, a report of
alternate states of awareness would be quite normal. Therefore, John's
capacity for visions is not the distinctive feature of the work.

1.1. THE HELLENISTIC UNIVERSE

Even a perfunctory reading of Revelation shows that from beginning to end, from John's opening vision of someone who looks like a

man with seven stars in his right hand (1:13) to the final vision of a new Jerusalem coming down from the sky (21:9ff.), all that the prophet observes takes place in the sky or is viewed from the sky or as located in the sky. Since the prophet's attention is focused on and in the sky, and since he reports phenomena relating to the sky, what more obvious way to get to understand his work than to understand how the original audience of this book perceived the sky. What did first-century Mediterraneans expect to see in the sky? How did they envision the universe? And why should an Israelite prophet with allegiance to Jesus as the Messiah see what he did in the sky?

Modern readers might find it difficult to recapture the first-century sense of the sky. Most of us know that the ancient earth-centered perception of an encapsulating sky was displaced by a sun-centered conception of the world (16th–18th c.), which was, in turn, dissolved by a galaxy-centered point of view (18th–19th c.). This last model itself has given way to a non-centered sky system (20th c.; see Krafft 1990). Consequently, we must recover some adequate ancient model of an earth-centered total system of the universe to be considerate readers of Revelation.

To make matters worse, many historically minded Bible readers learned their first ancient model of the world and its cosmic appurtenances from the book of Genesis. In the model required to imagine the scenes in the ancient Israelite creation story, the earth was flat and stable, rooted in place by means of solid pillars, surrounded by water and containing some underworld within. This flat earth was covered by the vault of the sky that was stretched out something like a half-circular tent. The vault of the sky separates the waters above from the waters below. And the stars are affixed to this vault, while sun and moon make their way across it.[1] This conception of the world, while certainly

---

[1] From the many biblical passages dealing with sky-earth relations, it is most often impossible to tell the shape of the sky the author has in mind. Consider the following sampling.

Since God dwells above the created world, descriptions of divine interaction move from beyond the world into the world. Thus we read how God himself talks from the sky (Exod 20:22; Neh 9:13); later an angel of the Lord calls from the sky (Gen 21:17; 22:11, 15); God looks down from the sky (Deut 26:15; Ps 14:2; 33:13; 53:2; 80:14; 102:19; Isa 63:15; Lam 3:50); God sends from the sky to save (Ps 57:3); God thunders from the sky (2 Sam 22:14); God throws down great stones from the sky (Josh 10:11); God answers David with fire from the sky to the altar (1 Chron 21:26) and for Solomon (2 Chron 7:1); God is expected to hear from the sky, his dwelling place (2 Chron 6:21, 23, 25, 30, 33, 35, 39), and he says he will (2 Chron 7:14) and does (2 Chron 9:28).

In Israel's older cosmology, rain comes from the sky's open windows (Deut 28:12; Isa 24:18; 45:8; Ps 78:23; Mal 3:10). When items "fall" or "come down" from the sky, they do so at God's behest: bread falls from the sky (Exod 16:4; Ps 105:40; John 6:31, 32, 33); rain comes from the sky (Deut 11:11; Neh 9:27; Isa 55:10; Acts 14:17); powder and dust rain from the sky (Deut 28:24); spirit descends from the sky

biblical perhaps for the Priestly tradition of the fifth century B.C., was not the prevailing elite one from the Hellenistic period on (ca. 333 B.C.). Concerned people changed their views of the cosmos in antiquity just as people do today. And while the change may not have been radical by Galileo's standards (after all Hellenistic people still believed in an earth-centered universe), yet it was appreciably different from the more ancient one it displaced.

> Great strides were made in astronomy during the Hellenistic age and in the philosophical schoolrooms there was a broad consensus on the nature of the cosmos. The earth is a sphere, remaining motionless at the center of the universe, and all the other heavenly bodies were likewise spheres. Surrounding the earth are the seven planets (which include sun and moon), each moving in its own sphere, and these in turn are enclosed by an eighth sphere containing the fixed stars. This general picture of the universe was very common, and worked its way into popular philosophy so that calling the cosmos "the whole eight" became an adage (*paroimia*) (Scott 1991: 55).

Consequently, as we shall see, the Hellenistic concept of the universe changed significantly from that in vogue in ancient Israel.

> From the fourth century B.C. almost all the Greek philosophers maintained the sphericity of the earth; the Romans adopted the Greek spherical views; and the Christian fathers and early medieval writers, with few exceptions, agreed. During the Middle Ages, Christian theology showed little if any tendency to dispute sphericity (Russell 1991: 69).[2]

(John 1:32; 1 Pet 1:12); fire and sulfur rained from the sky over Sodom (Luke 17:29); light falls from the sky (Acts 9:3; 22:6; 26:13); a sheet descends from the sky (Acts 11:5).

While such traditional events continue to occur, now the wrath of God has been revealed from the sky (Rom 1:18). And toward the New Testament period there seem to be more interpersonal interactions noted, much like when "the heavens open" for Ezekiel (Ezek 1:1); so too for Jesus (Mark 1:10; Matt 3:16; Luke 3:21), for Stephen (Acts 7:56), for Peter (Acts 10:11), and frequently in the book of Revelation.

People hear a voice from the sky (Dan 4:31; Matt 3:17; Mark 1:11; Luke 3:22; John 12:28; Acts 2:2; 11:9; 2 Pet 1:18). Just as the stars once fought from the sky (Judg 5:20), so now there are signs from the sky (Matt 16:1; Mark 8:11; Luke 11:16); warnings from the sky (Heb 12:25); stars fall from the sky (Matt 24:29; Mark 13:25; Luke 21:11 call these great signs from the sky).

Individuals see sky beings: Daniel sees a Watcher, a Holy One, coming down from the sky (Dan 4:13.23); others see the angel of the Lord (Matt 28:2; Gal 1:8); Jesus sees Satan fall like lightning from the sky (Luke 10:18). And fire comes down from the sky as sign for Elijah (2 Kings 1:10, 12, 14), as it does to devour Job's goods (Job 1:16); so too James and John can bid fire come down from the sky (Luke 9:54).

The Son of man once descended from the sky (John 3:13, 31; 6:38, 41, 42, 50, 51, 58) and will be seen descending (John 1:51). This is not unlike the Second Man who is both from the sky and of the sky (1 Cor 15:47; 1 Thess 1:10; 4:16). Jesus is revealed from the sky with his mighty angels (2 Thess 1:7).

[2] As Russell (1991) has demonstrated, the main source of the falsehood that people from antiquity to the time of Columbus believed in a flat earth was Washing-

Further evidence for this belief is to be found in the portrayal of the universe in ancient map-making. In those representations the earth is a sphere surrounded by a sphere of rotating planets in their own pathways and a rotating vault of fixed stars that encapsulates the whole.

> The importance of the Hellenistic period in the history of cartography in the ancient world has thus been clearly established. Its outstanding characteristic was the fruitful marriage of theoretical and empirical knowledge. It has been demonstrated beyond doubt that the geometric study of the sphere, as expressed in theorems and physical models, had important practical applications and that its principles underlay the development both of mathematical geography and of scientific cartography as applied to celestial and terrestrial phenomena. With respect to celestial mapping, the poem about the stellar globe by Aratus (though removed in time from Eudoxus) had encouraged the more systematic study of real globes such as that on the archetype of the Farnese Atlas or those constructed by Archimedes. The main constellations on these artifacts were equated with religious beliefs or legends, mainly in human or animal form. This practice in turn had stimulated a closer study of the sky and its groups of stars. By the end of the Hellenistic period, the celestial globes, although they were artistically decorated, were regarded as credible scientific representations of the sky that in turn could be given astrological uses, as in the compilation of horoscopes, in Greek society at large. In the history of geographical (or terrestrial) mapping, the great practical step forward was to locate the inhabited world exactly on the terrestrial globe (Dilke 1987: 277).

As Russell summarizes: "In the first fifteen centuries of the Christian era, five writers seem to have denied the globe . . . but nearly unanimous scholarly opinion pronounced the earth spherical, and by the fifteenth century all doubt had disappeared" (Russell 1991: 26). The five writers are: Lactantius (ca. 265–345) [in order to deny the antipodes], perhaps Theodore of Mopsuestia (ca. 350–430) and perhaps Diodore of Tarsus (d. 394); and finally Severian of Gabala (ca. 380) and Cosmas Indicopleustes (ca. 540), because "the Bible said."

1.2. KNOWING THE FIRST-CENTURY UNIVERSE

As is well known, the book of Revelation begins with the Greek word ἀποκάλυψις (apokalypsis). This word is transliterated as "apocalypse" and translated as "revelation." The reason for the translation is

---

ton Irving. Irving wrote a novelistic biography of Columbus, published in 1828, in which he set forth this lie. The heyday of Irving's propagandistic story was 1870–1920, during the period of conflict over evolutionism. Historically, there is no evidence of debate about the earth's roundness in Columbus' day. At that time the roundness of the earth was well known and taken for granted.

that in the last centuries B.C. the verb form (ἀποκαλύπτω, *apokalyptō*) commonly meant: "to make known something secret about someone; to reveal secrets about someone" (Smith 1983: 12). The social context of the original usage of the word was interpersonal communication, revealing secrets about human beings. But at about the same time that the word began to be used in the social, interpersonal sense, Babylonian astronomical and/or astrological knowledge was spreading throughout the Mediterranean world (see Florisoone 1950; 1951; and the earlier work of Brown 1899; 1900). This Babylonian knowledge moved westward, largely mediated through eastern Mediterranean coastal ethnic groups: Phoenician, Israelite, Egyptian. As people acquired this new knowledge, they either directly or, more usually, indirectly increasingly contributed to the local production of astronomical and astrological lore. And so secrets about things and persons divine rooted in the new knowledge could now be made known. It would seem that the newly appropriated "Chaldean" (meaning "Babylonian") lore greatly stimulated awareness that the god(s) had vitally important secrets readily discernible to those who could read the sky. Hence to assimilate this knowledge and thus to learn about cosmic phenomena and their impact on earth's inhabitants enabled those who studied them to make this information known to others. Since "revelation" was already the common word for the process of revealing interpersonal or personal secrets, our author uses it for revealing these astronomical and astrological secrets as well, for celestial entities such as stars were equally regarded as living, "personal" beings.

> Aside from the Epicureans, all the major philosophical schools in the Hellenistic era believed in the divinity of the stars. Even the notorious atheist Euhemerus (flourished 300 B.C.) acknowledged that they (at least) were gods. . . . If one supposes, as later Platonism usually did, that stars were composed of soul and body, of sensible and intelligible, of superior and inferior, of ruling and ruled, one would think that only the soul of the star would be divine, and not its body. One response was to say that in the case of the stars, soul was perfectly adapted to body, and the lower and visible part to a higher intelligible part. The "secondary" gods exist through the higher invisible gods, depending on them as the star's radiance depends on the star. In the star the divine soul exercises a perfect supremacy (Scott 1991: 55 and 57; see Taub 1993: 135–46).

Mediterranean thinkers of this period referred to astral divinities in a wide variety of ways. With these references people sought to underscore the intermediate divine quality of these beings which were superior to humans but inferior to the supreme divinity. Popular metaphors, like those derived from Plato, expressed this relationship by referring to God and the stars as a king with his subjects or as a commander with his troops. Of course this is the same as the designation "Lord God of hosts" (Yahweh Sabaoth) in the Israelite tradition. Celestial beings, whether stars or demons, angels or archangels, were said to be made of fire (hence visible at night). And depending on ethnic theology, the supreme God was either made of light, dwelling in the ether, or was uncreated and dwelling in inaccessible light (Jas 1:17, for whom God is the "Father of lights"; and 1 Tim 6:16, for whom God alone is "immortal and dwells in unapproachable light"; see Scott 1991: 59).

Just as the stars were innumerable, so were the myriads of entities that populated the region above the earth and below the fixed stars. Listen to how the Hellenistic author Philo of Alexandria explains the situation:

> It is Moses' custom to give the name of angels to those whom other philosophers call demons (or spirits), souls that is which fly and hover in the air. . . . For the universe must needs be filled through and through with life, and each of its primary elementary divisions contains the forms of life which are akin and suited to it. The earth has the creatures of the land, the sea and the rivers those that live in water, fire the fire-born which are said to be found especially in Macedonia, and heaven has the stars. For the stars are souls divine and without blemish throughout, and therefore as each of them is mind in its purest form, they move in the line most akin to mind—the circle. And so the other element, the air, must needs be filled with living beings, though indeed they are invisible to us, since even the air itself is not visible to our senses (*On the Giants* 6–8, LCL).

Philo was a "Judean," a member of the house of Israel, living outside of Judea in Alexandria, Egypt, at the turn of the first century A.D. Of course he has much more to say about these beings who inhabit the air. "They are consecrated and devoted to the service of the Father and Creator whose wont it is to employ them as ministers and helpers, to have charge and care of mortal man" (*On the Giants* 12, LCL). And just as there are good and wicked people, so too there are good and wicked demons and angels (*On the Giants* 16, LCL). "For so far is air from being alone of all things untenanted, like a city it has a goodly population, its citizens being imperishable and immortal souls equal in number to the stars" (his conclusion to the same argument in *On Dreams* 1.133–137, LCL). Philo's perception of the air as fully populated was common in the Hellenistic period. The general principle was: "There is no void of any sort, there cannot be a void and there will never be a void." And the reason for the principle: "For all parts of the universe are absolutely full, and the universe itself is full and perfectly replete with entities (*corpora*) of diverse form and quality and each having its own shape and dimensions" (*Asclepius* 33, Festugière-Nock 2.342). What makes such a void impossible is the ubiquitous presence of "intelligible beings, much like their divinity," or in more modern terms, "persons" of some sort, nonhuman and/or human. The void, then, does not refer so some absence of matter as in our physics. Thus in line with Philo's statement, we learn: "No part of the universe is empty of demons" (*Corpus Hermeticum* IX, 3, Festugière-Nock, 197).

For those who, like Philo, shared the traditions of Israel, the problem with astrology in terms of Chaldean sky lore was that "the cosmos was not God's work, but itself God." One must pass from

> astrology to real nature study . . . from the created to the uncreated, from the world to its Maker and Father. Thus the oracles tell us that those whose views are of the Chaldean type have put their trust in the sky, while he who has migrated from this home has given his trust to him who rides on the sky and guides the chariot of the whole cosmos, God (Philo, *Who is the Heir* 98–99, LCL).

Just like the other Mediterranean peoples of the period, however, the house of Israel used the new found astronomical lore to learn about its deity's activities. Only for Israelites, the presumption was that their deity, the YHWH God of their ancestors, was the supreme deity. While not at all denying the reality of the gods of those other nations, Israelites were forbidden to call them "god." Instead they used other Mediterranean designations for the cosmic beings inhabiting the sky and impacting the earth, i.e., spirit, demon, or angel. Though they changed the names, the way of perceiving the reality and function of those beings remained the same from one end of the world (Indus Valley) to the other (Spain). Israelites also readily identified planets with angels or good demons and saw the function of such astral beings either to act as deities or to serve as agents or assistants of the "Most High" God. Now in the Israelite tradition, this God could be known both from traditions deriving from the prophet Moses and from reading the sky. After all, did not Adam's antediluvian offspring, Enoch, distinguish himself by such sky readings (see Heb 11:5 and the books ascribed to Enoch). Israelite elites knew this from the ancient traditional sky lore preserved in writing, just like the words of the prophet Moses himself (see Milik 1976; for a full listing of those writings see Collins 1979; for English translations see *Old Testament Pseudepigrapha* 2 vols., ed. Charlesworth 1983 and 1985).

A range of ethnic groups in the Hellenistic age saw a proliferation of information deriving from observing celestial phenomena. It seems as though all Mediterranean peoples gratefully accepted the accumulated star lore developed in the ancient Mesopotamian region. Yet reading the sky, like reading in general, took place in terms of scenarios brought to the object to be read by the reader. All students of the sky would perceive the sky in terms of their distinctive ethnic traditional story, whether Babylonian, Phoenician, Israelite, Egyptian, Greek, Roman, or whatever. For example, the planet ascribed to the goddess Venus by the Romans, would be ascribed to Aphrodite by the Greeks, to Isis by the

Egyptians, to Anatu/Ashtarte by Phoenicians or Israelites, and to Aph-rodite/Anaitis by Hellenistic Babylonians. Yet the impact and influence of this planet were quite similar for nearly all these peoples. The distinc-tive ethnic traditional stories would be expanded by any other informa-tion available to the astronomer/astrologer, yet invariably these were appropriated in terms of the foundational ethnic tradition. In other words, a prophet of the house of Israel would envision the sky in terms of the traditional Israelite story enshrined in the Torah and the Prophets yet enlightened by the latest information from other celestial observers.

A solid example of this process is reported by Hippolytus (d. 235), a Christian writer living in Rome at the turn of the third century. He tells us how some (ostensibly of the Israelite tradition) interpreted the sky with the Bible and in order to understand the Bible. These inter-preters began with the scholarship of the period provided by Aratus in a famous astronomical poem called *The Phenomena*:

> Aratus says that there are in the sky revolving, that is, gyrating stars, because from east to west, and west to east, they journey perpetually, (and) in an orbicular figure. And he says [5.45–46] that there revolves towards "The Bears" themselves, like some stream of a river, an enormous and prodigious monster, (the) Serpent; and that this is what the devil says in the book of Job to the Deity, when (Satan) uses these words: "I have traversed earth under heaven, and have gone around (it)" [Job 1:7], that is, that I have been turned around and, thereby have been able to survey the worlds. For they suppose that towards the North Pole is situated the Dragon, the Serpent, from the highest pole looking upon all (the objects), and gazing on all the works of creation, in order that nothing of the things that are being made may escape his notice. For though all the stars in the firmament set, the pole of this (luminary) alone never sets, but careering [*sic*] high above the horizon, surveys and beholds all things, and none of the works of creation, he says, can escape his notice (*Refutation of All Heresies* 4.47, *ANF* 5.42–43).

This sort of interpretive process permitted the emergence of ethnically specific astral prophecy within a common Hellenistic matrix. The results are readily visible in Israelite revelations rooted in sky readings (Collins 1984: 20).

Of course the secrets revealed by the God of Israel might be answers to particular problems. It was common in the period to read the sky for information about nations as a whole or prominent individuals such as kings; or some sought general information about when to begin certain activities, such as house building, buying and selling, and travel-ing (see Cramer 1954; examples in Neugebauer and Van Hoesen 1959). The apostle Paul, too, states that his second trip to Jerusalem after his experience of Jesus the Messiah was dictated by revelation (Gal 2:2). Later he promises the Philippians that God will reveal to them the truth of competing opinions (3:15). In Revelation, John follows the path of many of his contemporaries and records his "readings" of the sky. As the document indicates, the prophet John stands within the traditions of Second Temple Israel and reads the sky in terms of the Yahwism that was Israel's elite ideology. Yet John belonged to that Israelite group that believed Jesus of Nazareth was crucified and raised from the dead by the God of Israel to be the Messiah. Consequently, it was not surprising that his celestial observations put him face to face with a humanlike being identified with Jesus the Messiah of Israel. This cosmic personage is later more specifically called the celestial Lamb, a being characterized by qualities typical of the Israelite king David and embodied by Jesus the Messiah.

1.3. THE INADEQUACIES OF TRADITIONAL READINGS

The approach to the book of Revelation adopted in this book in terms of the Hellenistic conception of the sky is a radically historical one. The goal is to understand the document in terms that would have made sense to a first-century A.D. audience. Only such a historical approach can be considered fair and adequate to the prophet's concern about "anyone taking away from the utterances of the scroll of this prophecy" (21:19). The task of helping a modern audience understand the book of Revelation, however, faces numerous obstacles. As is the case when working with all ancient documents, the obstacles derive not from the book of Revelation itself, but from both nonprofessional and professional students of the Bible who bring their own scenarios to their reading of the book (see Malina 1991). On the one hand, the historically minded interpreter must overcome the nonprofessional's uncritical acceptance of spurious information both about the genre or type of the work and about the experience it purportedly describes. For many nonprofessionals the book of Revelation has become a repository of predictions concerning the end of the world. This has been a quite common perspective ever since Pharisees and Christians sought to determine the "true" age of creation to determine the beginning of the seventh millennium—the Sabbath of the cosmos (see Landes 1988).

On the other hand, the basic difficulty with interpreting this book for a modern scholarly audience is the spurious familiarity with which modern scholars are burdened. Scholarly spurious familiarity derives from nineteenth-century northern European ideology and categorization, from attempts of recent scholars to maintain continuity with that nineteenth-century tradition, from theological ideology, and from attempts to find this book relevant in terms of that ideology. People who are ideologically indisposed invariably adhere to the "Received View" (see Malina 1986). Furthermore, the overflow of religious and biblical common knowledge and scholarship has trickled through to more than a few social scientists, especially those interested in modern deviant religious forms. From these social scientists we learn to speak of "millenarian movements," that is, "religious movements that expect imminent, total, ultimate, this-worldly collective salvation" (Talmon 1968: 349). Here "this worldly" means that it "offers not an other-worldly hope, nor a purely spiritual salvation, but the fulfillment of the divine purpose in a new universe and a new social order" (Talmon 1966: 167). Even the study of collective behavior, as the "apocalyptic" tradition indicates, was about "people going crazy together" (Martin 1920, cited by Gamson 1992: 54). Thus modern scholarship even outside the biblical guild has directly or indirectly derived from the received, scholarly interpretation of this book.

When modern scholars classify the book of Revelation as "apocalypse," they are indicating its literary type or genre. It was the German scholar F. Lücke (in 1852) who decided to use "apocalypse" as a label for the genre or category of this document and documents similar to it, such as the book of Daniel and those Israelite writings called Enoch, Ezra, and Baruch (Kvanvig 1989: 40, 56). Aside from the precedent of our ancient and medieval ancestors who often chose the first word(s) of a writing to serve as a title, it is difficult to understand why this label has been maintained by historical scholarship since the revealed quality of the information provided in these books was hardly noted.

Furthermore, it is true that early Christian groups often sought to set themselves apart from other groups in their social environment. And often they insisted on maintaining their in-group boundaries by constantly consoling one another with the hope of Jesus' coming as Messiah with power as well as by threatening the out-group with a "just you wait and see" message. Yet there seems little value in calling this perspective "eschatology." "Eschatology" derives from a Greek word that means the study of the end, of final things, usually the study of the presumed end of the world.[3] This term was coined in 1804 by K. G. Bretschneider and taken up by F. Oberthür in 1807–1810, and thence to the rest of

---

[3] Eschatology is not so much about life after death, the future, as about life now, in the present. In general, descriptions of future life (eschatology) function socially to set the limits and rules for life in the present and to provide a foundation for perspectives of personal responsibility. In particular, the eschatological doctrine in death-facing situations facilitates the bargaining/compromise situation by providing social certainty to the process (e.g., in the Kübler-Ross process: denial, depression, bargaining, compromise, acceptance). Finally, the eschatological doctrine in mourning-grieving situations functions to enable those who grieve to assess, on the basis of eschatological norms, where the deceased might presently be located, and thereby help in the process of patching the social rift caused by a person's death. Thus the various present focuses include: behavior in the present, motivation in the present, present bargaining while facing death, present grieving.

German-speaking theologians; a group of Alsatian theologians natural-
ized it in France in 1828; and it appeared in England in 1844, or even
sooner (see Carmignac 1979: 133–34).

While the terms "apocalypse" or "eschatological apocalyptic" sound
duly esoteric and learned, the terms shed little light on the sort of book
this last document of the New Testament really is. Perhaps some scholars believe that such labels appropriately categorize the work both in
the history of scholarship and in terms of appropriate categorical distinctions; however, it seems, rather, that "apocalypse" and "eschatology"
are simply part and parcel of the theological jargon of the past century
that fossilize perception and misdirect interpretation. Thus, while the
Greek word "apocalypse" (ἀποκάλυψις) originally meant the process of
revealing or making known something secret about persons, the word is
inadequate to describe the book of Revelation. Moreover, while it is
true that all information imparted by the sky-oriented prophets and
seers of antiquity consisted of uncovered secrets, not all revelations or
secrets were or are derived from the sky. As a matter of fact, the book
of Revelation and works like it (e.g., the books of Enoch) are really a
subset of the astronomical and astrological literature of antiquity.

1.4. THE BOOK OF REVELATION AS ASTRAL PROPHECY

The Greek philosopher Theophrastus (ca. 370–287 B.C.), often
credited for creating the label "economics," did indeed call the study of
the stars and their impact on the earth and its inhabitants "astronomics"
(τὰ ἀστρονομικά, ta astronomika) (On Weather Signs 1.1, LCL). This
label admirably fits the general category of sky study, since the ancients
made no distinction between astronomy and astrology (Hübner 1989).
The terms "astronomy" and "astrology" referred to the same sort of
scholarly concern as "astronomics," for both "astronomy" and "astrology" referred to the study of celestial phenomena with a view to
accumulating and applying practical information for the welfare of human beings. This professional task was not unlike the thrust behind a
farmer's accumulated knowledge of the sky required for determining
the best times for planting, harvesting, and the like. Obviously, however, the practical information sought by astral prophets included more
than agriculture.

The first person to insist that Revelation can be properly understood only with astronomy and astrology was Charles François Dupuis,
who wrote at the end of the eighteenth century. Dupuis was a true
Enlightenment figure, much concerned with the ultimate sources or
origins of religion. His deductions led him to say many "right" things,
but for the wrong reasons. His many valid insights rested on what we

today would consider invalid arguments. For example, in general he believed all religions were rooted in the worship of the sun. Hence anything attending the sun, such as the stars lying in the sun's path through the sky, would be connected with religion (e.g., the zodiac). With his focus on the sun, Dupuis urged serious consideration of the sky and its arrangements in any understanding of religious writings. He singled out the book of Revelation as rooted in astronomy. And it seems he was quite correct in this particular insight.

It is thanks to a number of dauntless scholars early in this century that we have an abundance of information about ancient astronomics. At the turn of the century, the Belgian Franz Cumont put together a team to catalogue all ancient Greek astrological documents in European libraries; representative samples of each were published (*Catalogus Codicum Astrologicorum Graecorum* 1898–1953). In addition to classical scholars, who produced critical editions of standard ancient astronomical and/or astrological works along with critical studies, one scholar, Franz Boll, attempted an astronomic interpretation of the major scenarios of the book of Revelation in 1914. Boll's contribution to ancient star lore is truly amazing, but he was not a biblical scholar or theologian. It seems it was largely for this reason that his work was discounted after the First World War, especially following a monograph by theologian Joseph Freuendorfer (1929; see Gundel 1950: 831–36). The works of Wilhelm Gundel, Wilhelm Kroll, and Andre Festugière, among others, however, continued to point to the value of astronomics for understanding the first-century A.D. view of the cosmos and, hence, the genre of the book of Revelation.

When Boll wrote his monograph on Revelation in 1914, he of course shared in the academic passion of the period to find the document's antecedent written sources. This goal still characterizes many of our contemporaries who seem to believe that finding sources would explain more than examining the chronological situation of the document. And it is true that Boll did overstate the case for John's having employed direct and distinct literary sources. Thus Freundorfer's critique was surely on target when he concluded:

> At the time of Revelation, the Babylonian worldview and the Athenian worldview were so closely fused together into a new worldview which now governed the beliefs, ways of dealing with the world and ways of considering fate in the whole civilized world that it would surely be false to turn one's attention solely toward the ancient Near East and derive everything from there for the interpretation of the scenarios and images of the apocalypticist. Now we found that Boll established too many points of contact that were too direct. Generally, when he endeavors to demonstrate that the seer's visions were "literary fictions," purely literary constructs and translations of astral objects, motifs, etc., his proofs fail and become quite artificial. To explain the visions, literary connections are not required, nor

is the assumption that the author would have creatively reshaped astral images into apocalyptic descriptions; rather those features are to be explained from what was commonly known among the people and from there became the property of the imagination of the seer. The four scenarios, beginning with εἶδον, *eidon* or ὤφθη, *ōphthē* (6:1; 8:2; 9:1; 12:1) remain fully understandable as genuine visions (Freuendorfer 1929: 146).

Freuendorfer was correct on a number of counts. First of all, by the time of Revelation, ethnic distinctions were generally insignificant for the civilized, that is, Hellenized, person. "[I]t is no exaggeration to say that by 60 B.C. Syrian, Greek, Iberian and Roman had become one" (C. H. Oldfather in his Introduction to *Diodorus of Sicily*, vol. 1, LCL). To use Paul's phraseology, "both Judean and Greek," that is, the "Set Apart" and the "Civilized," shared in a common Mediterranean fund of values and perceptions that can be labeled "Israelite" and "Hellenic" on the basis of the syntax, grammar, and language forms used to express them. But this would not hold for the meaning of the reality so labeled, since all shared a common social system: Mediterranean. By the first century of our era, Mediterraneans had more in common in terms of values and perceptions than they had differences.

Yet Freuendorfer and those discounting Boll failed to keep in mind that the prophet's visions were visions of the sky, celestial visions, of celestial beings. And Boll was surely correct in insisting that one must know what the sky was like and what was to be seen in the sky in the first century to understand the astral prophet, John. The study of the sky "fascinated the Hellenistic world and held with a paralyzing grip the Hellenistic mind" (C. K. Barrett 1961: 35). And thus "many of us (historians of antiquity) lack the training or the particular type of imagination necessary to enable us to understand a horoscope or an astrolabe, but none of us can with impunity regard astrology as a peripheral matter" (Nock 1972: 1.502). The fact is, as MacMullen has noted:

> From the period of the Roman Empire alone, the surviving astrological corpus matches in bulk the entire historical corpus; and though examined in detail by students of ancient religion, language, and science, it has been quite neglected by the social historian (MacMullen 1971: 105).

Of course the same is quite true of the house of Israel. Given the pervasive nature of astronomic concerns in Israel, it would be surprising indeed if there were nothing of astral prophecy in the New Testament, for as previously noted, everyone believed the sky was filled with celestial personages. Philo again is typical when he writes: "For the stars are souls divine and without blemish throughout, and therefore as each of them is mind in its purest form, they move in the line most akin to mind—the circle" (*On the Giants* 6–8, LCL). Hence persons adhering to the tradition of Israel would be well aware of astronomic impact on their lives. For example, from Israel's traditions we know of sky servants intervening on behalf of humans at God's command.

> But, uttering threats, Apollonius went on to the temple. While the priests together with women and children were imploring God in the temple to shield the holy place that was being treated so contemptuously, and while Apollonius was going up with his armed forces to seize the money, angels on horseback with lightning flashing from their weapons appeared from heaven, instilling in them great fear and trembling. Then Apollonius fell down half dead in the temple area that was open to all, stretched out his hands toward heaven, and with tears besought the Hebrews to pray for him and propitiate the wrath of the heavenly army (4 Macc 4:8–11).

Just as they professed that the Lord their God was one God (the prayer called the *Shema*, based on Deut 6:4ff.), so too could the stars:

> The stars shone in their watches, and were glad; he called them, and they said, "Here we are!" They shone with gladness for him who made them. This is our God; no other can be compared to him! (Baruch 3:34–35).

The stars then are nonhuman personages obedient to God and of service to God. The same is true of sun and moon and other celestial beings:

> For sun and moon and stars, shining and sent forth for service, are obedient. So also the lightning, when it flashes, is widely seen; and the wind likewise blows in every land. When God commands the clouds to go over the whole world, they carry out his command. And the fire sent from above to consume mountains and woods does what it is ordered. But these idols are not to be compared with them in appearance or power. Therefore one must not think that they are gods nor call them gods, for they are not able either to decide a case or to do good to men. Since you know then that they are not gods, do not fear them. For they can neither curse nor bless kings; they cannot show signs in the heavens and among the nations, or shine like the sun or give light like the moon (Epistle of Jeremiah 60–67).

Reverencing the statues of gods was forbidden since, as elite Israelites believed, statues are really dead entities. But reverencing the living celestial personages and God's sky servants seemed to have been proper behavior.

The Jerusalem temple and its appurtenances served as a massive, nationally known, billboard for astronomic lore. With such an endorsement, it would be difficult not to take astronomics seriously. Josephus describes the temple as follows:

> The gate opening into the building was, as I said, completely overlaid with gold, as was the whole wall around it. It had, moreover, above it those golden vines, from which depended grape-clusters as tall as a man; and it had golden doors fifty-five cubits high and sixteen broad. Before these hung a veil of equal length, of Babylonian tapestry, with embroidery of

blue and fine linen, of scarlet also and purple, wrought with marvelous skill. Nor was this mixture of materials without its proper significance: it typified the universe [literally: "an icon of the whole"]. For the scarlet seemed emblematical of fire, the fine linen of the earth, the blue of the air, and the purple of the sea; the comparison in two cases being suggested by their color, and in that of the fine linen and purple by their origin, as the one is produced by the earth and the other by the sea. On this tapestry was portrayed a panorama of the heavens, the signs of the Living Beings excepted (*War* 5.210–214, LCL).

Concerning the Holy Place, Josephus writes in the same context:

The first portion, partitioned off at forty cubits, contained within it three most wonderful works of art, universally renowned: a lampstand, a table, and an altar of incense. The seven lamps (such being the number of the branches from the lampstand) represented the planets; the loaves on the table, twelve in number, the circle of the Zodiac and the year; while the altar of incense, by the thirteen fragrant spices from sea and from land, both desert and inhabited, with which it was replenished, signified that all things are of God and for God (*War* 5.216–218, LCL).

The ingredients of the spices in the incense likewise have cosmic meaning. For example, Philo (*Who is the Heir* 197, LCL) has the four spices of Exod 30:34 standing for the four elements of the universe: air, earth, fire, and water. (But while Exod 30:34 has four, Jubilees 16:24 has seven, and Sirach 24:15 alludes to seven).

Josephus believed the temple service was of "cosmic significance," with its priests "reverenced by visitors to the city from every quarter of the earth" (*War* 4.324, LCL). Again, Josephus describes the booty taken from the temple by the Romans, and mentions:

a lampstand, likewise made of gold, but constructed on a different pattern from those which we use in ordinary life. Affixed to a pedestal was a central shaft, from which there extended slender branches, arranged trident-fashion, a wrought lamp being attached to the extremity of each branch; of these there were seven, indicating the honor paid to that number among the [Judeans] (*War* 7.149, LCL).

For Josephus' view of the cosmos, consider his allegorical interpretation of the temple and its appurtenances (see also Philo, *Moses* 2.88, 117ff.); Thackeray says this was "fairly widespread"):

For if one reflects on the construction of the tabernacle and looks at the vestments of the priest and the vessels which we use for the sacred minis-try, he will discover that our lawgiver was a man of God and that these blasphemous charges brought against us by the rest of men are idle. In fact, every one of these objects is intended to recall and represent the universe, as he will find if he will but consent to examine them without prejudice and with understanding. Thus, to take the tabernacle, thirty cubits long, by dividing this into three parts and giving up two of them to the priests, as a place approachable and open to all, Moses signifies the earth and the sea, since these too are accessible to all; but the third portion he reserved for God alone, because heaven also is inaccessible to men. Again, by placing upon the table the twelve loaves, he signifies that the year is divided into as many months. By making the candelabrum to consist of seventy portions, he hinted at the ten degree provinces [δεκα-μοιρία, *dekamoiria*] of the planets, and by the seven lamps thereon the course of the planets themselves, for such is their number. The tapestries woven of four materials denote the natural elements: thus the fine linen appears to typify the earth, because from it springs up the flax, and the purple the sea, since it is incarnadined with the blood of fish; the air must be indicated by the blue, and the crimson will be the symbol of fire. The high-priest's tunic likewise signifies the earth, being of linen, and its blue the arch of heaven, while it recalls the lightnings by its pomegranates, the thunder by the sound of its bells. His upper garment, too, denotes universal nature, which it pleased God to make of four elements; being further interwoven with gold in token, I imagine, of the all-pervading sunlight. The *essên*, again, he set in the midst of this garment, after the manner of the earth, which occupies the midmost place; and by the sash wherewith he encompassed it he signified the ocean, which holds the whole in its embrace. Sun and moon are indicated by the two sardonyxes wherewith he pinned the high-priest's robe. As for the twelve stones, whether one would prefer to read in them the months or the constellations of like number, which the Greeks call the circle of the zodiac, he will not mistake the lawgiver's intention. Furthermore the head-dress appears to me to symbolize heaven, being blue; else it would not have borne upon it the name of God, blazoned upon the crown—a crown moreover of gold by reason of that sheen in which the Deity most delights (*Antiquities* 3.180–187, LCL).

The ready acceptance of astrology among Judeans is further intimated by Josephus. He offers an overview of sky sightings and sky readings which presented besieged Jerusalemites with a whole range of signs that won the credence of the people (*War* 6.288–313, passim, LCL).

Further, Israelites at Qumran, along the shores of the Dead Sea, were equally devoted to astronomics. This is attested to by the large number and large variety of astronomic documents drawn up and used by them. First of all, there are several copies of the book of Enoch attesting to concern with sky servants, with holy ones and sky Watchers, and with the problem of their giant offspring (see Milik 1976). The remains of the *Genesis Apocryphon*, a Qumran document, begins with Lamech's concern about whether Noah was fathered by a giant. Then there are some books for interpreting thunder (βροντολογία, *brontologia*), several physiognomic horoscopes, and a document describing the new Jerusalem that descends from the sky (see Vermes 1987).

Throughout this book, we shall encounter various astronomic works written by authors in the Israelite tradition, such as the *Treatise of Shem* and its twelve-year cycle, the *Testament of Adam* with its description of what goes on in the sky during the course of a day, or the *Letter of Solomon to Roboam* with its zodiacal and planetary information for dealing with plants. This last-named work likewise offers advice on how to approach and to deal with those sky servants called angels and demons, alluding to the angel worship typical of Israelite tradition (see Charles 1920 2.224–25). And there is much astronomic information in early Judean traditional collections such as the *Testament of Solomon* (trans. Dennis Duling, *OTP* 1.935–87) or the anonymous Judean *Book of Decans* (trans. Gundel 1939: 385–90 from CCAG VI, 73–78). Israelite astrological interest continued well into the period of the beginning of the Jewish religion with the Talmud. Writing about this post–New Testament period, Lieberman notes concerning the pharisaic scribal tradition:

> The wisdom of the east (adopted by Greeks and Romans) could not be entirely ignored. A learned and cultured man of those times could not reject the science of Astrology, a science recognized and acknowledged by all the civilized ancient world. To deny at that time the efficacy of Astrology would mean to deny a well established fact, to discredit a "science" accepted by both Hellenes and Barbarians (Lieberman 1965: 98).

Indeed even with the emergence of the Jewish religion (ca. the fifth to the sixth century A.D.), Lieberman continues, "some of the Rabbis did not indeed deny the efficacy of Astrology."

But practical astronomic concern in Israel should come as no surprise. After all, all Mediterraneans sought the signs of the times[4] in atmospheric and celestial events (see Matt 16:3; and Theophrastus, *On Weather Signs*) and believed sky entities were alive, with sky events caused by celestial personages. Furthermore, while some Christians held that Jesus ascended through the celestial spheres to God (Acts 1:9), others had visions of Jesus in the sky (standing: Acts 7:55–56; seated: Col 3:1; Heb 8:1; 12:2), and all took the presence of God's sky servants, the "angels," for granted. Since we can be sure that there were Christian prophets, (Agabus, Acts 11 and 21; Paul, 1 Cor 12), there must have been Christian astral prophets after the manner of John the seer as well.

1.5. HOW ANCIENT PEOPLES HEARD SUCH DOCUMENTS

Obviously to consider John, the prophet of Patmos, as an astral prophet will require a perspective for the reading of the report he

---

[4] Note that in much contemporary theology, the signs of the times are social. Hence theological biblical commentaries presume the existence of salvation history, the revelation of God in social process or human history. Such, of course, was not the case in any period that might be called "biblical times."

authored quite different from the perspective usually adopted. In what follows, I will assume that John is an astral prophet and that his work consists of astral prophecy. Astral prophecy refers to those ancient narratives reporting the interaction of prophets and seers with star-related, celestial personages and the outcomes of that interaction. These narratives might describe both the initial circumstances of such interactions (i.e., visions, dreams, ecstasies and other altered states of consciousness), the interactions proper (what the prophet or seer hears and sees, i.e., alternative realities, the very secrets to be revealed), as well as the outcomes of the interactions (impact or meanings of celestial phenomena).

Clearly the cosmic beings in control of the earth, ranging from God, the other deities, and the various celestial beings, all dwelt in the sky. The sky was an immense region, variously imagined by persons in antiquity. But no matter who described the sky, there was one feature all agreed on: the universe was a closed system, closed in by a celestial vault or firmament. This was true even when the earth was represented as the central sphere of the cosmos. This sphere was ultimately surrounded by the sphere of the firmament or vault of the sky. Most often some high god or god(s) might be said to dwell beyond this firmament. It would be rare to have someone insist that all sky beings were enclosed within the vault. The fixed stars moved along the face of this vault or firmament. This vault or firmament was outfitted with an opening of sorts that allowed access to the other side (for a full second century A.D. description of the universe beginning with the spherical form of the earth and of the universe, along with the celestial circles and stars and planets, see the third section of the handbook of mathematics prepared by Theon of Smyrna, ed. E. Heller 1878, trans. R. and D. Lawlor 1979).

The firmament or vault encompassed in shell-like fashion all the observable or experienced sky phenomena or sky beings. The earth was in the center of this magnificent shell. In the Hellenistic period, learned elites imagined the earth to be a ball or sphere. Around the earth moved the moon, the sun, and the five visible planets (and for some, two other invisible ones). These celestial bodies passed over the segment of the earth where humans lived, then passed under the earth to emerge from the other side. The earth hung still and stable in the center of the whole rotating system.

The moon and sun were counted among the planets; thus there were seven visible planets with seven circuits marking off seven spheres surrounding the earth. The most significant planetary courses were those of the moon and of the sun. Their courses marked pathways; constellations in their path were considered especially significant. On the other hand, the celestial equator, a projection onto the firmament of the earth's equator, was equally significant for the orientation of the sky.

Eventually it was the sun's course which the other planets were also said to traverse. The sun's course through the sky marked a pathway called the ecliptic. In the time-span of a year, the sun made its way over this pathway once. All the stars it passed along its pathway were considered especially significant and were interpreted as forming, in combination, large sky figures (ζῴδια, zōdia in Greek). In the Hellenistic period, the larger western Mediterranean world of Greeks and Latins learned about the Babylonian sequence of twelve constellational living beings forming a belt or zodiac through which the sun passed. There was likewise a lunar zodiac, a belt of constellations through which the moon passed. As previously noted, scholars of the day learned Babylonian lore from the eastern Mediterranean as mediated by Phoenicians, Israelites, and Egyptians. By the time of the Hellenistic period, then, the older Babylonian system and its appropriations by Phoenicians, Israelites, and Egyptians, as well as Greeks and Romans, were developed, largely in unsystematic and contradictory fashion, to make sense of the sky and its impact on life.

Mediterranean society at this period knew of two types of persons who devoted themselves to knowledge of the sky (see Dahl 1975). On the one hand were those called "the wise men, the learned, the scholars." These people were in awe of the sky and insisted that no one could really grasp the greatness and magnificence of the celestial spheres. The best posture was to stand in awe of the creator. They thought that as far as celestial phenomena were concerned, one need only pay attention to traditional lore about weather, farming, sailing, and the like. A generic understanding of the constellations and their major stars suffices (in this regard, see the various illustrated Roman calendars in Stern 1981).

On the other hand there were those who believed one could surely get to understand what impact the sky and celestial beings had on human societies. This group included Babylonian (Chaldean *magi*), Greek, Roman, Egyptian, and Israelite astronomers, astrologers, prophets and/or seers. This group, including Israelite prophets or seers, sought information about their human groups from and concerning those living beings who controlled the skies. Of course, as noted previously, their perception of the sky and their descriptions of those perceptions followed from their ethnic stories and ideologies. Thus for Israelites in the Hellenistic period, there would be God and a whole range of living sky beings, good and evil, never labeled as deities even if they performed the functions of deities. For the others, there were God, gods, lesser deities, and demons. All who read and experienced sky phenomena perceived the various servants of God(s) (e.g., angels and demons, spirits good and bad) and the range of celestial forces (e.g., the planets, stars, comets, shooting stars, falling stars), as well as thunder, lightning, earthquakes, sky rumblings, hail, rain, sulfur rain. Apart from traditional weather lore, however, information concerning the sky beings and their impact on human living was not readily apparent. To discern those sky beings, to understand their behavior and intent, and to know how to ward off any untoward effects of their activity required access to a body of information that was not available in any evident and obvious way. In fact it was hidden information, something like the traditional understanding of biological and chemical processes. For centuries the study of these processes were the province of alchemists who sought to unlock their secrets. So too with the sky beings. Those who studied them with a view to discerning their effects upon human societies produced esoteric, secret knowledge, mysteries (Festugière 1939: 50, n. 1).

How did first-century Mediterranean astral prophets come to know the celestial secrets they reported? From both study (contemplation rooted in information provided by astronomers, astrologers, philosophers) and from direct contact with the sky personages (ecstasy, visions, dreams and sky trips; hence alternate states of awareness). The information thus gathered was handed down within families (father to son, teacher as fictive father to disciple as fictive son) as well as from seer to significant person (prophet to king).

The role of prophet or seer existed essentially because such information concerning the sky and its inhabitants was considered crucial for human well being. Ancients envisioned no split or division between the cosmos and human affairs, between some supposedly "supernatural" sphere and the natural (see Saler 1977). The role of "prophet" in the Hellenistic world was a social one performed usually on behalf of a whole society. And given the structure of society, the role of prophet was usually a political role exercised on behalf of a king, emperor, general or the like. But at times the role was performed on behalf of a smaller group. In Revelation, the astral prophet John communicates to or for his "brothers" (see Malina 1993).

That John calls his fellows by such a family term indicates he belonged to a group whose members interacted much like a first-century Mediterranean family, even though they were not related physically or legally. However, since celestial events generally affect whole regions and ethnic groups, they were not simply family matters, even a "church" family. Rather, the social grouping to which John refers seems to have resulted from the fact that the group in question could not form a political unit of its own. It was a family by default, so to speak. The reason for saying this is that astral revelations are essentially public. Since they are about power in the cosmos affecting regions populated by human beings and their institutions, such revelations are always political. Politics deals with the public use of power. Hence revelations, especially celestial ones, were invariably directed to persons of high public status, notably kings and priests. If we situate John within the context of Second Temple Yahwism, that is, within the Israelite tradition, then his revelation should have been for some Judean king or perhaps the high priest. Thus his delivering a prophecy to his "brothers" implies that the Israelite polity no longer served as mooring for Christian groupings, either because John and his "brothers" were ejected from Israel or because the kingdom of Judea was dissolving or simply no longer existed.

Consequently, it will become obvious, as Grabbe has recently argued (1989), that there is no necessary connection between a writing like Revelation and groups looking forward to an imminent transformation of the world. As a matter of fact, astronomical and astrological writings, including Revelation, do not necessarily arise in times of crisis, nor are they always, if ever, a product of the oppressed, marginalized, and powerless. Rather, astral prophecy was usually produced by figures within some philosophical or scribal establishment for political elites. From the perspective of social function within a polity, prophecy, wisdom, and worship may be closely associated.

1.6. THE IMAGERY OF THE BOOK

Ancient astral prophecy is always concerned with the social situation of the political groups to which Hellenistic prophets and seers belonged and/or with whom they interacted. There was no separation between the cosmos and society, no gulf between celestial events and human history, no distinction between supernatural and natural. If the social situation were positive, then astral prophetic information simply explained the reason for the status quo and its positive qualities. But, if the social situation were negative, then astral prophecy presented information from the celestial domain to explain the dismal situation and divulged information about the transformation of that situation in the forthcoming scenarios. Most often biblical scholars refer to the perception of the present situation as dismal coupled with a hope for eventual transformation as "apocalyptic" or "apocalyptic ideology." Perhaps it would be better to refer to this ideology as social crisis management. In an effort to "manage the crisis," the seer insists on the inevitable social transformation that would follow upon the passing of a dismal social situation. Such social transformation was forthcoming, organically flowing from the resolution of the dismal social situation, much as in our culture, young adulthood flows from the resolution of the confusions of puberty.

Of course the narrative likewise intimates what the seer advises and expects of his "brothers" in their situation. In Revelation, the seer advises endurance. Now this endurance has as its goal the radical restructuring of society. This is what the "new Jerusalem" is about. Hence endurance looks to a true social revolution wrought by extra-terrestrial forces. For the seer, then, the best of times is imminent, right around the corner. This is quite obvious from what has already occurred in the sky. After all, celestial events control human fortunes, and it is these events that the astral prophet reports. Since, as will become apparent, the significant events are past, endurance is the proper attitude in the present.

A final point about the astral prophet's role and ideological hegemony ought be noted. Ideological hegemony refers to an order in which a certain way of life and thought is dominant and to the ways conceptions of reality diffuse throughout all of society's institutional and private manifestations. Hegemony is established by the dominant stratum of society which controls the means of coercion and symbols of loyalty. These ways of conceiving reality become so diffused and accepted that they are equated with common sense knowledge. Hegemony is established to the extent that the world-view of the rulers is also the worldview of the ruled. The worldview of the social elites is perceived simply as current "social values" and as the natural state of existence. Hegemony implies the active engagement of individuals with the ideology of the dominant sectors of society and therefore active cooperation in their own domination.

From the perspective of ideological hegemony, the purpose of astral prophecy was to exert control over contemporary understandings and descriptions of the sky. Just as the understanding and description of the earth are called geography (from the Greek word for earth, γή, $g\bar{e}$), the understanding and description of the sky are called uranography (from the Greek word for sky, οὐράνος, *ouranos*). Uranography refers to the more or less systematic understanding of the sky. It also seeks to understand the stars and the celestial beings who control the stars and their effect upon human life. A close study of the text of Revelation indicates that while the seer may have been in Patmos, he learned the grammar, vocabulary, and syntax of reading the sky in the Semitic world. His constellations are Hellenized, traditional, Semitic ones. He describes what he sees and what he hears on the basis of Israel's Scriptures. Finally, the being enthroned at the center of the cosmos is the God of Israel, often geographically centered in Jerusalem and its temple, along with the cosmic Lamb of God, identified with the Messiah of Israel, Jesus of Nazareth.

What astral prophecy does is seek out the recurrent causes that determine the outcomes of social interaction. And it seeks these causes in celestial phenomena and personages. Once such causes are discovered, they are formulated in terms of laws deriving from the predictable behavior of celestial personages. These personages produce effects which eventually regulate the objects of human social concern. As we shall see, such formulations can be found in ancient thunder books, lightning books, earthquake books, beginning of the year books and the like (in scholarship, all of these have esoteric Greek names, and a number of them have been found at Judean Qumran). The activity of celestial beings constantly impacts on human social interactions. And these social interactions are all interconnected in a part-to-part relationship, something like a giant jigsaw puzzle with regularly fitting parts, but with no overall plan derived from the parts. The plan is latent, implicit because it is controlled from above. In analyzing data from the celestial field, prophets and/or seers generally produce facts that fall into an integral, whole picture of the partial regularities that they began with. All facts can be reduced to such piecemeal and partial regularities. As for the book of Revelation, we shall see that, thanks to the traditional story of Israel, especially that part presenting the events of cosmic and human origins, the author can provide a solution to the present situation affecting his part of the world in general and his "brothers" in particular, on the basis of what has happened in the sky in the past and what is happening there in the present.

It is my purpose, then, to lead the readers of this book on a tour through the chapters of Revelation, to identify some of the sky phenomena encountered by the seer and to note the significance of some of their activities. Such a tour should acquaint readers with the scenarios experienced by the author and will perhaps allow us to see them as a first-century audience would. But first, consider some of the characteristics of astral prophecy.

2

Sky Visions and Sky Trips: The Characteristics of Astral Prophecy

The book of Revelation describes John's experience in and with the sky. In the mind of a first-century observer, the type or genre of this sort of writing was "prophecy." This is rather obvious since the author calls his book "words of the prophecy" (Rev 1:3). The concluding chapter explicitly repeats the label three times: "How honorable is he who keeps the words of the prophecy of this book" (22:7, 10, 18; "the words of the book of this prophecy," 22:19). In this vein, a celestial being addressing the seer ranks him as among the prophets ("your brethren the prophets," 22:9), just as the seer is told that he "must again prophesy about many peoples and nations and tongues and kings" (Rev 10:11), although there is no indication about when and before whom he is to perform this role.

Yet John's style of prophecy surely differed from that of John the Baptist and Jesus, who were also ranked as prophets. And consider the prophecy of persons variously called mantics, oraclists, diviners, and interpreters of ancient texts (e.g., the *Odyssey* or the *Iliad*, or Genesis or Isaiah). Now what is distinctive of John, the seer of Patmos, is that his prophecy was rooted in reading the sky. Like others before and after him, John described the impact of stars on the earth. Such prophets read the sky by means of observations, sky visions, and sky trips.

2.1. What is Astral Prophecy?

It seems rather obvious that writings about visions in the sky, involving celestial events and celestial phenomena, belong to the category of sky description. In fact the events and entities described in the book of Revelation are not very different from what is generally called "astronomical" or "astrological" literature. However, the author of the book of Revelation claims to be a prophet; he ranks his work among the prophecy of his day and age. Consequently, by his own estimation, his writing would be a subset of the genre or type of astronomical and/or astrological literature, but of a prophetic sort, for there were other writings that formed other subsets of astronomical and/ or astrological literature. For example, there were writings on the meaning of thunder (βροντολογία, *brontologia*), forecasts for the year based on given constellations of the zodiac (δωδεκαετηρίς, *dōdekaetēris*), writings indicating which planets and their deities or angels are in control of hours of the day; and of course there were horoscopes indicating the best "hour" to begin a trip, to start a business, build a house, and the like. But none of these claimed to be prophecy the way John's work does.

The main concern of ancient sky scholars was the impact of celestial bodies on human beings. The chief difference in scholarly attitudes today is that our scholars view the world as impersonal, inert, and lifeless. The ancient sky observer believed in living cosmic beings who controlled sky entities and sky phenomena and their effect on human social interaction, especially politics. Stars were personages to be reckoned with. And for the ancients, the term "stars" referred to all visible celestial bodies, i.e., planets, constellations, single stars, comets, meteors.

Now the main characteristic of those ancient producers of astral prophecy was that they were given divinely guided interpretations of celestial phenomena. Their astral prophecy consisted of information imparted by means of experience with celestial entities: stars, singly or in constellations, personages such as angels or demons, and God (gods). When written down, this experience takes the shape of a type or genre of writing, for example, an oracular utterance, a story of the experience, or a list of events shortly to occur. Distinctive of the astral prophecy in Revelation (and other writings like it) is that the prophet describes events in story form, that is, in a narrative.

So we may say that as a genre or type of writing, astral prophecy, like that in the book of Revelation, is a type of astronomic writing with a narrative framework which sets forth information derived from the prophet's interaction with celestial entities.

2.2. DID JOHN REALLY SEE WHAT HE SAID HE SAW?

How can one assess whether John really saw what he said he saw? Did he simply imagine the whole thing? Did he sit down one day and decide to author a work of religious science fiction? How do people judge the factuality or nonfactuality of what they read? Consider how people in the habit of reading a newspaper generally come to their reading with rather fixed presuppositions about what they will find in the paper. They expect to find the news. But the news is not all of one type. Sports news is different from the obituaries, and these are both different from food ads or editorials. Newspaper readers know all about the various types of writing in a newspaper, and most do a credible job of interpreting this complex genre. The newspaper is indeed a complex genre whose many different literary forms or patterns require many different ways of assessing their message. "Genre" refers to the type or category of writing to which the document in question belongs. Thus the newspaper genre or type differs from the phonebook type. And novels differ from newspapers and arithmetic textbooks. This may be obvious, but all of us had to learn about different types of writings. Most of us will not confuse a "Dear Occupant" letter with a letter from a loved one even though both call us "dear." The point is that the genre of a writing derives directly from the social system. We believe that newspapers are a form of writing about the news because in social ways we have learned to expect that from newspapers. If a paper presents a total fabrication as a news story, it would be impossible to distinguish it from a factual news story solely on the basis of the way it is written, given where it is presented, the news page. Similarly, it is impossible to tell the difference between a historical account and historical fiction solely on the basis of the way they are written. Both a history book and a historical novel may describe the same characters at the same point in time in the same country with the same customs. Whether the author is a journalist or a novelist, the only way to know that one author intends to describe "what actually happened," while the other wants to tell a factually rooted fictional story, is by the storytellers telling what they are up to. The same is true with news clips on television news programs. It is as easy to show fictional footage as it is to show the factual. So to determine genre, a reader has to learn how to inquire of persons who live out the roles, values, meanings, and structures that constitute the social system, for it is these people and their social system that maintain a given type of writing as factual, meaningful, and useful. Just as this is true in our society, it is no less true of ancient ones. And the ancients could assess astral prophecy because they lived in a social system in which sky readings were significant for understanding human existence.

John took his sky readings while "in spirit" (1:10; 4:2; 17:3; 21:10). Whether one translates this phrase by ecstasy or trance, the point is that John himself insists he fell into an altered state of awareness and came to experience an alternate reality. This may be difficult for us to believe because we have been enculturated to be selectively inattentive to such states of awareness except in dreams. Pilch (1994: 233) has noted:

> The physician-anthropologist Arthur Kleinman offers an explanation for the West's deficiency in this matter. "Only the modern, secular West seems to have blocked individual's access to these otherwise pan-human dimensions of the self." What is the western problem? The advent of modern science in about the seventeenth century disrupted the bio-psycho-spiritual unity of human consciousness that had existed until then. According to Kleinman, we have developed an "acquired consciousness," whereby we dissociate self and look at self "objectively." Western culture socializes individuals to develop a metaself, a critical observer who monitors and comments on experience. The metaself does not allow the total absorption in lived experience which is the very essence of highly focused ASCs (= alternate states of consciousness). The metaself stands in the way of unreflected, unmediated experience which now becomes distanced.

If we recall that "objectivity" is simply socially tutored subjectivity, we might be more empathetic with persons of other cultures whose perceptions we find incredible because they are socially dysfunctional for us. Be that as it may, our astral prophet does report altered states of awareness and alternate perceptions of reality as he journeys to the sky (4:2), or to some nameless wilderness (17:3), and to an unnamed high mountain (21:10). How are we to assess John's statements? Anthropologist Felicitas Goodman has studied persons who have perceived alternate realities like those reported by John. She observes that it is not difficult to teach individuals how to fall into trance states, but that trance experiences are generally empty unless filled with culturally significant and expected scenarios (1990: 17).

What this means is that if John's experiences are so rich in imagery and action, it is only because he was culturally prepared to have such experiences. Hence any interpretation of John requires the interpreter to delve into the stories in Israel's tradition concerning events occurring in an alternate dimension of reality and involving people or beings who straddled the two dimensions. Ezekiel, Zechariah, Daniel, and the book of Enoch are excellent examples of such stories. Furthermore Goodman lists four requisite conditions common to the "trance journeys": (1) The traveler needs to know how to find the crack between the earth (ordinary reality) and the sky on the horizon (alternate reality). (2) The human body is an intruder in that alternate reality. By bodily posture, the seer must tune the physical self to the alternate reality in order to perceive it properly. (3) The seer needs the readily learnable proper angle of vision. (4) The event perceived in the experience of the alternate reality is sketched out very hazily. Therefore, to appreciate a particular experience it must be recognized by means of the general cultural story as well as any specific story (Goodman 1990: passim, summarized by Pilch 1994).

In sum, John is well educated in contemporary star lore and his culture's traditional stories. His story of this interpretation of the sky and its personages during his sky journey is his astral prophecy.

2.3. The When's and Where's of Astral Prophecy

As far as time is concerned, the information in John's astral prophecy has two dimensions: past and present. First of all, it is past in that the prophet's experience derives from sky settings rooted in the period of creation. The constellations are fixed at the time of creation. The planets, too, have been regularly traversing their irregular pathways since creation. Furthermore, these sky settings continue to impact the earth and its inhabitants even in the present.[1] Moreover, the astral prophecy is spatial in that it involves the effect of the sky (and its inhabitants) upon specific regions of the earth and the inhabitants of those regions. As a rule, the ancients do not report any celestial phenomena that impact on the whole earth. Astral prophets knew that sky phenomena were specific to a given region.

Of course the approach to reading the sky was rooted in a shared perception of the appurtenances and inhabitants of the sky. Sky readings in antiquity were never undertaken simply to satisfy curiosity or accumulate knowledge. All people believed they were controlled by forces greater than themselves, and these forces were fundamentally intelligent beings, hence person-type forces. Every significant effect was caused by some intelligent being, human or nonhuman. People were group-oriented and group-encapsulated, and groups were affected by sky phenomena. Thus ordinary people did not ask about "me," but about "us," when it came to sky forces. Only highly placed elites, such as princes, kings, or Roman senators, were sufficiently "individual" enough to expect to be the object of some celestial personage's concern. The problem for affected and concerned groups or elites was to determine what motivated a celestial person(s) to act against or for us (or "me" if an elite).

Since the book of Revelation deals exclusively with displays of astronomical power directed to groups and political elites, it would seem it is indeed about politics. Politics has power as its essential symbolic and social medium; however, since those wielding celestial power were intelligent beings who determined the meaning of events,

---

[1] This is not unlike Hellenistic "readings" of plays. In Rome, for example, Corcoran notes: "The Roman audience tended to interpret lines even from old plays as having a reference to current events and scandals, and the actors deliberately stressed such lines" (in Seneca, *Natural Questions* 1, LCL, 1971: 83, note 1).

Revelation equally deals with religion. But this religion is embedded in a political system (see Malina 1986b). Furthermore, since the work presents a revelation of political fortunes visible in celestial phenomena but unknown to the principal political entities involved, this further confirms the sense of calling this type of writing "astral prophecy." Thus there is every good reason to keep the ancient label of prophecy for this sort of writing, providing one keep in mind that the context is Hellenistic astronomics, hence "astral prophecy."

In sum, astral prophecy is a conventional, imaginative description of an experience in terms of celestial scenarios. Such prophecy is not assessed in terms of true and false, fact or non-fact, but in terms of the adequacy or inadequacy of the significance of the information it imparts. It is revelation in that astral prophets make known what most persons did not know. And most ancient persons simply did not know enough about sky lore and techniques for acquiring it to learn such information. Astral prophecy is astrological and/or astronomical prophecy. It differs from other forms of prophecy in that it describes visions of, and interactions with, sky beings and sky phenomena that impact upon regions of the earth. In the first-century Mediterranean, sky beings were commonly believed to be in control of human social realities: life and death, war and peace, climate and fertility, and the like.

2.4. ASTRAL PROPHECY AND REVELATIONS

To appreciate the distinctiveness of astral prophecy, we compare this form of divine revelation with a number of other forms attested to in antiquity. Astral prophecy was but one way of obtaining information from the world of God(s). The range of writings from the period that attest to divine revelations indicates that divine secrets had been acquired both directly and indirectly. On the one hand, divine secrets could be learned directly by prophets and seers through dreams or trance states (seeing and hearing), from a god (seeing and hearing), from a newly discovered book or stele (hearing by reading), and from signs in the sky (seeing and hearing). Direct revelations come from a sky source and involve the receiver's sight and hearing. John's astral prophecy belongs to this category of direct revelation.

On the other hand, indirect revelations are those handed down from recipient to recipient. In this scenario, hearing alone is involved (the ancients read aloud: see Rev 1:3). Indirect revelations are those given by a seer, sage, or prophet to a king or some other elite person, and those given to a learning community, i.e., his (her) children, fellow believers. Indirectly, one could learn divine secrets from those who received them directly, such as sages and seers, or one's parent and mentor (hearing by instruction or reading).

2.4.1. Revelation in the course of a dream or an ecstasy

Dream revelations should be familiar to readers of the Bible (see Fox 1987:102–67; Hanson 1980, Del Corno 1978). The revelations to Joseph in Matt 1:18–25 take place in dreams and include a birth oracle typical of generic horoscopes. Philosophers explained the rationale behind such revelations (e.g., Aristotle's treatise *On Prophecy in Sleep* 462b, 12–464b, 18). Greek and Roman priests were expected to interpret dreams, while some wrote books to facilitate such interpretations (a most famous manual is that of Artemidorus of Daldis in Lydia of the 2d c. A.D.). Such dream revelations have much in common with ecstatic visions (Hanson, 1980, even collapses the two). Thus the physician Thessalos, at a loss to understand a treatment, leaves Alexandria for the desert of Egypt and resolves either to discover the secret of the treatment or to commit suicide. He states: "Just as my soul incessantly foretold to me that I would have commerce with the gods, I continually raised my hands toward the sky, begging the gods to grant me, by a vision in a dream or by divine spirit [= sky power], a favor of this sort" (CCAG VIII, 3, p. 135, 29–30; see Festugière 1939; Smith 1977).

Revelation by means of "divine sky power" (= holy spirit) usually entails ecstasy, that is "leaving oneself." This is the burden of Paul's description in 2 Cor 12:2–4 (for antiquity, see also Johnston 1992: 303–5). Another good example is that of the *Potter's Oracle*, preserved in a Greek papyrus of the third century A.D., although the prophetic message reflects Ptolemaic Egypt of ca. 130 B.C. In the scenario, however, the prophet is presented as a prophet of Isis and Osiris during Amenophis' reign (14th c. B.C.). He is a rich person, possessing house and fields. One day he sells all his goods to take up the potter's trade. By this action he dishonors the priestly role and proves himself impious. People then consider him a fool (frag. 1, lines 1–10). The text that follows is damaged but can be summarized as follows. The population, irate at the man's lack of respect for the gods, breaks into his workroom and destroys all his things. He then falls into ecstasy (lines 14–5), and possessed by divine power ("god borne," line 15; "knowing from the sky" line 16), he begins to prophesy.

> The broken pots, he claimed, symbolized the destruction of Egypt. The evil god Typhon-Seth (i.e. the Greeks) will dominate the land, the Nile will provide no water, and men will suffer famine. Total chaos will prevail. Alexandria itself will be destroyed and will become a place where fishermen dry their nets. After the destruction of Alexandria (the Greek stronghold) the gods Agathos Daimon and Knephis will go to Memphis, the new

capital. The era of peace and prosperity will then be introduced by a divinely appointed king:

> And then Egypt shall blossom when the king who has been in good favor for fifty-five years shall appear from the sun, a dispenser of good things, established by the great goddess [Isis], so that the living will pray that the dead will be resurrected to share the good things. And at the conclusion of this period [the plants] will put forth leaves, and the empty Nile shall be filled with water, and discordant winter shall change and run in its regular cycle. And then the summer also shall resume its regular cycle. And the storm winds shall be gently diminished into well ordered breezes (cited from Aune 1983: 77).

This is a prediction of the collapse of the social order of Ptolemaic Egypt, with hope of its reestablishment by a king who will rescue the populace.

The trip to the sky is also common in dreams. Thus Artemidorus, in his well-known book, *On the Interpretation of Dreams*, tells us: "for example, Plutarch dreamt that he ascended into the sky with Hermes as his guide" (4.72, trans. R. J. White 215). We are informed of a similar ecstatic receiving revelation from gods in the Paris Magical Papyrus. This person first makes proper incantations, after which he is told:

> Then open your eyes, and you will see the doors open and the world of the gods which is within the doors, so that from the pleasure and joy of the sight your spirit runs ahead and ascends. So stand still and at once draw breath from the divine into yourself, while you look intently. Then when your soul is restored, say: "Come, lord etc . . . " (*PGM* 4.625–31, Betz 50).

Toward the end of the experience, the person is told:

> After you have said these things, he will immediately respond with a revelation. Now you will grow weak in soul and will not be in yourself, when he answers you. He speaks the oracle to you in verse, and after speaking he will depart. But you will remain silent, since you will be able to comprehend all these matters by yourself; for at a later time you will remember infallibly the things spoken by the great god, even if the oracle contained myriads of verses (*PGM* 4.724–31, Betz 52).

Thus, as Paul indicates, trips to the sky can occur in ecstasy. And Artemidorus notes how this can happen in dreams as well. A most famous sky traveler of this sort was the Egyptian King Nechepso. The second century A.D. author Vettius Valens, speaks of sky travel (οὐρα-νοβατέω, *ouranobateō*) in which ecstatic persons leave the earth behind and move into the realm of the immortal, where they become privy to the divine and sacred. His main witness for such revelation is Nechepso, who said: "It seemed to me that I traveled all night through the air . . . and someone in the sky echoed to me, someone enveloped in a dark *peplos*, proffering obscurity" (*Anthologiae* VI, preface, ed. Kroll 241,

16–19). In the Israelite tradition, Enoch is the sky traveler par excellence (1 Enoch 12:1). And, of course, so is the seer John in this book (1:10; 4:1–2; 16:3; 21:10).

Significantly, those who make sky trips still keep their feet on the ground. Philo, the Hellenistic philosopher of Alexandria, notes in his *On Dreams*: "And why, treading as you do on earth, do you leap over the clouds? And why do you say that you are able to lay hold of what is in the upper air when you are rooted on the ground?" (1.54, LCL). Note also the epigram said to come from Ptolemy: "I know that I am mortal, a creature of a day; but when I search into the multitudinous revolving spirals of the stars my feet no longer rest on the earth, but standing by Zeus himself, I take my fill of ambrosia, the food of the gods" (*Greek Anthology* 9.577, LCL see Taub 1993: 135–45)

2.4.2. Revelation through conversation with a sky being

Luke reports conversations with sky servants, held by Zachariah, Mary, and shepherds (Luke 1:11–22; 1:26–38; 2:9–14). The women going to the empty tomb likewise meet up with a sky servant(s) who gives them information (Mark 16:1–8; Matt 28:1–8; Luke 24:1–10). To meet and converse with a god or some other celestial being is a phenomenon which was simply not very surprising or unheard of in the Greco-Roman period. Consider Acts 14:11–12: "And when the crowds saw what Paul had done, they lifted up their voices, saying in Lycaonian, 'The gods have come down to us in the likeness of men!' Barnabas they called Zeus, and Paul, because he was the chief speaker, they called Hermes."

Josephus, too, reports something similar as normal among the Pharisees of his experience. He mentions that they were able to predict events and then goes on to describe their relationship with the wife of a certain Pheroras: "In return for her friendliness they foretold—for they were believed to have foreknowledge of things through God's appearances to them—that by God's decree Herod's throne would be taken from him, both from himself and his descendants, and the royal power would fall to her and Pheroras and to any children that they might have" (*Antiquities* 17.42, LCL).

In his travels through Phoenicia and Palestine, Celsus, a philosopher of the second century, reports that he had listened to prophets who addressed crowds inside temples and outside, in cities and in the countryside, with the following sort of revelation discourse:

I am God or God's Son or Spirit of God. Here I have come for the cosmos will soon be destroyed, and you as well, human beings, because of your injustices. But I want to save you. Hereafter you will see me elevated with heavenly power. Blessed is the one who now worships me! Upon all others I will cast eternal fire, on all their cities and countrysides. And those human beings who do not recognize the punishment that awaits them will repent and groan in vain. But those who believe in me I will protect forever (Celsus, *Against the Christians* [cited from Origen, *Against Celsus* 7, 9] Biblioteca Universale Rizzoli 238–41).

The second-century astrologer Vettius Valens, for example, notes how many times, "it seemed to me that divine beings conversed with me, and I then felt my understanding was fully clear and cleansed for my investigations" (*Anthologiae* VI, preface, ed. Kroll 242, 17–18).

A typical feature of this type of revelation is the claim that the outcome of the experience was a book "dictated" by the god or angel. The physician Thessalos brought along writing materials for his meeting with Asclepios (CCAG VIII, 3, p. 136, 27). This feature is found in various revelatory genres. Thus Ezekiel (2:9ff.) is told to eat the book which a divine hand gave him and which would be reproduced in his preaching (as though his stomach worked like a VCR or tape recorder). Likewise the author of our book is told to write (1:11–19). The basic idea is the same. The words pronounced or written by the prophet are divine; the wisdom he teaches has been revealed to him. Lucius, the hero of Apuleius' *Metamorphoses*, was quite distressed on the occasion of a vision "not to have tablets and a stylus to write down such a marvelous story" of Psyche; the distress derives from the same expectations (Apuleius, *Metamorphoses* 6.25, LCL).

2.4.3. Revelation by the discovery of a (divine) book or stele

In the Hellenistic period, it was common knowledge that there were books or steles of divine origin. In the Israelite tradition, people knew of the stone tables or steles "written by the finger of God" which the God of Israel gave to the prophet Moses (Exod 31:18). Such divinely inscribed tables were not rare. For example, Diodorus of Sicily (end of the first century B.C.) reports an account from Euhemerus' work entitled *Sacred Scripture* (ἱερὰ ἀναγραφή, *hiera anagraphē*), from about 300 B.C. According to this account, in the Zeus temple of the Pancheans

> there is a couch of the god which is six cubits long and four wide and is entirely of gold and skillfully constructed in every detail of its workmanship. . . . And on the center of the couch stands a large gold stele which carries letters which the Egyptians call sacred, and the inscription recounts the deeds both of Uranus and of Zeus; and to them there were added by Hermes the deeds also of Artemis and of Apollo (*Library of History* 5.46, 7, LCL; same information repeated in 6.1, 6–7, LCL).

It seems that Lactantius knew this tradition, for he writes:

> Euhemerus composed his history on the basis of the holy inscriptions which were contained in very ancient temples, and especially in a shrine of

Jupiter Triphylius, where, as the inscription stated, Jupiter himself had set up a gold stele on which he had written an account of his deeds, to serve posterity as a monument of what he had accomplished (*Divine Institutions* 1.11, LCL; cited by C. H. Oldfather *ad locum*).

Diodorus himself previously noted that the Pancheans had ancient traditions of their origin from Cretans, and "it has been their practice, in corroboration of these claims, to point to inscriptions which, they said, were made by Zeus during the time he still sojourned among men and founded the temple" (*Library of History* 5.46, 3, LCL).

Similarly, Diodorus relates:

> Now I am not unaware that some historians give the following account of Isis and Osiris: the tombs of these gods lie in Nysa in Arabia, and for this reason Dionysus is also called Nysaeus. And in that place there stands also a stele of each of the gods bearing an inscription in hieroglyphs. On the stele of Isis it runs: "I am Isis, the queen of every land, she who has instructed Hermes, and whatsoever law I have established, these can no man make void. I am the eldest daughter of the youngest god Cronus; I am the wife and sister of the king Osiris; I am she who first discovered fruits for mankind; I am the mother of Horus the king; I am she who riseth in the star that is in the Constellation of the Dog; by me was the city of Bubastus built. Farewell, farewell, O Egypt that nurtured me." And on the stele of Osiris the inscription is said to run: "My father is Cronus, the youngest of all the gods, and I am Osiris the king, who campaigned over every country as far as the uninhabited regions of India and the lands to the north, even to the sources of the river Ister [= Danube], and again to the remaining parts of the world as far as Oceanus. I am the eldest son of Cronus, and being sprung from a fair and noble egg I was begotten a seed of kindred birth to Day. There is no region of the inhabited world to which I have not come, dispensing to all men the things of which I was the discoverer" (*Library of History* 1.27, 4–5, LCL).

In the first century B.C. the author of the *Axiochos* explains the fate of the dead, relating his information to a revelation of the magus Gobryes, whose grandfather found it on Delos during the expedition of Xerxes, inscribed on two bronze tablets brought from the Hyperboreans (Ps-Plato, "Axiochus or On Death," in *The Works of Plato*, vol. 6, trans. George Burges, London: Bohn, 1854, 52–55).

Similarly, Plutarch states in his *The Face of the Moon* that the story he narrates about the fate of the souls on the moon comes from a stranger who "spent a great deal of time in Carthage . . . and he discovered certain sacred parchments that had been secretly spirited off to safety when the earlier city was being destroyed and had lain unnoticed in the ground for a long time" (Plutarch, *Moralia* 942 C, LCL).

The *Potter's Oracle* had also been dictated and set down in hieroglyphs in the presence of the king and the priests by the prophet in his trance. It was deposited by order of Amenophis in the sacred archives of Heliopolis where all might consult them (frag. 3, lines 17–20).

The prestige of ancient books for astrological study was so great that Ptolemy notes in his *Tetrabiblos*:

> Recently, however, we have come upon an ancient manuscript much damaged, which contains a natural and consistent explanation of their [the planets'] order and number. . . . The book was very lengthy in expression and excessive in demonstration, and its damaged state made it hard to read, so that I could barely gain an idea of its general purport; that too, in spite of the help offered by the tabulations of the terms, better preserved because they were placed at the end of the book (1.21, 48, LCL).

Then there is the tradition of Kyranides dating to the first century A.D. In the original prologue, the author states: "This book was engraved in Syriac letters on a column (or stele) of iron" (*Liber physicalium virtutum*, ed. Delatte, Ip.13). Harpocration's account of learning about this book is worth citing:

> This is the story, my daughter. Now the third time it happened that I came upon a certain old man very wise in foreign subjects and Greek letters. He said he was Syrian, but he had been made a captive and lived there [at Seleucia on the Tigris or in a nearby town]. This old man then took me on a full tour of the city, and he showed me everything. Now, having arrived at a place some four thousand paces from the city, we saw next to a great tower a column which the inhabitants had brought for themselves from Syria [= Assyria] and placed there for the health and healing of the inhabitants of the city [= a talismanic, miracle-producing tower, a sort of sacred stone]. When looking at it up close, I saw that this column bore an inscription in foreign letters. After that the old man, of whom I made the request, agreed to explain the thing to me, and I heard his story about the column, while he readily translated the barbarian letters aloud for me into the Aeolic [= Greek] language. "You see, my son," he said, "the three towers laid out in such a way that one of them stands at a distance of five thousand paces, the other two and a half thousand paces, the third four thousand paces. They have been built by the Giants who wished to ascend into the sky; because of this foolish impiety some were struck by lightning or others stricken with insanity for the rest of their days by the judgment of God, while still others God, in his anger, cast into the island of Crete." The old man who showed me these things ordered me to measure with a line the size of the stone [=of the tower?]. I then measured the one which was the closest and found the height of 32 cubits, breadth of 78. The tower stairs consisted of 208 steps. We also saw the sacred enclosure: in the middle of the enclosure there was a temple with stairs of 365 steps of silver, and another of 60 steps of gold. We climbed them to pray to God. The old man then told me the mysteries of the divine power, which it is not fitting to repeat. As for me, in spite of my desire to learn about it longer, I left the remainder for later and asked only about the column. The old man then took away the covering of linen and showed me the inscription

in alien and foreign letters. Since I am learned in my own letters, I requested and beseeched him to explain the text to me clearly and without envy. This is what was to be read on the column (*Liber physicalium virtutum*, ed. Delatte, 15–17).

The *Compendium aureum* of Flaccus Africus, said to be a compilation extracted from the *Kyranides*, presents the same motif with this variant: the book was found in a tomb this time:

> Flaccus Africus, a disciple of Belben [=Balinas = Apollonius of Tyana], to Claudius of Athens the calculator (?), good continuation of studies and good success in your investigations! After the books of the ancient Kyranides which are known to you and which are related to your colleague Harpocration, I have discovered in the city of Troy, hidden in a tomb with the bones of the first king Kyranos, this work entitled, *Golden Compendium*, because it is a summary of extracts, compiled with care, from the most important book of the Kyranides (ed. Delatte, 213).

Finding books of revelation in ancient tombs is a well-known, popular theme: the tombs of Cleopatra, Alexander the Great, Hermes Trismegistes, among others, all yielded books, just as in this case of Kyranos king of Persia (see Boll 1914: 136–37). In conclusion, consider the following passages from the magical papyri purporting to relate information from various inhabitants of the sky: "Lunar spell of Claudianus and [ritual] of heaven and the north star over lunar offerings: This papyrus itself, the personal property of the Twelve Gods, was found in Aphroditopolis [beside] the great goddess, Aphrodite Urania, who embraces the universe" (*PGM* 7.862–66, Betz 141). In a prayer to Hermes, we find: "Your true name has been inscribed on the sacred stele in the shrine at Hermopolis where your birth is" (*PGM* 8.41–42, Betz 146). " 'Great is the Lady Isis.' Copy of a holy book found in the archives of Hermes" (*PGM* 24a.4, Betz 254). "A copy from a holy book" (*PGM* 3.424, Betz 29).

2.4.4. Revelation received by means of signs in the sky

Persons today consider events in the sky that impact on the earth and its inhabitants as atmospheric phenomena. Lightning, tornadoes, thunder, sudden cloudbursts, and the like are simply all part of the weather. The ancients, however, considered such events as signs and sought social meanings in them. For the ancients, nothing could possibly happen in the sky that did not in some way impact the earth and its inhabitants. For example, the account of Moses' meeting with God on Sinai is replete with atmospheric phenomena. Smoke is interpreted as indicating God's presence ("because God came down upon it in fire"); thunder is interpreted as God's voice ("God replied to him in thunder").

Sky effects such as thunder, lightning, dense clouds, and earthquakes, indicate God's local presence (Exod 19:16–19). Over the centuries, the meanings of such atmospheric phenomena were compiled in collections relating to earthquakes (σεισμολόγιον, *seismologion*), thunder (βρον-τολόγιον, *brontologion*), and the like. Consider, now, the passage in the "Thunderbook of Hermes Trismegistus," a rather ancient source since it is used by the Roman Fonteius, who is prior to Varro (first century B.C.):

> In the month of January. If there is thunder or lightning, that same country must be attentive so that it not be devastated by a tyrant; the land will not bear fruits; there will not be a rising of the Nile due to lack of water; Egypt will subjugate its own masters; then the peoples of the West will live without care and in luxury; and the king of Persia will be free of cares. If this occurs at night, then the peoples of the West will live without cares and in luxury, but there will be upheavals; some kings will wage war; among those of the West, certain men will be held in honor; there will be wars in the country [= Egypt]; many will perish in the sea; the temperature will be good (CCAG VII, 226)

A pre-Constantinian poem, "On earthquakes," frequently attributed to Orpheus, lists its forecasts according to the position of the sun in the zodiac, beginning with Aries (April). Here are the first ten lines:

> Learn this material, my child: everything occurring when the dark haired Earthquaker (Poseidon) shakes the earth foretells for mortals good or bad fortune. When it comes at the equinox of springtime and the sun is journeying through Aries, if then the god embracing the earth shakes it violently during the night, that foretells great revolts in the city [= Alexandria]. If he shakes it during the day, this announces sadness and curses, a plague will strike a foreign people, and there will be for us affliction and sufferings (CCAG VII, 167).

This poem exists in prose form as well, and begins as follows:

> April. The sun being in Aries, if the earth quakes during the day, those who approach kings will be mutually involved in snares; the nearby cities will be shaken by great troubles and will experience acts of violence and murders; an illustrious person will perish and his followers will be in danger; there will be great rains; the fruits of the earth and trees will prosper. If the earth trembles at night, there will be quarrels among the people, and they will revolt against the tyrant of the place; because the soldiers of the tyrant will mutiny, they will oppose him and rebel against their own king; there will be troubles and revolutions among the people, the tyrants of the West will perish; there will be great rains; planted fields will multiply. In Egypt there will be famine and lack of water in the Nile (CCAG VII 167).

And in a thunderbook from Qumran, we find:

If it thunders in the sign of Taurus, revolutions (in) the wor[ld . . .] problems for the cities and destru[ction in the cour]t of the King and in the province of [. . .] there will be, and for the Arabs [. . .] famine. And some will plunder others [. . .] If it thunders in the sign of Gemini, fear and distress of the foreigners and of [. . .] (4Q318.2, col. 11, 6–9, ed. Garcia Martínez 452).

2.4.5. Types of indirect or transmitted revelations

One of the characteristic features of Hellenistic revelation litera-ture is that revelations are given only for those few of rather lofty ascribed status. This means revelations are really directed solely to well born persons, persons who are divine, god-like, or who tower above ordinary humans on the basis of their origins. For example, Aristotle has trouble admitting the existence of genuine revelations in dreams essentially because even persons who are not "the best" or "the wisest" have dreams. It is hardly possible for them to have revelations. To quote his own words: "For, apart from its improbability on other grounds, it is absurd to hold that it is God who sends such dreams, and yet that He sends them not to the best and wisest, but to any chance persons" (*On Prophecy in Sleep* 462b, 20–23, LCL). And again: "There is proof of this [that dreams are not sent by God]: for quite common men have prescience and vivid dreams, which shows that these are not sent by God" (*On Prophecy in Sleep* 463b, 15, LCL). Thus God or the gods do not direct their revelations to commonplace persons, persons of inferior social type!

2.4.6. Instructions of a sage or seer to a king/elite

A revelation that comes through reading sky signs is much the same as a dream; it too is for the elite: "Who could know the sky save by the sky's gift, and discover God save one who shares himself in the divine" (Manilius, *Astronomica* 2.116, LCL). Persons to whom signifi-cant celestial phenomena are directed have, by nature, a social status lofty enough to come in contact with the realm of the divine, the sky. This category belongs almost exclusively to royalty, to kings. The con-vention that kings were preeminent among human beings as worthy objects of divine contact was deeply rooted in the ancient Mediterra-nean, a conviction well portrayed in ancient sculpture (see L'Orange 1982 reprint of 1947). As the dictum had it: "The king is the last of the gods as a whole, but the first of human beings" (*Corpus Hermeticum* III Fragment XXIV, 3; ed. Festugière-Nock, 53; this whole fragment deals with the question of how regal persons are produced). Thus revelations are meant for the socially "worthy," and the most worthy person in the ancient world was the king. Consider the evaluation of Manilius:

> Moreover nature proffered her aid and of her own accord opened up herself deigning first to inspire those kings whose minds reached out to heights bordering on heaven, kings who civilized savage peoples beneath the eastern sky, where the stars return to view and soar above the cities of dusky nations (*Astronomica* 1.39–43, LCL).

Priests rank in second place:

> Then priests who all their lives offered sacrifice in temples and were chosen to voice the people's prayer secured by their devotion the sympathy of God: their pure minds were kindled by the very presence of the powerful deity and the God of heaven brought his servants to a knowledge of heaven and disclosed its secrets to them (ibid., 1.44–50)

In other words, the task of astral prophets and those occupied with astronomics, if they are not elites themselves, is to mediate their findings to persons of lofty status. Hence it is not surprising when John reminds his audience that Jesus the Messiah "has made us a kingdom, priests for God and his Father" (Rev 1:6), for only high status people are worthy of astral prophecy.

Consider these instances. When the buried secrets of Hippocrates are found they are delivered directly to the emperor. The list of royal personages who discovered concealed revelations is impressive. It includes Alexander, Kyranos of Persia, Ostanes, Cleopatra, Nero, Zoroaster of Bactria, Solomon, Atreus and Thyestes, Philip, Ammon of Egypt, Hermes as King, and Josiah (2 Kings 22). In the Hellenistic period, the king is often described as having recourse to astral prophets (προφήτης, *prophētēs*) for some information or other. And at times the astral prophet is a priest (the first priest of Isis is a prophet), while the famous duo, Nechepso (king) and Petosiris (priest/prophet), are often cited together. The point here is that the "worthy" are normally royal personages, although at times priests have sufficient ascribed status to receive revelation themselves. Usually, however, a non-elite prophet or seer served as intermediary, with the task of handing on revelations to higher status worthies; for example, Daniel mediates for Nebuchadnezzar and Belshazzar (on this see Boll 1914: 136–37).

This perception of worthiness deriving from ascribed status can be found in the Gospel story. Consider Luke 10:23–24: "Turning to the disciples he [Jesus] said privately, 'How honored are the eyes which see what you see! For I tell you that many prophets and kings desired to see what you see, and did not see it, and to hear what you hear, and did not hear it.' " Of course prophets and kings are singled out here because they are the normal recipients of revelations. Thus 2 Macc 2:13 notes how Nehemiah "founded a library and collected the books about the kings and prophets. . . . " Similarly, consider how the prophet's task is to search and inquire: "The prophets who prophesied of the grace that was to be yours searched and inquired about this salvation" (1 Pet 1:10); the prophet's function is not unlike that of the sage and the scribe, hence the collocation in Matt 23:34: "Therefore I send you prophets and wise men and scribes. . . . "

Similarly, the new information characteristic of the Jesus movement is a revelation since it has to be delivered to kings, here in the person of the messengers carrying that information: "and you will stand before governors and kings for my sake, to bear testimony before them" (Mark 13:9; Matt 10:18; Luke 21:12).

It is interesting to note that the passage parallel to Luke 10:23–24 and preserved in Matthew's Gospel has the following: "But how honored are your eyes, for they see, and your ears, for they hear. Truly, I say to you, many prophets and righteous men longed to see what you see, and did not see it, and to hear what you hear, and did not hear it" (Matt 13:16–17). Thus instead of prophets and kings as statuses worthy for the revelation, it is prophets and righteous persons. Similarly, consider Matt 11:13: "For all the prophets and the law prophesied until John"; and Matt 10:41: "He who receives a prophet because he is a prophet shall receive a prophet's reward, and he who receives a righteous man because he is a righteous man shall receive a righteous man's reward." The point here is that if the collocation of "prophet and king" designates those who are worthy by status to receive revelations, then for Matthew's community, the status-worthy are "prophets and the righteous." That is why "he who is least in the kingdom of heaven is greater than he [John the Baptist]" (Matt 11:11). Thus for Matthew, followers of Jesus have been ascribed a status worthy enough for revelation. The same is true for our astral prophet, John, and his community.

Furthermore, in line with the common view expressed by Aristotle (*On Prophecy in Sleep,* LCL, previously cited) that only "the best" and "the wisest" received revelations from God, Matthew notes how the magi (Matt 2:12) and Pilate's wife (Matt 27:19) get such dream-revelations. Yet as with the previously noted instance, Matthew ranks "the righteous" among the status worthy. Thus the righteous Joseph, "a just man" (Matt 1:19), receives a number of dream-revelations (Matt 1:20; 2:13, 19, 22; Acts 2:17 traces dream-revelations to Joel's forecast).

Finally, as regards the wisdom of the recipients of revelation, note the parallel between the astrological work ascribed to Apollonius of Tyana and Luke's Gospel. "For the wise conceal these things like a treasure in the earth and in their hearts, because the spirit of wisdom is in them" (Ps. Apollonius, CCAG VII, 179, 25–26). In Luke 10:21 God conceals revelations from the wise: "In that same hour he [Jesus] rejoiced in the Holy Spirit and said, 'I thank you, Father, Lord of heaven and earth, that you have hidden these things from the wise and understanding and revealed them to babes; yea, Father, for such was your gracious will.'"

Those who receive astrological revelations learn other positive powers. For example: "Therefore one must, as stated, preserve these things carefully, if one generally wishes to free up all living beings upon the earth from the yoke of Fate, to loosen trees and to bind birds and wild animals and serpents and blowing winds and flowing rivers" (Ps Apollonius, CCAG VII, 176, 11–14). And Luke 10:17–19 informs us concerning Jesus' disciples: "The seventy returned with joy, saying, 'Lord, even the demons are subject to us in your name!' . . . 'Behold, I have given you authority to tread upon serpents and scorpions, and over all the power of the enemy; and nothing shall hurt you' " (further, see Boll 1914: 136–37).

It is true that prophets and sages who mediate revelation can be more perspicacious than the worthy persons for whom the revelation is destined: "Of these things, child, I have declared to you the easy and godly solution which not even kings were able to grasp" (*PGM* 13.225, Betz 178). And significantly, "worthiness" is not a moral attribute, but a social attribute based on social standing. Other instances of intermediary seers and their worthy recipients: Petosiris to Nechepso; Letters to Philip; Bothros to a king; Nephotes to Psammeticus; Pitys to Ostanes; Thphe to Ochos; Pnouthios the prophet to Keryx (not a king); and again, Daniel to Nebuchadnezzar and Belshazzar (Festugière 1950: 327–32).

2.4.7. Know-How as Kinship Assets

Ancient historians tell how among the various peoples of the East, the secrets of all knowledge and wisdom were handed down from father to son. Know-how, technique, technological innovation, and a range of information about those matters that we call "technical knowledge" or "specialized information" were family assets. One learned these matters from one's father. If an expert had no children or wanted more children to share his skills and insights, he might take on a "disciple" or two, and treat them like a father treats a son. Thus Diodorus of Sicily informs us:

> Among the Chaldeans the scientific study of these subjects is passed down in the family and son takes it over from father, being relieved of all other services in the state. Since, therefore, they have their parents for teachers, they not only are taught everything ungrudgingly [lit. without envy], but also at the same time they give heed to the precepts of their teachers with a more unwavering trust. Furthermore, since they are bred in these teachings from childhood up, they attain a great skill in them, both because of the ease with which youth is taught and because of the great amount of time which is devoted to this study (*Library of History* 2.29, 4, LCL).

The same was true of Egypt.

> For speaking generally, the priests [of Egypt] are the first to deliberate upon the most important matters and are always at the king's side, sometimes as his assistants, sometimes to propose measures and give instructions, and they also, by their knowledge of astrology and of divination, forecast future events, and read to the king, out of the record of acts preserved in their sacred books, those which can be of assistance. For it is not the case with the Egyptians as it is with the Greeks, that a single man or a single woman takes over the priesthood, but many are engaged in the sacrifices and honors paid the gods and pass on to their descendants the same rule of life (*Library of History* 1.73, 4–5, LCL).

For the Persians, we have the report of Ammianus Marcellinus:

> When Zoroaster had boldly made his way into the unknown regions of Upper India, he reached a wooded wilderness, whose calm silence the lofty intellects of the Brahmins control. From their teaching he learned as much as he could grasp of the laws regulating the movements of the earth and the stars, and of the pure sacrificial rites. Of what he had learned he communicated something to the understanding of the Magi, which they, along with the art of divining the future, hand on from generation to generation to later times. From that time on for many ages down to the present a large class of men of one and the same descent have devoted themselves to the service of the gods (*The History* 23.6, 33–34, LCL).

Of course the same was true in the Israelite tradition, which also shared this Hellenistic and Mediterranean cultural value.

> They handed down from the very beginning such information concerning the combination of the stars, the names of the months and of the years, and everything that can still be said about sky beings. For Seth, the son of Adam, had inscribed this information in the Hebrew language on wooden tablets, himself instructed by an angel of God. Then after the dispersion of tongues, Ammon the Greek advanced this science farther, and others after him. They also say that Enoch, the seventh after Adam, inscribed in Hebrew on stone tablets a prediction about the forthcoming wrath of God; after the Deluge, some of these tablets were found on a mountain, and later, carried away into Palestine (CCAG VII, 87).

Mention of "the seventh after Adam" indicates that the author considered a continuous transmission. In *The Testament of Adam* 2 (*OTP* 1.994), Adam is the discoverer of astrology and hands it on to Seth.

These observations of the ancient Greek, Roman, Syrian, and Israelite historians can be confirmed from the writings of other eastern Mediterranean peoples. The generally held view was that in the East knowledge and wisdom were transmitted from father to son. Aside from being the "natural" instructor of his son in adult matters, the father was in charge of the family's knowledge and wisdom, a sort of sacred deposit which was passed on, a secret (*mystērion*, μυστήριον) which was not to leave the family. Because the development and preservation of knowledge was a kinship function, as early as the New Empire in Egypt when scribal schools originated, students who evidently were not of the same family were called "sons" of the teaching scribes. They thus become heirs of the scribal patrimony, like the scribes' own sons. Consider the opening of the Words of Ahiqar (6th cent. B.C.): "These are the words of one Ahiqar, a wise and skillful scribe, which he taught his son. Now he did not have offspring of his own, but he said: 'I shall nevertheless have a son!'" (*OTP* 2.494). The same was true in Babylon and Assyria, and eventually in Israel (see the title: "my son" in the wisdom tradition: Prov 1:8, 10, 15; 2:1; 3:1, 11; 4:10, 20; 5:1, 7, 20; 6:1 etc.). The relationship between Elijah and Elisha was like a father and son (see 2 Kings 2–3).

In this setting, the word of the teacher-father was believed to have creative and saving value (like the word of a father). This conception of the effectiveness of the word is most striking in the Hellenistic period. For example: "Hear, O my son Nadan . . . and be mindful of my words as the words of God" (the late version of *The Story of Ahikar* 2:1, Charles *APOT* 1.728). And in the Septuagint tradition of Proverbs, we find: "My words have been uttered by God. . . . What will you preserve, my son? What? The words of God! My first born son, I am telling you this!" (Prov 31:1 LXX). Consequently, we find the effectiveness of the words: "So shall my word be that goes forth from my mouth; it shall not return to me empty, but it shall accomplish that which I purpose, and prosper in the thing for which I sent it" (Isa 55:11). This wisdom is "a tree of life to those who lay hold of her" (Prov 3:18). And so, "A multitude of wise men is the salvation of the world" (Wis 6:24).

There are countless illustrations of this theme of hidden knowledge being passed from father to son, fictive or otherwise, e.g., Hermes to Asklepios; Pythagoras to Telauges; Solomon to Roboam; Apollonius of Tyana to Postumus; Kyranis; and Orphic literature (conveniently to be found in Festugière 1950: 336–54).

2.5. ONGOING CONCERNS FOR REVELATION

In sum, ancient human groups and their representatives sought to diagnose and deal with the socially unknown that impacted on their lives. Groups and persons believed they had access to those cosmic personages who controlled the socially unknown. And they gained this access either through the initiative of the celestial beings themselves (e.g., the appearance of a deity) or through human initiative (e.g., a person prepares for ecstasy). Hence by means of such access, one might, on behalf of a group or its central persons (e.g., the king), contact those controlling beings and, thanks to their help, enter their space by means of visions, sky trips, and the like, with a view to learning directives and obeying. Such access was part of the social role of prophets, seers, magicians, astrologers, and astronomers. At times such access agents simply observed events as they unfolded, while at other times they attempted to coerce such controlling beings to do their own bidding. In either case the information sought was not about some distant future but about the present and forthcoming events that would impact their lives. In other words, there was nothing "eschatological" about astral prophecy, at least not in any usual sense of the "study of the last things." What mattered were existing, present things. Questions that concerned people included: What is happening at present? What has caused or is causing present conditions? What are the immediate and forthcoming outcomes of the present situation? What should one do in the present to prepare for this rather proximate outcome? The time concern is not the remote or distant future, but the past, the present and the immediate forthcoming. And what bothered people was not the end of the world, but what forthcoming events held in store for the group. Of course astral prophets had only positive and encouraging information for their in-group. It was the enemy, the out-group, who would be afflicted with negative events, and this largely because of what happened in some distant past.

This way of thinking was rooted in the belief that revelation and revealed wisdom are significant for the rescue of human beings from their cosmic situation, set in place due to some remote events. The word "salvation" means rescue from a difficult situation. This is an important perspective found in the Israelite writings of the post-exilic period. At times this revelation comes from wise ones—sages, who discover the revealed wisdom by delving into the Torah of Moses (Sirach 24; 39 [2d c. B.C.]; 4 Ezra; Qumran pesher writings; the role of scribes). At other times the revelation is the outcome of cosmic visions (The Epistle of Enoch = 1 Enoch 92–105 [2d c. B.C.], explaining the first part of the book; 1 Enoch 1–5 [3d c. B.C.], rooted in Num 24:15–17 [Balaam's oracle] and Deut 33:1–2 [Moses' Blessing]; Parables of Enoch = 1 Enoch 37–71).

In the Jesus movement, revelation of wisdom was likewise crucial. Statements in Q (Matt 11:25–27; Luke 10:21–22), Mark (4:11–12), and Matthew ("I/my" phrases, for example: "I say to you"; "my church"; "all that I have commanded") point to Jesus as revealer of the requisite wisdom. But in the Christian movement, Jesus is himself the revelation of God (thus John, Paul). As a matter of fact, the nature of the appearances of the raised Jesus becomes a crucial issue for Christians in the post-apostolic generations. This issue is already underscored in the Gospels, for the Gospel traditions record the appearances of the resurrected Jesus in straightforward descriptions of an actual historic incident: the (Eleven) disciples gathered as a group to interact with the resurrected

Jesus who appears just like they knew him before the crucifixion: physical, touchable, sharing food with them. Dodd categorized these accounts
as "concise." On the other hand, in some accounts Jesus appears suddenly and unexpectedly to one or two distraught individuals. Jesus
addresses them so that eventually they recognize him (e.g., Mary Mag-
dalene in John 20:14–18; Emmaus disciples in Luke 24:13–35). Dodd
labels these accounts "circumstantial" (Dodd 1957: 9–15). These circumstantial appearances of the Gospel tradition are like those appearances
to Paul (Acts 9:3–7), Stephen (Acts 7:55–56), and the astral prophet
John (Rev 1:10–18). In the New Testament story, such circumstantial
appearances occur after Pentecost, with Jesus appearing from or in the
sky in brilliant light and perceived through some internal faculty (see
Acts 7:55–56; 9:7; 22:9) or in an ecstatic condition (Rev 1:10; Acts 10:10)
(see Pagels 1978: 415–18).[2]

In the book of Revelation, the risen Christ appears to John of
Patmos in an exalted state, as a sky figure. The description of this Jesus
as sky figure is like that in Daniel and, as we shall see, in the older
Salmeschoiniaka (earlier than 150 B.C., see ch. 4). The cosmic Christ
reveals information directed to "the angels of the seven churches." John
makes us privy to this celestial, cosmic information.

At this point, however, instead of considering that information, let
us turn to a consideration of a general map that might direct us through
John's cosmic scenarios.

---

[2] Pagels (1978) observes quite to the point that it was the concise type of
appearance that was recognized and required in early Christianity as the basis for
apostolic authority in Christian movement groups, with apostolic meaning: normative, legitimate, legal. Paul, of course, did not experience such an appearance of Jesus,
only circumstantial type vision(s). The circumstantial type of appearance in a vision
later became common coin among Gnostics for establishing their authority in face of
competing apostolic claims wielded by non-Gnostic bishops. Gnostics claimed continuing revelation through visions. To eliminate Gnostic claims to authority, yet to
include Paul and Revelation, non-Gnostic leadership set up a canon of Scripture.
Henceforth no other visions of Jesus could bear meanings of public import to
Christians, especially if their message deviated from the canon.

3

SKY JOURNEYS:
MAPS FOR A TOUR THROUGH REVELATION

On any reading of Revelation, John, the Prophet of Patmos, saw a range of sky phenomena and sky beings. This he did, he tells us, as he mounted into the sky, or moved to a nameless wilderness, or observed from a cosmic mountain. He presumably did all of this from his vantage point on the island. What the seer observes and thus unmasks for his readers is the true source and cause of particular events that have occurred and are occurring on certain parts of the earth. John's "revelation" unveils the cosmic forces behind particular social events observable by earth-bound persons and their historians. His purpose is to prevent his "brothers" from being deceived, from being taken in by the outsiders with whom they interact. Revelation is necessary to prevent deception.

The phenomena John regards occur above the earth. They are to be seen either on the vault of the sky, in the space between the earth and the vault, or beyond the vault of the sky. As I previously noted, the first-century cosmos was a gigantic, but limited, area. It might be imagined to be like one extremely huge, ball-shaped shell. The earth was in the center of this magnificent shell. In the Hellenistic period, learned elites such as Theon of Smyrna (early second century A.D.) could say quite confidently: "The entire cosmos is a sphere and the earth, which is itself a spheroid, is placed in the middle . . . the earth is the center of the universe, and it is but a point in relationship to the size of the universe" (*Mathematics Useful for Understanding Plato* 3.1, trans. R. and D. Lawlor 81). Furthermore, "the celestial sphere turning around its immobile poles and the axis which joins them, at the middle of which is fixed the earth, and all the stars carried by this sphere and all the points of the sky, describe parallel circles, that is to say, circles everywhere equidistant, perpendicular to the axis, and drawn from the poles of the universe as centers" (ibid., 3.5, trans. R. and D. Lawlor 86). Thus the earth was a sphere surrounded by the sky that served as pathway for various celestial bodies. All fixed stars were "constellated." They were not arbitrary arrangements but were living beings that impacted on each other and on the earth. Then there were those other visible and non-visible rational beings that filled the sky: planets and the atmospheric phenomena they produced, along with deities, demons, angels, and spirits of various sorts.

The earth hung still and stable in the center of the whole rotating system. The inhabited earth (the οἰκουμένη, *oikoumenē*) was only one-fourth of the earthly sphere. It looked like a Greek soldier's cloak, a χλαμύς, *chlamys* (see Aujac 1981), which was shaped like a curved trapezoid. This inhabited earth ran from the Atlantic in the west to the Indus River in the east and was entirely surrounded by impassable water. Furthermore, to the north was bitter and impassable cold and to the south unbearable and impassable heat. The inhabited earth was divided into three segments: Europe, Asia, and Libya (or Africa).

What marked off the universe were great circles "described by the stars" in the sky, as Theon of Smyrna says:

> There is one [circle] above us, around the always apparent and visible pole. It is called the arctic (= Bear) circle, because of the constellations of the Bears which it crosses. Another, on the opposite side, equal to the first, circles the pole which we never see, is itself always invisible to us and is called the antarctic (= Counter Bear) circle. The one in the middle, which is a large circle, divides the whole sphere into two equal regions and is called the equator, because on these corresponding regions of the earth, there is an equality between the days and nights; for other places in which one sees the sun rise and set according to the general movement of the universe, the durations of the day and night are equal when the sun describes this circle. Between the equatorial circle and the two arctic circles there are two tropics, the tropic of summer situated for us on this side of the equatorial circle, and on the other side, the tropic of winter. The sun, in its revolution, sometimes moves near to one and sometimes to the other. The zodiac is in fact obliquely extended between these two circles. The zodiac is a great circle. It touches each tropic at one point: the tropic of summer at a point in Cancer and the other tropic at a point in Capricorn. It cuts the equatorial circle into two equal parts and is itself also divided by this circle at a point in Aries and at a point in Taurus. It is this zone that the sun, moon and other planets move (*Mathematics Useful for Understanding Plato* 3.5, trans. R. and D. Lawlor, 87).

On the following page, there is an illustration that depicts the ancient image of the earth surrounded by the pathways in the sky (Fig. 1). Of course any tour through the scenarios of the book of Revelation must begin with an awareness of how the ancients viewed the universe.

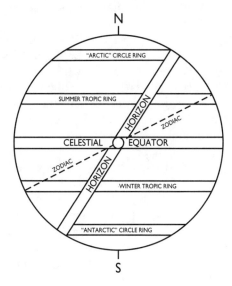

Figure 1: The Universe as Theon of Smyrna describes it. The perspective is that of God, standing outside the whole! Such a perspective was typical of all the celestial globes produced in the Mediterranean from the sixth century B.C. on (for a history from antiquity to the onset of Islam, see Savage-Smith 1985: 1–60).

3.1. A BASIC ORIENTATION FOR THE BOOK OF REVELATION

Given the general cosmic setting, perhaps the first item our tour requires is an overall map providing a quick orientation. The book of Revelation moves its readers through five sectors.

Sector 1: *The Cosmic Role of Jesus the Messiah*
Sector 2: *How God Controls the Universe and Deals with Israel*
Sector 3: *The Cosmos Before the Flood: Why the Present Condition*
Sector 4: *The First Postdeluvian City of Humankind: Babel and Its Fate*
Sector 5: *The Final City of Humankind: Celestial Jerusalem*

Each sector reveals the following:

Sector 1: The Cosmic Role of Jesus the Messiah. The book's introduction is followed by a letter introduction, which is in turn followed by an introductory vision of "one like a son of man," identified as Jesus, the Messiah. As cosmic Lord, he announces seven letters in edict form (chs. 1–3). What John learns about here is the cosmic role of Jesus, the Messiah soon to come.

Sector 2: How God Controls the Universe and Deals with Israel. Next comes the seer's vision of the other side of the sky where God dwells. The presentation starts with the cosmic Lamb's opening seven seals, which is followed by seven trumpets. The scene closes with a brief description of the fall of Jerusalem followed by a vision of God's sky temple (chs. 4–11). The sector begins with the notice of an opening in the sky (4:1), while it closes with the notice that God's temple in the sky opened (11:19). This conclusion likewise marks the start of the following sector. What John reports here is how God, controller of the universe, deals with the inhabitants of the land (of Israel, of course). At the close John learns rather briefly about why Jerusalem was to fall in A.D. 70.

Sector 3: The Cosmos Before the Flood: Why the Present Condition. Next follow three celestial signs: a Pregnant Woman, a Dragon and attendants, and Seven Bowls. Each sign involves some antediluvian cosmic interaction, duly described, with negative consequence for humans (chs. 12–16). The close of this sector is likewise marked with the notice that the sky tent of witness opened (15:5) allowing for the third sign of seven bowls to unfold. What John tells us here is about the situation of the cosmos and its impact on human society from the time of creation.

Sector 4: The First Postdeluvian City of Humankind: Babel and Its Fate. Babylon or Babel (they are the same word) is humankind's first city after the Flood. Now destroyed, it is the Babylon of the wilderness. John describes its former role, its supporters, and its dire fate, along with the fate of its cosmic backers, the Dragon and the two Beasts. Again, this sector has the sky opening to enable the rider on a white horse to emerge and lead the final battle (19:11). This is followed by a final judgment of all humankind (chs. 19–20). John thus learns about humankind's first postdeluvian city and its fate—along with the reasons for its destruction.

Sector 5: The Final City of Humankind: Celestial Jerusalem. Finally, God's new creation, specifically a new Jerusalem descending from the sky, is described, and the work quickly closes (chs. 21–22).

In all of these sectors, John considers the sky and elements in the sky both in themselves and in their repercussions upon the earth. To be faithful to John's perspective, in the course of this work I will employ terminology befitting sky surveillance. I use this terminology in the translation of this work. Thus God, whom the seer sees enthroned on the other side of the vault of the sky, dwells in the sky but beyond that vault. Jesus taught us to pray to this God as "Father who is in the sky" (I will refrain from speaking of "heaven" because for Americans it is an ambiguous term in Bible contexts). Our Father in the sky is attended by countless sky servants (= angels) who do his bidding. The gigantic figures that John sees in the sky are the same figures his ancient peers saw in the sky; they are those living beings known to us as constellations. Hence I will consider all the following figures as constellations: the son of man, the four living creatures opposite each other facing the celestial throne of God, the lamb, the altar in the sky, the "locust" plague controlled by constellational characters, the Woman and Child, the Dragon, the Beast rising over the sea, the Beast rising over the land, even the Wedding of the Lamb. Furthermore, given that horses, horses' manes, trumpets, and bowls are, among other labels, common names for comets, and comets invariably have negative effects on human beings, I shall consider the various media used by God's celestial sky servants as comets.

The book of Revelation presents an Israelite interpretation of the sky by an astral prophet who accepts Jesus as Messiah and as cosmic Lamb. We find in the work the normal astronomic cast of characters including constellations, stars, falling or otherwise, sun and moon, as well as the cosmic abyss in the southeastern sky. All this pertains to the cosmic furniture, so to say. But we also find reference to the distinctive tradition of Israel as contained in its sacred writings and its sacred lore.

For most modern readers, however, a more significant question has to do with time and timing. What exactly is the seer viewing in the sky? There are countless indications that the sky scenarios seen by the seer are those of the period covered by the creation stories of Genesis. Every Israelite knew that the sky as we know it was created by God "in the beginning" (Gen 1–2). Yet between that beginning and before the destruction of the giant offspring (Gen 6) of the sons of God and human females with the Flood (Gen 8), something happened. The beginnings of human civilization, marked by the construction of the first postdeluvian city, Babel, was under the direction of Nimrod, himself a deviant offspring of those sons of God and human females (Gen 10). For example, Philo notes that the first human being to desert from God after the Flood was Nimrod. "It was Nimrod who began this desertion. For the lawgiver says: 'he began to be a giant (γιγάς, *gigas*) on the earth (Gen 10:8), and his name means 'desertion' . . . And therefore to Nimrod Moses ascribes Babylon as the beginning of his kingdom" (*On the Giants* 66, LCL).

In Israelite tradition, those sky beings who did not have sexual relations with human females were called "holy ones." The problem of defilement, of course, is not because of human male sexual relations with human females. Rather, those sky beings called "sons of God" in Gen 6:2 crossed the natural boundaries between sky creatures and earth creatures. Following this same Israelite tradition, John identifies the fiery Dragon with the old serpent, the Devil and Satan, hence with another personage from Genesis. It is a general principle of anthropology that the functional purpose of creation stories is to explain the present, to make the present livable. And it seems our astral prophet, too, goes to the sky to learn about primeval origins in order to explain the present political situation, his present, in order to protect his "brothers" from deception, and thus help them to endure. I shall note this feature later when I speak of time in this book.

In sum, then, the burden of the book of Revelation deals with the role of Jesus Messiah in the cosmos, with God's punishment of the inhabitants of the land of Israel for their lack of repentance, with the origins of the present cosmic situation and of the cosmic evil that impacts the earth, and with reasons for the expected elimination of this evil by means of a cosmic renewal. John interprets his sky trips in terms of Israel's story of human beginnings in Genesis and the new human beginnings with Jesus Messiah.

3.2. A GENERAL MAP THROUGH REVELATION

The foregoing map provides a fundamental orientation to Revelation's sky interpretation. To become more familiar with the scenarios in the work, consider this slightly fuller map of the various sectors of the book:

Sector 1: The Cosmic Role of Jesus the Messiah. The work begins with three introductions or inaugural points. First, there is the general introduction to the book as a whole (1:1–3), followed by a specific introduction to the letters comprising chs. 2–3 (1:4–8). John follows with a description of his introductory or inaugural vision (1:10–20), duly noting his personal condition (altered state of awareness) and the time (the Lord's Day). Next follows the interaction in which an astral being of constellational proportions (like a "son of man," hence like a human being in shape) directs him to write orders to the controlling sky servants (angels in English texts) of seven specific Christian groups called churches (chs. 2–3).

Sector 2: How God Controls the Universe and Deals with Israel. The inaugural sequence is followed by another opening vision, this time a vision of the other side of the vault of the sky (ch. 4). Passing through "an open door in the sky" (4:1), the author sees the proper realm of God at the controlling center of the cosmos. God's throne, attended by seven spirits (4:1, 5), is surrounded by the thrones of twenty-four sky entities, that is, stars known as *"decans,"* but here called "elders" (4:4). At four equidistant and opposing points along the cosmic circle around the throne, there are four living beings, that is, constellations in animate shape (4:6–7). The seer is privileged to see the cosmos from God's point of view, from the other side of the vault of the sky. Along with seeing the vision, John hears singing, as one might expect in the upper reaches of the sky. The first song (4:8) unceasingly tells of the exclusivity and uniqueness of God; the second (4:11) praises the eternal God as creator.

This opening glimpse of the other side of the vault of the sky yields to the start of the book's cosmic drama with the cue provided by notice of the sealed scroll at God's right hand (5:1). One of God's "mighty" sky servants (the "mighty" type of angel is mentioned here and at 10:1 and

18:21) proclaims a search for some being of sufficiently exalted status (this is worthiness) to be privy to God's secrets (5:2). One of the decans (elders) then tells the seer that the one of sufficient eminence for the task is "the Lion of the tribe of Judah, the root of David, the one who conquered" (5:5). This personage, he sees, is none other than the "Lamb standing as though slaughtered," and located in the center of the decans (5:6). This Lamb is the constellation Aries, which was always pictured in the most ancient representations of the sky with head turned so as to be facing directly over its back to Taurus. John perceives Aries as having a broken neck to see backward, yet standing, thus was "slaughtered" yet standing. Once this eminent personage accepts the scroll, the whole cosmos breaks out in song. First the twenty-four decans and four living being constellations sing of the cosmic preeminence (worthiness) of the Lamb (the book's third song 5:9); then God's entourage equally hymns the preeminence of the Lamb (the fourth song 5:13), and finally all created beings second the judgment of all those prominent sky beings by singing of the honor of both God and the Lamb (the fifth song 5:13).

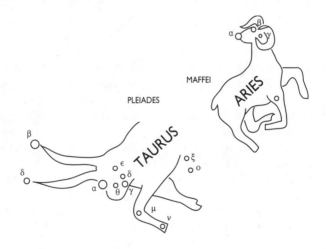

Image 1: Taurus and Aries from a modern sky chart.

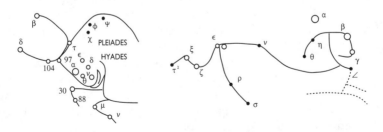

Image 2: Taurus and Aries from Ptolemy's description
(second century A.D.; from Brown 1900 2.229–30).

With the scenarios of God enthroned and the Lamb ready and waiting amid cosmic singing, the action is ready to begin. Chapters 6 to 11 set before us what God has decreed in the scroll, now disclosed by the Lamb as it opens the scroll. Any expectations that the scroll might hold a word of peace and prosperity are quickly dispelled as the first living being thunders out a command: "Come" (6:1). The rather surprising result is that a horse and rider gain ascendancy. The object of this ascendancy is presumably some unnamed opponent of God worthy of God's cosmic attention. And given that the whole series of events unleashed here ends up with the partial destruction of "the great city . . . where too their Lord was crucified" (11:8), the sector obviously deals with the land of Israel, that is, the territories of Galilee, Perea, and Judea, along with the capital city, Jerusalem. The second horse and rider's response to the command of the second living being indicates that the conquest is directed to the land. In context, this is the land of Israel. The third horse and rider, following the command of the third living being, point to food shortages in the land, while the fourth horse and rider, at the behest of the fourth living being, usher in death over a fourth of the land (6:2–9).

Without question the horses and their riders are celestial beings. Now among common names for comets, as we shall see, are "horse," "trumpet," and "bowl." Comets invariably bode ill for the inhabitants of the land over which they appear. These first four horses do indeed indicate evil outcomes for the land of Israel and its inhabitants. The fifth seal, on the other hand, allows the seer's murdered colleagues, now located under the constellation "Altar" (where the Milky Way passes), to get a hearing with God so as to make their case for vindication of honor, from the "inhabitants of the land" (6:10). While we are not yet explicitly told which land is in question, it is obviously a land about which God is concerned enough to issue pertinent decrees; hence its inhabitants stand in some relationship with God. Now the opening of the sixth seal results in upheaval among the natural appurtenances forming the human environment: sky and land. Social standing affords little security (6:15) against the judgment of God and the revenge of the Lamb (6:16).

However, before this judgment and revenge take place, presumably with the opening of the seventh seal, the seer tells of an intermission in the action (ch. 7), marked by the restraining of the four sky servants at the four corners of the earth (7:1). The purpose of the interlude is to "seal the slaves of our God upon their forehead" (7:3). Those thus rescued from judgment and revenge include a limited number of Israelites (only 144,000) and a limitless number "from every nation and tribe and people and tongue" (7:9). These join in song to God and the Lamb to acknowledge their rescue (7:6, the sixth song). Their song provokes a response in song by God's cosmic entourage

(7:12). After this the seer is informed by a decan as to who the non-Israelites were and of their relationship to the Lamb (7:13–17).

Finally (8:1), the opening of the seventh seal initiates a new stage of activity marked by seven trumpet-shaped comets. Like comets, the trumpets portend negative events on the land, carried out by remark-able celestial beings (8:2–9:19). The final three trumpet blasts are un-derscored as particularly shameful and dire, marked by three woes (8:13). After the sixth trumpet, we are finally told what it is all about; there is no change of heart forthcoming from those who offend God and their fellow humans (9:20–21). Chapter 10 presents an interlude before the final trumpet blast. During this interlude, the seer performs a pro-phetic symbolic action, indicating that he must further "prophesy con-cerning peoples and nations and tongues and many kings" (10:11).

Chapter 11 begins with another prophetic symbolic action, a sort of census of Israelites in God's (Jerusalem) sanctuary (11:1–2). Then two prophets appear who are specifically to witness against this Jeru-salemite population about the evil in its midst (sackcloth points to this). These stand before the Lord of the land (11:4), protected by God with authority over fertility-giving water (11:6–7). Ultimately they are killed by an animal, shamed by being left unburied, but raised from the dead by God, then taken to the sky (11:8–12). All of this transpires in the same great city "where their Lord was crucified," Jerusalem, which is said to have the qualities of Sodom (inhospitality) and Egypt (idolatry, 11:8). With the removal of the prophets, it is time for the final trumpet blast (11:14–15) when the rule of God and God's Messiah over the land is inaugurated. This is announced by sky dwellers, then acknowledged in a cosmic song (the book's seventh) by the twenty-four decans around God's throne (11:15–18). The upshot of it all is the opening of God's sky temple, so much so that one could see the ark of the covenant there (11:19). This closes the second set of scenarios presented by John. The reason for this is that another set begins immediately, which has little direct relation with what preceded.

Sector 3: The Cosmos Before the Flood: Why the Present Condi-tion. The new set of scenarios beginning with ch. 12 has the seer under the vault of the sky. There he sees a great sign (the first of three) of a constellation described as a Pregnant Woman with the sun passing through it (12:1–2). This is followed by the sign of a constellational Dragon with falling stars in its wake in the southern sky (12:3–4), waiting for the Pregnant Woman's child. What ensues is a set of "his-torical" interpretations explaining these constellations and their inter-action. In other words, the seer tells us what happened in the past with these signs. First, we find out that the cosmic Child was taken up to God and seated on God's throne (12:5). Then we are informed about the Woman's having been sent into some unnamed wilderness (12:6). Finally, we are told about the ancient battle of the sky servant Michael

and his cohort, who warred against the southern Dragon and cast it
from the sky (12:7–8). The Dragon is the Great Dragon, none other
than the Devil and Satan, a figure from Israel's tradition. These verses,
of course, explain Satan's presence in the Garden of Eden; he was
ejected from the sky early in the creation of the universe (12:9). Now a
loud sky voice situates the Dragon and his present role (12:10–12).
Finally, we are told of the Dragon's interactions with the cosmic
woman also now on earth; the "seed" of this woman are none other
than Christians (12:13–17). Hence, they too must have been with God
from the time of creation, a viewpoint held, it seems, by Pauline Christians who saw themselves chosen in Christ "before the foundation of
the world" (Eph 1:4).

Next, two more constellations are noted. The first rises in the sky
over the horizon of the sea (13:1), and the second rises in the sky over
the horizon of the land (13:11). The sea Beast serves as viceregent of the
Dragon, taking on "the holy ones," while the land Beast substitutes for
the sea Beast and leads earthlings to deceptive worship through controlled food rationing (by branding).

Meanwhile, the seer recounts a whole series of new scenarios.
First, the cosmic Lamb "sets" over Jerusalem, with an entourage of
144,000 holy ones. These, we are told, are the "sons of God" or sky
servants who were undefiled by the women mentioned in Gen 6:1–4
(14:1–5). Second, a trio of sky servants make quick announcements: the
first goes to the zenith of the sky to proclaim good news: the hour of
God's judgment has come (14:6–7). Next, a second sky servant quickly
proclaims the fall of Babylon the Great (14:8). Then a third sky servant
warns against any trafficking with the sea Beast (14:9–11). And finally,
two sickle-shaped comets, at the direction of two sky servants, "harvest"
the earth, a first harvest of presumably various produce, a second of
grapes, representing blood (14:14–20). Harvesting is a traditional symbol of judgment (Matt 3:12; 13:30; Luke 3:17; see Joel 3:13–14).

Now another (the third) sign appears: seven bowl-shaped comets
yielding seven plagues or injuries (ch. 15), depicting God's vindication.
Chapter 16 tells of the seven injuries, and concludes with the splitting of
Babylon/Babel into three (16:19), thus heralding its fate.

*Sector 4: The First Postdeluvian City of Humankind: Babylon/Babel
and Its Fate.* Chapter 17 tells of a sky servant who explains the significance of the judgment on Babylon/Babel, the first city of humankind
built after the Flood. The city is personified as a woman, both because
this was customary in the Hellenistic period and because Babylon's
protecting star at that period was Aphrodite (Venus, Isis, Ishtar). The
sky servant carries off the seer (17:3) to see the personified city and
then interprets the various relationships among the Beasts and the
Lamb and the city (17:4–18). Chapter 18 opens with another sky servant
announcing the fall of Babylon (18:1–3), and still another inviting his

protégés to leave the city (18:4–8). Finally, we are presented with a set of persons who regularly interacted with the city: kings of the earth, merchants, sailors (18:9–20). At the close, another "mighty" sky servant's action symbolizes the fate of crushed Babylon (18:21–24).

The first eight verses of ch. 19 narrate the cosmic chorus of praise evoked by God's just judgment. The seer is then directed to write, hence announce, the supper of the Wedding of the Lamb (19:9). But before that occurs, another "supper" of sorts takes place. The mounted "King of kings and Lord of lords," along with his army, vanquishes the (sea) Beast with its kings, tribunes, the mighty and their horses, freedmen and slaves, small and great. All of these cadavers serve as the supper of the birds of the sky. But the (sea)Beast and its false prophet (the land Beast) are thrown into the burning sulphurous pool (19:11–21).

With the two Beasts vanquished, it is finally the Dragon's turn. The seer sees a sky servant bind the Dragon with a chain for one thousand years (20:1–3), that is, for a "day" in the sight of the Lord ("But do not ignore this one fact, beloved, that with the Lord one day is as a thousand years, and a thousand years as one day," 2 Pet 3:8). During this period, those who witness to Jesus live and reign with him (20:4–6). But at its close, a final period is ushered in with the release of Satan for destruction with the Beasts (20:7–10) and with God's judgment of humankind (20:11–15).

Sector 5: The Final City of Humankind: Celestial Jerusalem. The seer then sees a new creation: a new sky and new earth along with a new Jerusalem (21:1–5). Up in the sky, a sky servant shows John the Lamb's bride, the new Jerusalem (21:9–22:6).

The work ends with multiple attestation as to its veracity. The first attestation is by John (21:8). Upon seeing/hearing all this, the prophet attempts once more (see 19:10) to worship the sky servant, but is again repulsed (22:8–9). The second attestation is by God (22:13), and the third, Jesus (22:16). The author concludes with an ending typical of a letter (22:19–21).

3.3. A SKY MAP FOR JOHN'S REVELATION

With the foregoing general map for our tour of John's Revelation in hand, we might briefly view the types of celestial bodies and beings the seer encountered. In the sky map that follows, the common, modern names of the constellations and stars are used. In the fuller treatment of each sector that follows, the reasons for singling out particular star sets will be presented in full. Here the sky map is offered for general orientation and quick reference.

SECTOR 1: THE COSMIC ROLE OF JESUS THE MESSIAH

Appearance in Sky	Where	When
Humanlike constellation	Above Patmos, the seer's location	Before A.D. 70

SECTOR 2: HOW GOD CONTROLS THE UNIVERSE AND DEALS WITH ISRAEL

Appearance in Sky	Where	When
Set 1: Constellations	Over land of Israel; specifically over Jerusalem	Before total destruction
Throne		
Aries		
Leo		
Taurus		
Scorpio-man		
Thunderbird		
24 Decans		
Set 2: Four comets	Over land of Israel; specifically over Jerusalem	Before total destruction
Horses from E, S. N, W —influenced by: Jupiter (white Mars (red) Mercury (black) Venus (pale white) —sent out over four years in sequence: year of Leo, Virgo, Libra, Scorpio		
Set 3: Constellation	Over land of Israel; specifically over Jerusalem	Before total destruction
Altar		
Milky Way		
Set 4: Seven comets	Over land of Israel; specifically over Jerusalem	Before total destruction
Trumpets Falling Star Winged Archers Centaurs —Sky location: Abyss by Altar Sky River Colossal Sky Servant Decans Temple in the Sky		

SECTOR 3: THE COSMOS BEFORE THE FLOOD: WHY THE PRESENT CONDITION

Appearance in Sky	Where	When
Set 1: Constellations	Some chaotic wilderness	Before Creation is complete
Pregnant Virgo		
Old Scorpio (Libra +		
Scorpio)		
Cosmic Child		
Orion		
Set 2: Constellations	Over the antediluvian earth, probably Mesopotamia	Before the Flood
Cetus		
Lupus		
Triangle		
Set 3: Constellation	In the sky, around the Throne	Before the Flood
Aires rising over		
celestial Zion		
Set 4: Constellation	Over the earth and around the city (= Babylon)	Before the Flood
Humanlike constellation preceded by three sky servants and followed by three sky servants wielding sickle-shaped comets		
Set 5: Seven Sky Servants at Sea of Glass	In the sky over the earth	Before the Flood
Set 6: Six bowl-shaped comets	In the sky over the earth	Before the Flood, when earth divided into three
Altar		
Old Scorpio		
Cetus		
Lupus		
Sun		
Frog stars		
Set 7: Seventh bowl-shaped comet	In the sky over the earth	Before the Flood, when earth divided into three

SECTOR 4: THE FIRST CITY OF HUMANKIND: BABEL AND ITS FATE

Appearance in Sky	Where	When
Set 1: Planetary Venus setting over Cetus Jupiter	In the wilderness, at Babylon	Right after the Flood
Set 2: Destruction and *Lamentation*	In the sky	After the destruction of Babel
Set 3: Constellations Throne Decans Four Living Beings, Wedding of the Lamb	Between sky and earth	At time of destruction of the two prehistoric constellations
Set 4: Comets and *constellations* White Horse comet, controlled by humanlike constellation Sky army and comets Cetus and Lupus Sky Abyss	In the sky	When Old Scorpio's influence put in abeyance
Set 5: Constellations Old Scorpio Sky Abyss Milky Way	Between the sky and the earth	When Jerusalem was destroyed
Set 6: Constellations Gog Magog Old Scorpio	In the sky	At God's final judgment
Set 7: Constellations Throne Death-and-Hades Sky Abyss	In the sky	At God's final judgment

SECTOR 5: THE FINAL CITY OF HUMANKIND: CELESTIAL JERUSALEM

Appearance in Sky	Where	When
Set 1: Constellations	In the sky: descending	Already now
Astral Jerusalem		
Wedding of the gods	In the sky	Already now
Set 2: Constellations	In the sky	Already now
Throne of God and the		
Lamb		
Tree of Life		

Such then is a general conspectus of the types of celestial formations encountered by the seer during his sky visions and sky trips.

3.4. SOME FREQUENT PERSONAGES IN THE BOOK

A number of personages feature frequently and prominently in the scenarios of Revelation from the first sector on. These include angels, the holy ones, spirits, and sky personages, such as the one "like a son of man" in the opening vision. Below we will examine their role in John's message.

3.4.1. Sky Servants or Angels

Angels are common in the Bible. They are often thought to be messengers from God to humans if only because the Greek word ἄγγελος (*angelos*) means "messenger." However, angels often do far more than carry messages. They not only bring and announce information, but they often carry out God's directives. This aspect of their nature is intimated by the Hebrew word for angel, *mal'ak*, meaning "a person who carries out a prescribed task." The experience of angels seems to have been common throughout the Mediterranean. Even the ancient Mesopotamians knew of them and depicted them in their sculpture. The Greeks called them *demons* (δαίμων), among other things, and the Romans called them *genii*. Since they inhabit the sky and are delegated by superior beings to carry out tasks, I will call them *sky servants*. In other words, everywhere the Greek word ἄγγελος appears in the text of Revelation, I will translate with "sky servant" (for a listing of the various sky servant labels in the Israelite tradition, see Davidson 1992: 325–42).

Note that the first result of such a translation is that it sounds odd, hence perhaps capable of dislodging spurious familiarity. The second result is that our scenario is no longer a churchly or churchy one, with chubby cherubs and tiny wings or vaporous larger winged persons. Sky servants are not theological creations in the first-century Mediterranean world. Created by God, they populate the region between earth and firmaments and are simply there doing what they must, like other ethnic groups and other categories of living beings. We might once more listen to Philo's explanation:

> It is Moses' custom to give the name of angels to those whom other philosophers call demons, souls that is which fly and hover in the air. . . . For the universe must needs be filled through and through with life, and each of its primary elementary divisions contains the forms of life which are akin and suited to it. The earth has the creatures of the land, the sea and the rivers those that live in water, fire the fire-born which are said to be found especially in Macedonia, and heaven has the stars. For the stars are souls divine and without blemish throughout, and therefore as each of them is mind in its purest form, they move in the line most akin to mind—the circle. And so the other element, the air, must needs be filled with living beings, though indeed they are invisible to us, since even the air itself is not visible to our senses (*On the Giants* 6–8, LCL).

> They are consecrated and devoted to the service of the Father and Creator whose wont it is to employ them as ministers and helpers, to have charge and care of mortal man (ibid. 12, LCL).

What sky servants must do is obey those who charge them with a task. In the drama of Revelation, the enthroned God has an endless supply of these sky servants. On the other hand, we find that the cosmic Dragon of ch. 12 likewise has a number of its own sky servants to do its bidding. The reader, however, is never told where these beings come from, when or where they were created, or even how the Dragon obtained these servants, or what exactly it bids them to do. Sky servants were living beings made of fire. Hence for those who know how to perceive alternate reality, sky servants were always radiant, easy to see, vested in brilliant white, indicating their provenance from the sky. In any event, significant members of the cast of characters in Revelation are the nameless sky servants.

3.4.2. The Holy Ones

There is another category of celestial beings who seem to do much the same thing as sky servants do, yet this category should probably be distinguished from sky servants in general. These are the "holy ones." For example, when the cosmic Lamb takes the scroll from the right hand of the throne, the attendant cosmic beings show their profound respects to the Lamb with song and incense (5:8). We are then told that the incense is the prayers of the "holy ones." This designation of "holy ones" for one category of God's sky servants derives from Deut 33:2 (see also Jude 14; and Milik 1976: 186). It is the normal name in the book of Enoch for God's sky servants, beginning at 1 Enoch 1:9 and continuing throughout the work.

What do these sky servants do? They accompany God! In Mediterranean society, among the many ways elites proclaimed their honor to one and all was to serve as patrons and to be accompanied at all times by an entourage of clients and slaves. This ever-present entourage told the world that a prominent, honorable person was present. God is a prominent, honorable person par excellence since God is always surrounded and accompanied by tens of thousands of holy ones. Thus, for example, 1 Enoch 9:1 observes: "When he comes with the myriads of his Holy Ones to execute judgment against all, he will destroy the wicked and will convict all flesh with regard to all their works and with regard to all the proud and hard words which wicked sinners have spoken against him" (Milik 1976: 185; "the proud and hard words which wicked sinners have spoken against" God is what blasphemy means).

What gave these sky servants the privilege of attending God or the cosmic Lamb or other high status cosmic personages? The book of Enoch provides the insight. To understand what the early parts of Enoch explain, one must keep in mind that for nearly all Mesopotamian and Mediterranean peoples, the creation of the world was followed by a cosmic flood, not unlike the Flood reported in Genesis. That means that the earth bears evidence of two sorts of beings: those that existed from creation until the Flood, which were subsequently annihilated, and those that existed from creation and survived the Flood. Among the events occurring on earth but before the Flood, the book of Genesis (6:1–4) reports:

> When men began to multiply on the face of the ground, and daughters were born to them, the sons of God saw that the daughters of men were fair; and they took to wife such of them as they chose. Then the Lord said, "My spirit shall not abide in man for ever, for he is flesh, but his days shall be a hundred and twenty years." The Nephilim (giants) were on the earth in those days, and also afterward, when the sons of God came in to the daughters of men, and they bore children to them. These were the mighty men that were of old, the men of renown.

This tradition concerning the existence of giants on the earth in the days before the Flood is equally a common Mesopotamian and Mediterranean one. The book of Enoch, in turn, offers an explanation typical of the Israelite tradition as found in Gen 6:1–4. Among the Dead Sea Scrolls, the retelling of the Genesis story in the Genesis Apocryphon intimates explicit worry about the sexual doings of Watchers, holy ones and sons of God and their "gigantic" offspring. In the case of Noah, for example, Noah's father, Lamech, is much concerned about whether he truly is the child's father. He adjures his wife to tell him, as we read in the following, somewhat damaged, fragment:

> Behold, I thought then within my heart that conception was due to the Watchers and the Holy Ones . . . and to the Giants . . . and my heart was troubled within me because of this child. Then I, Lamech, approached Bathenosh my wife in haste and said to her: ". . . by the Most High, the Great Lord, the King of all the world and Ruler of the Sons of Heaven, until you tell me all things truthfully . . . by the King of all the worlds until you tell me truthfully and not falsely" (1QapGen 2, trans. Vermes 252).

In the course of this book, I shall have occasion to cite these traditions, for it is rather certain that John knew the book of Enoch and traditions of the antediluvian population of the earth.

In any event, 1 Enoch informs us that the "sons of God" that descended from the sky to the earth were sky servants, "angels." But not all of them defiled the boundaries between sky beings and earth beings by sexual union with women (apparently all sky servants are males). Those that did not were specially rewarded by God. Now it is these meritorious sky servants, victorious veterans of an event that took place before the Flood, who are henceforth honorably labeled "holy ones." Their fellows, as we shall see, were duly vanquished by a group of chief sky servants and their colleagues. On the other hand, the offspring of the union of sons of God and women were the giants responsible for stone structures of gigantic proportion (Mediterranean dolmen and menhir, like Stonehenge) and their skeletons are still found at times (dinosaur remains identified as the bones of giants).

3.4.3. Spirits or Controlling Sky Winds

Another intriguing cosmic being is the *spirit* (Greek: πνεῦμα, *pneuma*). This seems to be a typically Semitic being, with a Semitic pedigree, who exerted power on behalf of the deity. The ancient world never managed to harness the wind. The wind was, therefore, uncontrolled and uncontrollable, invisible and most often unexpected, frequently powerful enough to damage humans and animals alike. This powerful, unknown, and unpredictable wind pointed to the activity of God. It was God at work on the earth, notably if it were beneficial. Harmful sudden winds were evil, as their activities indicated. Since our author distinguishes between spirit (Greek: πνεῦμα, *pneuma*) and wind (Greek: ἄνεμος, *anemos*), I will call *spirits* "sky winds," winds in and from the realm of the vault of the sky. This sky wind demonstrates God's power; however, the cosmos likewise had plain, old earth wind housed at the corners of the trapezoidal earth. Earth's winds blew predictably in various seasons and from various directions. These had their own name, as we shall see, and belonged to the category of ἄνεμος, wind.

To understand how wind worked, it is important to recall that wind (and spirit), like water and fire, was a liquid of sorts. We know this because of the way the ancients spoke of wind, water, and fire: all were poured out or poured in. "Infused" is a well-known church term which means "poured in."

We learn from 1:4 that before God's throne there were "the seven sky winds," undoubtedly ever ready to act on God's behalf. In this passage they must be intelligent beings since they send wishes of favor and peace to seven churches. Then at 1:10 John describes his visionary ecstasy as "being in a sky wind [πνεῦμα, *pneuma*]," carried along into powerful, unknown, and unpredictable realms by divine power. Pétrement notes concerning the seven:

> The idea that there are seven principal angels was not foreign to Judaism, or to the earliest form of Christianity. The passage in the book of Tobit where the angel Raphael says: "I am one of the seven holy angels who present the prayers of the saints and enter into the presence of the glory of the Holy One" (Tobit 12:15) has often been quoted. These seven archangels appear again in the literature concerning Enoch (1 Enoch 20; 81:5; 87:2; 90:21–22). A fragment of a liturgical work discovered near the Dead Sea mentions the seven "supreme Princes" (in Greek, the seven Archons) who are the highest dignitaries of the angelic hierarchy. Similarly, the Apocalypse speaks of "the seven Spirits who are before his throne," of "seven Spirits sent throughout the earth" (Rev 1:4; 5:6; cf. 3:1; 4:5; 8:2). In the Testament of Levi (8; in Greek), which is probably a Jewish-Christian work, seven angels appear to Levi in the form of seven men dressed in white. Hermas (3:4; 9:6, 12) speaks of six angels, "the first created": "It is to them that the Lord entrusted all his creatures, to make them prosper, to organize and govern them as masters." In some passages he depicts them as surrounding the "Son of God," who seems to be regarded as a seventh angel, though far superior to the six others. In Clement of Alexandria angels called *protoctistoi* or *protogonoi* who are seven in number are found again, on more than one occasion. Clement attributes them with "the greatest power" and calls them "archons of the angels" (1990: 65–67).

For Pétrement, the seven derive from either the round number of fullness or the seven days of creation over which each angel was set.

Be that as it may, the first outcome of John's altered state experience is his encounter with a cosmic being, a constellation that looked like a human being, "a son of man" (1:13). It is to this first encounter that we now turn as we consider Sector 1 of the book of Revelation.

4   SECTOR 1: THE COSMIC ROLE OF JESUS THE MESSIAH

1[1]A revelation of Jesus Messiah which God gave to him to show to his slaves what has to happen soon; and he indicated by means of signs, having sent (them) through his sky servant to his slave John, [2]who attests (as) the utterance of God and (as) the witness of Jesus Christ, all the things that he saw. [3]How honored are the reader and the hearers of the utterances of the prophecy and who keep the things written in it, for the time is near. [4]John to the seven churches which are in Asia. Grace to you and peace from the one who is and who was and who is coming, and from the seven sky winds which are before his throne, [5]and from Jesus Messiah, the trustworthy witness, the first-born of the dead and the ruler of the kings of the earth. To the one who is attached to us, and who has freed us from our sins by means of his blood, [6]and who has made us a kingdom, priests for God and his Father—to him glory and power unto the aeons of aeons. Amen.

       [7]"Behold he comes with the clouds,
       and every eye shall see him,
       especially those who pierced him,
       and all the tribes of the earth shall mourn over him."
       "Indeed! Amen!"

[8]"I am the Alpha and the O[mega]," says the Lord God, "he who is and who was and who is to come, the Almighty." [9]I, John, your brother and sharer in the distress and the kingdom and the perseverance in Jesus, was on the island called Patmos because of the utterance of God and the witness of Jesus. [10]I was under the control of a sky wind on the Lord's day, and I heard behind me a loud voice, like a trumpet [11]that said:

       "What you see, write down on a scroll
       and send (it) to the seven churches,
       to Ephesus and to Smyrna and to Pergamum
       and to Thyatira and to Sardis and to Philadelphia
       and to Laodicea."

[12]And I turned around to see the voice which was speaking with me; and when I turned I saw seven golden lamp stands, [13]and in the middle of the lamp stands one like a son of man, clothed in an ankle length garment and girded with a golden belt about his chest; [14]now his head and his hair [were] white like white wool, like snow, and his eyes like a flame of fire; [15]and his feet [were] like brass, like that fired in a furnace, and his voice [was] like the voice of many waters. [16]and [he was] holding in his right hand seven stars, and from his mouth proceeded a sharp, two-edged sword, and the sight of him [was] like the sun shining at full strength. [17]And when I saw him, I fell to his feet like a dead man; and he put his right hand upon me saying: "Stop being afraid; I am the First and the Last, [18]and the Living One; and I was dead and behold I am alive unto the aeons of aeons, and I have the keys of Death and of Hades. [19]Therefore write down what you see and what is and what is going to happen after that. [20]As to the hidden meaning of the seven stars which you saw in my right hand, and of the seven golden lamp stands: the seven stars are the sky servants of the seven churches, and the seven lampstands are the churches."

Our tour of the book of Revelation begins by considering John's opening vision. The whole work begins with three introductory or inaugural points. First, there is the general introduction to the book as a whole (1:1–3), followed by a specific introduction to the letters comprising chs. 2–3 (1:4–8). Next, John relates his introductory or inaugural vision (1:10–20), duly noting the circumstances of his personal condition (altered state of awareness) and time (the Lord's day). Then follows the interaction in which an astral being of constellational proportions (like a human being in shape) directs him to write orders to the controlling sky servants (angels) of seven specific Christian groups called churches (chs. 2–3).

4.1. UNDERSTANDING THE INITIAL SCENARIO

The first vision that the seer experiences is that of a being situated amid seven golden lamp stands. The description of that being is worth repeating.

> One like a son of man, clothed in an ankle length garment and girded with a golden belt about his chest; now his head and his hair [were] white like white wool, like snow, and his eyes like a flame of fire; and his feet [were] like brass, like that fired in a furnace, and his voice [was] like the voice of many waters. And [he was] holding in his right hand seven stars, and from his mouth proceeded a sharp, two-edged sword, and the sight of him [was] like the sun shining at full strength (Rev 1:13–16).

The being in question is a cosmic being on the vault of the sky since it holds seven stars in its right hand. It is like a human being in shape; and like a number of other constellations, it has a sword, while overall it shines like the sun. It is a wonder that the seer could see it. This cosmic being was located amid a lamp stand with seven golden lamps, undoubtedly a menorah-like arrangement of the seven planets. What the seer sees, then, is a constellation in human shape framed in by the seven planets. In his alternate state of reality, he interprets, hence sees, the vision as he describes it: a cosmic human-like entity standing before a cosmic menorah or lamp stand (for depicted scenarios of such cosmic beings, see L'Orange 1982 reprint of 1953).

Most Bibles send the reader off to the book of Daniel (7:13–14) for an instance of a similar being. Thus,

> I saw in the night visions, and behold with the clouds of heaven there came one like a son of man, and he came to the Ancient of Days and was presented before him. And to him was given dominion and glory and kingdom, that all peoples, nations, and languages should serve him; his dominion is an everlasting dominion which shall not pass away, and his kingdom one that shall not be destroyed (Dan 7:13–14).

Now those biblical scholars intent on finding sources for John's descriptions agree that the description of the appearance of "one like a son of man" (1:13) and the related "mighty" sky servant (10:1) derive for the most part from the book of Daniel. The first figure is named in Dan 7:13, but John's description of this human-like entity closely matches the "Ancient of Days or Ancient One" of Dan 7:9. The second figure is presented in Dan 10:5–6. Consider these descriptions:

> And the Ancient One took his throne, his clothing was white as snow, and the hair of his head like pure wool; his throne was fiery flames and its wheels were burning fire. A stream of fire issued and flowed out from his presence (Dan 7:9–10).

> I looked up and saw a man clothed in linen, with a belt of gold from Uphaz around his waist. His body was like beryl, his face like lightning, his eyes like flaming torches, his arms and legs like the gleam of burnished bronze, and the sound of his words like the roar of a multitude (Dan 10:5–6).

Yet where does Daniel get the descriptions? To whom would these descriptions make sense? On what basis? There are truly countless ancient descriptions of astral divine beings that are similar to these portrayals. For example, consider the following from an astrological manual entitled *Salmeschoiniaka* (also: *Salmeschniaka*; *Salmesachanaka*; see Cramer 1954: 16), used by Nechepso-Petosiris, hence dating to before 150 B.C. A second-century A.D. copy of the *Salmeschoiniaka* contains a description of the astral deities that control every five degrees of the celestial circumference and every five days. One of these seventy-two deities is described as follows:

> The goddess of the month of Aphthynsint[?]; she is called the face of the sun. Her appearance is that of a statue of genuine lapis lazuli; a woman seated on a throne, having eyes, one like [. . .] and the other Typhon-like, her countenance golden, hands on [her breast], adorned, a royal diadem on her head (cited from Boll 1914: 52).

The collection *Oxyrhynchus Papyri* (Grenfell and Hunt 3, 1912: 126–37) contains a significant fragment of the *Salmeschoiniaka*. The opening description runs as follows:

> Aquarius that is the month of Pharmouthi 16–20: The presiding deity of that period, his name is Nebu, of which the interpretation is that he is the lord of wars and reason. He is represented by an upright statue with the face of a vulture, wearing a diadem upon his head, and with the face of a serpent behind, having two wings and the feet of a lion and holding four swords, both faces being of gold. He signifies that the governor will . . . evils; there shall be war, dislike and battle, and he will take counsel with the people as a friend. And during his rule there shall be a rebel and there shall be war, and many cities of Egypt with perish on account of the rebel, for the signs of the time are war and dislike and battle, and there shall be destruction (of many?). In this time many shall live by stealth (?), and some shall live by singing and dancing, and some by chanting in the temples, and some by singing at banquets with sweet voices and they end well. This deity causes by reason the conqueror to be conquered and the conquered to conquer, and many live by receiving gratuities and registering and collecting from men what they have drunk up, and some live by . . . as servants. He causes men to be lame because one foot . . . The sickness in this season is in the intestines and bowels, and there shall be many deaths (loc. cit. 135).

Another example from the *Salmeschoiniaka*, chosen as a random excerpt by Cramer:

> The Lord of Flame. His image is an upright statue of a man with the face of a . . . towards the back, however that of a piglet having a snout in front of its face. Having swords in his hands, four, and a knife. His tongue and face of fire. He indicates that this period makes many find their livelihood as advocates, others as wizards, many as singers of gods and kings, and many as translators of languages and many . . . and from place to place migrating and men earning much without labor nor worry how it was earned . . . are eaten up. Many, however, consume the substance of others. He makes many passive homosexuals, and many cohabiting with their aunts and stepmothers, so as to debauch them . . . (Cramer 1954: 17).

Further, a work dating to the end of the first century A.D., *The Sacred Book of Hermes to Asklepios* (Ruelle 1908) lists thirty-six star deities. These are the so-called decans, divinities of each ten degrees of the zodiac and also of each ten days of the year (I shall deal with the decans later, when considering the twenty-four elders). Concerning the twenty-fourth star deity, we read:

> This one has the name Nephthimes. He has the figure of a man [often there are also animal-headed figures], who stands at a well which has two streams coming together, feet close together, girded from chest to ankles, [radiant] flecks in his beard, and a water vessel in his right hand (Ruelle 1908: 264).

Finally, consider the fourth-century description of Mithra from the so-called *Mithras Liturgy*:

> Now when they take their place, here and there, in order, look in the air and you will see lightning bolts going down, and lights flashing, and the earth shaking, and a god descending, a god immensely great, having a bright appearance, youthful, golden-haired, with a white tunic and a golden crown and trousers, and holding in his right hand a golden shoulder of a young bull: this is the Bear which moves and turns heaven around, moving upward and downward in accordance with the hour. Then you will see lightning bolts leaping from his eyes and stars from his body (*PGM* 4, 694–704, Betz 51–52).

Our one "like a Son of Man" also has in his right hand a seven-starred constellation. There are a good number of seven-starred constellations. The best candidate, though, is the Pleiades, traditionally called "The Seven" in the ancient Middle East, and very often depicted on various cylinder seals and steles. It was a basic sky sign for planting, hence for fertility and human survival. Be that as it may, the human-like figure that the seer sees has a two-edged sword protruding from his mouth. Constellational figures often have swords, but almost never protruding from the mouth. Yet mention of such a sword from the mouth would be quite easy in a period when people imagined a celestial Perseus with sword and Gorgon's head, or Orion with sword in his belt or in his hand. Cultured Greeks shared such images.

The point of these parallels is to illustrate how "normal" the figure of the cosmic, constellational son of man would be in the ancient Mediterranean within the context of astronomic perception. So it is to astronomic literature that one ought turn in order to situate and understand the perspective of the astral prophet, John.

4.2. THE ROLE OF THE COSMIC JESUS

In summary, John's first vision is that of a human-like constellation, one like a human being. This being has the ability to emerge from the sky and to put its hand on the seer. It can even speak with a sword in its mouth. In 1:17–18, it reveals who it is: The First and the Last, the Living One who was dead and is now alive forever. This description recalls 1:5, where Jesus the Messiah is described as the firstborn of the dead and preeminent ruler of the kings of the earth, and 1:7, where he is described as one whom every eye shall see. And the purpose for "every eye" seeing Jesus is so that "all the tribes of the land shall mourn on account of him."

This is a significant passage since it is the first hint of the specific orientation of the book of Revelation. The reference to mourning is generally seen as a reference to Zech 12:10–11. Now if John does channel his expectations in terms of Zechariah's scenario, then we learn several things. First of all, this passage from Zechariah tells that "the house of David and the inhabitants of Jerusalem . . . when they look on him whom they have pierced, they shall mourn for him," and that "on that day the mourning in Jerusalem will be as great as the mourning for Hadad-rimmon in the plain of Megiddo." The royal house of Israel, the city of Jerusalem and its inhabitants, and Megiddo allude to later scenarios in the book and relate the destruction of Jerusalem in Sector 2 ("the great city . . . where too their Lord was crucified," 11:8) and the destruction of that other great city, Babylon (mention of Megiddo = "Harmagedon," 16:16) in Sector 4.

Furthermore, the passage from Zechariah indicates that one of the author's aims is to proclaim Israel's need to mourn over Jesus' death (in Jerusalem). "To mourn" means to make a public protest over the presence of some evil, such as death, famine, or any other significant disaster or catastrophe. It is the behavior typical of those personally afflicted with evil and developed into a social ritual. For example, should a spouse die, as a rule the surviving spouse cannot eat, or sleep, and does not care about personal grooming, and the like. This inability to eat is ritualized into fasting; the inability to sleep is ritualized into keeping vigil all night, while apathy for grooming leads to the ritualized use of clothing made from sacking material (that is, sackcloth) and ashes. The Hebrew name for this sort of mourning means "(self) humiliation." And the behavior is clearly indicated in Joel 1:14; 2:15, where the prophet urges all to "sanctify a fast" (see 1 Kings 21:9 for a similar proclamation).

The point is that to mourn the crucifixion of Jesus is to admit that his death was wrongful, that his execution was an evil and shameful act, marking a disaster for Israel. In this perspective, the purpose of Revelation is to get all the tribes of the land (Israel, of course) to acknowledge publicly the wickedness of Jesus' execution. Of course there is more involved, for what indicates the propriety of such an acknowledgment is the present condition of Jesus. Early Christian theology began with the attempt to deal with the experience of Jesus' death and subsequent appearance. It is the appearance of Jesus after death that provoked questions, for his appearance to the Twelve (less one) was quickly interpreted as a resurrection effected by God. God raised Jesus from the dead. The normal question was: why him and not some other very good person? Moreover, Jesus did not simply die by falling off a roof. He was publicly humiliated, shamed, and rejected by God's people, the very persons who were to acknowledge him. The manner of his death pointed to rejection by God, for he was crucified, hence presumably cursed by God (Deut 21:23). Yet God honored him by raising him from the dead. And although he once appeared after death and interacted with the core group of his followers, he was no longer in their midst. Where could he be found, what was he doing, how does he fit into the scheme of reality created and governed by God the creator of all? It was these sorts of questions that lay at the source of Christian theology.

Given the roles ascribed to Jesus in the book of Revelation, it would seem that John's astral prophecies are likewise meant to answer these latter questions. In other words, John presents a theological perspective concerning Jesus' relationship to God, a perspective often called "Christology." In the opening chapter of the book we encounter some of the personages involved in formulating this perspective: John the astral prophet, sky servants, John's communities, those who pierced Jesus, the cosmic Jesus and God. John's description of God and God's activities forms the theology of the book.

In the course of this book I hope to set out the theology of the book of Revelation as it emerges from the perspective of astral prophecy. While Revelation seeks to allay deception and to appeal for endurance among first-century Christians, our ancestors in faith, what it has left us with is a set of brilliant images of what God is like and what God does for those who believe in his Messiah, Jesus.

Furthermore, of course, the role of Jesus as cosmic Messiah is heightened in a way that is impressive and moving. From the outset, in the first celestial scenario, Jesus the Messiah is presented as Lord of the pole of the universe, with the pivotal cosmic stars in his control, in his "right hand." To control the cosmic pole is to be in charge of all that happens on earth. Jesus is *Polokrator,* controller of the pole of the universe already now, and is not merely Israel's forthcoming Messiah. His actual role far surpasses the narrow and confining role ascribed to him by his earthly followers.

In the next sector, we shall find that this cosmic Lord of the pole of the universe is identified with the zodiacal Lamb/Ram. This is the sky being that has preeminence and primacy over all celestial beings. The Lamb/Ram, as first of the zodiacal constellations, received this primacy before the outfitting of the earth when the Creator filled the sky with the cosmic beings found there. Furthermore, it was generally believed that when the sky returned to the position that it had at its inception with creation, the whole universe would be transformed. The exalted Jesus now occupies this cosmic center associated with the Lamb/Ram.

Of perhaps even greater religious importance is the fact that this cosmic Jesus appears to the seer specifically to give directives to seven named Christian churches. At the time John writes, these Christian groupings were surely not very large. And yet the personage wielding cosmic power is concerned with these socially insignificant communities. It is because Jesus is now Polokrator, controller of the pole of the universe. It is important to note that the word "pole," did not refer simply to that abstract, mathematical point that marks the place where the earth's imaginary axis passes. This is our meaning of the word. For the ancients, the word "pole" referred to that central pivot plus all the sky connected with it that rotated around the earth due to the power applied at the pole (see Le Boulluec 1981: 147). In other words, for the earth's inhabitants, the "pole" was like a huge umbrella consisting of the northern half of the firmament that in fact covered the known inhabited earth. (This known, inhabited earth consisted of only one-fourth of the surface of the earth, from the Atlantic to the Indus Valley, as all learned people knew. It was separated from the south by an impassable torrid zone, from the west by an impassable ocean.) Hence as controller of the pole of the world, the risen Jesus controlled the firmament that covered all the inhabited earth. He can now encompass the whole earth within his purview and single out his own.

Hence the fact of his having a message for the seven Christian groups underscores their significance in his eyes. We leave our consideration of these ancient Asian churches and their problems for the final chapter of this book. Before proceeding to Sector 2 and its vision beyond the vault of the sky, we pause to consider briefly how John reads his sky visions.

4.3. A BRIEF PAUSE: JOHN'S MODE OF INTERPRETING THE SKY

It is curious, first of all, that here (v. 20) the cosmic Jesus himself, rather than some sky servant, explains the meaning of some of the items in John's vision, specifically items unrelated to the book of Daniel. The seer is told that the seven-star constellation equates with a set of sky messengers directed to the seven churches, while the celestial planetary menorah refers to the seven churches themselves. In 7:13–17, a decan (elder) explains a feature of the seer's sky vision, while in 17:8–18 it is a sky servant that offers explanation. However unlike the direct explanation in 7:13–17, both here and in 17:8–18 the explanation is allegorical. The sights really stand for something or someone else. Such allegorical explanation is quite rare in this work. But it was rather usual in the astronomics of those deviants labelled as "heretics."

In the perspective of early Christians who compiled listings of heretics, Israelites who rejected Jesus as Messiah were quintessential heretics. Among this group, the Pharisees were remembered for their devotedness to astrology: "Fate and astrology were quite popular notions with them," writes Epiphanius (*Panarion* 16.2.1, trans. Philip Amidon 1990: 51). Epiphanius further recounts how they possessed a vocabulary of their own in Hebrew for the zodiac and other celestial beings.

Hippolytus reports knowing persons, "heretics" of course, who read constellations in terms of Israel's biblical tradition. They assimilate the doctrines of an Aratus, for example, to those declared by the Scriptures, thus "exhibiting a strange marvel, as if the assertions made by them were fixed among the stars" (Hippolytus, *Refutation of All Heresies* 4.46, *ANF*, 5.42). For example:

> And near the head itself of the Dragon is the appearance of a man, conspicuous by means of the stars, which Aratus styles a wearied image, and like one oppressed with labor, and he is denominated "Engonasis." Aratus (*Phenomena* 5.63ff.) then affirms that he does not know what this toil is, and what this prodigy is that revolves in the heaven [-sky]. The heretics, however, wishing by means of this account of the stars to establish their own doctrines, (and) with more than ordinary earnestness devoting their attention to these (astronomic systems), assert that Engonasis is Adam, according to the commandment of God as Moses declared, guarding the head of the Dragon, and the Dragon (guarding) his heel. For so Aratus expresses himself: "The right-foot's track of the Dragon fierce possessing" (*Refutation of All Heresies* 4.47, *ANF* 5.42–43).

> But Aratus says: here this (constellation) is Cepheus; and Cassiopeia, and Andromeda, and Perseus, great lineaments of the creation to those who are able to discern them. For he asserts that Cepheus is Adam, Cassiopeia, Eve, Andromeda the soul of both of these, Perseus the Logos, winged offspring of Jove, and Cetos, the plotting monster (*Phenomena* 5.353ff.). Not to any of these but to Andromeda only does he repair, who slays the Beast; from whom, likewise taking unto himself Andromeda, who had been delivered (and) chained to the Beast, the Logos—that is Perseus— achieves, he says, her liberation. Perseus, however, is the winged axle that pierces both poles through the center of the earth, and turns the world around. The spirit also, that which is in the world, is (symbolized) by Cygnus, a bird—a musical animal near "The Bears"—type of Divine Spirit, because that when it approaches the end itself of life, it alone is fitted by nature to sing, on departing with good hope from the wicked creation, (and) offering up hymns to God (*Refutation of All Heresies* 4.49, *ANF* 5.44).

The heretics opposed by Hippolytus interpret the Scriptures allegorically. The Scriptures do not mean what they say literally, but refer to something else (this is allegory). Furthermore, these heretics likewise interpret the stars allegorically, using the fixity and regularity of the stars to give credence to their interpretations:

> some persons, assimilating these (doctrines of astronomics) to those declared by the Scriptures, convert (the holy writings) into allegories, and endeavor to seduce the mind of those who give heed to their (tenets), drawing them on by plausible words into the admission of whatever opinions they wish, (and) exhibiting a strange marvel, as if the assertions made by them were fixed among the stars (*Refutation of All Heresies* 4.46, *ANF* 5.42).

How does John's astral prophecy differ from the procedure alluded to in Hippolytus? The obvious answer is that John's reading of the sky takes place in an altered state of awareness, with the aid of sky servants, and not by the learned effort evidenced in the foregoing examples. Furthermore, the only instances of allegory are ascribed to visionary beings: the exalted Polokrator in 1:20 and the sky servant in 17:8–18. John himself takes the biblical stories and what he sees in the sky not allegorically but literally. For example, God creates everything, including the Dragon, who is Satan, a personage known from the creation story; and Babylon/Babel did exist as the first city after the Flood, being eventually destroyed at God's command. As for the Christian story, Jesus is risen Lord, now ascended to God in the sky; he is the Lamb of God; and God rules the cosmos from beyond the vault of the sky.

Now it is only with reference to the interpretation of seven stars and lamp stands in the opening scenario (1:20) and the scenario of Babylon (17:8–18) that we find allegory in the work. Perhaps these allegorical interpretations are not from the original seer, but from others in early Christian groups who used John's revelation to find some significant "hidden meaning." For the allegorizations detract from the original scenarios and suggest to readers to search the work for further hidden meanings. This is the procedure that early Christian deviants followed.

Apart from 1:20 and 17:8–18, John's approach to the Scriptures, to the stars, and to his visions is direct and straightforward. He sets forth the plain meaning. If he alludes to Israel's Torah and Prophets, it is not so much to cite prophetic Old Testament sources or to demonstrate the fulfillment of prophecy. Rather, his ruminations through Israel's sacred writings provided him with information about what might be expected when one has altered states of awareness involving cosmic journeys. These expected sights and interpretation of sights were known from Isaiah or Ezekiel or Zechariah or Daniel, as well as from Enoch, and they could be articulated in borrowed words. John was not concerned with allegory at all. Consequently, it seems that 1:20 and 17:8–18 are early insertions into John's work, perhaps by one of his "brother" astral prophets, intended to make his astral prophecy relevant for some later Christian group or other.

5 SECTOR 2 BEGINS: THE SCENARIO OF THE THRONE IN THE SKY

4 [1]After these things, I saw and behold an open door in the sky, and the previous voice that I heard [was] like a trumpet speaking with me saying: Come up here and I will show you what must happen after these things. [2]I was immediately in a sky wind; and behold a throne was placed in the sky and someone seated on the throne, [3]and the one seated [was] like the sight of jasper and carnelian stone, and a rainbow round about the throne [was] like the sight of emerald. [4]And round about the throne [were] twenty-four thrones, and on the thrones [were] seated twenty-four elders clothed in white garments, and on their heads golden wreaths. [5]And from the throne proceeded lightnings and voices and thunders; and seven torches of fire burning before the throne, which are the seven sky winds of God, [6]And before the throne [was something] like a sea of glass like crystal.

And in the middle of the throne and around the throne [were] four living beings filled with eyes in front and in back.

[7]and the first living being similar to a lion, and the second living being similar to a young bull, and the third living being having the face like a human, and the fourth living being like a flying eagle. [8]And the four living beings each of them having six wings each round about them and within full of eyes.

And they have no pause, day and night, saying:

Holy, holy, holy
Lord God Almighty,
who was and who is and who is coming.

[9]And whenever the living beings will give glory and honor and acknowledgment to the one sitting on the throne, the one who lives into the aeons of aeons,

[10]the twenty-four elders will fall before the one seated on the throne, and they will prostrate themselves before the one who lives into the aeons of aeons, saying:

[11]"Worthy are you our Lord and God,
to receive glory and honor and power,

because you created everything,
and because of your good-pleasure, they were,
and were created."

5 [1] And I saw on the right hand of the one seated on the throne a scroll written within and without, sealed up with seven seals. [2] And I saw a mighty sky servant proclaiming in a loud voice: "Who is worthy to open the scroll and to break open its seals?" [3] And no one—[neither] anyone in the sky nor on the earth nor below the earth—was able to open the scroll or to look into it. [4] And I wept much because no one worthy was found to open the scroll or to look into it. [5] And one of the elders says to me: "Stop crying! Behold the lion of the tribe of Judah, the root of David, conquered [in order] to open the scroll and its seven seals." [6] And I saw in the middle of the throne and of the four living beings and in the middle of the elders a lamb standing as though slaughtered, having seven horns and seven eyes, [which are the {seven} sky winds of God sent upon the whole earth]. [7] And he went and he accepted from the right hand of the one seated upon the throne. [8] And when he received the scroll, the four living beings and the twenty-four elders fell down before the lamb, having each of them a lyre and golden broad-flat-bowls full of incense, which are the prayers of the holy ones. [9] And they sang a new song saying:

"Worthy are you to accept the scroll
and to open up its seals;
because you were slaughtered and bought for God with your blood from every tribe and
tongue and people and nation;
[10] And you made them for our God a kingdom and priests and they will rule upon the earth."

[11] And I saw and I heard a voice of many sky servants around the throne and of the living beings and of the elders, and the number of them was ten thousands of ten thousands, and thousands of thousands, [12] saying with a loud voice:

"Worthy is the slaughtered Lamb
to receive power and wealth and wisdom and
strength and honor and glory and praise."

[13] And every creature—the one in the sky and upon the earth and below the earth and upon the sea and all those in the seas—I heard saying:

"To the one seated upon the throne and to the Lamb
praise and honor and glory and might
into the aeons of aeons."

[14] And the four living beings said: "Amen."
And the elders fell down and prostrated themselves.

While most presentations of Revelation follow the consideration of the opening chapter with an explanation of the seven letters, I suggest moving on to Sector 2 of the tour. This keeps us in the sky, now situating us with the prophet before the throne of God, and affords a cosmic orientation for all that has happened so far and for all that is yet to happen. For if John has any message at all, it is that the one God is in control of the universe. In chs. 4–5 John describes his experience of the presence of God. However, he does so not simply to tell his fellow believers what God's "throne room" is like. This they would know from traditions like those in 1 Enoch. Rather, John describes God's controlling location to provide the setting for the cosmic action he witnessed and now feels impelled to recount: the fate of the land of Israel and its center, Jerusalem.

Through an opening in the sky, our astral prophet sees a throne with seven torches in its vicinity, twenty-four elders ensconced around the central throne, and four living creatures at opposing corners. He likewise witnesses the acclamation of the cosmic Lamb. Meanwhile cosmic songs are directed to God and to the Lamb. The whole scenario is readily understandable from Hellenistic astronomic knowledge. But the meaning of the scenario derives from John's interpretation, based on his Israelite expectations and Christian profession.

John's second vision, then, is a vision of the other side of the vault of the sky (ch. 4). By passing through "an open door in the sky" (4:1) the prophet can see the proper realm of God at the controlling center of the cosmos. Since John undertakes his sky trip within the framework of Israelite tradition, he naturally interprets what he sees in terms of that tradition as understood within his elite circles in the first century A.D. Thus he sees the throne of the sole and unique God. The throne is attended by seven spirits (4:1.5), the seven stars that in Pharisaic astrology constitute God's chariot. This central throne is surrounded by the thrones of twenty-four sky entities, that is, stars known as "decans," but here called "elders" (4:4). At four equidistant and opposing points along the cosmic circle around the throne, there are four living beings, that is, constellations in animate shape (4:6–7). The seer is privileged to see the cosmos from God's point of view, from the other side of the vault of the sky. Along with seeing the vision, John hears singing, as one might expect, in the upper reaches of the sky. The first song (4:8) unceasingly tells of the exclusivity and uniqueness of God; the second (4:11) praises the eternal God as creator.

This first scenario of what transpires on the other side of the vault of the sky moves toward the book's cosmic drama signaled by the sealed scroll at God's right hand (5:1). One of God's "mighty" sky servants proclaims a search for some being of sufficiently exalted status (this is worthiness) to be privy to God's designs (5:2). One of the decans or elders then tells the seer that the one worthy enough for the task is "the Lion of the tribe of Judah, the root of David, the one who conquered" (5:5). This personage, he sees, is none other than the "Lamb standing as though slaughtered," and located in the center of the decans (5:6). This Lamb, of course, is the well-known celestial Lamb, the constellation

Aries. As will be explained later, the Latin and Greek names of this constellation (Latin: *Aries* and Greek: *Krion* both mean "ram") are rather recent. The traditional name of this zodiacal being (Phoenician: *Telah,* Israelite: *Taleh,* Arabic: *Al-Hamal*) was "Male Lamb." From Babylonian times on, those who actually looked at the sky always pictured Aries with a "reverted head, that is, with head twisted in such a way that the Lamb looked directly over its own back to Taurus" (Brown 1899: 1.337). This is how Aries appears in the most ancient representation, and this is how Manilius describes that entity in his poem: "Resplendent in his golden fleece, first place holder Aries looks backward admiringly at Taurus rising" (*Astronomica* 1.263–264, LCL). A being with its head turned directly backwards as the celestial Aries might easily be judged to have a broken neck, much like a "slaughtered" lamb. And yet it remains standing in spite of its "reverted head." Clearly, Aries was an obvious choice to be perceived in terms of the Christian story according to which God's Lamb was slaughtered yet continues to stand.

Image 3: Taurus and Aries with decans (elders) below from an early second century Roman coffin lid (now in the British Museum; see p. 95)

Once this eminent personage accepts the scroll, the whole cosmos breaks out in song. First the twenty-four decans and four living being constellations sing of the cosmic preeminence (worthiness) of the Lamb (the book's third song 5:9); then God's entourage equally hymns the preeminence of the Lamb (the fourth song 5:13); and finally, all created beings second the judgment of all those prominent sky beings by singing of the honor of both God and the Lamb (the fifth song 5:13).

5.1. THE OPENING IN THE SKY

The opening in the sky enables the prophet to enter the other side of the sky. That the sky had such an opening was common knowledge in antiquity. For example, consider the opening in the roof of the magnificent Pantheon in Rome. This opening is usually given a functional explanation; it was made to let light enter the structure. The fact is it does let in light, but in replication of the light that comes from the realm of God on the other side of the vault of the sky. The present roof and walls date from the time of Hadrian, "a passionate practitioner of astrology" (Cramer 83). Dio Cassius, who knew the Pantheon in its Hadrianic restoration, gives his view for the choice of name: "It has this name, perhaps, because it received among the images which decorated it the statues of many gods, including Mars and Venus; but my own opinion of the name is that, because of its vaulted roof, it resembles the sky" (*Roman History* 53.27.2–3, LCL). This vaulted roof has an opening in the dome, called *oculus* in Latin (meaning "eye"). And this "eye" in the dome replicates the opening in the actual sky. One can observe a similar structure in the Roman ritual pit called the *mundus* (literally: the world), which had an altar over its opening in the center of its vaulted roof (illustrated in Meslin 1978: 33).

Through an opening, John gains access to the other side of the vault of the sky and begins to observe. What was to be found on the other side of the vault of the sky? Long before John, Plato had the following to say about "the back of the world" where God (or gods) dwelt, in the Phaedrus 247C–E (cited from Hackforth 1952: 77–80):

> And now there awaits the soul the extreme of her toil and struggling. For the souls that are called immortal, so soon as they are at the summit, come forth and stand upon the back of the world: and straightway the revolving heaven carries them round, and they look upon the regions without. Of that place beyond the heavens none of our earthly poets has yet sung, and none shall sing worthily. But this is the manner of it, for assuredly we must be bold to speak what is true, above all when our discourse is upon truth. It is there that true Being dwells, without colour or shape, that cannot be touched; reason alone, the soul's pilot, can behold it, and all true knowledge is knowledge thereof. Now even as the mind of god is nourished by reason and knowledge, so also is it with every soul that has a care to receive her proper food; wherefore when at least she has beheld Being she is well content, and contemplating truth she is nourished and prospers, until the heavens' revolution brings her back full circle. And while she is borne round she discerns justice, its very self, and likewise temperance, and knowledge, not the knowledge that is neighbor to Becoming and varies with the various objects to which we common ascribe being, but the veritable knowledge of Being that veritably is. And when she has contemplated likewise and feasted upon all else that has true being, she descends

again within the heavens and comes back home. And having so come, her charioteer sets his steeds at their manger, and puts ambrosia before them and draught of nectar to drink withal (for Plato's astronomics, see Rivaud 1970: 52–63: "Le système astronomique de Platon"; and for life in the sky, see Robin 1933: lxxxii–lxxxvi: "La vie céleste des âmes et le lieu au delà du ciel").

A number of ancient globes depicting the constellations do so from the vantage point of this other side, so that only the backs of the constellational beings are visible to the observer (see Thiele 1898). This perspective from the other side seems to be where philosophers imagined themselves to be situated as they developed their theological speculation as well. Aujac (1981: 14, n. 28) has observed:

> One cannot but think that Plato had artificial spheres in mind when speaking of the procession of souls, he writes: "For the souls that are called immortal, so soon as they are at the summit, come forth and stand upon the back of the heavenly vault (ἐπὶ τῷ τοῦ οὐρανοῦ νώτῳ, *epi tōitou ouranou nōtō*) and straightway the revolving heaven carries them round, and they contemplate what is beyond the heavens" (*Phaedrus* 247E). Likewise, the first unmoved mover of Aristotle, situated beyond the sphere of the cosmos, would well have originated from reflection on certain mechanical models of the world.

Knowledge concerning the other side of the sky, then, was not exactly esoteric. But it was not a uniform body of knowledge, since experience of this other side depended on the cultural traditions that held the observer.

John obtained access to the other side thanks to his prophetic ability to perceive alternate reality. But such ability was not always required. According to the Israelite tradition of the period, when God created Adam, God "created for him an open heaven, so that he might look upon the angels singing the triumphal song. And the light which is never darkened was perpetually in paradise" (2 Enoch 31:2–3, *OTP*). Subsequently, of course, this sky aperture was either closed or concealed. Israelite tradition, as a rule, held this opening to be closed. However, it obviously could be opened at God's command.

Ezekiel, perhaps the first great astral prophet in Israel, tells of his vision thanks to an opening in the sky (Ezek 1:1). The sky likewise opened, we are told, at Jesus' baptism (Mark 1:10; Matt 3:16; Luke 3:21). Peter has a vision of food descending through such an opening (Acts 10:11). And ancient Christian accounts tell of persons seeing Jesus standing before God (Stephen in Acts 7). This posture is that of an avenger rising to his feet to exact vengeance for dishonor done to God (see Derrett 1988). Usually Jesus (the Son of man) was envisioned as seated at the right hand of God (after Ps 110:1; thus Matt 26:64/Luke 22:69 Q; Acts 2:33–36; Col 3:1; Eph 1:20–33; Mark 16:19; Heb 1:3, 13;

8:1; 10:12–13; 12:2; cf. Rom 8:34; 1 Pet 3:22; Barn 12:10–11). This vision interprets Jesus as co-regent or ruler with God. In either case, to see Jesus with God requires an opening in the sky.

Where exactly is this opening to the realm of God? Was it anywhere God directed his sky servants to open the vault, or was it in a fixed location? Some believed it was a fixed, if concealed, location. Ulansey has argued that Mithraism provided information about access to such an opening for the devotees of Mithra, alias Perseus, who is situated above Taurus (Ulansey 1986; 1987; 1989a; 1989b). Thus to describe the way persons determined the location of this opening to the other side of the vault of the sky would require some information about the structure of this vault. This question might not have been an entirely idle one. Jesus' ascension to God in Jerusalem required him to pass through such a door, although Acts simply reports a cloud enveloping him as he is taken up (Acts 1:9). Hence the opening in question was undoubtedly directly above Jerusalem, Israel's center of the world. As in the uranography of many ancient peoples, the true dwelling of any God is to be found in the sky directly above the God's earthly temple. So too in Israel. And there was no contradiction in observing God's throne at the pole above the inhabited earth as well as directly above God's temple in Jerusalem.[1]

As with Paul's experience in 2 Cor 12:2, persons in altered states of awareness found no difficulty in this period to remain on earth while traveling in the sky. Philo the Alexandrian reports:

> We have the testimony of those who have not taken a mere sip of philosophy but have feasted more abundantly on its reasonings and conclusions. For with them the reason soars away from the earth into the heights, travels through the upper air and accompanies the revolutions of the sun and moon and the whole heaven and in its desire to see all that is there finds its powers of sight blurred, for so pure and vast is the radiance that pours therefrom that the soul's eye is dizzied by the flashing of the rays. . . . So then just as we do not know and cannot with certainty determine what each of the stars is in the purity of its essence, we eagerly persist in the search because our natural love of learning makes us delight in what seems probably, so too though the clear vision

---

[1] Perhaps the easiest way to understand how such perception is possible is to work through what Jean Piaget says about a child's conception of geometry, space, and the world (Piaget et al. 1960; 1967; 1979). For the perception of space, Sack (1986: 21) suggested Piaget's works for understanding all classification by space. And Dean Chapman (1995) elaborated Piaget's insights in a map describing Mark's view of geography. While no one would say the ancient Mediterranean authors were children or thought like children, the fact is all extant maps of antiquity (e.g., in the representative collection of Harley and Woodward, 1987) are much like maps drawn by children in Piaget's sampling. For ancient Mesopotamia and the book of Enoch, see the map drawn up by Grelot (1958) which I later use for Revelation.

of God as He really is denied us, we ought not to relinquish the quest. For the very seeking, even without finding, is felicity in itself (*Special Laws* 1.37, 39, LCL).

Likewise from Egypt, we read in a traditional collection of lore known as the *Poimandres of Hermes Trismegistos*:

> For none of the sky gods [stars] will come down to the earth, leaving the boundary of the sky; rather man will go up into the sky and measure it and he knows what in the sky is on high, what is down below, and he grasps all the rest with exactness and supreme wonder; he does not even have need to leave the earth to get up above, that is how far his power stretches! (*Corpus Hermeticum* X, 25, Festugière-Nock 1.126).

And further on:

> Command your soul to fly into the sky and it will have no need of wings. Nothing can be an obstacle to it, neither the fire of the sun, nor the ether, nor the revolution of the sky, nor the body of other stars; but cutting through space, it will climb up in its flight to the last [sky] body. And if you wish to get through above the whole universe and contemplate what is on the other side (if there be an "other side" of the universe), you can (*Corpus Hermeticum* XI, 19, Festugière-Nock 1.155).

And again:

> On the contrary, all who partake in the gift coming from God, when one compare their works with those of other categories, are immortal and no longer mortal for they have embraced all things by their intellect, those on earth, those in the sky and those, if any, above the sky (*Corpus Hermeticum* IV, 5, Festugière-Nock 1.51).

In the Hellenistic period, some Stoics held that there was nothing above the sky, a position Cleomedes refutes: "Those saying that there is nothing outside the cosmos are babbling" (Cleomedes, *On the Circular Motion of Celestial Bodies*, I, 1, 3–4, ed. Ziegler 6.26–8.14). Thus astral prophets and other ecstatics can in fact be in two places at one time through "astral projection." They can see things above and below.

Later on in the work, John informs us about other occasions when he sees through an opening in the sky. To begin with, he tells about how he looks through the opening to see God's temple, itself open to enable one to see the ark of the covenant there (11:19). Israelite tradition knew that the true temple of God, of which the earthly one is but a pale reflection, is in the sky (see Exod 25:40; Ezek 40–42 for this tradition). Like the vault of the sky, the doors of the sky temple must be opened so that the seer can see God's divine decrees. Thus in our book we read: "Then God's temple in the sky was opened, and the ark of his covenant was seen within his temple; and there were flashes of lightning, voices, peals of thunder, an earthquake, and heavy hail" (11:19). Similarly,

John notes: "After this I looked, and the temple of the tent of witness in the sky was opened, and out of the temple came the seven angels with the seven plagues, robed in pure bright linen, and their breasts girded with golden girdles" (15:5–6). Then too the sky opens to let the white horse and rider come through for the final cosmic conflict (19:11). Finally, at the new creation, it presumably opens over the site of Jerusalem to enable the new Jerusalem to descend (Rev 21).

5.2. THE STRUCTURE OF THE VAULT OF THE SKY

Knowledge of the sky in antiquity was cumulative. Those who studied the subject always built on what predecessors said. And even if they disagreed with those predecessors, they included previous learned opinions anyway. This chain of learning about the vault of the sky can be traced to Mesopotamia. While there is evidence that all ethnic groups took celestial events seriously, it seems that the systematic study of the sky behind the astral prophecy of Revelation is in the tradition rooted in Assyro-Babylonian lore. This learning was mediated to the Mediterranean by means of Phoenicia, Israel, and Egypt. Now even before the zodiac was established, Assyro-Babylonian devotees of astronomics charted the sky in terms of three bands, called the pathways of En-lil, Anu, and Ea. En-lil was the Lord of All (equivalent to Baal and Zeus); Anu, the Sky God and Lord of the Firmament (equivalent to El, Elohim); and Ea, the King of the Deep, earthly and watery (like Poseidon). These pathways ran along and parallel to the equator of the earth, with the various constellations distributed in three groups along the pathways of their movement:
(a) the stars of the pathway of En-lil included the constellations in the northern sky, covering the north polar region down to about 17 degrees;
(b) the stars of the pathway of Anu covered the central band over the equator and lying between +17 degrees and -17 degrees;
(c) the stars of the pathway of Ea covered the southern sky, covering the area from about -17 degrees of the southern declension to the south polar region (see Floorisone 1950 and Figure 2 below).
For ancient Mesopotamian scholarship the original significant band of constellations of paramount concern was an equatorial band, with parallel pathways above and below the central equatorial band. The constellations along the equatorial pathway of Anu formed an equatorial zodiac. Subsequently, another band was developed, following the pathway of the sun. It was along this pathway that eclipses took place, and the path was called the "ecliptic." Constellations lying along this path counted as the "zodiac." On a globe, the ecliptic runs at an angle

relative to the North Pole and the equator. It therefore crosses the equator at two points. The resulting cross shape is a cosmic sky cross, of great significance to Plato as well as to early Christians. It was the celestial manifestation of the cross of Jesus, perhaps the very spot through which one passed to enter the other side of the vault of the sky (Daniélou 1964: 265–92). This cosmic cross was equally significant to Gnostics and Mithraists. It would seem that fundamental to this significance is the later preference for understanding the impact of the sky in terms of the ecliptic and its twelve zodiacal constellations. From this arrangement the number "twelve" gained in symbolic importance. During the Hellenistic period, this arrangement increased in significance as the arrangement of preference for the tradition running from Assyria and Babylon to Egypt, Greece, and Rome.

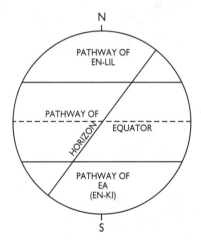

Figure 2: The Babylonian world, after Floorisoone 1950:257

However, the equatorial arrangement lent itself to a description of the sky in terms of a central point and four "corners." On a globe, the sky equator was a celestial projection of the earth's equator. It divided the universe into two equal parts. If one imagines the resulting hemispheres as half-global umbrellas, then from the northern perspective the central topmost point was the polar star, with the firmament forming a half-global, umbrella-like dome resting on the celestial equator. Along this equator at four equidistant points lie the four "corner" points, marked by constellations to be seen along the earth's horizon. Along this horizon, the vault of the sky touches the seas surrounding the inhabited world. The resulting five-fold arrangement (center and four corners) gave greater prominence to the constellations along the equator, rather than to the zodiac. This earlier arrangement was

1. Daily Movement of Sun and Cosmos

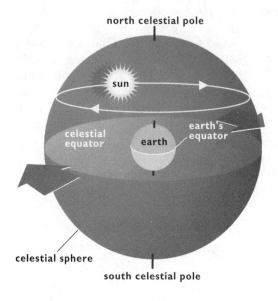

2. Sun's Annual Movement through Zodiac

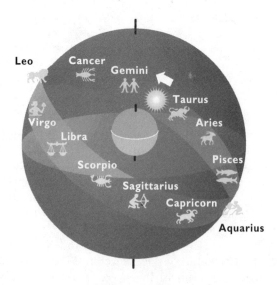

Figure 3: An ancient view of the sky and the
zodiac's movement across the sky.

3. Spring Equinox

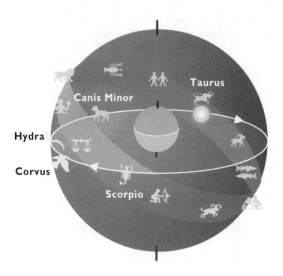

4. Movement of the Equinox

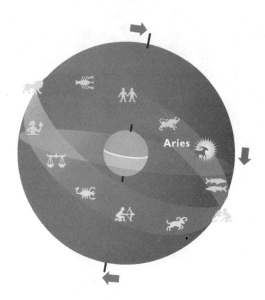

the arrangement of preference for the tradition running from China and Persia to the Middle East. Persian influence in general, and on Judea in particular, seems to account for the prominence of this arrangement in Ezekiel, Zechariah, and here in Revelation. From this arrangement, the number "four" gained its symbolic importance. De Saussure notes: "[T]he planet associated with the pole, center of the skies, and with the supreme divinity is found to be Saturn, to which the Greeks attributed the name of the supreme divinity who presided over time. The Emperor on high, as the earthly emperor, being placed in the center, is surrounded by twelve signs and four cardinal points which mark the revolution of the stars in time and space" (de Saussure 1924: 214).

In the Hellenistic period, both the equatorial and ecliptical systems were variously fused and applied so as to be available to learned students of celestial phenomena. And in both systems, the sun, moon, and five planets were of fundamental importance. It is these seven wandering celestial bodies that endowed the number "seven" with its symbolic importance.

Now in the scenario described by John here in ch. 4, the arrangement is that of central point (throne) and four corner points (living beings). Then along the equatorial pathway are twenty-four star beings surrounding the central point (the elders or decans). The final celestial entity in this scenario is the Lamb. See Figure 4 for a sketch of this scenario.

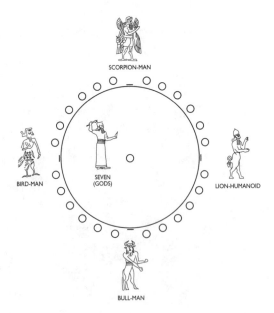

Figure 4: The arrangement of the sky as seen by the seer, standing outside the globe of the universe, at the top of the celestial globe, with the north at the center. The circle around the center are the locations of the 24 decans; the circle at the center is the throne location.

Figure 5 presents Brown's (1900: vol. 2, frontispiece) sketch of a Sumero-Semitic Euphratean Planisphere with constellations of the sort known in Hellenistic times.[2]

5.3. THE CENTRAL AGENTS

Our task in this chapter is to consider the central cast of characters, chiefly to find out what was expected of them in the world of first-century astronomics. These include the occupant of the central throne, the occupants of the twenty-four surrounding thrones, the four living creatures, and the cosmic Lamb.

---

[2] The abbreviations are: S.-A.: Sumerian-Akkadian; B.-A.: Babylonian-Assyrian; Ph.: Phoenician.

5.3.1 The Central Throne and Its Occupant

The first object the visionary sees in the sky is a throne. The presence of a throne constellation is well known. There is a globe on which the chief constellations of the second-century B.C. are depicted with their backs to the viewer, the famous Farnese sphere, an ancient copy of an even more ancient sculpture (for photographs and explanation see Thiele 1898: passim; excellent photographs of this sphere can also be found in the *Encyclopedia of World Art* II, Pl. 23). Near the North Pole over Leo and Cancer the throne is depicted, the *thronus Caesaris*. Pliny mentions the constellation "that in the reign of his late majesty Augustus received the name of Caesar's Throne" (*Natural History* 2.178, LCL). The group of stars in which appeared the *sidus Iulium*, the comet embodying the divine Caesar after his death, was designated as his "throne." Another well-known "throne" in the sky is one on which Cassiopeia sits. For Hellenistic Egyptians this throne is in the constellation of Virgo-Isis. This throne stands in the "atrium," that is, in an open celestial temple. All this was perceived in or on the sky. And Jupiter himself is often depicted as an enthroned celestial ruler in the zodiac, especially on coins. (Thiele 1898: 41). It was also current to depict a figure or a single star sitting on a throne formed of other stars. Hence the scenario of God's throne in the sky or of twenty-four elders enthroned there was really quite known. Surely it was not esoteric or knowledge available only to some privileged initiates.

Our author says nothing further about how big God's throne in the sky was thought to be. It might embrace the whole sky or a part of it. But Isa 66:1 (LXX: "Thus says the Lord: the sky is my throne") speaks in favor of the first view (cf. Matt 5:34; 23:22; see Boll 1914: 31–32). John's astral prophetic model, Enoch, likewise saw a throne in his visions:

> And as I shook and trembled, I fell upon my face and saw a vision: and behold there was an opening before me and a second house which is greater than the former, and everything was built with tongues of fire. And in every respect it excelled the other—in glory and great honor—to the extent that it is impossible for me to recount to you concerning its glory and greatness. As for its floor, it was of fire and above it was lightning and the path of the stars; and as for the ceiling, it was flaming fire. And I observed and saw inside it a lofty throne—its appearance was like crystal and its wheels like the shining sun; and I heard the voice of the cherubim; and from beneath the throne were issuing streams of flaming fire. It was difficult to look at it. And the Great Glory was sitting upon it—as for his gown, which was shining more brightly than the sun, it was whiter than any snow. None of the angels was able to come in and see the face of the Excellent and the Glorious One; and no one of the flesh can see him—the flaming fire was round about him, and a great fire stood before him. No one could come near unto him from among those that surrounded the tens of millions that stood before him. He needed no council, but the most Holy Ones who were near to him neither go far away at night nor move away from him (1 Enoch 14:15–24, *OTP*, 1.20–21).

The one on the throne looked like jasper and carnelian to the seer (4:3). These stones are yellowish, the color of the polar star. The polar star marks the central spot proper to the one in charge of the cosmos. It is important to note, once more, that in antiquity the pole was not simply a point marking either end of an imaginary axis through the earth. Rather it was a sort of encapsulating and enveloping, hemispheric cover that embraced everything in the sky and caused the sky to move the way it does (see Le Boulluec 1981: 147). Hence the arrangement here is that of that central, pivotal point of control, the pole marking the center of the vault of the sky, and four equidistant points located along the equator. We find this arrangement in Ezekiel's description of a central throne in the sky: "And above the firmament over their heads there was the likeness of a throne, in appearance like sapphire" (Ezek 1:26). Ezekiel describes the color of the polar star as that of sapphire, both here and later on: "Then I looked, and behold, on the firmament that was over the heads of the cherubim there appeared above them something like a sapphire, in form resembling a throne" (Ezek 10:1). Sapphires, of course, are largely yellow (Sanskrit, *saniprya* "Beloved of Saturn," the yellow planet); but they are often blue, at times even orange. Here presumably the seer beholds the yellowish polar star. The throne John sees is surrounded by an arc (like a rainbow) of emerald green light. Ezekiel once saw the same scenario: "Like the appearance of the bow that is in the cloud on the day of rain, so was the appearance of the brightness round about" (Ezek 1:28).

In the Israelite tradition, whenever God makes an appearance, a range of atmospheric phenomena marks the events. "Lightning" here refers to silent lightning flashes, like summer heat lightning. "Thunder" refers to sky sounds usually following lightning flashes, while "thunderbolts" are simultaneous lightning and thunder. "Sounds" refers to a range of audibles perceived as coming from the sky, from rumblings to all sorts of echoes. Even the pathway of the sun, the ecliptic, is called a sound or voice in ancient Mesopotamia. As a matter of fact, " 'voice' frequently occurs in Akkadian star names, the stars being the 'voices' (proclaimers) of the heaven" (Brown 1900: 2.15). All such phenomena were believed to be caused by sky beings of various types, with some significance for humans living in regions from which these phenomena can be perceived. While their significance was admitted, the quality of this significance was debatable. Yet even a person who doubted the value of horoscopes and the ability to foretell the course of a person's life from stars (such as Pliny the Elder or Hippolytus) nevertheless believed in the significance of celestial phenomena such as lightning, comets, sky sounds, and thunder claps. Pliny tells us that lightning comes from three planets:

> Most men are not acquainted with a truth known to the founders of the science from their arduous study of the heavens, that what when they fall to earth are termed thunderbolts are the fires of the three upper planets particularly those of Jupiter which is in the middle position—possibly because

it voids in this way the charge of excessive moisture from the upper circle (of Saturn) and of excessive heat from the circle below (of Mars); and that this is the origin of the myth that thunderbolts are the javelins hurled by Jupiter. Consequently heavenly fire is spit forth by the planet as crackling charcoal flies from a burning log, bringing prophecies with it, as even the part of himself that he discards does not cease to function in its divine tasks. And this is accompanied by a very great disturbance of the air, because moisture collected causes an overflow, or because it is disturbed by the birth-pangs, so to speak of the planet in travail (*Natural History* 2.18, 82, LCL).

Pliny further observes that in his day,

knowledge has made such progress even in the interpretation of thunder-bolts that one can prophesy that others will come on a fixed day, and whether they will destroy a previous one or other previous ones that are concealed: this progress has been made by public and private experiments in both fields (*Natural History* 2.54, 141, LCL).

Thunderbolts, then, communicate information from the sky and the beings that control it. "[Lightning] flashes on the left are considered lucky, because the sun rises on the left-hand side of the firmament" (*Natural History* 2.55, 142, LCL). Thus Pliny presupposes that the proper stance for observation is facing south. And so does Varro: "Of that heavenly division (*templi*) four parts are named: left to the east, right to the west, before to the south, behind to the north" (*On the Latin Language* 7.7, LCL).

The "seven torches of fire" are directly identified with "seven sky winds of God" (see Pétrement 1990: 65–67, cited on p. 65 above). In context, the torches themselves refer to the seven stars in the vicinity of the pole. These are perhaps the seven Great Ones ("Kabirim"), the stars that comprise Ursa Minor (Brown 1900 2.187), even though the most famous seven form the constellation Ursa Major, known in Mesopotamian tradition as "The Great Chariot" (Brown 1899: 1.268–69). These stars are known variously as simply the "Seven Stars"; or as "Septem Triones," the seven oxen that plow or thresh around the pole (in Latin, a common word for northern is "seven-oxen-ward," *septemtrionalis*); or "the Turner" (*Helike*) (Le Boeuffle 1977: 82–89). "The Pole-star, of course, stands alone as a sacred unit, whilst the seven prominent stars of the *Great Bear* form a *Chariot* naturally enough, and are reduplicated in the seven stars of the *Lesser Bear*. These two heavenly Chariots guard the Pole" (Brown 1900: 2.236). In the same vein, we find a tradition in Clement of Alexandria about the cherubim on the ark of the covenant: "Undoubtedly these golden statues with six wings each indicate either the two Bears, as some would have it, or rather the two hemispheres of the earth . . . " (*Stromata* 5.6,35,5, Sources Chrétienne p. 82 n. 278). This tradition points to the ark's mercy seat (Exod 25:19), where God was to be experienced as a replication of cosmic reality. The whole derives from Ezekiel's perception of the sky: "Then I looked, and behold, on the firmament that was over the heads of the cherubim there appeared above them something like a sapphire, in form resembling a throne" (Ezek 10:1).

Before (and behind and around) the throne is a sea of glass like crystal. This sea of glass is the vault of the sky. Hence the scenario is like that of Ezekiel: "Over the heads of the living creatures there was the likeness of a firmament, shining like crystal, spread out above their heads" (Ezek 1:22). Milik notes:

> The author of Revelation is no doubt thinking of the pavement in front of the throne, a pavement in transparent ice like that is the antechamber of the throne-room in En 14:10 (our line 24 of column vi). A number of other elements common to the book of Revelation and to Enoch make it clear that the Christian writer had first-hand knowledge of the Book of Enoch, probably the Greek translation of it; cf. En 22:12 and Rev 6:9–10; En 86:1 and Rev 9:1 and 11 and 8:10; En 91:16 and Rev 21:1. For a similar influence of the description of the new Jerusalem on the book of Revelation, see DJD [Documents of the Judean Desert] iii, p. 186 (Milik 1976: 199).

5.3.2. The Twenty-Four Thrones

In 4:4, around the control throne, making a circle in the sky along the celestial horizon, were twenty-four thrones. On the astral thrones are twenty-four gold-wreathed persons clothed in garments of light, called "elders." The astral thrones themselves mark off twenty-four segments of the horizon. While the central throne of God might readily be identified with a constellation, from where do the twenty-four thrones derive? And what is a throne in this case?

To begin with, Ptolemy recounts:

> [The planets] are said to be in their own "chariots" or "thrones" and the like when they happen to have familiarity in two or more of the aforecited ways with places in which they are found; for then their power is most increased in effectiveness by the similarity and cooperation of the kindred property of the signs which contain them (*Tetrabiblos* 1.23, LCL).

Similarly, "in the Michigan astrological roll (P. Mich. 149, col. 3A, 22–34) the 'thrones' are identified with the (astrological) exaltations and the depressions of the planets are called their 'prisons'; upon the thrones the planets have 'royal power,' in their prisons they 'are abased and oppose their own powers' " (F. E. Robbins in his notes to Ptolemy, *Tetrabiblos* 1.23, LCL). In sum, thrones are positions of power in the sky. Now why twenty-four?

Diodorus of Sicily, writing shortly before the Christian era, observes relative to Babylonian astronomy:

> Beyond the circle of the zodiac they (the Babylonians) designate twenty-four other stars, of which one half, they say, are situated in the northern parts and one half in the southern, and of these those which are visible

they assign to the world of the living, while those which are invisible they regard as being adjacent to the dead, and so they call them "Judges of the Universe" (*Library of History* 2.31, 4, LCL).

Interestingly, this passage offers traditional information about twenty-four star personages encircling the sky, with twelve who will judge the world. Our seer does not play up this feature (see 5:8 for the activity of these twenty-four).

In terms of celestial personages, these elders on their thrones of power would fit the profile of those truly significant astronomic beings of antiquity, the astral deities known as decans. The word "decan" (from the Greek: δέκα, *deka*, "ten") is a creation of the Hellenistic period to designate the astral deities who dominate over every ten (δέκα) degrees of the circle of the zodiac. These deities are far more ancient than the Hellenistic period, since the decans derive from Egypt in Pharaonic times. The deities in question often varied in number from seventy-two to twenty-four, although thirty-six was the proper decan number, given a circle of three-hundred-sixty degrees. In ancient Egypt they were associated with constellations or single stars (e.g., Sirius, Orion, Kyon, Prokyon, Hydra), rising about ten days apart along the pathway of the sun and covering some ten degrees of one of the constellations of the zodiac (see Neugebauer 1983 [1955]). However, this solar pathway for the Egyptians and Babylonians was not the circle of the ecliptic but the pathway of Anu mentioned previously. The pathways of Anu referred to the large band extending from one tropic to the other in breadth, with the celestial equator (a projection of the earth's equator onto the vault of the sky) forming its middle line (see Festugière 1950: 115–16). As astral deities, the decans exerted tremendous influence on the earth and its inhabitants.

Here in Revelation we have only twenty-four elders, not the thirty-six of Babylonian sky lore. But the lower number fits the Hellenistic situation. Neugebauer notes:

> We must now come back to the "decanal hours." Obviously these "hours" determined by the rising of stars on horizons with constant longitudinal difference are neither constant nor even approximately 60 min. in length. They vary as the oblique ascensions of the corresponding sections of the ecliptic and are about 45 min. long because during each night eighteen decans rise and set. Thus twelve decanal hours seem too short to measure time at night. In so arguing, one forgets, however, that each decan has to serve for ten days as indicator of its hour. If we furthermore require that these "hours" of the night never should be part of twilight, we get a satisfactory covering of the time of total darkness by means of only twelve decans during ten consecutive days, especially for the shorter summer nights. Again for the sake of consistency a simple scheme which held true for Sirius near the shortest summer nights was extended to all decans and all nights, thus making the number of "hours" twelve for all seasons of the year. And finally the symmetry of night and day, of upper and nether

world, suggested a similar division for the day. This parallelism between day and night is still visible in the "seasonal hours" of classical antiquity. It is only within theoretical astronomy of the Hellenistic period that the Babylonian time-reckoning with its strictly sexagesimal division, combined with the Egyptian norm of 2 x 12 hours led to the twenty-four "equinoctial hours" of 60 min. each and of constant length (Neugebauer 1983: 208–9).

Herodotus records this particular point when he writes that "the Greeks learned about the sundial and the gnomon and the twelvefold division of the day from the Babylonians" (*Histories* 2.109, LCL). Perhaps it was Anaximander who mediated this information since he also constructed a celestial globe showing distances in terms of the Babylonian sexagesimal system (Kahn 1960). The point is, by the fifth century B.C., the civilized world from Babylon to Greece knew of twelve lunar months of thirty days (with regular intercalations as needed). Then on the analogy of the year, the day (daylight plus night time) was divided into twelve larger "double hours," and 360 smaller units. And these time units were connected with the circular course of the sun, the moon, and the stars, in terms of the same procedure; a circle's circumference consisted of twelve equal "double segments" and 360 lesser units (see Eggermont 1973: 119–24).

Thus by the time of John's Gospel, it is no surprise when Jesus asks rhetorically: "Are there not twelve hours in the day?" (John 11:9). These twelve hours corresponding to the twelve divisions of the celestial circle are in fact double hours, hence twenty-four in all. Consequently, our seer could see twenty-four elders about the central throne of God, each presumably in charge of one hour of the day. It is well known that "the division of the priesthood into twenty-four courses, each of which did service for one week in Jerusalem from Sabbath to Sabbath . . . was the system prevailing at the time of Jesus" (Jeremias 1969: 199). It would seem that there was some connection between these twenty-four courses and the decanal arrangement of Hellenism, for even in the older portion of the *Testament of Adam* (chs. 1–2, *OTP* 1.993), we find a worship horarium according to which the twenty-four hours of the night-day cycle are parceled out among various superearthly beings, including various elements, as their distinctive time frame.

In the British Museum's Egyptian collection, the twenty-four decans are duly featured on the coffin lids of the Roman Cornelius Pollios and of his son Soter (wall cases 47 and 49), from Sheikh Abdu'l-Qurna, West Thebes, and dating to the early second century A.D. These lids are painted with a large representation of the sky goddess, Nut, surrounded by the twelve signs of the zodiac arranged clockwise about her body. On the right are Leo, Virgo, Libra, Scorpio, Sagittarius, and Capricorn. On the left are Aquarius, Pisces, Aries, Taurus, Gemini, and Cancer. On the sides of the cover are, to the left, the twelve decans of the day, and to the right the twelve decans of the night (see Image 3, p. 79).

The author of Revelation calls the twenty-four beings enthroned around the throne of God "elders" (Greek: πρεσβύτεροι, *presbyteroi*). What connection might there be between decans and elders? The fact is that in a number of Israelite inscriptions from around the Mediterranean, a council of elders was called a *gerousia* (γερουσία), or *dekania* (δεκανία), while a member of this council was called *presbytēs, presbyteros* (πρεσβύτης, πρεσβύτερος) synonyms for the Latin *decurio,* and the Greek *dekanos* (δεκανός; see Kant 1987: 694–95). Thus it took very little imagination to connect the terms *presbyteros* with *dekanos,* since both mean "council member; elder." Yet in terms of celestial personages, these elders on their thrones of power fit the profile of those truly signigicant astronomic beings of antiquity, the astral deities known as decans.

In Revelation, the elders are celestial personages ("clad in white" 4:4), of exalted rank ("golden crowns" 4:4) and power ("enthroned" 4:4), forming a core group about the central throne. They regularly worship God, submitting their crowns to God and participating in celestial songs of praise to God (4:10; 5:11, 14; 7:11; 11:16; 19:4). They are privy to God's cosmic plan and can impart those secrets to prophets (5:5; 7:13). They likewise surround the cosmic Lamb (5:6), give their homage to the Lamb, and mediate the homage of other beings (5:8). These decanal thrones undoubtedly belong to the category of "thrones, dominions, principalities, and powers" over which Jesus Messiah has preeminence in Colossians 1:16.

The fact that the elders occupy God's inner circle, close to the center of power, likewise indicates their decan-like celestial location. While the explanation of the nature and quality of decans in Hellenistic writings is contradictory (see Gundel 1936a), one can make some generalizations. To begin with, the decans are located between the vault of the sky and the equatorial zodiacal circle, thus supporting that vault and delimiting the path of this zodiac. While they may be said to accompany the planetary gods who inhabit the same zodiacal domain in the outmost pathway of the universe, they are nonetheless superior to planetary deities. The reason for this is that decans know neither planetary stations nor retrograde movements. Rather, they keep above such change. They are sovereign astral beings, embracing the whole cosmos in the course of one night and one day, keeping watch over everything. In Revelation, the author sees the decans as twenty-four elders about the throne of God. In this way, the decans are perceived from and appropriated into an Israelite-based Christian perspective. And they thus continue to maintain their previous astronomic dignity, for in previous perceptions the decans were considered guardians and rescuers of the whole cosmos, at the same rank as the highest of astral deities, beings of power and might second only to the highest god(s). It would seem the elders here, now in monotheistic context, are much the same (for particulars, see Gundel 1936a, and Festugière's excursus in *Corpus Hermeticum* II; 1946: xxxviii–lxi). As astral deities, the decans were perceived to exert tremendous influence on the earth and its inhabitants. In the tradition deriving from Paul, reference to the powers that rule over the world points to the decans as negative forces (see Pétrement 1980: 51–64). Without further explanation, we are told of the negative impact of "principalities" (ἀρχαί, *archai*), of "dominations" or "authorities" (ἐξουσίαι, *exousiai*), of "powers" (δυνάμεις, *dynameis*), and "lordships" (κυριότητες, *kyriotētes*; see Rom 8:38; 1 Cor 15:24; Col 1:16; 2:10, 15; Eph 1:21; 6:12). In the later Christian perspective deriving from this assessment, the decans were identified with demons. Thus in the *Testament of Solomon*, while the positive nature of decans is recognized, they are largely responsible for human afflictions and are in the control of sky servants such as Michael. Yet these constellational beings (στοιχεῖα, *stoicheia*) are called "cosmic regents" (οἱ κοσμοκράτορες, *hoi kosmokratores*) (*Test Sol* 18:2, *OTP* 1.977).

Given the central importance of the decans in antiquity, I offer a summary statement of the ancient traditions concerning these beings and their role from Firmicus Maternus in Appendix A, pp. 269–71.

5.3.3. The Four Living Creatures

As noted above, with our seer we look upon the scenarios from God's perspective. We stand atop and on the other side of the vault of the sky, looking down at everything from the perspective of the throne. This perspective was afforded by celestial armillary spheres. An armillary sphere was an arrangement of rings (Latin: *armillae*) each of which was the circle of a single sky sphere, e.g., the course of the moon, the celestial equator, the ecliptic. This arrangement of rings was intended to show the relative position of the principal celestial circles. Of course spheres before Copernicus, such as that of Theon of Smyrna in Figure 1, above, have an immovable earth at the center.

Now looking down from the throne but within the cosmos, the seer sees on each side of the throne four major constellations. He depicts them for us as these constellations face the throne. Constellations, of course, are constituted of stars, and in the Hellenistic period, stars singly or constellated were regarded as animate beings, like persons or animals for the most part. Supposedly inanimate objects, such as the scales of Libra or the cup of Crater, were often seen as held by animate beings, usually persons. Now what John sees are constellations that he interprets in line with Israelite tradition, as we see, for example, in Ezekiel. It seems that Ezekiel once had the same experience, but from another vantage point. Ezekiel seems to be situated above the whole cosmos, since all four constellations move at once:

> [A]s I was among the exiles by the river Chebar, the heavens were opened, and I saw visions of God. . . . As I looked, behold, a stormy wind came out of the north, and a great cloud, with brightness round about it, and fire flashing forth continually, and in the midst of the fire, as it were gleaming bronze. And from the midst of it came the likeness of four living creatures. And this was their appearance: they had the form of men, but each had four faces, and each of them had four wings. Their legs were straight, and the soles of their feet were like the sole of a calf's foot; and they sparkled like burnished bronze. Under their wings on their four sides they had human hands. And the four had their faces and their wings thus; their wings touched one another; they went every one straight forward, without turning as they went. As for the likeness of their faces, each had the face of a man in front; the four had the face of a lion on the right side, the four had the face of an ox on the left side, and the four had the face of an eagle at the back. Such were their faces. And their wings were spread out above; each creature had two wings, each of which touched the wing of another, while two covered their bodies (Ezek 1:1, 4–11).

The astral prophet reports the vision once more, this time indicating that the ox-shaped being is what the cherubim looked like:

> And as for their appearance, the four had the same likeness, as if a wheel were within a wheel. When they went, they went in any of their four directions without turning as they went, but in whatever direction the front wheel faced the others followed without turning as they went. And their rims, and their spokes, and the wheels were full of eyes round about—the wheels that the four of them had. As for the wheels, they were called in my hearing the whirling wheels. And every one had four faces: the first face was the face of the cherub, and the second face was the face of a man, and the third the face of a lion, and the fourth the face of an eagle. And the cherubim mounted up. These were the living creatures that I saw by the river Chebar (Ezek 10:10–15).

The point is John perceives the same four constellations at four opposite points of the equatorial zodiac. As in Ezekiel, the creatures marked out by the constellations are full of eyes, that is full of stars in front and behind. Stars are frequently called "eyes." For example, Manilius sets forth various theories of the origin on the universe and notes:

> Possibly the universe was constructed out of fire and flickering flames (so Empedocles), which have formed the eyes of the sky and dwell throughout the whole system and shape the lightning which flashes in the skies (*Astronomica* 1.132–134, LCL).

Plutarch, in turn, notes:

> At the same time, observing that the sky was dotted with stars, and the moon was rising bright and clear, while the sea everywhere was without a wave as if a path were being opened for their course, he bethought himself that the eye of Justice is not a single eye only, but through all these eyes

of hers God watches in every direction the deeds that are done here and there both on land and on the sea (*Dinner of the Seven Wise Men* 161E–F, LCL).

Again, because stars are called "eyes," the four living creatures "full of eyes" would be constellations, "full of stars," in both John's vision and in Ezekiel 1 and 10. In this scenario, it seems they bear up the throne on the back of their bodies, while the fronts of their bodies face inward.

Boll explains these astral beings both here and in Ezekiel as the four Babylonian seasonal constellations: Scorpio-man, Leo, Taurus, Pegasus (1914: 35). His selection of these four is due to the fact that they each bear a "royal star." Firmicus Maternus tells us: "In all signs we find bright stars shining with awesome majesty, but regal ones in four—in Leo, Scorpio, Aquarius and Taurus" (Firmicus Maternus, *Mathesis* 6.2.1, trans. Rhys Bram 183). The main star of Leo (Greek star catalogs begin with this constellation) is *Regulus*, meaning "Royal Star," which was of the highest significance in Babylonian and Greek astrology. The brightest stars of Taurus and of Scorpio (Aldebaran and Antares) are repeatedly noted as lying opposite each other (ἀντικείμενοι, *antikeimenoi*) along the equator/horizon. They too are royal stars whose appearance brings princely might and imperial sway. In the Babylonian tradition, Scorpio has a human face since it is a "Scorpion Man," as in the Gilgamesh epic, who guards the gate of the sun in the west (see Jacobsen 1976: 204). As for the royal star in Aquarius, Firmicus Maternus writes in this context: "the twentieth degree of Aquarius is similarly adorned with majestic brilliance" (ibid., 6.2, 3, loc. cit.) referring to a royal star. However, the sky reference does not fit Aquarius, but rather the star labeled *alpha* Pegasi (see Boll 1914: 37, n. 3). Firmicus Maternus has the right star, but the wrong constellation. Boll further cites a Babylonian inscription in which Pegasus is called "the leader of the stars from the divinity Anu," that is, the stars of the equator. This constellation was the Babylonian "Thunderbird" (see Jacobsen 1976: 128–29). Thus each of these constellations bears a "royal" star—that is enough to prove their special note in Hellenistic astrology, which follows Babylonian sources in this case.

These four constellations are likewise depicted in a Babylonian source as designating the four directions of the sky, for they lie about ninety degrees from each other. In this position, they duly circumscribed the whole vault of the sky, and in our scenario, the reference to "the throne of God" would refer to the entire sky. Furthermore, these constellations stood at the equator opposite each other (see Boll 1914: 37). John's phrase, "in the middle of the throne and around the throne," makes sense, for the equator both cuts the sky in half and goes around it.

Image 4: A warring Scorpio man on a Babylonian
land grant stone (now in the British Museum).

Given this arrangement, John's "flying Eagle" is thus to be identified with the constellation called Hippos in the Greek sky, Pegasus by
the Romans, Thunderbird by the Babylonians. The constellation occurs
again in 8:13. In Babylonian lore, traceable to the seventh century B.C.
the Thunderbird (our Pegasus) is "the leader of the stars of Anu," the
first celestial configuration on the celestial equator (see Bezold, Kopff,
and Boll 1913: 23). On the ecliptic, on the other hand, Aries was the
first of the zodiac constellations: "The Wool-Bearer leads the signs"
(Manilius, *Astronimica* 2.34, LCL).

Be that as it may, in the alternative, older system that considered
the equator as the foundational cosmic belt, it was the Thunderbird
(the Roman winged horse, Pegasus) that stood at the beginning of the
equatorial constellational sequence, positioned in mid-heaven at the
center of the sky. Taurus was then located on the eastern horizon, Scorpio
on the western horizon. Now should the Thunderbird (Pegasus) take a
position in mid-heaven once more, then the stars of the universe would
all occupy the positions they once had at the time of creation. Such a
restoration marked the "Great Year," "when all the stars return to the
place from which they at first set forth, and, at long intervals, restore
the original configuration of the whole heaven" (Cicero, *The Republic*
6.24, LCL).

In sum, the four living creatures, like a lion, a bull, a human-faced
being, and a flying eagle, refer to the constellations along the celestial
equator (a projection of the earth's equator onto the vault of the sky)
and located opposite each other. And the best candidates for the four
are the constellations now called Leo (the lion), Taurus (the bull),
Scorpio (the human-faced) and Pegasus (the flying eagle).

5.3.4. The Cosmic Lamb

In 5:6 John introduces the cosmic Lamb who will play a significant role in what follows. This Lamb is situated in the middle of the throne of God, hence in the middle of the sky, with the four animate beings at four opposite points on the horizon and the twenty-four elders marking points along the horizon. It is a Lamb, "as though slain," having seven horns and seven eyes. These latter, we are told, are likewise the seven sky winds.

In this scenario, we further learn that the Lamb takes control of the land by opening the scroll (5:7ff.). Subsequently, we find out that it is male (e.g., his spouse is a bride 19:9) and that he receives obeisance along with God (5:8 and often). He is a warrior, soon to get satisfaction for what was done to him and his ("the wrath of the Lamb," 6:16), eventually overcoming demonic powers (17:14). As warrior he establishes the rule of peace (7:9) on the sky mountain (14:1) and judges (14:10). In the end he is acknowledged as the Lord of lords and King of kings (19:16), ruling his followers from the throne of God (22:1, 3). And right before being presented here, he is said to be "the lion of the tribe of Judah, the root of David, who conquered" (5:5). Thus all the imagery associated with the Lamb is that of power, force, control, and conquest. If anything, the Lamb is depicted as a powerful, young male, hence as a young ram.

Furthermore, it is true that horns may stand for power and eyes for knowledge, while "seven" can mean fullness, totality; however, it seems insufficient here to state simply that the Lamb possesses the fullness of power and of knowledge. The real question is why seven horns and seven eyes, and how are we to imagine what the seer saw? If the Lamb stands in the middle of the sky and of the four constellations and twenty-four elders, then clearly the seven horns and seven eyes must relate to some sky phenomenon and thus relate the Lamb to some constellation.

The constellation labeled "Aries" by the Latins was originally considered to be a male lamb (even the word *aries* derives from Greek ἄρης, *arēs*, "lamb," or ἔριφος, *eriphos*, "young ram, kid"). The ancient Phoenician name for Aries was *Teleh*, "male lamb, young ram" (Brown dates this name to Tyre ca. 1200 B.C., Brown 1899: 1.119 and Figure 4, above). This label for the constellation was adopted by Second Temple Israel. It was used by Pharisees for this constellation according to Epiphanius (*Panarion* 16.2.1, trans. Philip Amidon 1990: 51). Naturally in later Jewish zodiacs the constellation in question was always called *Taleh*, meaning "male lamb, young ram; young man" (see the visuals in Hachlili 1977: 61–77). Arab astronomers maintained this Semitic designation, naming the constellation *Al-Hamal*, "the young ram" (Savage-

Smith 1985: 162). Given this tradition, it is no surprise that the cosmic Lamb behaves like a young ram. The Greeks had little difficulty in identifying Aries with a young ram. Lucian has one of a pair of contending brothers behave as follows: "Thyestes then indicated and explained (σημενούμενος, sēmenoumenos) to them the Ram (κριός krios) in the sky, because of which they mythologize that Thyestes had a golden Lamb (ἄρην, arēn)" (On Astrology 12, LCL). Further, Aries (the Ram) is the first in the zodiac, the center and head of the cosmos as the astrologers say (see Boll 1914, p. 44, n. 2; there he cites Nigidius Figulus, first century A.D., who calls Aries "the leader and prince of the con-stellations"; the Scholia in Aratum 545, relating that "the Egyptians [Nechepso-Petosiris] say Aries is the head"; and Nonnos who says that Aries "is the center of the whole cosmos, the central navel of Olympus"; Vettius Valens, Rhetorios, and Firmicus Maternus are quite similar. Further, the Greek words for lamb, sheep, and ram are often used synonymously, even in the same tradition. Boll cites the tradition of the "ram of Pelops" called variously lamb and sheep (1914: 45, n. 6). And in Ps 113:4, 5, ram and lamb are used in parallel.

Aries is the leader of the stars of the ecliptic: "The Wool-Bearer leads the sign for his conquest of the sea" (Manilius, Astronomica 2.34, LCL). According to astrological lore that focused on the zodiac and its eclipitc belt, at the beginning of the universe Aries stood in mid-Heaven (μεσουράνημα, mesouranēma, is an astronomical technical term), that is, at the "head" of the cosmos, at the summit of it all. For example, Firmicus Maternus writes:

> We must now explain why they began the twelve signs with Aries. . . . In the chart of the universe which we have said was invented by very learned men, the mid-heaven is found to be Aries. This is because frequently—or rather, always—in all charts, the mid-heaven holds the principal place, and from this we deduce the basis of the whole chart, especially since most of the planets and the luminaries—the Sun and the Moon—send their influ-ence toward this sign (Mathesis 3.1.17–18, trans. Rhys Bram 75).

Ancient Israel likewise recognized the prominence of Aries in it New Year celebration connected with its foundational event, the Exodus (Exod 12:2: the Exodus occurs in the first month of the year). And the ritual marking the Exodus involved a male lamb, Aries itself.

There is an ancient representation of Aries with a distinctive ring around its chest, "designating the equinox" (Thiele 1898: 108; for a similar ring inscribed with stars around Taurus, see Noll 1980, tables 16 and 20). This ring is like the wheel or circle (τροχός, trochos) which surrounds the throne of God in 1 Enoch 14:18: "a lofty throne, its appearance like crystal and its wheels like the shining sun." The wheel then serves as a nimbus or halo, much used by ancient art long before its Christian usage (for ancient Christian depictions of the Lamb relating to our book, see Boll 1914: 45, 144; and especially Leclercq 1924: the lambs in illustrations nos. 195 and 197, cols. 880 and 881–82).

As for the horns and the eyes, a number of constellations have their horns and eyes consisting of stars, for example Taurus or Capricorn. On the other hand, the image presented here is not that clear. As already noted, eyes in the sky readily refer to stars. Now since the horns here are not described as consisting of stars, we might note that "horns" is one of the many names for comets, which the ancients likewise called "stars." Undoubtedly, the listing of seven horns and seven eyes derives from the author's use of numbers (unless he counted the stars in the constellation he regarded as the Lamb).

Note that Daniel 8 describes a fight between a ram and a goat. The seer's interpretation in Dan 8:20 states that the ram with the horns is the king of the Medes and Persians, while the goat is the king of the Greeks. This ascription points to the oldest form of zodiacal geography, where Persia fits under Aries, while Syria, the Hellenistic kingdom of the Seleucids, under Capricorn. Boll presents the oldest series of peoples and their corresponding constellations, following the usual zodiacal sequence (1914: 46 n. 5):

Country	Constellation	Country	Constellation
Persia =	Aries	Libya and Cyrene =	Libra
Babylon =	Taurus	Italy =	Scorpio
Cappadocia =	Gemini	Cilicia and Crete =	Sagittarius
Armenia =	Cancer	Syria =	Capricorn
Asia =	Leo	Egypt =	Aquarius
Hellas and Ionia =	Virgo	Red Sea and India =	Pisces

The situating of Persia in first place would date this sequence to a time before Alexander's conquest. However, such zodiacal geography was not constant. A first-century sequence from Manilius, *Astronomica* 4.744–817 (LCL ad loc. and Goold's note on xci–xcii) is as follows:

Constellation	Region
Aries	Hellespont, Propontis, Syria, Persia, Egypt
Taurus	Scythia, Asia, Arabia
Gemini	Euxine, Thrace, India
Cancer	Ethiopia
Leo	Phrygia, Cappadocia, Armenia, Bithynia, Macedonia
Virgo	Rhodes, Ionia, Greece, Caria
Libra	Italy
Scorpio	Carthage, Libya, Hammonia, Cyrene, Sardinia, other islands
Sagittarius	Crete, Sicily, Magna Graecia
Capricorn	Spain, Gaul, Germany
Aquarius	Phoenicia, Tyre, Cilicia, Lycia
Pisces	Euphrates, Tigris, Red Ocean, Parthia, Bactria, Asiatic Ethiopia, Babylon, Susa, Nineveh

In conclusion, we might note that astral lore was well known in the social world of our author. To call the Messiah "the light of the world" or to designate him as leader at the head of the periodic changes of the universe in the form of the constellation Aries would not be very different things. On the other hand, the seven "eyes" of the Lamb (5:6) were given the more specific interpretation in the document of the seven sky winds of God, perhaps at a later date. Yet in 4:5 these sky winds are identified with seven torches or stars.

5.4. Cosmic Hymns

We encounter many hymns throughout this sector, probably because it was commonly assumed in the first-century Mediterranean world that music filled the cosmos. The reason we on earth cannot hear this constant music is that our ears are as unfit to hear that music as our eyes are unfit to look into the sun. As an instance of this opinion, consider Cicero:

> After recovering from the astonishment with which I viewed these wonders, I said: "What is this loud and agreeable sound that fills my ears?" "That is produced," he (Scipio the Elder) replied, "by the onward rush and motion of the spheres themselves; the intervals between them, though unequal, being exactly arranged in a fixed proportion, by an agreeable blending of high and low tones various harmonies are produced; for such mighty motions cannot be carried on so swiftly in silence; and Nature has provided that one extreme shall produce low tones while the other gives forth high. Therefore this uppermost sphere of heaven, which bears the stars as it revolves more rapidly, produces a high, shrill tone, whereas the lowest revolving sphere, that of the moon, gives forth the lowest tone; for the earthly sphere, the ninth, remains ever motionless and stationary in its position in the center of the universe. But the other eight spheres, two of which move with the same velocity, produce seven different sounds, a number which is the key of almost everything. Learned men, by imitating this harmony on stringed instruments and in song, have gained for themselves a return to this region, as others have obtained the same reward by devoting their brilliant intellects to divine pursuits during their earthly lives. Men's ears, ever filled with this sound, have become deaf to it; for you have no duller sense than that of hearing. We find a similar phenomenon where the Nile rushes down from those lofty mountains at the place called Catadupa; the people who live near by have lost their sense of hearing on account of the loudness of the sound. But this mighty music, produced by the revolution of the whole universe at the highest speed, cannot be perceived by human ears, any more than you can look straight at the Sun, your sense of sight being overpowered by its radiance" (in the section recounting Scipio's dream in *The Republic* 6.18–19, LCL).

However, just as our seer can discern what is happening in constellations and stars, and just as he can look directly upon beings in the sun, so too he can hear the music of the spheres.

There were a number of astronomic explanations for the celestial concert that everyone in the field knew had gone on since creation. Theon of Smyrna (early second century A.D.) quotes Alexander of Aetolia (third century B.C.) in detail about how "the seven spheres give the seven sounds of the lyre and produce a harmony because of the intervals which separate them from one another" (*Mathematics Useful for Understanding Plato* 3.15, trans. R. and D. Lawlor, 91–92); he then cites Eratosthenes and ends with his own explanation.

In the Israelite tradition, a similar witness to the music before God's throne is found as early as Isa 6:3 and 49:13. For Second Temple Israel, we find the same in a document called *Testament of Adam*, in a section dating perhaps to the second century A.D. This work tells of God's praise during the night and the day:

The Hours of the Night:

The first hour of the night is the praise of the demons; and at that hour they do not injure or harm any human being. The second hour is the praise of the doves. The third hour is the praise of the fish and of fire and of all the lower depths. The fourth hour is the "holy, holy, holy" praise of the seraphim. And so I used to hear, before I sinned, the sound of their wings in Paradise when the seraphim would beat them to the sound of their triple praise. But after I transgressed against the law, I no longer heard that sound. The fifth hour is the praise of the waters that are above heaven. And so I, together with the angels, used to hear the sound of mighty waves, a sign which would prompt them to lift a hymn of praise to the Creator. The sixth hour is the construction of clouds and of the great fear which comes in the middle of the night. The seventh hour is the viewing of their powers while the waters are asleep. And at that hour the waters (can be) taken up and the priest of God mixes them with consecrated oil and anoints those who are afflicted and they rest. The eighth hour is the sprouting up of the grass of the earth while the dew descends from heaven. The ninth hour is the raise of the cherubim. The tenth hour is the praise of human beings, and the gate of heaven is opened through which the prayers of all living things enter, and they worship and depart. And at that hour whatever a man will ask of God is given to him when the seraphim and the roosters beat their wings. The eleventh hour there is joy in all the earth when the sun rises from Paradise and shines forth upon creation. The twelfth hour is the waiting for incense, and silence is imposed on all the ranks of fire and wind until the priests burn incense to his divinity. And at that time all the heavenly powers are dismissed. The End of the Hours of the Night.

The Hours of the Day:

The first hour of the day is the petition of the heavenly ones. The second hour is the prayer of the angels. The third hour is the praise of the birds.

The fourth hour is the praise of the beasts. The fifth hour is the praise which is above heaven. The sixth hour is the praise of the cherubim who plead against the iniquity of our human nature. The seventh hour is the entry and exit from the presence of God, when the prayers of all living things enter, and they worship and depart. The eighth hour is the praise of fire and of the waters. The ninth hour is the entreaty of those angels who stand before the throne of majesty. The tenth hour is the visitation of the waters when the spirit descends and broods upon the water and upon the fountains. And if the spirit of the Lord did not descend and brood upon the waters and upon the fountains, human beings would be injured. and everyone the demons saw they would injure. And at that hour the waters (are) taken up and the priest of God mixes them with consecrated oil and anoints those who are afflicted and they are restored and healed. The eleventh hour is the exultation and joy of the righteous. The twelfth hour, the hour of the evening is the entreaty of human beings, for the gracious will of God, the Lord of all (*Testament of Our Father Adam 1–2, OTP* 1.993).

In this vein of constant cosmic praise in song, this sector of the book tells of a first song (4:8) which unceasingly hymns the exclusivity and uniqueness of God and a second (4:11) which praises the eternal God as creator. Then the twenty-four decans and four living being constellations sing of the cosmic preeminence (worthiness) of the Lamb (the book's third song 5:9). Then God's entourage equally sings of the preeminence of the Lamb (the fourth song 5:13). Finally, all created beings second the judgment of all those prominent sky beings by singing of the honor of both God and the Lamb (the fifth song 5:13). The limited number of Israelites (only 144,000) and a limitless number "from every nation and tribe and people and tongue" (7:9) likewise join in song to God and the Lamb to acknowledge their rescue (7:6, the sixth song). Their song provokes a response in song by God's cosmic entourage (7:12, the seventh song). The rest of the work tells of various cosmic songs.

5.5. SOME FURTHER FEATURES OF THIS SECTOR

The "voice like a trumpet" should be distinguished from the later seven trumpets that unleash woes upon the earth. The focus here is not on the trumpet but on the voice. Now, why a voice like a trumpet in 4:1? The trumpet, whether of metal or of animal horn, was the loudest controlled sound humans could produce at the time. Hence to hear any loud and controlled sound was to hear something "like a trumpet." Trumpets were not musical instruments, but rather instruments to signal power, whether in temples (where they could summon God and people) or in battle and court (where they could summon king, soldiery and people). And naturally since a cosmic being was speaking, it could only sound extremely loud, "like a trumpet" in the ancient world.

Why are the living creatures outfitted with wings in 4:8? Wings are likewise characteristic of the living celestial creatures from earliest time in the Middle East, no less than in later traditions such as those of Ezek 1 and 10. Wings in the ancient world were the main way to describe the ability to propel oneself through the air with phenomenal speed, like a bird. Of course the six-wing configuration is found in Isa 6, but is equally common on Mesopotamian sculptured figures and seals as well (see Black and Green 1992, 64–65 and passim).

With the scenarios of the God enthroned and the Lamb ready and waiting amid cosmic singing, the action in the sky is ready to begin.

6

SECTOR 2 CONTINUES:
OF SCROLLS, SEALS, AND COMETS

6 [1]And I saw when the Lamb opened the first of the seven seals, and I heard the first of the four living begins saying as with the voice of thunder: "Come!" [2]And I saw, and behold a white horse, and the one seated upon it having a bow and a wreath was given to him and he went out a victor and in order to conquer. [3]And when he opened the second seal, I heard the second living being saying: "Come!" [4]And another horse came out, a fire-red one. And to the one sitting upon it was given to take peace from the land and so that they slaughter each other and a great sword was given to him. [5]And when he opened the third seal, I heard the third living being saying: "Come!" And I saw and behold a black horse. And the one seated upon it having a scale in his hand. [6]And I heard like a voice in the middle of the four living beings saying: "A measure of wheat for a denarius," and "Three measures of barley for a denarius." "But do not harm the oil and the wine." [7]And when he opened the fourth seal, I heard the voice of the fourth living being saying: "Come!" [8]And I saw and behold a pale horse, and the one sitting upon [it], his name Death, and Hades followed along with him. And authority was given to them over one fourth of the land, to kill with a sword and with famine and with death, and by wild animals of the land. [9]And when he opened the fifth seal, I saw under the Altar the souls of those slaughtered on account of the word of God and on account of the witness which they had. [10]And they shouted out with a loud voice saying:

> "Until when, O Holy and Truthful Master,
> Do you not judge and avenge our blood,
>   from among the inhabitants of the land?"

[11]And a white robe was given to each of them, and it was told to them to rest still a little while, until both their fellow slaves and their brothers who are going to be killed just like they [were] are filled. [12]And I saw when he opened the sixth seal and a great earthquake took place, and the sun became black like hair cloth, and the whole moon became like blood. [13]And the stars of the sky fell onto the land, like a fig tree drops its unripe figs when shaken by a great Wind. [14]And the sky was moved aside like a rolled scroll, and every mountain and island was moved from their places. [15]And the kings of the land and the nobles and the tribunes and the wealthy and the powerful and every slave and free man hid themselves in caves and in the rocks of the mountains. [16]And they say to the mountains and the

rocks: "Fall upon us" and "Hide us" from the face of the one sitting on the throne and from the wrath of the Lamb. [17]Because the great day of their wrath came, and who can stand?

7[1]After this I saw four sky servants standing upon the four corners of the earth, holding the four winds of the earth so that the wind not blow upon the land nor upon the sea nor upon any tree. [2]And I saw another sky servant coming up from the rising of the sun, having a seal of a living God, and he shouted with a loud voice to the four sky servants to whom it was given to them to injure the land and the sea, [3]saying: "Do not injure the land or the sea or the trees until we seal the slaves of our God upon their forehead." [4]And I heard the number of the sealed, a hundred forty-four thousand sealed, from every tribe of the sons of Israel:

> [5]from the tribe of Judah, twelve thousand sealed,
> from the tribe of Reuben, twelve thousand,
> from the tribe of Gad, twelve thousand,
>
> [6]from the tribe of Asher, twelve thousand,
> from the tribe of Nephtali, twelve thousand,
> from the tribe of Manasse, twelve thousand,
>
> [7]from the tribe of Simeon, twelve thousand,
> from the tribe of Levi, twelve thousand,
> from the tribe of Issachar, twelve thousand,
>
> [8]from the tribe of Zebulon, twelve thousand,
> from the tribe of Joseph, twelve thousand,
> from the tribe of Benjamin, twelve thousand sealed.

[9]After these things, I saw and behold a great crowd which no one was able to count it, from every nation and tribes and peoples and tongues, standing before the throne and before the Lamb, clothed in white robes and a palm branch in their hands, [10]And they shout with a loud voice, saying:

> "Rescue (due) to our God seated upon the throne and to the Lamb."

[11]And all the sky servants were standing around the throne and (around) the elders and (around) the four living beings, and they fell down before the throne upon their faces and they prostrated themselves before God, [12]saying:

> "Amen! Praise and glory and wisdom and acknowledgment and honor and power and
> strength to our God unto the aeons of aeons. Amen!"

[13]And one of the elders answered, saying to me: "Those clothed with the white robes, who are they and from where do they come?" [14]And I answered him: "My lord, you know!" And he said to me: "Those are they who came from the great distress, and they rinsed their robes and whitened them in the blood of the Lamb.

> [15]"Because of this they are before the throne of God
> and they worship him day and night in his temple,
> and the one seated upon the throne will pitch a tent over them.
>
> [16]"They will not still hunger, nor will they still thirst,
> nor will the sun beat down upon them,
> nor any heat-wave,
>
> [17]because the Lamb that is in the middle of the throne will shepherd them,
> and will guide them over to water wells of life;
> and God will wipe away every tear from their eyes."

The initial cosmic action in the book of Revelation derives from God's decree contained in a sealed scroll written on the inside and on the outside, and located at the right hand of the one seated on the throne. The immediate problem forestalling the action is the absence of anyone worthy to open the scroll, obviously to read the contents. To reveal God's will is to set it under way, for good or ill. And only someone worthy can reveal God's will. The cosmic Lamb, who has the qualifications, opens the seals and sets the action under way. What makes worthiness a qualification, and what made the Lamb worthy? And what do the seals have in common with comets? In this section of our tour, we note again that in antiquity, revelations were meant only for the worthy; and "worthy" was a status designation, not an assessment of moral quality. Further, the dire sevens that issue from the sky—that is, the outcome of the seven seals, the seven trumpets and the seven bowls—all referred to comets in antiquity.

6.1. WORTHINESS AND THE LAMB

The last cosmic songs that closed the throne scenario mention the worthiness or exalted status of the Lamb. As previously explained, revelations from the deity are essentially directed to the high-status persons who control society: the king or the emperor or some other eminent elite personage. "Worthiness" thus is not a moral reference but a status reference. This means that worthiness derives not from being good or from doing something good, but from social rank or from social standing within a community. To be "worthy" means to have the appropriate status, to be recognized as appropriately honorable due to ascribed status. Ascribed status refers to socially ranking people on the basis of their birth or appointment by a higher ranking person rather than on the basis of some achievement or ability. For example, the child of a king is noble by birth; the child of a billionaire is rich by birth; U.S. presidential appointees to cabinet posts are in charge due to their appointment. In each case such persons are ranked as noble, rich, or in charge not due to any proven ability or achievement on their part. They have ascribed status rather than achieved status. Now worthiness in antiquity was essentially due to ascribed status. Thus only persons whose ascribed social standing sets them above ordinary mortals are "worthy" to receive revelations. As a matter of fact, one of the characteristic features of Hellenistic revelation literature is that revelations are directed solely to persons whose ascribed status is lofty. Such persons are usually divine, godlike, or superhuman.

As previously noted (see p. 39–42, above), this perspective explains why Aristotle, for example, has trouble with the divine authenticity of any dream revelations. The essential problem for the philosopher is that unworthy persons have dreams, and since they are persons of low social status, their dreams could not possibly be revelatory. Low status persons simply could not be recipients of divine revelations, either by dreams or in any other way. Revelations of God come only to the best and wisest. The point is that revelations belong solely and only to the socially prominent, the socially worthy. And the cosmic Lamb is such a worthy recipient of God's secrets.

Two features in the presentation of the Lamb underscore the Lamb's worthiness. To begin with, as we previously noted (see p. 101–4, above), the cosmic Lamb is the constellation Aries which "stands as though slaughtered." In the sky, Aries seems to have a broken neck, having its head turned directly backward to face Taurus. "Resplendent in his golden fleece, first place holder Aries looks backward admiringly at Taurus rising" (Manilius, *Astronomica* 1.263–264). Yet it is not a dead being; rather, it stands and acts, located "in the middle of the throne and of the four living beings and in the middle of the elders" (5:6), with "seven horns and seven eyes, which are the [seven] sky winds of God sent upon the whole earth," hence with God's very knowledge (eyes) and power (horns) over the world. It would he harder to find any other being with higher status in the cosmos.

However, what is distinctive of our astral prophet's message is what he learns from one of the powerful decans. The cosmic Lamb is identified with "the lion of the tribe of Judah, the root of David" (5:4). This designation intimates that the twelve tribes of Israel each fall under a different zodiacal constellation (hence there will be only twelve tribes). It further suggests that the protective constellation of Judah is Leo, with its enormous royal star, Regulus. On the other hand, in the tradition of Israel, a Judean "Leo" (Gen 49:9–10) of the Davidic family (Isa 11:1, 10) is God's Messiah. In this book, God's Messiah has already been identified in ch. 1 with Jesus, the one whom "they" pierced and whom God raised. And this is not Leo, but the cosmic Lamb.

The celestial presence of the cosmic Lamb marks the beginning of Israel's year: "This month shall be for you the beginning of months; it shall be the first month of the year for you" (Exod 12:2). Judaism, with its endless cultural borrowings, gave up this ancient custom in favor of the Babylonian autumnal New Year (see Parpola 1993: 174, n. 64). The eating of a lamb that replicates the first constellation of the spring New Year further marks a beginning; Aries being male requires a male lamb, "either of sheep or goat" (Exod 12:5; as previously noted, the Semitic traditional name of the constellation is Taleh, "male lamb or kid). And it is because the month is under the control of the first of the constellational signs, that Israel must ingest a lamb, not a calf, chicken, or dog.

Furthermore, the cosmic Lamb is connected with all the events commemorated on the traditional four nights of the Passover. It was set at the head of the cosmos at creation (in Gen 1), and then promised by God to Abraham at the sacrifice of Isaac, but kept back and replaced by a ram (Gen 22). In the Exodus Passover itself, as just noted, it is under the aegis of this cosmic sign that the lambs of the Exodus were slaughtered to save Israel (Exod 12). Finally it serves as the cosmic sign of all Passovers to follow, including the one at which Jesus the Messiah died. The book of Revelation is replete with this sort of cosmic symbolism deriving from the stars (see Le Déaut 1963).

6.2. SCROLLS AND COMETS

What sort of relationship might there be between the divine scroll and comets?

A reading of Rev 6:1–7:17 (above, p. 108–10) makes it obvious that what triggers the unfolding action in Revelation is a scroll at the right side of God's throne. Given the action that follows, the scroll contains directives from God. Whatever God says happens. There is no gap between God's words and consequent activity. This seems to be the nature of the directives from the throne: once read, the orders are immediately realized. It is the sealed quality of the scroll that keeps the action desired by God in abeyance.

The nature of the action, however, is really no secret. A sealed scroll written on the inside and the outside is no first-century anomaly. The contents of the inside of a sealed scroll were summarized on its outside, so its contents were apparent without breaking the seals. Of course, to read the scroll's contents, the seals must be broken. The problem of worthiness, here, is not so much about what would soon happen. After all, Israel's prophets, from Moses on, spoke of God's vindication of his divine honor in the face of repeated blasphemy and "adultery." Blasphemy refers to shaming or injuring the honor of another by means of words. "Adultery" or "fornication" was a prophetic code word for idolatry, that is, dishonoring God by social intercourse with other deities. As in human interpersonal relations, so too with God. To restore honor, the dishonored person must achieve satisfaction. To divert the social requirement of satisfaction and to patch up rifts in relations, the offending party has to have a change of heart.

Nevertheless, the contents of the scroll would be well known. What was required was the implementing of the scroll's events. This required a being of the status of the cosmic Lamb to open the scroll and thus to set the events under way. And as the seer observes, events scarcely keep up with themselves as one follows upon the other. The events that do occur follow upon the appearance of celestial phenomena: horses and riders, bowls, trumpets, and the like. The chain of command is as follows: the Lamb opens the scroll, a sky being gives an order, and the celestial phenomenon passes over the land of Israel. The outcome is something negative for the land of Israel and its inhabitants. The question here is, what sort of celestial phenomena pass over the land of Israel with negative results for its inhabitants and their environment. The first-century learned answer was, comets.

Consider the view of the second-century A.D. author Ptolemy:

> We must observe, further, for the prediction of general conditions, the comets which appear either at the time of the eclipse or at any time whatever; for instance, the so-called "beams" [δοκίδων, *dokidōn*], "trumpets" [σαλπίγγων, *salpingōn*], "jars" [πίθων, *pithōn*] and the like, for these naturally produce the effect peculiar to Mars and to Mercury—wars, hot weather, disturbed conditions, and the accompaniments of these; and they show, through the parts of the zodiac in which their heads appear and through the directions in which the shapes of their tails point, the regions upon which the misfortunes impend. Through the formations, as it were, of their heads, they indicate the kind of the event and the class upon which the misfortune will take effect; through the time which they last, the duration of the events and through their positions relative to the sun likewise their beginning; for in general their appearance in the orient betokens rapidly approaching events and in the occident those that approach more slowly (*Tetrabiblos* 2.90–91, LCL).

Comets invariably mark negative events. Pliny reports:

> There are also *faces* (= firebrand shaped) that are only seen when falling, for instance one that ran across the sky at midday in full view of the public when Germanicus Caesar was giving a gladiatorial show. Of these there are two kinds: one sort are called *lampades*, which means "torches," the other *bolides* (missiles)—that is the sort that appeared at the time of the disasters of Modena [44 B.C. Antony besieged Decimus Brutus there]. The difference between them is that "torches" make long tracks, with their front part glowing, whereas a "missile" glows throughout its length and traces a longer path.

> There are also *trabes* (= beams), in Greek *dokoi*, for example one that appeared when the Spartans were defeated at sea and lost the empire of Greece [at Cnidus 394 B.C.]. There also occurs a yawning of the actual sky, called *chasma*, and also something that looks like blood, and a fire that falls from it to the earth—the most alarming possible cause of terror to mankind; as happened in the third year [349 B.C.] of the 107th Olympiad when King Philip was throwing Greece into disturbance. My own view is that these occurrences take place at fixed dates owing to natural forces,

like all other events, and not, as most people think, from the variety of causes invented by the cleverness of human intellects. It is true that they were the harbingers of enormous misfortunes, but I hold that those did not happen because the marvelous occurrences took place but that these took place because the misfortunes were going to occur, only the reason for their occurrence is concealed by their rarity, and consequently is not understood as are the risings and setting of the planets described above and many other phenomena (*Natural History* 2.96–97, LCL).

The collector of ancient lore, Isidore of Seville, reports more than thirty types of comets:

A star is called *cometes* (comet, Greek: body of hair) because hairs (*comas*) of light flow from it. This type of star, when it appears, signifies either pestilence or hunger or wars. In Latin, *cometae* are called *crinitae* (Latin: head of hair) because they shoot out flames that look like hair. The Stoics say that there are more than thirty different types of comets, and some astrologers have written about their names and effects (*Etymologies* III, 16–17, Biblioteca de Autores Cristianos 1.476).

Consider the descriptive types of comets that Pliny notes:

A few facts about the world remain. There are also stars that suddenly come to birth in the heaven itself; of these there are several kinds. The Greeks call them "comets" (Latin transliteration: *cometae*), in our language "long-haired stars" (Latin: *crinitae*), because they have a blood-red shock of what looks like shaggy hair at their top. The Greeks also give the name of "bearded stars" to those from whose lower part spreads a mane resembling a long beard. "Javelin stars" quiver like a dart; these are a very terrible portent. To this class belongs the comet about which Titus Imperator Caesar in his fifth consulship wrote an account in his famous poem, that being its latest appearance down to the present day. The same stars when shorter and sloping in a point have been called "Daggers"; these are the palest of all in color, and have a gleam like the flash of a sword, and no rays, which even the Discus star, which resembles its name in appearance but is in color like amber, emits in scattered form from its edge. The "Tub star" presents the shape of a cask with a smoky light all around it. The "Horned star" has the shape of a horn, like the one that appeared when Greece fought the decisive battle of Salamis. The "Torch star" resembles glowing torches, the "Horse star" horses' manes in very rapid motion and revolving in a circle. There also occurs a shining comet whose silvery tresses glow so brightly that it is scarcely possible to look at it, and which displays within it a shape in the likeness of a human countenance. There also occur Goat comets, enringed with a sort of cloud resembling tufts of hair. Once hitherto it has happened that a 'Mane-shaped' comet changed into a spear; this was in the 108th Olympiad, A.U.C. 408 (i.e. 346 B.C.). The shortest period of visibility on record for a comet is 7 days, the longest 80 (*Natural History* 2.89–90, LCL).

Thus from Pliny's list, one can cull the following list of eleven comet types, based on their names:

pogonia	bearded star
acontia	javelin
xiphia	dagger (glisten like a *gladium*)
disceus	discus
pitheus	tub (like *dolius*)
ceratia	horn (like *cornus*)
lampadia	torch (like faces)
hippeus	horse (like the *iuba equina*, horse's mane)
hircus	goat
iuba	mane-shape (like *hippeus* above)
hasta	spear

Another significant thing about comets is that they almost invariably result in negative outcomes for human beings, as Pliny intimates.[1]

---

[1]While the traditional interpretation of the significance of comets was overwhelmingly unfavorable, there was a single exception relative to the comet that appeared at the death of Julius Caesar. For the first time in Roman history there was now a widespread mood which saw in a comet the physical proof of a catasterism, that is, of the elevation of a mortal to become a star among stars. For Plutarch viewed it as a cosmic sign: "There was a great comet which showed itself for seven nights in great splendor after Caesar's murder and then disappeared, indicating the comet served to mark the murder" (*Caesar* 69,3, LCL). Dio Cassius preserved a more evolved tradition:

> When, however a certain star during all those days appeared in the north toward evening, which some called a comet, claiming that it foretold the usual occurrences, while the majority, instead of believing this, ascribed it to Caesar, interpreting it to mean that he had become immortal and had been received into the number of the stars, Octavius then took courage and set up in the temple of Venus a bronze statue of him with a star above his head. And when this act also was allowed, no one trying to prevent it through fear of the populace, then at least some of the other decrees already passed in honor of Caesar were put into effect. Thus they called one of the months July after him, and in the course of certain festivals of thanksgiving for victory they sacrificed during one special day in memory of his name. For these reasons the soldiers also, particularly since some of them received largesses of money, readily took the side of Caesar (*Roman History* 45.7, 1–2, LCL).

In his *Odes*, Ovid writes: "As the moon among the lesser lights, so shines the Julian star amid all others. O Father and Guardian of the human race, thou son of Saturn, to thee by fate has been entrusted the charge of mighty Caesar [Augustus]; mayst thou be lord of all, with Caesar [Augustus] next in power" (*Odes* 1.12, 46–52, LCL). And in his *Metamorphoses*, we read: "Scarcely has he spoken when fostering Venus took her place within the senate house, unseen of all, caught up the passing soul of her Caesar from his body, and not suffering it to vanish into air, she bore it towards the stars of heaven. And as she bore it she felt it glow and burn and released it from her bosom. Higher than the moon it mounted up and, leaving behind it a long fiery train, gleamed as a star" (*Metamorphoses* 15.843–51, LCL). Here, Caesar is born in the sky of pregnant Venus, like the child in chapter 12.

Cicero specifies the point in a listing of reasons why Stoics (and Cicero too) perceive the existence of the gods:

> Indeed our master Cleanthes gave four reasons to account for the formation in men's minds of their ideas of the gods. He put first the argument of which I spoke just now, the one arising from our foreknowledge of future events; second, the one drawn from the magnitude of the benefits which we derive from our temperate climate, from the earth's fertility, and from a vast abundance of other blessings; third, the awe inspired by lightning, storms, rain, snow, hail, floods, pestilences, earthquakes, and occasionally subterranean rumblings, showers of stones and raindrops the color of blood, also landslides and chasms suddenly opening in the ground, also unnatural monstrosities human and animal, and also the appearance of meteoric lights and what are called by the Greeks "comets," and in our language "long-haired stars" (*cincinnatae*) such as recently during the Octavian War [87 B.C.] appeared as harbingers of dire disasters, and the doubling of the sun, which my father told me had happened in the consulship of Tuditanus and Aquilius, the year in which the light was quenched of Publius Africanus, the second sun of Rome—all of which alarming portents have suggested to mankind the idea of the existence of some celestial and divine power. And the fourth and most potent cause of the belief he said was the uniform motion and revolution of the sky and the varied groupings and ordered beauty of the sun, moon and stars, the very sight of which was in itself enough to prove that these things are not the mere effect of chance (*On the Nature of the Gods* 2.13–15, LCL).

Of course, I have not cited everything the ancients said about comets. There will be more to come. But for the moment, consider that whatever the sky servants unleash into the atmosphere over the land, whether horses, or trumpets, or bowls, everything would be considered types of comets by anyone interested in astronomics. Now we turn to a consideration of the first four seals: the horses and their colors.

6.3. THE SEVEN SEALS

The first four seals command the emergence of four horses and riders. The four living beings at each of the four cardinal points of the sky call forth these phenomena. The fifth and sixth seals in turn relate to the sun and the moon; and the seventh to the throne. As we shall see, in the realm of the sky the constellations of the four living creatures correlate with the cardinal planets: Jupiter, Mars, Mercury, Venus. The planet Saturn, quite rightly, is omitted since it corresponds to the polar center; consequently, here it corresponds with the throne and the seventh seal (de Saussure 1926: 353).

The commands issue from the four living creatures about the throne, and this in succession. And the region over which the comets produce their dire outcomes is, of course, the land of Israel. The first living being in the sequence, described previously as the one like a lion, is the constellation Leo (4:7). Leo was the springtime constellation, and its bright star, Regulus, was the king of the stars. A horse comet would suggest dire events since in the ancient Mediterranean world, horses were essentially war animals, like tanks in our "civilized" warfare (see Hyland 1990). Thus the mention of comet horses indicates catastrophe such as only war can offer. The white color of this horse relates to the planet Jupiter.

The second living creature constellation, Taurus (also known in Ezek 10 as the winged ox called a "cherub"), summons the red horse. The red horse, from the south, has a rider with power to remove peace from the land. The planet Mars is here clearly designated by the color red and by the suggestion of war.

Subsequently it is the turn of the third living creature constellation, Scorpio. To the third seal corresponds a black horse, that is, a horse from the north. Its rider carries a balance in his hand. Not surprisingly, the balance constellation (Libra) derives from the claws of Scorpio. This rider speaks of the cost of food (one denarius for a measure of grain etc.). The planet Mercury, which in the Sino-Persian tradition corresponds to the color black, is here recognizable by the commercial scale typical of Mercury in Babylonian-Greek celestial interpretation.

To the fourth seal and fourth living creature constellation (the Thunderbird = Pegasus) corresponds a horse of a pale color, from the west. And the planet involved is pale white Venus. Corresponding to the role of Venus and the west in the Sino-Persian system, the rider of this horse is called Death; he is given power to kill those inhabiting the land with the sword, famine, and flood.

The opening of the fifth and sixth seals (6:9, 12) should present events affecting the sun and moon. But the series is interrupted by the abrupt mention of the sky Altar, a notice that seems rather obvious to the seer. In fact the presence of the Altar in the southern sky, specifically in the Milky Way, was well known. With the sixth seal, we learn that the sun becomes black, and the moon takes on the color of blood. The darkening of sun or moon or both points to the same phenomenon. The atmospheric darkening of the moon, characterized here by horror, the bloody color of the shadowed moon, and its "becoming blood" as in Joel 3:4 and Acts 2:20, was frequently noted among Greek and earlier authors (see Rochberg-Halton 1987: 333, and the text on 344–48). Here it stands immediately next to the atmospheric "blackening" of the sun (by clouds). The situation is similar in 9:2, where the darkening of the sun is due to smoke from the cosmic abyss.

Along with effects on sun and moon, falling stars strike the land like figs from a wind-shaken tree (cf. 8:10; 9:1; Mark 13:24–25). Yet the size of the stars is huge since when "a great star" falls from the sky, it hits a third of the rivers of the land (8:10). In antiquity all stars were considered larger than the earth. In Cicero's account of Scipio's dream, Scipio notes the following from his observation point on the Milky Way:

> When I gazed in every direction from that point, all else appeared wonderfully beautiful. There were stars which we never see from the earth, and they were all larger than we have ever imagined. The smallest of them was that farthest from the sky and nearest the earth which shone with a borrowed light [i.e., the moon]. The starry spheres were much larger than the earth; indeed the earth itself seemed to me so small that I was scornful of our empire, which covers only a single point, as it were, upon its surface (*The Republic* 6.17, LCL).

The seventh seal remains to be opened by the Lamb (in 8:1). At this point in our tour, we turn to the details of the seal sequence. First we consider the scenario of four horses and horsemen, then the significance of their colors, and then the type of ancient astral writings that fits such a sequence. In conclusion, we offer some information about the sky Altar in the Milky Way.

6.3.1. The Twelve-year Cycle in Antiquity

John's interpretation of the stars as the four riders of ch. 6 may be rooted in the scenarios of Zechariah 1 (four horses, one horseman) and Zechariah 6 (four chariots). Zechariah 6:1–8 affords a taste of that sky trip:

> And again I lifted my eyes and saw, and behold, four chariots came out from between two mountains; and the mountains were mountains of bronze. The first chariot had red horses, the second black horses, the third white horses, and the fourth chariot dappled gray horses. Then I said to the angel who talked with me, "What are these, my lord?" And the angel answered me, "These are going forth to the four winds of heaven, after presenting themselves before the Lord of all the earth. The chariot with the black horses goes toward the north country, the white ones go toward the west country, and the dappled ones go toward the south country." When the steeds came out, they were impatient to get off and patrol the earth. And he said, "Go, patrol the earth." So they patrolled the earth. Then he cried to me, "Behold, those who go toward the north country have set my Spirit at rest in the north country."

Here the chariots are the four winds of the sky (Zech 6:5), yet only three are specifically mentioned. Perhaps the tradition has been confused at this point. The passage in Revelation is both fuller and clearer. And, it would seem, traditional Hellenistic star deities, now appropriated in terms of Israelite perception, are involved in this scenario, for the events provoked by the riders are best explained with the insight that they bear typical traits of four sequential years of a recurring twelve-year series of zodiacal signs.

To begin with, one of the outstanding features of Hellenistic speculation on the meaning of the cosmos is the focusing of perception (that is, selective attentiveness) on cosmic change. Sky changes and their impact on human living, perceived in terms of specific time-frames running from the "hours" of a day through months and years to enormous time periods were the calibrated units of significance. Each significant unit was under the regimen and control of some specific star deity. Of these ancient calibrated units, only the most recent practice, beginning in the second century A.D., has come down to us. This "recent" practice commemorates the control of a given day by one of the planetary deities, as in our English names for the days of the week. These names derive from the Anglo-Saxon equivalents of ancient Mediterranean astral gods (thus Monday = the moon's day; Tuesday = Tuis or Mars; Wednesday = Woden or Mercury; Thursday = Thor or Jupiter; Friday = Friede or Venus; Saturday = Saturn; and Sunday = sun; see Beck 1988). Along with this newer practice of ascribing sequential days to astral deities, there was the earlier practice of ascribing sequential hours of the day to various deities; and ancient calendars likewise ascribed sequential years to the sway of specific planetary deities in seven-year cycles (thus the year of the sun, the year of the moon and so forth) or to zodiacal deities in twelve-year cycles (thus the year of Aries, the year of Taurus and so forth).

However, it was the recurring zodiacal twelve-year cycle that was preferred in the Hellenistic world. In fact this custom followed Sino-Persian usage (as in the Chinese calendar popularly known in the U.S., for example, the year of the Monkey), with each successive year governed by a specific zodiacal constellation. The ancient Mediterranean evidences a number of sources describing such twelve-year series, as previously noted. The Greek name for this twelve-year cycle was a *dodekaeteris*. (Boll 1914: 79 n. 3 mentions a 12,000-year Persian world period, and a 12,000,000-year Orphic world period). Occurrences over the whole year were then determined by the zodiacal sign in the ascendancy: weather and harvest, health and sickness of humans and animals, hunger and plague, and often, insurrection and war or peace. Everything depended on the influence of the zodiacal sign.

Furthermore, the prevailing new year winds were also often very significant indicators of cosmic meaning, much like in the Zechariah's cosmic experience. The initial winds of the year were called the starters or harbingers of the year. Thus in (Pseudo-)Eudoxos' ancient *Dodekaeteris* we have relative to Aries: "the southeast wind will guide the way and the rest of the winds will mix in . . . " (CCAG VII, 183, 6); the work goes on to describe the rest of the twelve-year zodiacal sequence. We find similar initial wind indications in these works, expressed with phrases such as "governed by . . . " as in: "governed by westerly winds" (CCAG II, 145, 1). Individual winds were related to given zodiac signs (see Boll 1914: 80, nn. for a list of such documents found in CCAG).

As an example from the period of Caesar Augustus, consider the following *Dodekaeteris*:

> Year of Aries. This year will begin with the northwind. The winter is cold, long, severe, snowy, will not pass easily, severe because of the wind. In the middle of winter on January 28 (= Octavius 27) big storms from the northeast will begin. Around the time of the Zephyr, after the spring equinox on March 28, the weather will change in three days to heavy rains and strong mild winds, and after the three days, until the rising of the Pleiades on April 27, the 25th (or 23rd) of Drusaios. Spring will be hot (after that winter), summer temperate, fall hot. This year the rivers will be greatly swollen. One must sow early and reap at the beginning of November and Agrippaios. If not, the winter sowing will bear little. The grain harvest will be better than the grape harvest. Shepherds will have a good period. and the year remains not unproductive, but fruitful (CCAG II, 144, 5–20).

This text then offers prophecies of weather and related significant items such as harvests and other agricultural production. Now consider an example of a more general *Dodekaeteris;* this one ascribed to Zoroaster. Here are some sentences from the year of Taurus: " . . . eye illnesses will dominate. . . . The year is not favorable for sea travelers. A famous man will die in this year. . . . One must pray that no earthquake or invasion occur" (*Geoponica* 1.12, cited from Boll 1914: 82, n. 1). In these texts, some years are richer, others poorer.

There are other works related to the *Dodekaeterides* that prophesy the occurrences of the year by the zodiacal location of the sun and moon during an earthquake, thunderclap, or darkening of the sky. A number of such ancient works were literal translations from Babylonian, and in some circles all *Dodekaeterides* were said to derive from Babylon.

An excellent example of an Israelite *Dodekaeteris* is the so-called *Treatise of Shem*, conventionally said to have been "composed by Shem, the son of Noah, concerning the beginning of the year and whatever occurs in it" (see Appendix B, pp. 272–75). The translator of this work, while unclear about its function (*OTP* 1.481, n. 1c), dates this document to the first century B.C.

To return to the passage in Revelation, it seems the riders on these starry horses (or comets) can be known from their allusions to constellational attributes. What these features point to are the successive deities of the zodiac, ruling for successive years. Such star deities in human form can be found not only for the twelve segments of the ecliptic zodiac, but also for all thirty-six decans that constitute the full picture of the sky (for representations of such zodiacal and decanal deities, see the *Encyclopedia of World Art* II, 1960: Pl. 20–2).

We find a similar division of the sky into twelve zodiacal and three-hundred sixty decanal beings in the Israelite tradition as well. For example, 1 Enoch mentions the twelve taxiarchs (rulers of ranks) by name, while alluding to the three-hundred sixty decans. The passage runs as follows:

> These are the names of those which lead the ones that come out and go down in their appointed seasons, which lead them in their respective places, orders, times, months, authorities and locations. The four leaders which distinguish the four seasons of the year enter first; after them enter the twelve leaders of the orders which distinguish the months; and the three hundred and sixty captains which divine the days and the four epagomenal days, and leaders which divine the four seasons of the year. These captains over thousands are added between leader and leader, each behind a place to stand; but their leaders make the division. And these are the names of the leaders, which divide the four seasons of the years which are fixed: Malki'el, Hela'emmemelek, Milay'ul and Narel. The names of those who lead them are 'Adnur'ul, 'Iyasus-'el, 'Elum'el . . . Malkiyal Tam'ayen, Berka'el, Zalebsa'el, Heluyasaf, Hela'emmemelek, Geda'iyal, Helya'el, Ki'el, 'Asfa'el . . . (1 Enoch 82:10–20, *OTP* 1.60–61).

These various sky servants are identical in function to the deities of the zodiac and the decans, the human-like "lords" of the circle of the sky. This astronomical passage leaves no doubt that the sky beings in question are astral deities. We have noted the activities of each hour of the day and night in *The Testament of Adam* 1 (*OTP;* there are lists of the beings in charge of each of these hours in a parallel presentation by Ps. Apollonius of Tyana, CCAG VII, 177, 3–180, 8). These *lords* and *mighty ones,* lesser deities of the decans, are characterized in Revelation by the features of the zodiacal sign to which they belong.

6.3.2. "The Four Horsemen of the Apocalypse"

Now we return to the scenario in Revelation. In order to appreciate what is going on here, consider the explicit mention of the scale (Libra) in v. 5. This is what the third horseman carries. If this verse refers to the year of Libra in a twelve-sign sequence, then the author must have the other signs in mind as well. The sequence is: Leo, Virgo, Libra, Scorpio. But our seer is not consistent. In v. 4 he mentions mutual slaughter before noting the sword that causes the slaughter. On the other hand, in v. 8 we are properly told first of the sword and then the detrimental activity that follows. Hence if the author is referring to Libra in relation to the third rider—as the horseman with a scale in his hand—and if we follow the zodiacal sequence, then Leo must be first,

Virgo second, and Scorpio fourth. From the perspective of the *Do-dekaeteris*, those features mentioned by the author under each sign must be characteristic for each year. For the sake of clarity, we leave aside the first rider for final consideration and begin with the second rider.

6.3.2.1. The Year of Virgo: the Second Rider

Consider now the second rider, given the sword, "to take peace from the land." In an astronomic context, this would be the *lord* of the year of Virgo. Now while such a lack of peace is seldom foretold of Virgo, yet the sun in Virgo, when darkened, effects, "evil in many places; much thievery, violence, and many incursions will occur . . . there will be in Asia the rotting of many places and destruction and slaughter and killing by sword and hunger, and so forth" (from Nechepso-Petosiris, 150 B.C., CCAG VII, 136, 12–137, 3). According to another document with far fewer threats, we find, "the Sun being in Virgo, if an earthquake occur in the day, there will be wars and swords" (CCAG VII, 169, 21; yet earthquakes usually bring peace and fortune, see CCAG VII, 170, 4). Similarly during subterranean thunder "there will be slaughter" (CCAG VIII, 3, 186, 19). We find a like analysis in John Lydus (*De ostentis* 52, 22: civil wars; 60, 19: war attacks and captures; and more specifically in 105, 3–5: "they will carry off unmarried and married women as during war"). There are two reasons for these prophecies for the usually peaceful sign of Virgo. First of all, it was believed that celestial Virgo once lived on earth but departed to the sky. Since she left the earth, the earth is now in the worst of conditions. She attempts to take peace entirely from the earth: "and the virgin Astraea, last of the celestial beings, abandoned the lands soaked in blood due to slaughter" (my literal translation of: "et virgo caede madentes ultima caelestum terras Astraea reliquit," from Ovid, *Metamorphoses* 1.149–150, LCL; Ovid is based on Aratus, *Phenomena* 97ff. where Virgo speaks).

Secondly, next to Virgo's location in the sky is the sword (μάχαιρα, *machaira,* or ξίφος, *xiphos*; further, the Greek προτρυγητήρ, *protrygētēr,* "vine dresser's knife," is a name of a star in Virgo). Astrologers called the image of Virgo itself ξιφέρης, *xipherēs,* "sword-bearing" (Sarapion, student of Hipparchus, hence ca. 100 B.C., CCAG V, 3, 97, 7; Hekate is also called ξιφέρης).

6.3.2.2. The Year of Libra: the Third Rider

The third rider has a scale in his hand and shouts his message in the sky in the midst of the four living creatures. The measure of grain was the daily food requirement. Now there is a Babylonian text that states: "When Libra is dim [sad], the scales will not . . . 2 shekels will be worth only ½ shekel" (translated by Bezold and cited by Boll 1914: 85; the normal price of a measure of wheat, χοῖνιξ σίτου, *choinix sitou,* was an eighth of a denarius). Hence the hunger of v. 8 derives from this rider. Most of the evidence points here to the year of Libra. Some examples: "Year of Libra (yoke). There will be rot in the grain, euphoria of the Dionysiac" (CCAG V, 1, 176, 21). The same contrast between the grain harvest and the grape harvest. So too: "Libra ruling . . . seed sparing . . . wine much" (CCAG III, 31, 1). Or wine and oil taken together contrasting with grain; with thunder in the month of Libra (October): "if it should thunder, it reveals destruction of grain, but abundance of wine and oil" (CCAG VIII, 3, 125, 12).

It is thus clear why the liquid quality of oil and wine is contrasted with grain measured on the scale. In the year of Taurus, we have the opposite: oil will be expensive, while grain will be cheap (CCAG VII, 183, 18). The year of Libra then has power only over what is weighed, not over liquids. On the other hand, we find the ambiguity typical of prophecy as well; at times what is not weighed is even more expensive. In another passage liquid and weight in the year of Libra are connected: "what is sold by measure or weight will not be just" (John Lydus, *De ostentis*, 105, 11). In other words, Libra portends a great rise in prices, as in our book.

In the other years of the cycle too, harvest is always noted and contrasting conditions foreseen. As with grain and oil, so too, when vegetables are good, animals are bad and vice versa, or when the land is good, the king has it bad and vice versa. And barley (Greek: κριθή, *krithē*) is also mentioned. In one prediction, for the year of Sagittarius all the products mentioned in Revelation are listed, and a good year on the whole earth is predicted, or in one case, little wheat but lots of barley. That Revelation mentions only part of the land is also typical of these astrological documents. Hunger as a consequence of the rule of Libra is often expressly noted. And Revelation terminology (including ἀδικέω, *adikeō*, for "to damage" crops) is identical with these *Dodekaeterides* (see Boll 1914: 86, nn. 2–10).

6.3.2.3. The Year of Scorpio: the Fourth Rider

The next Revelation period is that of the rule of Death and Hades. This duo reflects the common pairing of deities (e.g., already in the Canaanite tradition of Ugarit: Gupanu-and-Ugaru, the messengers of Ba`alu, travelling in pairs as noted by de Moor 1.10, n. 54; also Kotharu-and-Khasisu; Zizzu-and-Kamathu, and finally the personal attendants of Athiratu/Asherah, Qidshu-and-Amruru). In the religious traditions of the eastern Mediterranean, the god Muth (Ugaritic: Mot = Death) was born of Kronos in pre-historical times; "the Phoenicians call him Death-and-Pluto" (Philo of Byblos, *The Phoenician History*, frag. 2, 34, cited from Attridge and Oden 57). "Pluto" and "Hades" are the same, both being personifications of the cosmic Abyss at the southern edge of the orb of the earth. "Death" is the injurious sky servant, the sky servant in charge of plague, epidemic injury itself. John mentions Death-and-Hades also in 1:18 and 20:13–14. And the witnesses of 6:9 fit this region of the dead in the southern sky very well, but that might be unintentional.

The location of Death-and-Hades in the direction of the cosmic Abyss fits the celestial region of Scorpio since ancient astronomic tradition places this constellation in the Hades region of the sky. Scorpio is a creature that deals out corruption, skin diseases, and pain, and points to poison (Vettius Valens, *Anthologiae* I, 2, ed. Kroll, p. 10, 27ff. CCAG VII, 205, 15f.). So when it rules, one expects sicknesses of all sorts as well as plague, and the texts bear this out. "Democrites says that the rivers will swell over their banks and there will be sickness about late autumn. It is necessary to pray that a pestilential sickness not happen" (*Geoponica* I, 12, p. 26,1). Scorpio threatens "corruption of men and grain" (John Lydus, *De ostentis* 53, 26). Summer in the year of Scorpio is "full of sickness" (ἐπίνοσος, *epinosos*) (CCAG II, 148,17 and also V, 1, 177, 11). According to Nechepso-Petosiris, when the moon is darkened in Scorpio, one must fear plague (CCAG VII, 132, 12). If in November, it thunders when the sun is in Scorpio; "there will be hunger and plague in the countryside . . . and there will be sickness among men" (CCAG VII, 166, 12, 16). These examples should suffice to point up the interpretation of Revelation.

Finally and fortunately, apart from war, famine, and plague, not all such atmospheric and social afflictions are of the same ferocity. That is why astral prophets can forecast various affliction in years other than those of Virgo, Libra, and Scorpio. Yet the injuries mentioned here and related to astral phenomena are slaughter by sword, famine, death, and wild animals (6:8). Of course these are also threats in Israelite tradition. For example, wild beasts kill cattle and children in Lev 26:22–23, or famine, sword, wild beasts, and pestilence are mentioned in Ezek 5:17, 14:21, and 33:27. While Rev 6:8 inverts the last two elements, it is most similar to Ezek 14:21 ("when I send upon Jerusalem by four sore acts of judgment: sword, famine, evil beasts, and pestilence, to cut off from it human and beast"). However, the calamities are typical here because they are related to the astral beings, God's sky servants, connected with the constellations.

6.3.2.4. The Year of Leo or of Sagittarius: the First Rider

Now consider the first rider with bow and crown, riding out to victory. As just noted, at the close of the series, the afflictions are listed as "kill with a sword, famine, death and wild animals" (6:8). The second rider used the sword, the third brought famine, while the fourth focused on death. Now what of the wild animals? Presumably, if the second, third and fourth riders ushered in sword, famine and death, wild animals must be left for the first rider. According to the zodiacal sequence of riders, the first rider preceding Virgo should be Leo. But according to the order of the afflictions listed in Rev 6:8, it should follow Scorpio; that is, it should follow "death" in the sequence of four, hence it must be Sagittarius.

Now what if the first rider is in fact Sagittarius? The bow fits this centaur creature. And according to Teukros of Babylon, the centaur has a royal face, hence is warlike and victorious (CCAG II, 151, 21). As centaur, Sagittarius belongs to the animal realm (CCAG VII, 206, 24, e.g.). Hence in his year one must especially expect a plague of wild animals. The reverse interpretation (CCAG VII, 170, 22) is that "wild animals will perish." The centaur is a human in star sagas identified with Chiron the wise.

While everything mentioned in Revelation fits what we know of Sagittarius, the possibility that the constellation Leo is involved must likewise be considered. Leo is animal, and there is more damage through wild animals in the year of Leo than in Sagittarius. For example, for Leo we find: "a manifestation of wild animals" (CCAG III, 30, 20); "there will be wild animals all over" (CCAG V, 1, 242, 2); "there will be damage to fruits by wild animals" (CCAG VII, 165, 19); "multiple damage to fields" (CCAG VII, 185, 2), or in the month of Leo, August: "the appearance of many wild animals and snakes so that there will be animal caused afflictions for men" (CCAG VII, 229, 22). One can see the direct relationship between constellation and effect in another passage: "lion will assault men in an even more bloody way in the regions in which they are located" (John Lydus, *De ostentis* 113, 8). Once more we have a range of typical interpretations.

What of the other characteristics of the first rider? All riders seem to resonate with the horses of Ezekiel and are in agreement with the taxiarchs of Enoch. Hence there is no reason to favor Centaur-Sagittarius on this score. What of crown and bow, and fighting and victory? Leo is regal, princely (Vettius Valens, *Anthologiae* I, 2, ed. Kroll p. 9, 15–16) because of the bright star in his chest which the Chaldeans called the kingly or royal star, "Regulus." It was believed that those born about the time of this star's rising had a regal horoscope. Hellenists believed that Leo ruled the sky. Obviously there is a crown or wreath as sign of the ruler. As for being victorious: "Those who have the ascendant in the second degree of Leo will be powerful kings. But whenever Mars or Saturn come to that space, they arouse danger of war" (Firmicus, *Mathesis* 8.23, Rhys Bram 287). At the third grade of Leo (i.e. without Mars or Saturn), we find concerning the conqueror: "[he] will be king of a double kingdom, dominating many provinces," hence in fact a "victor."

As for the bow, Teukros' *Sphaera barbarica* mentions "Dogface" or "Wolfface Bowman" or simply "Bowman" as rising with Leo. This is a combination of the old Babylonian name of Bowstar for the Greek Dog constellation called Kyon (Canis). It rises with Leo (on calendars the Dog Star and Leo are combined). Then, from this form there is an "Indian" representation of a partial god (decan) of Leo who "wears a wreath of white basil" and "holds a bow" (Boll 1914: 91).

Thus the scenario in Revelation fits both Sagittarius and Leo. Boll would choose Leo, as the leading rider, who brings a plague of animals. On the other hand, there is much to recommend the beginning of the series of four years with the year of Leo if only because this Babylonian "ruler of the stars" was originally put at the head of the series, as in Greek astrology as well. Thus the first animal in fact summons his deity of the year, and so with the others.

In sum, the first part of this sequence of seals reveals how John the seer experiences a range of cosmic elements: comets as horses (well known to Greeks as well); constellations that control the year (Leo, Virgo, Libra, Scorpio) naturally made into riders; the attributes of star deities including Regulus of Leo, the Vine-tender's Knife of Virgo, Scales of Libra, Death-and-Hades of Scorpio. These he perceives through lenses provided by Israelite tradition, with the details of the four noted afflictions. These afflictions are rooted in God's promise to punish apostasy to Israel in general (Lev 26:22–23) and in Jerusalem in particular (Ezek 5; 33:27). All this is quite traditional and yet appropriated in a distinctive way typical of astral prophecy.

6.4. THE COLORS OF THE HORSES

The horses and their respective riders bear attributes which, joined with the color of the horse, indicate the planet and the cardinal direction of the sky. This is not unlike the equine colors found in Zechariah. These colors are rooted in the astrological tradition of China as mediated to the Mediterranean by the Persians. The colors correspond to directions of the sky as shown on the chart on p. 128.

Shulman (1978: 51) presents Chinese grave figures of clay with a woman on the White Tiger of the west; a woman on the Dark Warrior (serpent and turtle) of the north; a woman on the Green Dragon of the east; a woman on the Red Bird of the south. Closer to the geographical location of our visionary, we find this directional labeling, for example, in place names such as the Black Sea (to the north), the Red Sea or Edom (= Red, to the south), White Russia or White Syria (that is, Cappodocia, to the west; see Brown 1899: 1.226). In the Sino-Iranian system the center is characterized by Yellow (hence the Yellow River). So too, the color of the polar stones in Rev 4:3 is yellowish.

To determine the planets involved in 6:2–8 as well as the directions noted by the colors in this passage, de Saussure (1926: 355) argues as follows. First of all, we note that the original scenario in this Sector 2 (in ch. 4) consists of a center and four points, the throne and four living creatures. Now in the Sino-Persian system from which this scenario ultimately derives, Saturn stands at the center, while the four cardinal planets Jupiter, Mars, Venus, and Mercury are situated at each corner. Ptolemy's color correlations give the Hellenistic consensus: "For the prediction of general conditions we must also observe the colors at the time of the eclipses . . . for if they [the luminaries involved] appear black or pale greenish yellow they signify the effects which were mentioned in connection with Saturn's nature; if white, those of Jupiter; if reddish, those of Mars; if (pale or golden) yellow, those of Venus; and if multi–hued, those of Mercury" (*Tetrabiblos* 2.89–90, LCL with adjustment for colors). De Saussure (p. 355) notes:

> Venus is more brilliant than Saturn, yet of a paler hue. In China, as noted previously, Venus corresponds to the west, to Evening, to Decline, to Death. Being associated with the west, it is yin, hence female, but it is not considered to symbolize love or fecundity. Being associated with the west, side of decline, of death and of the worship of ancestors, "it presides over killings," as we have seen: war corresponds to the west side and to autumn, season of metal, of punishments and of the color white. Thus Venus bore the name of the "planet of metal," and "The Great White."

Following this arrangement, our seer sees comets of war following the nature of the red planet Mars (south) and the pale white planet Venus (west). The Mars-influenced comet is thus characterized by the military action. The Venus-influenced comet, in turn, is characterized by killing in war and violent punishment.

Further, there are two white horses (comets) in this passage, one a *brilliant* white, the other a *pale* white. If this latter is influenced by Venus, the first can only be under the control of Jupiter. It is true that the corresponding color for the east ought be brilliant blue and/or green. But since there were no horses of this color, an adaptation of the rule is necessary here. Besides, the first influencing planet alluded to here should be brilliant Jupiter (from the east) since in the Sino-Persian system Jupiter stands at the head of the series of planets, corresponding to the first of the seasons, springtime. Furthermore, in the first century A.D. Leo was the actual springtime constellation, with its focal star, Regulus, the king of the stars. Jupiter being the first of the planets, Leo being the constellation of springtime, and springtime opening the course of the year, it makes logical sense for the horseman of the first horse to wear a crown and emerge with the desire to vanquish. Furthermore, in the eastern Mediterranean, springtime marked the end of the rainy season, hence the time for kings to go to war (cf. 2 Sam 11:1).

In spite of his contribution, de Saussure believed the colors of the horses in this passage were really not of concern to the author of Revelation, while they were to Zechariah. But colors were part of astrology. And the color-direction correspondence was well known. Thus in a treatise using ancient sources, the wind directions: south, east, north and west are red, yellow, black and white respectively (CCAG VII, 104–105). In Apuleius (*Metamorphoses* 11.3 LCL) we have the same four colors on the garment of Isis-Luna: "Her robe, woven of sheer linen, was of many colors, here shining with white brilliance, there yellow with saffron bloom, there flaming with rosy redness; and what most especially confounded by sight was a deep black cloak gleaming with dark sheen which was wrapped about her . . . "—white, saffron yellow, red, black. In Zech 6:2 LXX, the colors are: red, black, white, dapple grey.

To summarize, the opening vision has the following dimensions:

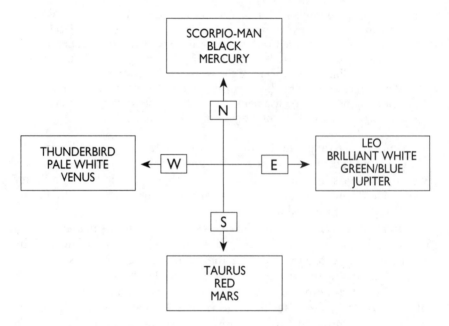

The sequence of horse-shaped comets, then, would be first from the east (white), second from the south (red), third from the north (black) and the fourth from the west (pale).

6.5. The Altar in the Sky

With the opening of the fifth seal, the author looks at the celestial Altar and sees under the Altar, white-robed witnesses killed because of the evidence they gave (6:9–10). John often sees this sky Altar (8:3, 5;

9:13; 11:1; 14:18). And in 16:7 the Altar itself speaks, attesting to the truthful and just quality of God's judgment in requiting the blood of these witnesses. This comes as no surprise since the Altar is a constellation, a living being. To return to the prophet's vision of witnesses under the Altar, the word "under" in Greek (ὑποκάτω, *hypokatō*) is a technical term in astronomy used for situating a celestial body (see Toomer 1984:16). Furthermore, the first-century Roman author Manilius, among others, tells of the Altar in the sky, as follows:

> Next has heaven a temple of its own, where its rites now paid, the Altar gleams after victory gained when Earth in rage bore forth the monstrous Giants against the skies. Then even the gods sought aid of mighty gods, and Jupiter himself felt the need of another Jupiter, fearing lest his power prove powerless. He saw the earth rising up, so that he deemed all nature was being overthrown; mountains piled on lofty mountains he saw growing; he saw the stars retreating from heights which were now neighbors, heights which brought up the armed Giants, brood of a mother they tore apart, deformed creatures of unnatural face and shape. Nor did the gods know whether anyone could inflict death upon them or whether forces existed greater than their own. Then it was that Jupiter set up the constellation of the Altar, which of all altars shines brightest even now (*Astronomica* 1.420–432, LCL).

In another passage he mentions: "the altar of the gods, at which Olympus pays its vows" (5.18, LCL). And quite appropriately, relative to the passage in Rev 6:9, he writes:

> At the side of Scorpio risen hardly eight degrees what of the Altar bearing incense-flame of which its stars are the image? On this in ages past the Giants were vowed to destruction before they fell, for Jupiter armed not his hand with the powerful thunderbolt until he had stood as priest before the gods. Whom rather than temple dignitaries will such risings shape and those enrolled in the third order of service, those who worship in sacred song the divinity of the gods and those who, all but gods themselves, have power to read the future? (5.339–347, LCL; Goold 328, note a, refers to *Digest* 33.1.20.1: " . . . priest and sacristan and temple-freedmen," where the "third order" would be the temple slaves or freedmen).

The Roman scenario of the sky, like the Greek, (both dependent on the Babylonians on this point), has the Altar in the southern sky, specifically in the Milky Way. The name of this constellation varies (in Greek: βωμός, *bōmos* or θυτήριον, *thytērion* or θυμιατήριον, *thymiatērion*; in Latin: *ara* or *turibulum*). The constellation was depicted either as an altar of sacrifice or as an altar of incense. It really does not matter whether this is an altar of sacrifice as in 8:3 or an altar of incense; see 6:9; 8:3; 14:18. What does matter is that this sky Altar is connected with the dead in "white garments," a ready first-century reference to stars in the Milky Way.

For while John indicates that this Altar was the place for the gathering of witnesses, both here and in 7:9, he tells of the dead in their white robes, noting that here they are under the Altar where the Milky Way in fact is to be found. Such a connection is ready at hand. Consider Cicero:

> Such a life is the road to the skies, to that gathering of those who have completed their earthly lives and been relieved of the body, and who live in yonder place which you now see (it was the circle of light which blazed most brightly among the other fires), and which you on earth, borrowing a Greek term, call the Milky Circle. . . . For the spirits (*animi*) of those who are given over to sensual pleasures and have become their slaves, as it were, and who violate the laws of gods and men at the instigation of those desires which are subservient to pleasure—their spirits, after leaving their bodies, fly about close to the earth and do not return to this place [the Milky Way] except after many ages of torture (*The Republic* 6.16, 29, LCL).

In turn, Manilius writes:

> Perhaps the souls of heroes, outstanding men deemed worthy of heaven, freed from the body and released from the globe of Earth, pass hither and, dwelling in a heaven that is their own [i.e. in the Milky Way], live the infinite years of paradise and enjoy celestial bliss.

Then follows a long list of those heroes. The list concludes with the following:

> Here are Cato and Agrippa, who proved in arms the one the master, the other the maker of his destiny; and the Julian who boasted descent from Venus. Augustus has come down from heaven and heaven one day will occupy, guiding its passage through the zodiac with the Thunderer [= Jupiter] at his side; in the assembly of the gods he will behold mighty Quirinus and him whom he himself has dutifully added as a new deity to the powers above, on a higher plane than shines the belt of the Milky Way. There is the gods' abode, and here is theirs, who, peers of the gods in excellence, attain to the nearest heights (*Astronomica* 1.758–808 passim, LCL).

This tradition is not alien to Israelite lore in which the elect have a similar fate:

> The sixth order, when it is shown to them how their face is to shine like the sun, and how they are to be made like the light of the stars, being incorruptible from then on (4 Ezra 7:97).

The pious mother of the martyred Maccabees is told her sons are already stars:

> Take courage, therefore, O holy-minded mother, maintaining firm an enduring hope in God. The moon in heaven, with the stars, does not stand so

august as you, who, after lighting the way of your starlike seven sons to piety, stand in honor before God and are firmly set in heaven with them (4 Macc 17:4–5).

As is well known this tradition is clearly expressed in the book of Daniel:

And those who are wise shall shine like the brightness of the firmament; and those who turn many to righteousness, like the stars for ever and ever (Dan 12:3).

Relative to the witnesses under the sky Altar in John's work, Boll (1914: 34) refers to the significance of the Storehouse of the south in Job 9:9 LXX: "The Lord is the one who makes the Pleiades and Hesperos and Arcturos and the Storehouse of the south." Job's Storehouse of the south is in fact the region under the sky Altar in the south. Here the four groups of stars mentioned point to stars situated at the four opposite directions of the sky. The Pleiades to the east, Hesperos in the west. And obviously the emerging polar star Arcturus designates the north, and the Storehouse in question is in the south. Now according to Aratus (*Phenomena* v. 405), the constellation that lies across from Arcturus is "Thyterios," the Altar, hence in the location of Job's Storehouse, thus "where the Altar lies low in the sky" (Ovid, *Metamorphoses* 2.139, LCL; in v. 403 Aratus notes that this constellation can be used to refer to the south; cf. also vv. 418, 429, 435). The south wind coming from the Altar is fearsome (Aratus, *Phenomena* v. 429). In Job 37:9 [LXX], the Storehouse of the south yields distress.

The Altar then is the locale of Job's Storehouse of the south. In Ezra and Baruch the persevering souls of the just are in the storehouse or chambers (for example: "Did not the souls of the righteous in their chambers ask about these matters, saying, 'How long are we to remain here? And when will come the harvest of our reward?' " 4 Ezra 4:35). Proverbs 7:27 likewise mentions the storehouse or "chambers of death." However, for John, the astral prophet, the dead are under the Altar, in the southern sky where this constellation touches the horizon of the earth. This region is likewise called "the Hades in the sky" (see Boll 1914: 71). The purely celestial localization of the Altar in Revelation, well understood in early Christian times, is important for the history of the altar in Christian churches. It stands behind the connection that early Christians made between their altar table and martyr's tomb in pre-Constantinian times (Boll 1914: 33–35).

In summary, if we read the Revelation of John as the work of an astral prophet, we find that he reads the sky through lenses provided by contemporary astronomics, its *Dodekaeterides*, and its cosmic directions, as well as Israelite expectations and his experience of recent events. It is the one on the throne, whose will is made known by the Lamb's opening of the scroll. It is God, not willful astral beings, who is behind what unfolds in the cosmos in general and the land of Israel in particular. God's forthcoming judgment on Israel is a thing of the past, something long ago determined by God. It is already in the stars, at hand at the throne of God, inaugurated by the cosmic Lamb, under command of the living beings at the four corners of the sky, carried out by comets of given shapes and colors. It is up to the astral prophet to make known what he has come to learn to read in the sky, and thus reveal God's purpose to his brothers and sisters.

7

SECTOR 2 ENDS: ON TRUMPET COMETS, FALLING STARS, AND COSMIC WOES

8 [1]And when he opened the seventh seal, there was silence in the sky for about a half hour. [2]And I saw the seven sky servants who stand before God and seven trumpets were given to them. [3]And another sky servant came and stood by the Altar, having a golden [incense] burner, and much incense was given to it so that he might give [offer it] for the prayers of all the holy ones upon the golden Altar before the throne. [4]And the smoke of the incenses went up with the prayers of the holy ones from the hand of the sky servant before God. [5]And the sky servant received the [incense] burner, and filled it with fire from the Altar and threw it onto the land; and there were thunders and voices and lightnings and earthquake. [6]And the seven sky servants having the seven trumpets prepared them in order to blow. [7]And the first one blew: and there was hail and fire mixed with blood, and it was cast upon the land, and a third of the land was burnt up, and a third of the trees were burnt up, and every green plant was burnt up. [8]And the second sky servant blew: and like a great mountain burning with fire was thrown into the sea; and a third of the seas became blood. [9]And a third of the creatures in the sea died, those having life and a third of the boats were destroyed. [10]And the third sky servant blew: and a great star burning like a torch fell from the sky, and it fell upon a third of the rivers and upon the source of water. [11]And the name of the star is called Absinth. And a third of the waters turned into absinth, and many of the persons died of the water because it became bitter. [12]And the fourth sky servant blew: and a third of the sun and a third of the moon and a third of the stars were struck, so that a third of them was darkened, and so that the day, a third of it, did not shine, and the night likewise. [13]And I saw and I heard an eagle flying in mid-heaven saying in a loud voice: Woe, Woe, Woe, to those dwelling in the land because of the remaining voices of the trumpet of the three sky servants who are going to blow.

9 [1]And the fifth sky servant blew: and I saw a star fallen from the sky onto the land, and the key to the pit of the Abyss was given to it. [2]And the pit of the Abyss was opened, and smoke ascended from the pit like the smoke of a great furnace, and the sun and the air was darkened from the smoke of the pit. [3]And from the smoke, locusts came out onto the land, and authority was given to them like the authority which the scorpions of the land have. [4]And it was said to them that they not injure the grass of the land nor any plant nor any tree, but only human beings who do not have the seal of God on their

foreheads. [5]And it was given to them so that they do not kill them, but that they be tormented for five months; and this torment like the torment of a scorpion, when it stings a human being. [6]And in those days human beings will seek death, and they will surely not find it, and will desire to die and death will flee from them. [7]And the likeness of the locusts [was] similar to horses made ready for war, and upon their heads like wreaths similar to gold, and their faces like faces of human beings, [8]And they had hair like the hair of women, and their teeth were like lions', [9]and they had armor like iron armor and the voice of their wings like the voice of many-horsed chariots running into battle. [10]And they have tails like scorpions and stingers, and with their tails their authority to injure human beings for five months. [11]They have over them a king, the sky servant of the Abyss; its name in Hebrew is Abaddon, and in Greek he has the name Apollyon. [12]The first woe has gone; behold still two woes come after these things. [13]And the sixth sky servant blew: and I heard the first voice from the horns of the Altar of gold before God, [14]saying to the sixth sky servant, having the trumpet: Let loose the four sky servants tied at the great river Euphrates. [15]And the four sky servants prepared for the hour and day and month and year were loosed so that they kill a third of human beings. [16]And the number of cavalry [was] twenty-thousand of ten thousands; I heard their number. [17]And thus I saw the horses in a vision and those seated upon them, having fiery [=red] and hyacinth [=violet] and sulphury [=yellow] armor, and the heads of the horses like the heads of lions, and out of their mouth came fire and smoke and sulphur. [18]And from these three injuries, a third of human beings were killed, from the fire and the smoke and the sulphur coming out of their mouths. [19]For the authority of the horses is in their mouths and in their tails. For their tails [are] like snakes, having heads, and they do injury with them. [20]And the rest of the human beings, those who were not killed with those injuries, did not change [their heart] from the works of their hands, so that they not prostrate themselves to demons and to golden and silver and bronze and stone and wood idols who can neither see nor hear nor walk, [21]And they did not change [their heart] from their murders or from their magical drugs or from their fornications or from their thefts.

10[1]And I saw another mighty sky servant coming down from the sky, clothed in a cloud, and a rainbow around his head, and his face like the sun and his feet like fiery columns, [2]And having in his hand an opened little scroll. And he placed his right foot on the sea and his left on the land, [3]And he shouted with a loud voice just as a lion roars. And when he shouted, the seven thunders spoke out their voices. [4]And when the seven thunders spoke out, I was going to write. And I heard a voice from the sky saying: Seal up what the seven thunders speak out, and do not write those things. [5]And the sky servant which I saw standing on the sea and on the land raised his right hand into the sky [6]and swore by the one living unto the aeons of aeons, who created the sky and what is in it and the land and what is in it and the sea and what is in it, that there is no longer time. [7]but in the days of the voice of the seventh sky servant, when it is about to blow, and the mystery of God, as announced to his slaves, the prophets, is being fulfilled. [8]And the voice which I heard from the sky to speak with me again and to say: "Go, take the open scroll in the hand of the sky servant standing on the sea and on the land." [9]And I went off to the sky servant, telling him to give me the little scroll. And he says to me: "Take and eat it up, and it will make your stomach bitter, but it will be as sweet as honey in your mouth." [10]And I took the little scroll from the hand of the sky servant and I ate it up, and it was sweet as honey in my mouth. And when I ate, my stomach became bitter. [11]And they say to me: "You must again prophecy concerning peoples and nations and tongues and many kings."

11[1]And a reed like a staff was given to me, saying: "Get up and measure the temple of God and the Altar and those prostrating themselves in it. [2]And leave out the outer court of the temple and do not measure it, but it is given to the nations, and they will trample down the holy city for forty two months. [3]And I will give my two witnesses, and they will prophecy for one thousand two hundred sixty days clothed in sackcloth. [4]These are the two olive trees and the two lamp stands standing before the lord of the land. [5]And if anyone wishes to injure them, fire will come out of their mouth and devour those hostile to them; and if anyone will wish to injure them, thus must he be killed. [6]These have the authority to close the sky, so that it does not rain for the days of their prophecy, and they have the authority over waters to turn them into blood and to strike the land with every sort of injury as frequently as they might wish. [7]And when they will have completed their witness, the wild animal coming up from the Abyss will do battle with them, and he will conquer them and kill them. [8]And their corpse in the square of the great city, named in a trance state as Sodom and Egypt, where too their Lord was crucified. [9]And [those] from among the peoples and tribes and tongues and nations look on their body for three days and a half, and their corpses are not permitted to be put into a tomb. [10]And those who dwell in the land rejoice over them and are glad, and send gifts to each other, because those two prophets tormented those who dwell in the land. [11]And after the three days and a half, a sky wind of life from God entered into them, and they stood upon their feet and a great fear fell upon those seeing them. [12]And they heard a loud voice from the sky saying to them: "Come up here!" And they went up into the sky by [means of] the cloud, and their enemies saw them. [13]And at that hour a great earthquake took place, and the tenth of the city fell, and names of seven thousands of human beings were killed by the earthquake, and the rest became terrified and they gave glory to the God of the sky. [14]The second woe went away. Behold the third woe is coming quickly. [15]And the seventh sky servant blew; and there were loud voices in the sky saying:

> "The kingdom of the world of our Lord and of his Messiah has happened,
> And he shall reign [as king] unto the aeons of aeons."

[16]And the twenty-four elders who are seated before God upon their thrones fell down upon their faces and prostrated themselves to God, [17]saying:

> "We thank [acknowledge] you, Lord God the Almighty, who is and who was,
> because you have assumed your great power and you reign [as king];

> [18]"And the nations were irate
> and there came your wrath,
> and the time of the dead to be judged,
> and to give reward to your slaves the prophets, and the Holy Ones and
> to those who fear your name, the small and the great,
> and to destroy those who destroy the land."

[19]And the temple of God in the sky opened and the ark of his covenant in his temple was seen. And there were lightnings, and voices, and thunders, and earthquake, and great hail.

With the opening of the seventh seal a new stage of activity unfolds. Seven trumpet-shaped comets mark this stage. Like previous phenomena signaled by comets, the trumpets also unleash negative events on the land, carried out by remarkable celestial beings (8:2–9:19). Three woes underscore the final three trumpet blasts as particularly distressing (8:13). After the sixth trumpet, we are finally told what it is all about. The people of the land refuse a change of heart and continue to offend

God and fellow humans (9:20–21). Shortly before the final trumpet blast, the seer performs two prophetic symbolic actions. The first indicates that he must further "prophesy concerning peoples and nations and tongues and many kings" (10:11). The second is a census of Israelites in God's Jerusalem sanctuary (11:1–2). Then two prophets appear who are specifically to witness against this counted population about evil in its midst (sackcloth points to this). The prophets stand before the lord of the land (11:4), protected by God with authority over fertility giving water (11:6–7). They are ultimately killed by an animal, shamed by being left unburied, but honored by being raised from the dead by God; then they are taken to the sky (11:8–12). All of this occurs in the same great city "where their Lord was crucified," hence Jerusalem, said to have the qualities of Sodom (inhospitality) and Egypt (idolatry) (11:8). With the removal of the prophets, it is time for the final trumpet blast (11:14–15). Here we would expect a description of the destruction of Jerusalem. Instead, the trumpet marks the inauguration of the rule of God and God's Messiah over the land. This is announced by sky dwellers, then acknowledged in a cosmic song by the twenty-four decans around God's throne (11:15–18). The outcome of it all is the opening of God's sky temple, so much so that one could see the ark of the covenant there (11:19). With this the second set of scenarios presented by John comes to a close.

7.1. Comets Like Trumpets and Bowls

When the cosmic Lamb opens the seventh seal (8:1), a period of silence in the sky ensues. This silence follows immediately upon the great praise by all the sky beings (7:11–12); thus the cosmic singing comes to a halt. Perhaps it is the last hour of the night, for the pause is not unlike that occurring at the end of the twelve hours of the night. In the previously cited *Testament of Adam* we read: "The twelfth hour is the waiting for incense, and silence is imposed on all the ranks of fire and wind until all the priests burn incense to his divinity. And at that time all the heavenly powers are dismissed" (1.12, *OTP*). A like pause of silence occurs in the *Testament of Pseudo Apollonius of Tyana* where at the twelfth hour of the night "the orders of the sky and the fiery orders pause" (CCAG VII, 179, 7–8). In these traditions, this pause takes place at the time of incense, just as in Rev 8:3. Again, we are at the sky Altar in the southern sky (8:5). The interval of silence marks a transition to a new start. Here the seventh seal ushers in a new sequence of seven, this time seven trumpets. These trumpets, of course, signal something negative, as war trumpets do for an invaded population.

What is the rhyme and reason behind the sequence of trumpets? Perhaps by comparing the similarities between the outcomes wrought by the trumpet-shaped (chs. 8–11) and bowl-shaped (ch. 16) comets and another Enochic document, we can see why John outlines events as he does.

We noted previously how Ptolemy explicitly remarked that trumpet-shaped and bowl-shaped comets

> naturally produce the effects peculiar to Mars and to Mercury—wars, hot weather, disturbed conditions, and the accompaniments of these; and they show, through the parts of the zodiac in which their heads appear and through the directions in which the shapes of their tails point, the regions upon which the misfortunes impend. Through the formations, as it were, of their heads they indicate the kind of the event, and the class upon which the misfortune will take effect; through the time which they last, the duration of the events; and through their position relative to the sun likewise their beginning (*Tetrabiblos* 2.90–91, LCL).

It has often been noted that the seer presents his forecast involving these trumpets and bowls in two sets, the first of four elements, the second of three elements. And the events follow a parallel sequence as follows:

The Seven Bowls (ch. 16)	The Seven Trumpets (chs. 8–11)
On the land. Boils.	Hail, blood, fire. On the land; a third of the trees and all grass burnt.
In the sea. It becomes blood.	In the sea, a type of fire mountain falls into the sea; it becomes blood.
In rivers and wells. They become blood. Recall of the blood of martyrs.	A great star falls into rivers and wells. They become bitter.
Against the sun. Extreme heat.	Against sun, moon, stars.
Against the throne of the animal. Darkness, pain and sores for people.	[Woe 1] The miraculous locusts against men, no greenery; pain and sores for people.
Against the Euphrates, which dries up. Three sky winds "like frogs" announce to the kings of the earth.	[Woe 2] Four sky servants at the Euphrates. The miraculous rider. The sky servant on the cloud.
In the air. Lightning, thunder, voices, earthquakes, hail. Prophecy of the fall of Babel.	[Woe 3] Voices in the sky, which opens up; lightning, voices, thunder, earthquake, hail.

Thus both series follow the same order: land, sea, rivers/wells, sky beings, pain/sores, Euphrates, air. From where does this order derive? In the first-century document called Slavonic Enoch (2 Enoch), God says:

And on the sixth day I commanded my wisdom to make man out of the seven components: first his flesh from the earth, second his blood from dew [some MSS. and sun], third his eyes from the sun [some MSS.: from the bottomless sea], fourth his bones from stone, fifth his reason from the mobility of the angels and the clouds, sixth his veins and hair from the grass of the earth, seventh his soul from my spirit and the wind (2 Enoch 30:8, *OTP* 1.150).

The passage continues with a list of seven properties given by God to the earthling: "hearing to the flesh, sight to the eyes, smell to the spirit, touch to the veins, taste to the blood, endurance to the bones, sweetness to the reason" (2 Enoch 30:9). This is followed by the well known anagrammatic analysis of the name "ADAM" in terms of the Greek: *A*natole (east), *D*ysis (west), *A*rktos (north), *M*esembria (south). Thus the first earthling, extensively and intensively, mirrors the whole world. Consider now the list in 2 Enoch 30:8 and the data in Revelation:

2 Enoch 30	Rev 16 (Bowls)	Rev 8ff. (Trumpets)
From earth: flesh.	Earth: boils.	Burning of a third of the earth, grass and trees.
From the bottomless sea: blood	Sea: blood.	Sea: blood
From dew: blood	Rivers and wells: blood	Rivers and wells: bitter
From sun: eyes.	sun: fire and heat.	sun: darkness.
From stone: bone	Throne of the animal (Rome), pains for man.	Locusts, that afflict man, not the grass.
From agility of sky servants and clouds: reason.	Three *pneumata* going forth from the mouth of the beast as messengers.	Four sky servants at the Euphrates, rider who kills with fire, smoke, sword. Sky servant on cloud.
From grass: veins and hair.	Lacking.	Lacking, but see 1 and 5 above.
From God's sky wind and the earth wind: human breath.	Air: lightning, thunder, hail, etc.	[Region of the air] lightning, thunder, hail, etc.

While the parallel is not perfect, it does indicate two things. Like 2 Enoch, the listing in Revelation is derived from a genre known in the culture. Furthermore, the listing intimates interest in speculation about the first human being as a microcosm, a miniature replication of the world (see Boll 1914: 57–67).

7.2. ON FALLING STARS AND PLANTS

Several times in the course of the work, the seer tells us about falling stars and their effects (6:13; 8:10; 9:1; 12:4). The third trumpet-shaped comet marks the event of a falling star hitting the land and effectively transforming a third of all potable water into poisonous water. This was due to this "great star burning like a torch" falling into the water. Falling stars impacting upon the land with nefarious results are well known. Rev 12:3 notes how the Dragon hits a third of the stars of the sky with its tail, causing a huge shower of falling stars. But here only a single star is mentioned. This is similar to the incident in the book of Enoch where a single star falls, later followed by a large number. The fallen stars of Enoch seem to be none other than the Watchers or the fallen sky servants who copulated with the daughters of men in pre-Flood times (as in Gen 6:1–4):

> Again I saw with my own eyes as I was sleeping, and saw the lofty heaven; and as I looked, behold, a star fell down from heaven but managed to rise and eat and to be pastured among those cows. Then I saw these big and dark cows, and behold they all changed their cattle sheds, their pastures and their calves; and they began to lament with each other. Once again I saw a vision, and I observed the sky and behold, I saw many stars descending and casting themselves down from the sky upon that first star. And they became bovids among those calves and were pastured together with them, in their midst. I kept observing, and behold, I saw all of them extending their sexual organs like horses and commencing to mount upon the heifers, the bovids, and they (the latter) all became pregnant and bore elephants, camels and donkeys. So (the cattle) became fearful and frightened of them and began to bite with their teeth and swallow and to gore with their horns. Then they began to eat those bovids. And behold, all the children of the earth began to tremble and to shake before them and to flee from them (1 Enoch 86:1–6, *OTP* 1.63).

But this third trumpet ushers in a well-known falling star related to a plant. Stars and plants (and stones) were often related in antiquity, especially for their positive and/or negative effects on people. The star here has the name of a Mediterranean plant called "Absinth" (Greek ἄψινθος, *apsinthos*, English: absinth, artemisia, or vermouth or wormwood). The plant grows all around the Mediterranean, and there were many varieties of absinth. Most were bitter. All the varieties of the plant were useful for a range of human ailments provided the juice was not taken unboiled and/or unmixed. Taken straight, "this juice is injurious to the stomach and head" (Pliny, *Natural History* 27.47, LCL). Not only that, it was a well know contraceptive and abortifacient (see Riddle 1992: 48–49; 83). About a Palestinian variety, we are told:

Wormwood, *Artemisia judaica*, Hebrew: *la'anah*, Greek: ἄψινθος, *apsinthos*, χολή, *cholē*. Description: A plant of the genus *artemisia*, which may grow to the size of a bush. There are several species and varieties. *Artemisia iudaica* is native to Palestine; its main stem has side shoots covered with small woolly green leaves. The juice of the leaves has a bitter taste and may, if drunk unmixed, be noxious, but mixed in right proportions it can be a useful medicine. In some passages wormwood symbolizes God's punishment, or suffering and sorrow. References: *la'anah*: Deut 29:18; Prov 5:4; Jer 9:15; 23:15; Lam 3:15.19; Amos 5:7; 6:12; ἄψινθος, *apsinthos*: Rev 8:11; χολή, *cholē*: Matt 27:34; cf. Acts 8:23 (Committee on Translations of the United Bible Societies, *Fauna and Flora of the Bible*, United Bible Societies: London, 1972: 198).

A star with this plant name is not found among any people. However, to name a star after its effects is not uncommon. The Arabs, for example, name one star "the Changer" because its rising marks sudden changes in the weather. And the star names "Pleiades," "Hyades," and "Orion" were explained in antiquity because of their effects on sailing and rain.

But how did absinth (artemisia, vermouth, or wormwood) come to be considered a poison? Perhaps the Stoic principle of stellar emanations might clarify the point. Just as the stars are nourished by the dampness of the earth, they in turn emanate sky winds (πνεύματα, *pneumata*), moist currents of fire, conceived of quite directly and physically, upon the earth. For example Proserpina, queen of the dead and moon goddess, who "illumines every city with your womanly light," is asked to: "nourish the joyous seeds with your moist fires and dispense beams of fluctuating radiance according to the convolutions of the sun" (Apuleius, *Metamorphoses* 11.2, LCL).

There is a whole lore dealing with the relationship of stars and plants (see Festugière 1950: 1.146–86, also the *Letter to Roboam*, Appendix C: On Plants and the Zodiac, pp. 276–80). For example, as far as its effects are concerned, the poison of hemlock derives from the planet Mars and the constellation Scorpio. Consequently, it is poisonous only in those countries which lie under the dominance of Scorpio in astrological geography, in this case Italy. In Crete, which is under another sign, it is even said to be the favorite vegetable: "the emanations of the gods (stars) can do this relative to various locations and time periods" (this is the teaching of the God Asklepios himself in CCAG VIII, 3, 137, 19ff.).

Now the plant called absinth falls under the control of poisonous Scorpio. On earth, the plant is effective against poisonous snake bites, poison neutralizing poison. But since here the absinth comes directly from the sky, it must necessarily be poisonous, not a neutralizing agent. But why does this flow of moist, fiery particles specifically influence rivers and wells, the human fresh water supply? The same idea has been associated with lightning strikes. Should such stormy beams of light strike a fruit tree or a river in a given month, "it will not damage each river or well; but it will afflict water, making the water noxious rather sporadically" (John Lydus, *De ostentis* 103, 8; see also 102, 17: "it will afflict water, and trembling will come upon the bodies of human beings"). This is the same sort of sporadic poisonous effect on rivers and wells, lethal for humans, as in our passage (see Boll 1914: 41–42).

If all this sounds a little esoteric, consider the first-century Israelite document known as the *Letter to Roboam* (cited from CCAG VIII, 2, 143ff.; see Carroll 1989). In this document, Solomon instructs his son how to pray to living beings controlling the planets, when to pray to whom, how to make seals to mark one's body for protection by these beings, and what plants to pick, for what purposes, while praying to the appropriate constellational or planetary angel. Appendix C: On Plants and the Zodiac reproduces the section on the plants that correlate with the zodiacal constellations and planets.

7.3. ON COSMIC WOES

The book of Revelation is notorious for its abrupt and unexplained mention of various items. The seer presumes all readers know about these items. This sort of authoring is called high context writing (see Malina 1991). The author supposes that his audience is quite well informed about everything to which he refers, such as the comets, the sky Altar or holy ones, and the like. As the fifth sky servant announces the first of three Woes, sending out another trumpet-shaped comet in ch. 9, John abruptly mentions the pit of the Abyss (or Abysmal Pit). This Abyss likewise figures prominently in later portions of the work (11:7; 17:8, 20:1, 3). After an introductory consideration of this cosmic Abyss, we shall move on to consider the three woes.

7.3.1. The Cosmic Abyss

To understand why there might be an Abyss in the sky at all, one must recall that the author presents earthly items and their matching entities in the sky. For example, the Jerusalem temple has its matching reality in the sky temple of God; the earthly Jerusalem has a corresponding celestial one: there are earthly services of worship, as well as one in the sky; and presumably some earthly throne exist in parallel with a celestial one. Now he sees a celestial Abyss corresponding to the traditional terrestrial pit of the ancient Mediterranean, whether Sheol, Hades, or Tartarus (Neugebauer 1983: 273, 278 has published a Byzantine copy of a map from ca. the second century A.D., that marks the location of the entrance to the underworld). Many Mediterranean sites were vaunted as entrances to the subterranean Abyss (see Rohde 1925: 186–87, nn. 23–26). Virgil, for example, describes the entrance as follows: "Just before the entrance, even within the very jaws of Hell" there are "many monstrous forms besides of various beasts are stalled at the doors, Centaurs and double-shaped Scyllas, and the hundredfold Briareus and the beast of Lerna, hissing horribly, and the Chimaera armed with flame, Gorgons and Harpies, and the shape of the three-bodied shade" (*Aeneid* 6.268–294, LCL).

This terrestrial Abyss likewise had a corresponding celestial equivalent. An ancient Mediterranean informant, Firmicus Maternus, among others, tells us the river Styx, the border of the celestial Hades, is found in the eighth degree of Libra, that is, in autumn at the beginning of the second half of the zodiac (*Mathesis* 8.12.2). Macrobius tells us that Assyrians and Phoenicians considered the second half of the zodiac, from the claws of Scorpio (Libra) to the end, as the Hades half of the sky. There the sun spends most of its winter time period:

> That Adonis too is the sun will be clear beyond all doubt if we examine the religious practices of the Assyrians, among whom Venus Architis and Adonis were worshipped of old with the greatest reverence, as they are by the Phoenicians today. Physicists have given to the earth's upper hemisphere (part which we inhabit) the revered name of Venus, and they have called the earth's lower hemisphere Proserpine. Now six of the twelve signs of the zodiac are regarded as the upper signs and six as the lower, and so the Assyrians, or Phoenicians, represent the goddess Venus as going into mourning when the sun, in the course of its yearly progress through the series of the twelve signs, proceeds to enter the sector of the lower hemisphere. For when the sun is among the lower signs, and therefore makes the days shorter, it is as if it had been carried off for a time by death and had been lost and had passed into the power of Proserpine, who, as we have said, is the deity that presides over the lower circle of the earth and the antipodes; so that Venus is believed to be in mourning then, just as Adonis is believed to have been restored to her when the sun, after passing completely through the signs of the lower series, begins again to traverse the circle of our hemisphere, with brighter light and longer days.
>
> In the story which they tell of Adonis killed by a boar the animal is intended to represent winter, for the boar is an unkempt and rude creature delighting in damp, muddy and frost covered places and feeding on the acorn, which is especially a winter fruit. And so winter, as it were, inflicts a wound on the sun, for in winter we find the sun's light and heat ebbing, as it is an ebbing of light and heat that befalls all living creatures at death.
>
> On Mount Lebanon there is a statue of Venus. Her head is veiled, her expression sad, her cheek beneath her veil is resting on her left hand; and it is believed that as one looks upon the statue it sheds tears. This statue not only represents the mourning goddess of whom we have been speaking

but is also a symbol of the earth in winter; for at the time the earth is veiled in clouds, deprived of the companionship of the sun, and benumbed, its springs of water (which are, as it were, its eyes) flowing more freely and the fields meanwhile stripped of their finery—a sorry sight. But when the sun has come up from the lower parts of the earth and has crossed the boundary of the spring equinox, giving length to the day, then Venus is glad and fair to see, the fields are green with growing crops, the meadows with grass and trees with leaves. This is why our ancestors dedicated the month of April to Venus (*Saturnalia* 1, 21, 1–6, trans. Davies 1969: 141–42).

More specifically, the celestial Hades must refer to a great constellation consisting of those stellar configurations now called Scorpio, Ophiucus (the Serpent Bearer), Sagittarius, the Altar, and the Centaur. It is in this region of the sky that one finds the sky entrance to Hades, located between Scorpio and Sagittarius (noted by Plutarch, *On the Genius of Socrates* 590B–592E, LCL).

And this Abyss clearly is to be situated in the southern sky. In the last cited work, Timarchus notes that "the celestial sea is extremely deep especially toward the south." DeLacy and Einarson, in their comment on Plutarch's *Genius of Socrates* 590D, observe: "The great deep in the south was suggested by the starless space around the invisible pole in Greek globes" (note d). This ignorance alone would allow for the bottomless Abyss to be located in the south! (For other witnesses, see Rohde 1925: 330, n. 111; there he cites Varro who tells of the ecstatic vision of Empedotimus who saw in the sky among other things three gates and three ways to the gods and the kingdom of the dead). An Akkadian (Hid Zuab Gal) and Assyrian (*Nahru apshi rabi*) name for the Milky Way was "River of the great Abyss" (Allen 1963: 475).

Scorpio and colleagues are guardians of the gate of Hades, with the power and duty of allowing entrance only to those permitted by God's decision (much like God's control of the earth wind by sky servants in 7:1; and his control of the temple entrance by seven sky servants in 15:8). Hence while people might wish to die, they cannot. Later in this passage (9:11) we find that this Abyss is in fact the pit of destruction. The pit exudes smoke, indicating fire. Now in this same region of the southern sky, it is the constellation Altar that is such a smoke-producing source.

Interestingly enough, the constellational beings located on either side of the Altar are Sagittarius and the Centaur. And near the Centaur one finds the Beast and in one tradition, a Sea Monster, along with the confluence of two rivers. Thus Manilius:

> And the Centaur of twofold form; he is half man, joined at the waist to the body of a horse. Next has heaven a temple of its own, where, its rites now paid, the Altar gleams after victory gained when Earth in rage bore forth the monstrous Giants against the skies. Then even the gods sought aid of

mighty gods, and Jupiter himself felt the need of another Jupiter, fearing lest his power prove powerless. He saw the earth rising up, so that he deemed all nature was being overthrown; mountains piled on lofty mountains he saw growing; he saw the stars retreating from heights which were now neighbors, heights which brought up the armed Giants, brood of a mother they tore apart, deformed creatures of unnatural face and shape. Nor did the gods know whether anyone could inflict death upon them, or whether forces existed greater than their own. Then it was that Jupiter set up the constellation of the Altar, which of all altars shines brightest even now. Next to it Cetus undulates its scaly body; it rises aloft upon a spiral of coils and splashes with such a belly as drove the sea beyond its proper shores when it appeared from the waves to destroy the daughter of Cepheus exposed upon the cliffs. Then rises the Southern Fish in the quarter of the wind after which it is named. To it are joined the Rivers which make their winding way along great curves of stars: Aquarius connects his waters with the upper reaches of the one stream, whilst the other flows from Orion's out-thrust foot; they meet each other and blend their stars together [i.e. the stream from Aquarius' urn and the River Eridanus] (*Astronomica*, 1.418–443, LCL).

7.3.2. The First Woe: Scorpion Locusts

When the falling star of 9:1 opens the Abyss, the smoky gloom spawns monstrous locusts. As a rule biblical commentators trace this locust plague to the book of the prophet Joel. The passage does have elements in common with Joel; however, the locusts bite like scorpions, and they afflict humans not greenery. Further, they are outfitted like war horses with human heads. In fact they are scorpion tailed, winged Centaurs. Such nefarious demons are not part of the scenario of earthly nature. They are, therefore, sky locusts emerging from the gloom of the cosmic Abyss in the south (for further indications of infernal elements among the stars usually associated with Scorpio/Libra, see Le Boeuffle 1977: 228–29; and Brown 1899 1.71–76).

Emerging from the southern sky, the sky locusts act like earthly scorpions but are intelligent beings, for they take orders to seek out only persons without God's seal on their foreheads and to afflict those persons with the pain of a scorpion sting. Three things are then noted concerning these locusts: first, their tormenting of human beings will not result in death (9:6); second, the locusts not only act like scorpions but look like centaurs (9:7–10); and third, they have a king over them, the fallen star who is sky servant of the Abyss (9:11). Further, the description of the locusts as scorpion-centaurs is marked off by mention of the duration of their assault, that is, five months (9:5, 10).

Five months' duration is an unusual time period in this book. Furthermore, the period does not pertain to the duration of an actual locust plague since, once the locusts eat up vegetation, they move on.

Given the imagery and the perspective of astral prophecy, it seems that the five months relate to celestially determined calendar duration. In Greek astronomy months were named after the corresponding zodiacal signs. Now since the locusts behave like scorpions, there would be a ready connection to the month of Scorpio. And if we count the months by their Greek names (of course, in Latin form), then the sequence is Scorpio, Sagittarius, Capricorn, Aquarius, Pisces. These are the final zodiac signs of the annual cycle. In other words, the locusts are to afflict men till the end of the year. While locust activity can occur at other times, locust activity befits the month of Scorpio:

> Should the moon while in Scorpio be fully eclipsed in the first or second hour, there will be severe batterings in Ethiopia and neighboring localities. Should it be fully eclipsed in Scorpio while in mid-heaven in the third, fourth, fifth or sixth hour, there will be many murders in Syria, Cilicia, and Libya and there will be many locusts. Should it occur in the eighth, ninth or tenth hour, there will be suffering in the land of the Persians and Euboia. In Egypt conflict among aristocrats and crowds will show no compliance with governors (Nechepso-Petosiris CCAG VII, 140, 8–22; John Lydus, *De ostentis* 75, 13).

These centaur-like scorpion locusts match the description of the centaurs of Babylonian boundary stones, later pictured in Hellenistic and Egyptian-Greek constellations. The Babylonian creatures are centaur archers, i.e., armed with bow and arrow, thus outfitted for war. At times they are two-headed, a human head coupled with another head, for example, a dog's head. They are also portrayed with powerful wings and a scorpion's tail above the horse tail or simply with a scorpion's tail. Such an image of Sagittarius can be found on nearly every Egyptian temple or coffin that depicts the celestial Archer.

While these images derive from late Hellenistic and Roman times, they are, with slight modification, rather consistent over the millennia. For example, consider Sagittarius depicted on the right corner of famous Hellenistic Dendera Zodiac. The scorpion tail is a remnant of an older Babylonian conception in which Sagittarius and neighboring Scorpio were fused, perhaps even with other constellations. The result was a broad picture of the southern sky. Along with such a centaur-shaped Scorpio-Archer, there was also Scorpioman (one of the four living creatures of ch. 4), a human-like equatorial constellation, with a human torso, animal lower body, lion-footed and scorpion-tailed (see the sketches of such "Scorpion people" in Black and Green 1992: 65 and p. 100, above). The bow carried by Scorpionman was said to derive from the fangs of Scorpio.

Now if one admits the identification of the agent of the first woe as the celestial Archer, imagined in terms of contemporary planispheres, there will be no need to bother with the prophet Joel. While the Babylonian Sagittarius sports a peaked cap or visor, the Egyptian constellation wears a double crown, and the Greek Archer, called the "crown bearer" (διαδηματοφόρος, *diadēmatophoros*) is a royal figure. A Greek replication of the crown is the wreath (στέφανος, *stephanos*), likewise the Greek name for the constellation Corona. For the Greeks, Sagittarius has a wreath at his feet. Astrologers said he dropped the crown while playing; hence he should be wearing it. For example, Hyginus, notes regarding the centaur Sagittarius, that "before its feet there are several stars in circular form, which some say was his crown that fell while he was playing" (*Astronomican* 2.2.27, ed. A. Le Boeuffle, Belles Lettres, 70). He also reports that this "centaurs crown had seven stars" (3.26, Belles Lettres 105).

A final feature to note here regarding the Abyss and the emerging scorpion locusts is the reaction of the people that John records. We are told that people will seek death, but death will flee from them (9:6). This sort of statement is idiomatic in the culture to underscore the hopelessness of the situation. Berger (1976: 76–77) lists twenty-five instances of the formula (e.g., Lam 1:19 LXX; Ezek 22:30; Ps 37:10; Prov 1:28; 4Q185 1.12ff.; 4 Ezra 5:10; Luke 15:16; 17:22. For specific instances of people praying for death and not finding it, Berger cites Apoc of Elias, ed. Steind. pp. 77, 79; Lactantius, *Div. Inst.* 7.16, 12; Jub 23:24; Arabic Apocalypse of Peter 2.271: "I will also fill the hearts of other men with fear and fright to such an extent that they will pray for death"). And John Lydus has a forecast based on the occurrence of thunderbolts when the sun is in Scorpio:

> The sun in Scorpio. Whenever it is found in Scorpio, if a thunderbolt strike down against a tree, wealth will be forthcoming to the owners of the tree, but tillage will diminish. A sailing voyage will be dangerous, and many thunderbolts together will fall down upon the sea, and many shipwrecks will occur. If a thunderbolt dart against a public place, a shameless youth will lay hold of the kingdom, while the profligate and corrupt flock together to him. But if a thunderbolt strike against city walls, there will be need to fear wars from neighboring regions and the corruption of the youth of the nation. Then hostile forces will come upon a myriad of the wicked so that death is recognized as something to be prayed for (*De ostentis* 105, 17–28).

In conclusion, then, there can be little doubt that the locusts are centaur-like creatures: human-headed, lion-toothed, long-haired, wreathed, winged war horses, with chests of iron and tails of scorpion stingers. It was such centaur-like constellations that John perceives invading the land. As we have noted, there were two such constellations in the ancient sky, Sagittarius and Centaur, located on either side of the Altar, in the southern vault of the sky. It was common to describe Sagittarius as a centaur, yet distinct from the constellation Centaur. Thus Manilius:

At the side of Scorpio risen hardly eight degrees, what of the Altar bearing incense-flame of which its stars are the image? On this in ages past the Giants were vowed to destruction before they fell, for Jupiter armed not his hand with the powerful thunderbolt until he had stood as priest before the gods. Whom rather than temple dignitaries will such risings shape and those enrolled in the third order of service, those who worship in sacred song the divinity of the gods and those who, all but gods themselves, have power to read the future?

After a further four degrees the Centaur rears his stars and from his own nature assigns qualities to his progeny. Such a one will either urge on asses with the goad and yoke together quadrupeds of mixed stock or will ride aloft in a chariot; else he will saddle horses with a fighter or drive them into the fight. Another knows how to apply the arts of healing to the limbs of animals and to relieve the dumb creatures of the disorders they cannot describe for his hearing. His is indeed a calling of skill, not to wait for the cries of pain, but recognize betimes a sick body not yet conscious of its sickness.

Him the Archer follows, whose fifth degree shows bright Arcturus to those upon the sea . . . (Manilius, *Astronomica* 5.339–363, LCL).

Now if the first woe is led by the Archer at one side of the Altar, the second is led by the constellational Centaur.

Centaur

7.3.3. The Second Woe: Lion-headed War Horses

From the sky Altar a celestial voice commands the sixth sky servant to let loose the four sky servants bound at the Euphrates. This is a curious command, for while invading hordes from the east usually came from the direction of the Euphrates (see 16:12), what would four sky servants be doing there bound? And given the progression of the vision in which sky locations provoke sky responses, perhaps something other than the geographical Euphrates is what the author has in mind. Actually astronomic tradition has a number of rivers in the sky. The Babylonian tradition counted seven mighty rivers on earth that were matched by seven in the sky. Among the seven celestial rivers, we find the following: (1) River of the Fish(es) flows from the Urn of Aquarius, where the Sea-horse, the Sea-goat, the Sea monster, the Dolphin, the two zodiacal Fish and the Southern Fish all swim. (2) River of the Bird(s) is that part of the Milky Way containing the constellations of the Swan, the Vulture (Lyre) and the Eagle. (3) River of the Sun-God is that of Ningirsu-Tammuz, the river of Orion, Eridanus. (4) River of Marduk is the Milky Way as it flowed through Perseus and past Capella. (5) River of the Serpent, the Nahru Martu (The Bitter River), i.e., the Ogen-Okeanos (Canal of water), the encircling Ocean stream. (6) River of the Goddess Gula (Great One), i.e., the Goddess Nisinna; this is the primeval Akkadian watery deep, the primordial abyss. (7) River of Gan-gal, the High Cloud, i.e., the Milky Way (Brown 1900: 2.203–5).

Moreover, while the Euphrates was lauded with a range of titles ("The Bringer of Fertility," "the King of the Plain of Eridu," "Strong One of the Plain"), it had a celestial equivalent as well. In the sky it was the River of Ningirsu-Tammuz, alias the river of Orion, the Eridanos (Brown 1900: 2.203). On the other hand, there was also "The River of Mighty Waters" that gave life to Gilgatil (the Enclosure of Life), found in the region marked off by the stars: beta, gamma, eta and zeta of Ursa Minor, fronting the Pole Star. Brown notes that this was "the special place in the universe which is in an occult and peculiar manner the abode of the essence and spirit of life; and it is equally natural to locate this spot in the heights of the north, ever crowned by the unsinking stars" (Brown 1900: 2.185). Perhaps it was to this sort of celestial river that John refers.

Be that as it may, it is from the sky that the unfettered four sky servants now command a veritable limitless celestial cavalry, charged with the task of killing one third of the land's inhabitants. Thus the trumpet comet unleashes a host of lion-headed, horse-shaped stars: red, violet, and yellow. Of course the red is due to fire, the violet to smoke, and yellow to sulphur. It is these elements that prove lethal, resulting in the death of a third of humanity. The snake tails of these horses make them similar to the scorpion tails of the previous centaurs.

Thus the second Woe (9:13–21) involves the death of a third of the unsealed inhabitants of the land by a cavalry of celestial beings, this time, lion-headed, serpent-tailed horses. Egyptian art witnesses to a double-headed centaur, with the heads of a human and a lion. The sky being involved now is the constellation at the other side of the sky Altar, Centaur. Centaur has the ability to muster a cavalry if only because, as Manilius notes, his protégés "will load horses with arms (that is his own, by being armed and mounted) or will drive them into arms (that is yoked to war-chariots)" (Goold's literal translation of

Manilius, *Astronomica* 5.351, LCL, note d). The quality of the earthly protégés derives from the qualities of their celestial protectors.

At the close of this scene (9:20–21), we are finally and indirectly informed about a reason for the cosmic carnage. It was to urge the two-thirds of the unsealed inhabitants of the land to a change of heart, specifically away from idolatry, murder, magic, fornication, and theft. The presumption, then, is that it was precisely for these crimes that the first third of the land's inhabitants perished.

7.3.4. The Third Woe: The Mystery of God

According to the astral prophet John, the third woe occurs at 11:15, with the sky servant's final trumpet blast. If this is so, then chs. 10 and 11 are essentially an intermezzo between the sixth and seventh trumpet. Chapter 10 begins with the seer's vision of the book's second gigantic celestial personage, "clothed in a cloud, and a rainbow around his head, and his face like the sun and his feet like fiery columns . . his right foot in the sea and his left foot on the land" (10:1–2). In Israel's tradition, such colossal sky servants are well known. Consider the description of the archangel Uriel, well-known from 1 Enoch 9:1; 10:1; 27:2, 33:4:

> Now when Joshua drew near to attack at Jericho, he lifted up his eyes and looked; and behold, an angel whose name was Uriel; his height was about from the earth to the sky, and his breadth was about from Egypt to Jericho. And in his hand was his sword drawn clear of the sheath. Then Joshua fell upon his face to the ground and asked of him: Did you come to help us or do you seek to kill for our enemies? And he said to him: I did not come to help and I am not for the enemies, but am an angel sent from before YHWH. I come now to punish you because last evening you neglected the daily burnt offering and today you neglected the study of the Torah. And he said: On account of which of these then did you come? And he said: I came on account of the neglecting of the Torah. And so Joshua fell upon his face upon the ground and said: Please do not forgive now the sins of your servant on account of his servants. And he said to him: Whatever is spoken from before YHWH against us must be accomplished and must be done. Then the angel sent from before YHWH said to Joshua: Let evil deeds pass away and convert and busy yourselves with the study of the Law which you neglected. . . . And Joshua heeded in his soul all that the angel sent from before YHWH said to him and did so (Tg. Josh. 5:13–15 [MS 607 [ENA 2576] Jewish Theological Seminary of New York] cited from Malina 1968: 79–81).

Why this gigantic stature? Undoubtedly something of the sort is implied in the story so briefly presented in Gen 6:1–9. It would seem from this passage that the proper stature of God's sky servants was indeed colossal. Here the sky servant gives his word of honor concerning the fact that time is running out and in the process mentions how "the mystery of God as announced to his slaves the prophets is being fulfilled" (10:7). The mystery of God in this context refers to everything that sky servants reveal. Consider, for example, 1 Enoch:

> And so to the Watchers on whose behalf you have been sent to intercede—who were formerly in heaven—(say to them), "You were (once) in heaven, but not all the mysteries (of heaven) are open to you, and you (only) know the rejected mystery. This one you have broadcast to the women in the hardness of your hearts and by this mystery the women and men multiply evil deed upon the earth" (1 Enoch 16:2–3, *OTP* 1.22).

> (Then) the angel said (to me), "This place is the (ultimate) end of heaven and earth: it is the prison house for the stars and the powers of heaven. And the stars which roll over upon the fire, they are the ones which have transgressed the commandments of God from the beginning of their rising because they did not arrive punctually. And he was wroth with them and bound them until the time of the completion of their sin in the year of mystery" (1 Enoch 18:14–16, *OTP* 1.23).

Given the locale of all the activity in this section of the book of Revelation, it would seem that our seer is to announce that year of mystery as now arriving!

The distinctive aspect of this appearance is that the gigantic sky servant has a "little scroll" in his hand. He then obliges the prophet to perform two prophetic symbolic actions. The first action is to eat the scroll (10:8–11); the second is to measure the Jerusalem temple's inner court (11:1–2). A prophetic symbolic action is an action commanded by God that inevitably produces the effects it symbolizes. Since actions can be quite ambiguous, the significance of such prophetic actions is always clarified. Such actions are quite numerous in the books of Jeremiah and Ezekiel. Jesus' taking bread at the Last Supper in the Synoptic Gospels is also a prophetic symbolic action. The words "This is my body" (Mark 14:22 par.) clarify the meaning of the action, just as the words "This is Jerusalem" clarify the meaning of Ezekiel's behavior in Ezek 5:5. These are declaratory formulas which accentuate the formal character of the statements. In the Israelite tradition, the distinctive feature about these actions is that their effects demonstrate the power of God who commands them.

Here the meaning of the prophet's eating the scroll refers to his task of "prophesying concerning peoples and nations and tongues and many kings" (10:11). And the meaning of his measuring the inner precinct of the temple, an in-group census of sorts, is to mark off the fated Jerusalem population because of its interaction with two prophetic witnesses (11:3–13). The narrative of this work does not connect the first prophetic action with anything explicit in the story that follows. However, the second prophetic action is related to what follows, for God's prophets appear in Jerusalem, where they are duly and shamefully dispatched. And the numbered population carries on as though it were a holiday, with gift-giving and all. The outcome was the partial destruction of the city at the very time God takes up his prophets: "And at that hour a great earthquake took place, and the tenth of the city fell, and names of seven thousands of human beings were killed by the earthquake, and the rest became terrified and they gave glory to the God of the sky. The second woe went away. Behold the third woe is coming quickly" (11:13–14).

Now given the fact that the scenario closes with a vision of the open cosmic temple of God, it would seem that the third woe somehow implies the total destruction of Jerusalem. "For all in the period, the uncontested and uncontestable principle, since it is affirmed by Daniel, is that the destruction of Jerusalem indicates the beginning of the end" (Gry 1939: 355, n. 1). The passage in Daniel is the following:

> And after the sixty-two weeks, an anointed one shall be cut off, and shall have nothing; and the people of the prince who is to come shall destroy the city and the sanctuary. Its end shall come with a flood, and to the end there shall be war; desolations are decreed (Dan 9:26).

So the city of Jerusalem and its temple had to be destroyed before the Messiah begins his rule over the land. While the author of Revelation does not tell us any more about the actual destruction of Jerusalem other than alluding that celestial armies were involved, Tacitus writes in his introduction to the Judean war: "Prodigies had indeed occurred . . . contending hosts were seen meeting in the sky, arms flashed and suddenly the temple was illumined with fire from clouds" (*Histories* 5.13, LCL, partly based on Virgil, *Aeneid* 8.528–529). And he continues: "Of a sudden the doors of the shrine opened and a voice greater than human cried: 'The gods are departing,' at the same moment the mighty stir of their going was heard" (ibid.; see Saulnier 1989). Now a parallel passage in Josephus, presumably deriving from the same source, relates:

> Thus it was that the wretched people were deluded at that time by charlatans and pretended messengers of the deity; they neither heeded nor believed in the manifest portents that foretold the coming desolation, but, as if thunderstruck and bereft of eyes and mind, disregarded the plain warnings of God. So it was when a star resembling a sword, stood over the city, and a comet which continued for a year (*War* 6.288–289, LCL).

> Again, not many days after the festival, on the 21st of the month of Artemisium [ca. May], there appeared a miraculous phenomenon, passing belief. Indeed what I am about to relate would, I imagine, have been deemed a fable, were it not for the narratives of eyewitnesses and for the subsequent calamities which deserved to be so signalized. For before sunset throughout all parts of the country chariots were seen in the air and

armed battalions hurtling through the clouds and encompassing cities (*War* 6.297–299, LCL).

Josephus offers a whole range of other signs as well (passim *War* 6.288–313). Surely Josephus, as well as the others he mentions, (e.g., the ecstatic Jesus, son of Ananias) witnesses to typical perceptions of the time. As John the seer tells us, celestial armies were involved indeed.

While the final comet-trumpet and the woe it intimates are passed by without further ado, the end of the woes ushers in God's expected dominion with his Messiah, hence with God's judgment entailing reward for prophets, holy ones, and all those who fear God (11:16). This scenario with God and his Messiah wielding dominion concludes with a vision of the open sky through which can be seen God's open temple, with the ark of the covenant prominently featured. Since the covenant previously dealt exclusively with Israel, presumably the new situation indicates the end to a covenant relationship rooted in people, land, and temple. Obviously what is at issue is a renewal of covenant relationships with God, but now open to all to whom the open sky is visible, that is, to all human beings. This is the outcome and result of the whole cosmic vision presented in this second sector of the book of Revelation. This is what the prophet has to reveal in this second sector to allay deception and to support endurance.

8   SECTOR 3: PREHISTORIC STAR WARS

12 ¹And a great sign was seen in the sky, a Woman clothed with the sun, and the moon under her feet and on her head a wreath of twelve stars. [2]And having in the womb, and she cries out having childbirth pains and tormented to give birth. [3]And another sign was seen in the sky, and behold a great fire-colored Dragon, having seven heads and ten horns and on its heads seven diadems. [4]And its tail sweeps away the third of the stars of the sky, and it threw them onto the earth, and the Dragon stands before the Woman about to give birth, in order when she gives birth to eat up her Child. [5]And she gave birth to a son, a male, who is going to shepherd all the nations with an iron rod. And her Child was taken up to God and to his throne. [6]And the Woman fled into the wilderness where a place is prepared by God there so that they nourish her there for one thousand two-hundred sixty days. [7]And there was a war in the sky, the Michael and his sky servants to do battle with the Dragon. And the Dragon did battle and his sky servants. [8]And he did not prevail nor was their place found any longer in the sky. [9]And the great Dragon, the ancient Serpent, the one called Devil and Satan, the one who deceives the whole inhabited world, was thrown out—he was thrown out into the earth, and his sky servants were thrown out with him. [10]And I heard a great voice in the sky saying:

> "The rescue and the power and the kingdom of our God and
> the authority of his Messiah has now been realized,
> because the Accuser of our brothers has been thrown out,
> the one accusing them before our God day and night.

[11]"And they conquered him because of the blood of the Lamb and
> because of the utterance of their witness."

[12]Because of this, be glad O skies and those tented in them;
> "Woe to the earth and the sea, because the Devil has come down
> o you, having great anger,
> Knowing that he has little time."

[13]And when the Dragon saw that he was thrown out into the earth, he pursued the Woman who gave birth to the male. [14]And there were given to the Woman the two wings of the great eagle, so that she

might fly into the wilderness, into her place, where she might be nourished there a time and times and a half of a time, away from the face of the Serpent. [15]And the Serpent threw water out of his mouth after the Woman, like a river, so that he might have her carried away by the river. [16]And the earth helped the Woman, and the earth opened its mouth and drank up the river which the Dragon threw out of his mouth. [17]And the Dragon was furiously angry at the Woman and went away to make war with the rest of her seed, those keeping the commandments of God and having the witness of Jesus. [18]And he stood at the sand of the sea.

Our tour through Sector 2 closed with the seer's looking into the vault of the sky at God's celestial temple and seeing the Ark it houses. That vision followed the last of the seven trumpets. The author now turns to another set of visions occurring, for the most part, under the vault of the sky. The celestial visions are punctuated by the word "sign." Sector 3 of the tour (chs. 12–16) has three such signposts: a first sign formed by a starry Pregnant Woman, a second constituted by a cosmic Dragon, and a third consisting of seven comets in the shape of bowls. Each sign, of course, involves some cosmic interaction, duly described, having negative consequences for human beings. The first and second signs quickly unfold into conflict, concluding with attention on the Dragon (ch. 12). Next follows a description of the activity of the Dragon and its companion constellations, two Beasts (chs. 13–14). The final sign once more removes us to a scenario of the open sky and the temple of God, this time to gaze at the open celestial Tent of Witness (15:5) from which the sky servants are about to pour out seven disastrous bowls. The action closes with the emptying of the last bowl and the collapse of "the great city," presumably Babylon or Babel, and its surround (16:19–20).

What John describes here is the situation of the sky during the early part of God's creation of the universe. This temporal location is obvious from the fact that John identifies the cosmic Dragon of the sky with the ancient Serpent of primordial earth, for, as is well known, in Israel's tradition, creation was a process taking place over "six days" leading up to the creation of the first human. However, when the human and his consort are situated in the Garden of Eden, the ancient Serpent is already on earth in the garden (Gen 2–3). Hence the cosmic Dragon must have been thrown down from the sky during that prehistoric creation period before the creation of the human. And even prior to the Dragon's ejection from the sky, John encounters a cosmic Pregnant Woman on the celestial vault who gives birth during that prehistoric period as well. What then is John describing? This sector concludes with the announcement of the destruction of the "great city," Babylon or

Babel—the very first postdeluvian city on our planet, again according to Genesis (ch. 10). The scenarios in this sector, then, are bracketed by events alluded to in Israel's stories of origin: cosmic creation (concluded with the prehistoric flood) and cultural creation (to be concluded presumably, with the posthistoric new Jerusalem). The author thus explains the whys and wherefores behind the destruction of the Flood generations followed by a similar explanation of the destruction of that seat of renewed civilization, Babel. In Sector 3 specifically, his attention is on the destruction of the Flood generation. Interestingly enough, it is with these generations that the Israelite book of Enoch is concerned. John's experience, again, falls within the same tradition. Recall our opening text segment that includes John's account of the first two signs (Rev 12:1–18).

8.1. THE FIRST AND SECOND SIGNS:
THE PREGNANT WOMAN AND THE DRAGON

This opening passage of Sector 3 stands as a centerpiece between chapter 11 with its presentation of two witnesses and chapter 13 with its presentation of two beasts. The passage unfolds by presenting a Pregnant Woman and a waiting Dragon, both said to be signs. Signs are both constellations and forecasts or indications of what is forthcoming, whether it be weather conditions or social events. After the two are presented, a series of actions in the sky follows: first, the birth of a cosmic Son who will lead; the Son is enthroned; then the wilderness flight of the woman for 1,260 days, and finally a sky war: Michael and his army vanquish the Dragon and his army, with the Dragon cast to the earth. The action closes with a pause marked by cosmic acclamation.

Then the action moves to the earth. First, the Dragon pursues the Woman who, now winged, flees to the wilderness for three and a half times (= years = 1,260 days). Then the Dragon spews out water to kill the Woman, the earth swallows the water and saves her. We are then told that the Dragon turns to war on the seed of the Woman, although no incidents are yet described. The action again closes with a pause, marked by the Dragon waiting at the seashore.

8.1.1. The Pregnant Woman

The constellation of the Pregnant Woman is a sky deity of gigantic proportions (the constellation Virgo is in fact one of the largest of the constellations). Indications of her colossal size are the facts that there

are twelve stars (or constellations) about her head, with her feet over
the moon and the sun contained within her contours. Like some other
female sky deities of the period, she gives birth and experiences the
pangs of the event. We are informed about the constellation of the
Pregnant Woman from Mesopotamian traditions. Brown notes: "Here,
Eritu ('the Pregnant-woman') a name of Istar = the constellation Andromeda. Istar-Aphrodite was called Mylitta (Herodotus, *Histories*
1.131) i.e. (Bab.) Mulidtu ('the [Child] Bearer'), and she should be the
original female figure afterwards called Adamath (=Andromeda) by the
Phoenicians" (Brown 1900: 2.22). What Herodotus says is that the Per-
sians learned "to sacrifice to the 'heavenly' Aphrodite from the As-
syrians and Arabians. She is called by the Assyrians 'Mylitta,' by the
Arabians 'Alilàt,' and by the Persians 'Mitra' " (*Histories* 1.131, LCL).
As for the identity of this heavenly Aphrodite, Godley, the translator of
Herodotus, observes: "The great goddess (Mother of Heaven and
Earth) worshipped by Eastern nations under various names—Mylitta in
Assyria, Astarte in Phoenicia: called Heavenly Aphrodite, or simply the
Heavenly One, by Greeks" (ibid., n. 1). Relative to this personage,
Herodotus tells of the following incident:

> when they [the Scythians] were in that part of Syria called Palestine,
> Psammetichus king of Egypt met them and persuaded them with gifts and
> prayers to come no further. So they turned back, and when they came on
> their way to the city of Ascalon in Syria, most of the Scythians passed by
> and did no harm, but a few remained behind and plundered the temple of
> Heavenly Aphrodite. This temple, as I learn from what I hear, is the oldest
> of all the temples of the goddess, for the temple in Cyprus was founded
> from it, as the Cyprians themselves say; and the temple on Cythera was
> founded by Phoenicians from this same land of Syria. But the Scythians
> who pillaged the temple, and all their descendants after them, were af-
> flicted by the goddess with the "female" sickness: inasmuch that the
> Scythians say that this is the cause of their disease, and that those who
> come to Scythia can see there the plight of the men whom they call
> "Enareis" (*Histories* 1.105, LCL, note to "Enareis": "The derivation of this
> word is uncertain; it is agreed that the disease was a loss of virility. In 4.67
> enares = androgynos").

John depicts the Pregnant Woman in a rather conventional way for a
sky deity. For example, consider Apuleius' description of the celestial
Isis in "the prayer of Lucius to Isis, his Patroness":

> O Queen of Heaven—whether you are bountiful Ceres, the primal mother
> of crops, who in joy at the recovery of your daughter took away from men
> their primeval animal fodder of acorns and showed them gentler nourish-
> ment, and now dwell in the land of Eleusis; or heavenly Venus (= Phoeni-
> cian goddess Astarte), who at the first foundation of the universe united
> the diversity of the sexes by creating Love and propagated the human race
> through ever-recurring progeny, and now are worshipped in the island

sanctuary of Paphos; or Phoebus' sister, who brought forth populous multitudes by relieving the delivery of offspring with your soothing remedies, and now are venerated at the illustrious shrine of Ephesus (= Diana/Artemis, also Lucina/Eileithyia); or dreaded Proserpina (= Hecate) of the nocturnal howls, who in triple form repress the attacks of ghosts and keep the gates to earth closed fast, roam through widely scattered groves and are propitiated by diverse rites—you who illumine every city with your womanly light, nourish the joyous seeds with your moist fires, and dispense beams of fluctuating radiance according to the convolutions of the sun—by whatever name, with whatever rite, in whatever image it is meet to invoke you: defend me now in the uttermost extremes of tribulation (*Metamorphoses* 11.2, LCL).

He continues with Lucius' description of his vision of Isis:

First of all her hair, thick, long, and lightly curled, flowed softly down, loosely spread over her divine neck and shoulders. The top of her head was encircled by an intricate crown into which were woven all kinds of flowers. At its midpoint, above her forehead, a flat round disc like a mirror—or rather a symbol for the moon—glistened with white light. To right and left the crown was bounded by coils of rearing snakes, and adorned above with outstretched ears of wheat. Her robe, woven of sheer linen, was of many colors, here shining with white brilliance, there yellow with saffron bloom, there flaming with rosy redness; and what most especially confounded my sight was a deep black cloak gleaming with dark sheen, which was wrapped about her, running under her right arm up to her left shoulder, with part of its border let down in the form of a knot; it hung in complicated pleats, beautifully undulating with knotted tassels at its lower edge. Along the embroidered border and over the surface of the cloak glittering stars were scattered, and at their center the full moon exhaled fiery flames. Wherever streamed the hem of that wondrous robe, a garland of flowers and fruits of every kind was attached to it with an inseparable bond (*Metamorphoses* 11.3–4, LCL).

Now Isis speaks to Lucius:

Behold, Lucius, moved by your prayers I have come, I the mother of the universe, mistress of all the elements, and first offspring of the ages; mightiest of deities, queen of the dead, and foremost of heavenly beings; my one person manifests the aspects of all gods and goddesses. With my nod I rule the starry heights of the sky, the health giving breezes of the sea, and the plaintive silences of the underworld. My divinity is one, worshipped by all the world under different forms, with various rites and by manifold names. In one place the Phrygians, first-born of men, call me Pessinuntine Mother of the Gods (= Cybele), in another the autochtonous people of Attica call me Cecropian Minerva (= Athene), in another the sea-washed Cyprians call me Paphian Venus; to the arrow bearing Cretans I am Dictynna Diana, to the trilingual Sicilians Ortygian Proserpina, to the ancient people of Eleusis Attic Ceres; some call me Juno, some Bellona, others Hecate, and still others Rhamnusia; the people of the two Ethiopias, who are lighted by the first rays of the Sun-God as he rises every day, and the Egyptians, who are strong in ancient lore, worship me with the rites that are truly mine and call me by my real name, which is Queen Isis (*Metamorphoses* 11.5, LCL).

Relative to the crown of twelve stars, note how a fifth-century author, Martianus Capella (I, 75, ed. Dick p. 34), describes Juno, consort of Jupiter: "She had a resplendent wreath about her, which rayed forth with the flames of twelve burning gemstones." This recalls the previous sector where we saw that there were plants and gemstones that corresponded with the stars, notably with the zodiacal constellations and the months of the year over which they presided.

For contemporaries of John, this description of this sky Woman with the sun as her garment, a crown of twelve stars and the moon at her feet would obviously and necessarily be related to some zodiacal constellation since it has the sun "clothing" it. The constellation thus stood in the pathway of the sun, on the ecliptic. In the vision she would be at the zenith of the sky, since the sun covers her. But her clothing would change every month with the course of the sun and moon through the zodiacal constellations. And the moon at her feet situates her toward the south of the ecliptic. Thus just as with the previous visions of Sagittarius, the Altar, and the Centaur, we are looking at the south of the sky. Further verification of this location is the *red* Dragon, red being the celestial color standing for the south.

How best to identify this constellation? The identification of this Pregnant sky Woman with the constellation Virgo dates back at least to Charles Dupuis in 1794, whom I cite (and translate) from Lehmann-Nitsche (1933: 202):

> The author of the Apocalypse turns his gaze to the heaven of the fixed stars, and specifically to the Zodiac, and on that part of the sky where at midnight the beginning of the year at the winter solstice was situated and which in springtime, at sunset, rose the first on the horizon of the Eastern Part. These constellations were vessels called Arca, and the Celestial Virgin, accompanied by the Serpent, which rose following her, and which appeared to pursue her in the Sky, while in the west the river of Orion seemed to be swallowed up by the earth and disappear with its setting. This then is the tableau with which the astronomical sky presents us at the time when the equinoctial year ends and when the sun of springtime shines, bringing the famous Lamb, chief of the twelve signs. What are the tableaux which Apocalypse presents here? A bow shining in the sky. A winged woman, like Virgo of our constellations, whom a serpent pursues, and a river which the earth swallows up. The mystical tableaux of the twelfth chapter which John views in the sky can be reduced to these (p. 247).

Lehmann-Nitsche notes:

For Dupuis, the constellation of the ship, preceding Virgo, must be the arc in the celestial temple to which the author refers in ch. 11. As for the zodiacal Virgo: "By rising at midnight, it presides over the opening of the solstitial year; and three months later, by its rising at six in the evening and at the beginning of the night, over the equinox of springtime. This connection with the two principal periods of time should have led it to enjoy a great role" (p. 251). . . . The crown of stars "designates the twelve months or the twelve signs through which the sun passes during a year and the moon in each of its revolutions" (p. 249).

However, to accept the identification of this woman with the Roman Virgo, the image must fit the story of the *Virgo coelestis*. And there are mythologies in antiquity that readily fit the scenario: Isis and her son Horus pursued by the Dragon Typhon; Leto about to give birth to Apollo, pursued by the Dragon Python, and the like.

Now in antiquity, the constellation which the Roman's called Virgo was identified with many deities: Aphrodite, Isis, Dike, Demeter, Magna Mater, Eileithyia, Tyche, Pax, Atargatis or Dea Syria, Iuno [Venus] coelestis of the Carthaginians (see Le Boeuffle 1977: 212–15). But most of our witnesses speak of the identity of Virgo with Isis. Isis is found holding or nursing her child Horus in the Hellenistic Egyptian sky maps (see the Dendera zodiac of the first to the second century A.D. in *Encyclopedia of World Art* II, Pl. 20). Teukros the Babylonian (first century A.D.) tells us that in the constellation of Virgo there emerges "a certain goddess, seated on a throne and nursing a child, of whom some say she is the goddess Isis feeding Horus" (Boll 1914: 110). We find the same portrayal in Egyptian temple pictures of the early Roman Empire, including the constellation on the ceiling of a Dendera temple and other paintings, gems, and coins. Apuleius calls her "mother of the stars, parent of the seasons, mistress of the whole world" (*Metamorphoses* 11.7, LCL).

Similarly, Typhon is found in the Hellenistic sky charts. Thus an early Egyptian text states: "The four northern (spirits?) that are the four deities of the servant. They hold back the attack of the gruesome one (sc. Typhon) in the sky. He is as a great fighter. . . . The front leg of Seth (Typhon) is found in the northern sky. It is the office of Isis, in the form of a hippopotamus to tend the chain" (Boll 1914: 110). In this scenario, Isis is depicted as a constellation near the North Pole that keeps Typhon (here: Ursa Major or Ursa Minor), a "seven starred" being, chained up with the help of ministering astral deities. In Egyptian lore, she is found in three different locales, near the constellation Canis, as Virgo, and near the North Pole.

Finally, in a passage from Apuleius where Psyche turns in prayer to Juno, she states:

> O sister and consort of great Jupiter, whether you dwell in the ancient sanctuary of Samos, which alone glories in your birth and infant wails and

nursing, or whether you frequent the blessed site of lofty Carthage, which worships you as a virgin who travels through the sky on the back of Leo, or whether you protect the renowned walls of the Argives beside the banks of Inachus, who proclaims you now the Thunderer's bride and queen of goddesses—you whom all the east adores as Yoker (Zygia) and all the West calls Bringer into Light (Lucina)—be you Juno Savioress to me in my uttermost misfortune (*Metamorphoses* 6.4, LCL).

The point is that in the mind of first-century Mediterraneans, the female statuses and roles of virgin, mother, and queen could thus readily reside in the same person. In Hermetic tradition, Isis is described as the Maiden of the Cosmos, the one who gives birth to the sun and the like.

Furthermore, the connection of that constellational configuration with the myth of Isis and Horus was made in the Hellenistic period in rather great detail. Thus it belonged to the world of our seer and was discovered long before his work was written. Now it is significant that John sees this constellation as a Pregnant Woman, while traditional lore has it as Mother and Child. What this means is that John views the constellation when it still formed a single entity, before the birth of the Child, hence as a cosmic Pregnant Woman. This vision places us in prehistoric times. As previously noted, since the Dragon is still in the sky, the scenario here considers the sky as it was early on at the time of creation. In sum, we are given a glimpse of the constellation in the way it once was. This temporal feature will become apparent as we consider the Dragon and the Beasts.

Snake-dragon

8.1.2. The Dragon

The second sign is the fire-colored Dragon. The color red locates it in the southern sky. It "stands" at the feet of the woman about to give birth. This is further indication of sky location since the Greek for "stands" (present perfect form: ἕστηκεν, *hestēken*) was a technical term for fixing and designating the location of a star or a constellation. And its present perfect grammatical form points to a condition enduring into the present. In other words, this constellation is where it has always been since some time in the past. The word "stands," then, is not used to describe behavior, as though the Dragon were elsewhere and then came and stood where we find it in this scenario. In sum, we are dealing with two fixed constellations, whose significance ("signs") is seen by the seer for the first time.

The fact that the Dragon's tail sweeps (present tense) away a third of the stars of the sky further points to a location generally lacking in stars compared to other sky locations. This, again, is the south, in the region of the Abyss. That these stars fall to earth points to a region known for falling stars. "For the unaided eye, there are segments of the sky that seem totally lacking in stars. Two notable ones lie above the constellation Leo and another, much smaller, between Virgo, Raven (Corax), Cup (Crater) and Leo. These are likewise regions of falling stars" (Lehmann-Nitsche 1933: 229, who also cites a shower of 14,000 stars on October 9, 1933 and notes the consternation it caused among people in Portugal).

The question we might pose now is, which constellation does John label as the red Dragon, the Dragon in the south? Obviously it is not Draco, which is found at the North Pole. Boll opts for Hydra, which "extends from Cancer to Libra (the claws of Scorpio), hence through four of the 12 zodia or a third of the sky (1914: 102–2)." Boll bases his judgment on the information offered by Vettius Valens, who does indeed state concerning Hydra that "its tail reaches to the claws of Scorpio while its head to the claws of Cancer" (*Anthologiae* 1.2, ed. Kroll 9, 28–30). Immediately above Hydra and accompanying it are the constellations of Corax (Raven) and Crater, which have seven and ten stars respectively. Corax with seven, corresponding to the number of heads, lies closer to Virgo. Crater with ten stars has the image of a projection of ten dorsal "fins" (horns), not spread over seven heads, but placed along the back of the Dragon. In antiquity Hydra was also called the Serpent as well as the Dragon (Le Boeuffle 1977: 142–43).

On the other hand, Lehmann-Nitsche (1933: 215) argues that the prototypical Dragon of the sky is really ancient Scorpio, originally a much larger set of stars than the present constellation. It was truly gigantic, even by celestial zodiacal standards, since it originally consisted of two zodiacal signs (Libra/Claws and Scorpio). It was only relatively recently, that is, about 237 B.C., that it was divided by the Greeks, when the claws originally holding an Altar were lopped off to become Libra. For the ancient Chinese tradition, the original Scorpio ran from Virgo to Scorpio and included horns, neck, heart, and tail.

Aratus has the tail extending into the Serpent Bearer (Ophiuchos); hence the image has a serpentine tail. Furthermore the Chinese call Scorpio "the Dragon." The present name and image of the constellation derives from Babylon ca. 3000 B.C. (for the stars that made up this constellation, see Lehmann-Nitsche 1933: 215–17; Brown 1899: 1.66–77). The Babylonians too saw horns where later students of the sky saw Scorpio's claws (Lehmann-Nitsche 1933: 223). And finally, Brown notes how in Babylonian tradition, Scorpio always stands for darkness, death, and evil. In sum, ancient Scorpio seems to be the Dragon in question. Consequently, the scenario described by John would consist of a Pregnant Woman (Virgo), with the traditional Heads (later Claws, now Libra) of the Dragon (old Scorpio) right at her feet awaiting her offspring's birth.

8.2. THE FIRST SERIES OF ACTIONS

The first piece of activity after the presentation of the characters is the birth of a son from the Pregnant Woman. The action, then, involves the separation of one constellation from another, with the removal of the new constellation to yet another called the son's throne, undoubtedly like the thrones of the elders/decans mentioned in the previous sector. Again, such thrones are not surprising. In Matt 25:31 we are told that the son of Man likewise has a throne in the sky: "When the son of Man comes in his glory, and all the angels with him, then he will sit on his glorious throne."

Of course interpreters have not refrained from trying to identify the celestial child. Boll (1914: 118–19) believes this scenario bears no reference to any actually occurring historic event or personage. The child born in the sky is a personage of the past, not of the future! However, Boll (1914: 115) does cite a Persian text (from A.D. 542) attributed to the ancient Teukros making the following reference to Mary and Jesus:

> In the first third (decan) of Virgo a virgin ascends which Teukros calls Isis. She is a pretty, pure virgin with long hair and fair of countenance; she has two spikes of wheat in her hand and sits on a throne covered with pillows. She awaits a small boy and gives him broth to eat in a place called the Atrium; some people call the boy Isu, i.e. Jesus.

This does not seem to be the perspective of the author of Revelation at all. As Boll notes, the only reference to the life of Jesus in this work are the following passages: 1:5, 7; 5:9; 12:11; and perhaps 11:8 if it is not interpolated.

In this context, we might note that the author is obviously more deeply involved with cosmic sky searching and prehistoric scenarios than with concern about a historic personage, yet there is such a prehistoric person of great later significance. Consider the Israelite traditions reported in 1 Enoch where the sage notes in one of his antediluvian visions:

> At that place I saw the One to whom belongs the time before time. And his head was white like wool, and there was with him another individual, whose face was like that of a human being. His countenance was full of grace like that of one among the holy angels. And I asked the one—from among the angels—who was going with me and who had revealed to me all the secrets regarding the One who was born of human beings, "Who is this and from whence is he who is going as the prototype of the Before-Time? And he answered me and said to me, 'This is the Son of Man', to whom belongs righteousness, and with whom righteousness dwells'" (1 Enoch 46:1–3, *OTP*).

Then Enoch saw

> that Son of Man was given a name, in the presence of the Lord of the Spirits, the Before Time; even before the creation of the sun and the moon, before the creation of the stars, he was given a name in the presence of the Lord of Spirits. He will become a staff for the righteous ones in order that they may lean on him and not fall. He is the light of the gentiles and he will become the hope of those who are sick in their hearts. All those who dwell upon the earth shall fall and worship before him; they shall glorify, bless, and sing the name of the Lord of the Spirits. For this purpose he became the Chosen One; he was concealed in the presence of (the Lord of the Spirits) prior to the creation of the world and for eternity. And he has revealed the wisdom of the Lord of the Spirits to the righteous and the holy ones, for he has preserved the portion of the righteous because they have hated and despised this world of oppression (together with) all its ways of life and its habits in the name of the Lord of Spirits; and because they will be saved in his name and it is his good pleasure that they have life (1 Enoch 48:2–7, *OTP*).

Enoch further sees God, the Lord of the Spirits, commanding the elites of this world (kings, governors, high officials and landlords) to recognize this Chosen One, "how he sits on his throne of glory," a point repeatedly underscored (1 Enoch 62:2, 3, 6). And Enoch notes how this "Son of Man sitting on the throne of his glory . . . was concealed from the beginning, and the Most High One preserved him in the presence of his power; then he revealed him to the holy and elect ones" (1 Enoch 62:7 *OTP*).

We are then told that this "Son of Man":

> shall never pass away or perish from before the face of the earth. But those who have led the world astray shall be bound with chains; and their

ruinous congregation shall be imprisoned; all their deeds shall vanish from before the face of the earth. Thenceforth nothing that is corruptible shall be found; for that Son of Man has appeared and has seated himself upon the throne of his glory; and all evil shall disappear from before his face; he shall go and tell to that Son of Man, and he shall be strong before the Lord of the Spirits (1 Enoch 69:27–29, *OTP*).

There can be little doubt that with the prehistoric birth of the sky Woman's son, enthroned with God early in the history of the cosmos, we are viewing with John the origins of Enoch's Son of Man. And there is equally no doubt that this Enochian Son of Man is the Messiah of Israelite expectation. "The Lord of Spirits and his Messiah" are mentioned in one breath at the end of the passage where this Son of Man is described (1 Enoch 48:10, *OTP*). And later we are told: "All these things which you have seen happened by the authority of his Messiah so that he may give orders and be praised upon the earth" (1 Enoch 52:4, *OTP*). While the story developed in this sector of the book of Revelation is not about the Messiah's activity, it seems John's vision of the Dragon's origin necessarily involves the Messiah's cosmic origin as well.

8.3. THE WOMAN IN THE WILDERNESS

The next action consists of the flight of the sky Woman into some "wilderness" (12:6). We are not directly told whether this wilderness was situated in the sky or on the earth. However, since we are subsequently told that the Dragon pursues the Woman after the Dragon is thrown to the earth, the sky Woman must now find herself on earth. Astronomers like Aratus knew that Virgo once was on earth, only to return to the sky due to the diffusion of evil among human beings. Now John's vision clarifies how the being called Virgo by the Romans originally came to earth at creation time. She was pursued by the Scorpio Dragon after she gave birth to the enthroned cosmic Child.

And how did she get back to the sky? Aratus begins his account of this tradition at the point John leaves off. For Aratus, Virgo, the deity of Justice (Dike-Parthenos) once lived on earth. She left for her present position in the sky (the constellation Virgo) to avoid the terrible earth which became wicked during the period of the third generation after Creation:

Beneath both feet of Bootes mark the Maiden (Parthenos), who in her hands bears the gleaming Ear of Corn. . . . But another tale is current among men, how of old she dwelt on earth and met men face to face, nor ever disdained in olden time the tribes of men and women, but mingling with them took her seat, immortal though she was. Her men called Justice (Dike); but she assembling the elders, it might be in the market-place or in the wide streets, uttered her voice ever urging on them judgments kinder to the people. Not yet in that age had men knowledge of hateful strife, or carping contention, or din of battle, but a simple life they lived. Far from them was the cruel sea and not yet from afar did ships bring their livelihood, but the oxen and the plough and Justice (Dike) herself, queen of the peoples, giver of things just, abundantly supplied their every need. Even so long as the earth still nurtured the Golden Race, she had her dwelling on earth. But with the Silver Race only a little and no longer with utter readiness did she mingle, for that she yearned for the ways of the men of old. Yet in that Silver Age, was she still upon the earth; but from the echoing hills at eventide, she came alone, nor spake to any man in gentle words. But when she had filled the great heights with gathering crowds, then would she with threats rebuke their evil ways and declare that never more at their prayer would she reveal her face to man. . . . And when, more ruinous than they which went before, the Race of Bronze was born, who were the first to forge the sword of the highwayman, and the first to eat of the flesh of the plowing ox, then verily did Justice (Dike) loathe that race of men and fly heavenward and took up that abode, where even now in the night time the Maiden (Parthenos) is seen of men established near to far-seen Bootes (*Phenomena* 96–136, LCL).

On the other hand, Seneca does describe how the starry Virgo comes down to the earth (see below). But this is an abandoned earth, the earth at the end of the present world order. John does not explain the descent of the starry Woman or tell of her fate. Rather, he simply says that God takes care of the woman in the wilderness for the next three and a half years.

Where might this wilderness be? Perhaps at this juncture it might be useful to present a map of the world that surely was known to John the seer. To begin with, some time ago Pierre Grelot developed a map of the world on the basis of 1 Enoch (1958). He went on to show that this map likewise fits the first-known Babylonian map (an excellent reproduction in Kahn 1960, pl. 1 opposite 88). The information in 1 Enoch well accords with the geographical information in Homer as well as in the Babylonian epic, the *Enuma Elish*. Hence it represented a common perspective for ancient elites from the Mediterranean to Mesopotamia. Milik (1976: 40) reproduces that map in his edition of the Qumran fragments of Enoch and further notes that John, the prophet of Revelation, knew Enoch rather well (ibid. 199). If this is so, then perhaps this traditional map as mediated by Enochian geographical indications provides a fundamental orientation for John as well. I present it in English below (Figure 5). The main adaptation to John's orientation is the placement of the Abyss and the celestial Prison in the south (rather than the north, where Milik has them).

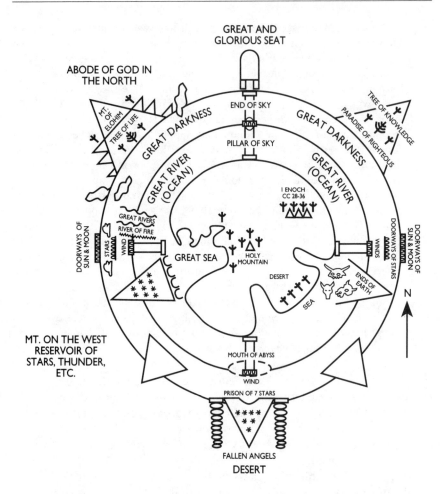

Figure 5: Map of the world in 1 Enoch 1–36, after Milik 1976: 40, after Grelot 1958. I place the Abyss and prison of the sky servants in the south.

8.4. Prehistoric Star Wars

The action in this opening scenario of our tour's third sector climaxes in a sky war after the cosmic Child is safely enthroned in the sky with God, and the Woman is duly taken care of in the wilderness (12:7–8). The motif of a prehistoric sky war is known throughout the Mediterranean region, and earlier in Mesopotamia. It is ready at hand in Giant and Titan stories, for example, as depicted on the great altar of Zeus in Pergamum (called the Throne of Satan in 2:13). The motif of casting down some or all of the stars of the sky in the process of such a war is likewise known at the time. Consider the following sampling. First, from the Sibylline Oracles:

I saw the threat of the burning sun among the stars
and the terrible wrath of the moon among the lightning flashes.
The stars travailed in battle; God bade them fight.
For over against the sun long flames were in strife,
and the two-horned rush of the moon was changed.
Lucifer fought, mounted on the back of Leo.
Capricorn smote the ankle of the young Taurus,
and Taurus deprived Capricorn of his day of return.
Orion removed Libra so that it remained no more.
Virgo changed the destiny of Gemini in Aries.
The Pleiad no longer appeared and Draco rejected its belt.
Pisces submerged themselves in the girdle of Leo.
Cancer did not stand its ground, for it feared Orion.
Scorpio got under its tail because of terrible Leo,
and the dog star perished by the flame of the sun.
The strength of the mighty day star burned up Aquarius.
Heaven itself was roused until it shook the fighters.
In anger it cast them headlong to earth.
Accordingly, stricken into the baths of ocean,
they quickly kindled the whole earth. But the sky remained starless
(*Sibylline Oracles* 5.512–531, *OTP*).

The next witness is Seneca:

But whatever this may be, would that night were here! Trembling, trembling are our hearts, sorely smitten with fear, lest all things fall shattered
in fatal ruin and once more gods and men be overwhelmed by formless
chaos; lest the lands, the encircling sea, and the stars that wander in the
spangled sky, nature blot out once more. No more by the rising of his
quenchless torch shall the leader of the stars, guiding the procession of the
years, mark off the summer and winter times; no more shall Luna, reflect-
ing Phoebus' rays, dispel night's terrors, and outstrip her brother's reins, as
in scantier space she speeds on her circling path. Into one abyss shall fall
the heaped up throne of gods. The Zodiac, which making passage through
the sacred stars, crosses the zones obliquely, guide and sign-bearer for the
slow moving years, falling itself, shall see the fallen constellations; the
Ram who, ere kindly spring has come, gives back the sails to the warm
west-wind, headlong shall plunge into the waves over which he had borne
the trembling Helle; the Bull, who before him on bright horns bears the
Hyades, shall drag the Twins down with him and the Crab's wide-curving
claws; Alcides' Lion, with burning heat inflamed, once more shall fall
down from the sky; the Virgin shall fall to the earth she once abandoned;
and the Scales of justice with their weights shall fall and with them shall
drag the fierce Scorpion down; old Chiron, who sets the feathered shafts
upon Haemonian chord, shall loose his shafts from the snapped bowstring;
the frigid Goat who brings back sluggish winter, shall fall and break thy
urn whoever thou art; with thee shall fall the Fish, last of the stars of
heaven, and the Wagon which was never bathed by the sea, shall be
plunged beneath the all engulfing waves; the slippery Serpent which gliding

like a river, separates the Bears shall fall and icy Cynosura, the Lesser
Bear, together with the Dragon vast, congealed with cold; and that slow
moving driver of his wagon, Arctophylax, no longer fixed in place, shall
fall (*Thyestes* 827–874, LCL).

And finally Nonnos (from about the fourth century A.D.):

Still there was no rest. The Giant turned back and passed from north to
south; he left one pole and stood by the other. With a long arm he grasped
the Charioteer, and flogged the back of hailstorming Aigoceros; he
dragged the two Fishes out of the sky and cast them into the sea; he
buffeted the Ram, that midnipple star of Olympios, who balances with
equal pin day and darkness over the fiery orb of his spring-time neighbor.
With trailing feet Typhoeus mounted close to the clouds: spreading abroad
the far-scattered host of his arms, he shadowed the bright radiance of the
unclouded sky by darting forth his tangled army of snakes. One of them
ran up right through the rim of the polar circuit and skipped upon the
backbone of the heavenly Serpent, hissing his mortal challenge. One made
for Cepheus' daughter (Andromeda), and with starry fingers twisting a
ring as close as the other, enchained Andromeda, bound already, with a
second bond aslant under her bands. Another a horned serpent, entwined
about the forked horns of the Bull's horned head of shape like his own,
and dangled coiling over the Bull's brow, tormenting with open jaws the
Hyades opposite ranged like a crescent moon. Poison spitting tangles of
serpents in a bunch girdled the Ox–drover. Another made a bold leap,
when he saw another Snake in Olympos, and jumped around the Ophiuchos' arm that help the viper; then curving his neck and coiling his
crawling belly, he braided a second chaplet about Ariadne's crown. Then
Typhoeus many-armed turned to both ends shaking with his host of arms
the girdle of Zephyros and the wing of Euros ragging first Phosphoros,
then Hesperos and the crest of Atlas. Many a time in the weedy gulf he
seized Poseidon's chariot and dragged it from the depths of the sea to land;
again he pulled out a stallion by his brine-soaked mane from the undersea
manger and threw a vagabond nag to the vault of heaven, shooting his shot
at Olympos—hit the sun's chariot, and the horses on their round whinnied
under the yoke. Many a time he took a bull at rest from his rustic plowtree
and shook him with a threatening hand, bellow as he would, then shot him
against the moon like another moon, and stayed her course, then rushed
hissing against the goddess, checking with the bridle her bull's white yoke-
straps, while he poured out the mortal whistle of a poison-spitting viper.
But Titan Mene would not yield to the attack. Battling against the Giant's
heads, like-horned to hers, she carved many a scar on the shining orb of
her bull's horn (=the moon as Isis-Hathor). And Selene's radiant cattle
bellowed amazed at the gasping chasm of Typhaon's throat. The Seasons
undaunted armed the starry battalions, and the line of heavenly Constellations in a disciplined circle came shining into the fray. A varied host
maddened the upper air with clamor and with flame: some whose portion
was Boreas, others, the back of Lips in the west, or the eastern zones or
the recesses of the south. The unshaken congregation of the fixed stars

with unanimous acclamation left their places and caught up their travelling fellows. The axis passing through the heaven's hollow and fixed upright in the midst, groaned at the sound. Orion the hunter, seeing these tribes of wild beasts (the heads of Typhoeus), drew his sword; the blade of the Tanagraian brand sparkled bright as its master made ready for attack; his thirsty Dog shooting light from his fiery chin, bubbled up in his starry throat and let out a hot bark, and blew out the steam from his teeth against Typhaon's beasts instead of the usual hare. The sky was full of din, and answering the seven-zoned heaven, the seven throated cry of the Pleiads raised the war-shout from as many throats; and the planets as many again banged out an equal noise. Radiant Ophiuchos, seeing the Giant's direful snaky shape, from his hands so potent against evil shook off the gray coils of the fire-bred serpents, and shot the dappled coiling missile, while tempests roared round his flames—the viper arrows flew slanting and maddened the air. Then the Archer let fly a shaft—that bold comrade of fish-like Aigoceros (Capricorn); the Dragon, divided between the two Bears, and visible within the circle of the Wagon, brandished the fiery trail of the heavenly spine; the Oxherd, Erigone's neighbor, attendant driver of the Wagon, hurled his crook with flashing arm; beside the knee of the Image (Engonasin) and his neighbor the Swan, the starry Lyre presaged the victory of Zeus (*Dionysiaca* 1.175–258, LCL).

The sky war theme, with presumably proper "apocalyptic" touches in terms of specific numbers, witnessed accounts, cast of characters, and the like, was known well enough in antiquity to warrant a rather full scale parody by Lucian (see his, *A True Story* 1.11–29, LCL). However, these stories are surely not "apocalyptic" or "eschatological," for they describe what occurred in the extremely distant past, in prehistoric times, often when human beings had not yet been created.

Such stories of the cosmic situation prior to the creation of human beings function to explain the culturally interpreted cosmic context of human existence. For example: is nature to be subjected to humans, or are humans to submit to the forces of nature? Should people strive to live in harmony with nature or fear nature as a source of evil for humans? What of the forces to evil that emerge in human social (as opposed to personal) interaction, such as genocide, war, chosen-peoplehood, ethnic and racial superiority to the detriment of others—from where do all such social attitudes and activities derive? Stories of cosmic beings in the past will explain the present both to make it understandable and to give it social warrant.

In the book of Revelation where the astral prophet reads the sky in terms of the traditions of Israel, the sky war in question is the celestial conflict between the colossus Michael and the starry Dragon. Traditionally in the region, the well-known constellational colossus that takes on evil is Orion. In the Israelite context, consider the statement in Isa 13:10: "For the stars of the sky and their constellations will not give their light; the sun will be dark at its rising and the moon will not shed its light." The word translated "constellations" here in the RSV is *kesilim* in Hebrew; the word means "strong ones" (see also Job 9:9; 38:31; Amos 5:8). In the ancient Greek version of the Bible this passage from Isaiah is translated as follows: "For the stars of the sky and Orion and the whole array of the sky will not give light; and it will be dark at the rising of the sun, and the moon will not give its light." In this Hellenistic context, Orion is singled out from the rest of the stars of the sky, the celestial army. Of course, according to the traditional Israelite reading of the sky, the sky servant of God ahead of and apart from the rest of the celestial army is Michael (the meaning of his name proclaims God's distinctiveness, since it asks: "Who is like God?"). Michael's battle with the Dragon at the dawn of creation is the Israelite reading of the well known fight between Orion and ancient Scorpio (see Lehmann-Nitsche 1933: 219). Thus Aratus writes:

> The winding River (Eridanus) will straightway sink in fair flowing ocean at the coming of Scorpion, whose rising puts to flight even the mighty Orion. Thy pardon, Artemis (moon), we crave! There is a tale told by the men of old, who said that stout Orion laid hands upon her robe, what time in Chios he was smiting with his strong club all manner of beasts, as a service of the hunt to that King Oenopion. But she forthwith rent in twain the surrounding hills of the island and roused against him another kind of beast—even the Scorpion, who proving mightier wounded him, mighty though he was, and slew him, for that he had vexed Artemis. Wherefore, too, men say that at the rising of the Scorpion in the east, Orion flees at the Western verge (*Phenomenon* 634–641, LCL).

The ancient tale here was of the fight between the strong Orion = sun/light and Scorpio = darkness. The tale was retold in historical times in terms of forces of light and darkness now replicated in constellations (see Brown 1989: 1.69). In this passage, of course, Scorpio keeps Orion at bay. Our astral prophet, however, perceives occurrences and person-ages of the cosmic sphere in terms of Israel's traditions. And perhaps the most explicit evidence for this comes at 12:9. Here the constella-tional Dragon is identified with the ancient Serpent of Genesis 2. And this Draco-Genesis Serpent is then equated with the Devil (in Greek: διάβολος, *diabolos*, meaning "accuser"), and Satan (in Hebrew *Satan*, a Persian loan word referring to a secret agent who tests loyalties for a king, for example, as in Job 1). This character, of course, is well-known from the book of Genesis. And according to Luke, Jesus, too, perhaps in an altered state of awareness like John's, mentioned that he also saw Satan (this Scorpion/Dragon) fall from the sky like lightning (Luke 10:18). From time immemorial, Satan's task has been precisely the task described here as his name: "the deceiver of the whole world." Such deceiving "secret police" were known in John's world. Consider the incidental remark of Epictetus, a first-century Stoic philosopher:

When someone gives us the impression of having talked to us frankly about his personal affairs, somehow or other we are likewise led to tell him our own secrets. . . . In this fashion the rash are ensnared by the soldiers in Rome. A soldier, dressed like a civilian, sits down by your side, and begins to speak ill of Caesar, and then you too, just as though you had received from him some guarantee of good faith in the fact that he began the abuse, tell likewise everything you think. And the next thing is—you are led off to prison in chains (Epictetus, *Discourses* 4.13, 1.5, LCL)

This indeed is how the Dragon is said to function. The motive behind his deceptive tactics is to test the loyalty of those he accuses. And the fact that the Dragon acts to deceive is significant for John, whose task as astral prophet is to allay the deception plaguing his "brothers" by revealing what he sees and experiences.

At what point of history do we stand in the story? The seer sees the Dragon and his sky servants thrown onto the earth as they battle with Michael and his sky servants. But when, according to Israelite tradition, did this actually occur? Since this personage is a celestial being and appears in the Israelite story of the creation as already on the earth when human beings appear, he must have been created with the stars of the sky and subsequently cast down to the earth, where he could attempt to deceive and test the loyalty of those first humans. Consequently, the whole sky war scenario takes us back to the early stages of creation, a time before human beings and the earth itself were created. Like other contemporary astral prophets, such as the author of the book of Daniel or Berossus the Babylonian, John perceives traces of the time before human time in the sky.

Our astral prophet now hears a victory song (12:10–12) acclaiming the joy in the sky thanks to the ejection of the Dragon in antediluvian times. However, the Dragon's dislocation from the sky means calamity for the earth and sea since the Dragon now resides there, even if only for "a little time."

Sky Servants

8.5. Concluding Actions

After the pause for the cosmic acclamation, a second set of actions resumes on earth, beginning with a scenario set up in 12:4. Now it is "meanwhile back with the Woman . . . " The first action of this second set is the Dragon taking up pursuit of the recently Pregnant Woman, this time on earth. We are again reminded of the Woman's location in the wilderness, taken care of by God for three and a half years.

We now find out that the Woman gets to the wilderness on the wings of the great eagle. Boll (1914: 14) notes how Virgo is always winged, while Isis often is. Perhaps the image derives from the winged Babylonian Ishtar. However, since the action is no longer occurring in the sky, Lehmann-Nitsche (1933: 212) suggests "the two wings of the great eagle" here on earth is the wind. The great eagle is the Babylonian Thunderbird (as in the four living creatures), who controls the north-wind. Hence it is on wings of the wind that the woman gets to her refuge in the wilderness (for a whole range of such wings, see the sampling provided by Parpola 1993: 201–2).

The second action scenario (12:15) is the threat against the Woman in the wilderness by a stream from the Dragon's mouth. The scenario is that of a rampaging river of water in a wilderness wadi, much like an arroyo in the U.S. Southwest. Such dry stream beds in the middle of a parched wilderness can become raging torrents should it rain in surrounding highlands or mountains. However, here, before reaching the Woman the river disappears into the earth. Perhaps John wants particularly to underscore how the Woman's safety is guaranteed by God, the controller of the cosmos. The Woman is significant in context not simply because she is, as her constellational name has it, "She Who Gives Birth" to the cosmic Child, but because she likewise has other earthly offspring, as we find out in the next scene.

The third action scenario (12:17) depicts the frustrated Dragon full of fury, on his way to wage an earth war. Against whom? The astral prophet abruptly and surprisingly informs us that the sky Woman has other offspring, called "her seed" (as in the case of Eve in Gen 3:15). These offspring are not prehistoric persons kept with God, but human beings in John's world who keep God's commandments and adhere to the witness of Jesus. However, their relationship to the cosmic sky Woman who gave birth to the cosmic Child enthroned with God before the foundation of the world intimates that these followers of Jesus likewise derive somehow from that ancient period. This is not unlike the Pauline tradition in which God is acknowledged for choosing the followers of Jesus "before the foundation of the world" (Eph 1:4).

Finally, the action pauses with the Dragon at the seashore. In the narrative, the pause focuses attention on the Beasts about to be introduced in the next chapter. In the sky scenario, we find our Dragon constellation setting, hence stretched out along the sky, viewed by the seer along a beach.

9

SECTOR 3 CONTINUED:
ANTEDILUVIAN LAND WARS

13 ¹And I saw a Beast coming up from the sea, having ten horns and seven heads, and on its horns ten diadems, and on its heads a name of blasphemy. ²And the Beast which I saw was similar to a leopard, and its feet like a bear, and its mouth like a lion's mouth. And the Dragon gave it its power and its throne and great authority. ³And one of its heads [was] as though slaughtered unto death, and its injury of death was healed. And the whole earth was astounded after the Beast. ⁴And they prostrated themselves before the Dragon because it gave authority to the Beast, and they prostrated themselves before the Beast saying: "Who [is] like the Beast, and who can do battle with it?" ⁵And it was given a mouth to speak great things and blasphemies, and it was given authority to act for forty-two months. ⁶And it opened its mouth for blasphemies against God, to blaspheme his name and his tent, those tenting in the sky. ⁷And it was given to it to do battle with the holy ones and to conquer them, and it was given to it authority over every tribe and people and tongue and nation. ⁸And they will prostrate themselves to it, all those dwelling on the earth, whose name is not written in the scroll of life of the Lamb slaughtered from the foundation of the world. ⁹If anyone has ears, let him hear.

> ¹⁰If anyone into captivity, into captivity he goes;
> If anyone to be killed by the sword, by the sword he is killed.
> Here is the endurance and the trustworthiness of the holy ones.

¹¹And I saw another Beast coming up from the earth, and it had two horns like a Lamb, and it spoke like a Dragon. ¹²And it exercises all the authority of the first Beast before it. And it makes [it] so that the earth and those dwelling in it prostrate themselves to the first Beast, whose injury of its death was healed. ¹³And it makes great signs, so that it makes fire come down out of the sky into the earth before human beings. ¹⁴And he deceives those dwelling on the earth on account of the signs which it was given to him to do before the Beast, saying to those who dwell on the earth to make an icon for the Beast who has the injury of the sword and lived. ¹⁵And it was given to it to give a sky wind to the icon of the Beast, so that the icon of the Beast might speak and act so that whosoever might not prostrated himself before the icon of the Beast would be killed. ¹⁶And it makes [it] so

that all—the small and the great, the wealthy and the poor, and the free and the slave—they might give to them a mark [branded] on their right hand and on their forehead. [17]And so that no one could buy or sell except having the mark, the name of the Beast or the number of its name. [18]Here is wisdom; the one having understanding let him calculate the number of the Beast, for it is a number of a human. And its number [is] six–hundred sixty-six.

14[1]And I saw and behold the Lamb standing on Mount Zion, and with him one hundred forty-four thousands having his name and the name of his father written on their foreheads. [2]And I heard a voice from the sky like a voice of many waters and like a voice of great thunder, and the voice which I heard like of lyre-singers lyring with their lyres. [3]And they sing as though a new song before the throne and before the four living beings and the elders; and no one could learn the song except the one hundred forty-four thousand, those bought from the earth. [4]These are those who have not been sullied with women, for they are virgins; these are those following the Lamb wherever he goes; these were bought from human beings a first-fruits to God and to the Lamb, [5]And in their mouth there was found no lie; they are blameless. [6]And I saw another sky servant flying in the high-point of the sky, having aeonic good news to announce over those seated upon the earth and over every nation and tribe and tongue and people. [7]Saying in a loud voice: Fear God and give him glory because the hour of his judgment has come, and prostrate yourselves to the one who made the sky and the earth and the sea and the sources of water. [8]And another second [sky servant] followed, saying: "Babylon the great fell, she fell, who gave all the nations to drink from the wine of the anger of her fornication." [9]And another third sky servant followed them saying in a loud voice: "If anyone prostrates himself to the beast and to its icon, and accepts the mark upon his forehead or upon his hand, [10]and he shall drink from the wine of the anger of God poured out undiluted into the cup of his wrath, and he shall be tormented with fire and sulphur before the holy sky servants and before the Lamb. [11]And the smoke of their torment goes up unto aeons of aeons, and they do not have a pause day and night, those prostrating themselves to the Beast and to his icon, and if anyone accept the mark of his name." [12]Here is the endurance of the holy ones, those keeping the commandments of God and the faithfulness of Jesus. [13]And I heard a voice from the sky saying: "Write"; How honorable are the dead who die in the lord from now on; Indeed, says the sky wind, let them take rest from their labors; for their works follow after them. [14]And I saw and behold a white cloud and seated upon the cloud like a son of man, having upon his head a golden wreath and in his hand a sharp Sickle. [15]And another sky servant came out of the temple, shouting in a loud voice to the one sitting on the cloud: Send your Sickle and harvest, because the hour to harvest has come, because the harvest of the earth has become overripe. [16]And the one seated on the cloud cast his Sickle upon the earth and the earth was harvested. [17]And another sky servant came out of the temple in the sky, having also a sharp Sickle. [18]And another sky servant from the altar, having authority over the fire, and he voiced with a loud voice to the one having the sharp Sickle saying: You too send your sharp Sickle and harvest in the bunches of the vine of the earth, because their grapes are ripe. [19]And the sky servant cast his Sickle upon the earth, and he harvested the vines of the earth and he cast into the great wine-press of the anger of God. [20]And the wine-press outside the city was trampled, and blood came out of the wine-press up to the bridle of a horse, for a thousand six–hundred stadia [190 miles].

15[1]And I saw another sign in the sky [that was] great and astonishing, seven sky servants having seven injuries, the last ones, because with them the anger of God is completed. [2]And I saw as a sea of glass mixed with fire and those who conquered over the Beast and over his icon and over the number of his name standing upon the sea of glass, having the lyres of God. [3]And they sing the song of Moses the slave of God and the song of the Lamb saying:

"Great and astonishing [are] your works O Lord God the Almighty;
Just and truthful are your ways, O king of the nations.
[4]"Who will not fear, O Lord, and glorify your name?
Because [you] alone are holy,
Because all the nations will come
And prostrate themselves before you,
Because your just-deeds have been manifested."

[5]And after these things I saw and the temple of the Tent of Witness in the sky opened. [6]And the seven sky servants having the seven injuries went out from the temple, garbed in resplendent pure linen and girded with golden belts around the chest. [7]And one of the four living beings gave to the seven sky servants seven golden bowls full of the anger of the God living unto the aeons of aeons. [8]And the temple was filled with smoke from the glory of God and from his power, and no one was able to enter into the temple until the seven injuries on the seven sky servants would be carried out.

16[1]And I heard a loud voice from the temple saying to the seven sky servants: Go and pour out the seven bowls of the anger of God into the earth. [2]And the first went off and poured out its bowl into the earth; and there occurred a bad and wicked ulcer upon the human beings having the mark of the Beast and prostrating themselves to his icon. [3]And the second poured out his bowl into the sea; and there occurred blood as of a dead person, and every living soul died, those in the sea. [4]And the third poured out its bowl into the rivers and sources of water; and they turned into blood. [5]And I heard the sky servant of the waters saying:

"Just are you, O he who is and who was, O holy one, because you judged things.

[6]"Because they poured out the blood of the holy ones and of the prophets
and you have given them blood to drink;
They are worthy."

[7]And I heard the altar saying:
"Indeed, O Lord God, the Almighty,
Truthful and just are your judgments."

[8]And the fourth poured out its bowl upon the sun; and it was given it to burn human beings with fire. [9]And human beings were burned with a great fire, and they blasphemed the name of God having authority over these injuries, and they did not have a change [of heart] to give him glory. [10]And the fifth poured out its bowl upon the throne of the Beast; and its kingdom became darkened, and they chewed their tongues due to the pain. [11]And they blasphemed the God of the sky because of their pain and because of their sores, and they did not have a change [of heart] from their deeds. [12]And the sixth poured out its bowl upon the great river Euphrates; and its water dried up so that the way of the kings from the rising of the sun might be made ready. [13]And I saw from the mouth of the Dragon and from the mouth of the Beast and from the mouth of the false prophet three unclean sky winds as frogs. [14]For they are sky winds of demons doing signs, which come upon the kings of the whole inhabited world, to gather them for war on the great day of God the Almighty. [15]Behold I am coming like a thief. How honorable is the one who watches and keeps his garments so that he not walk naked and they see his shame. [16]And he gathered them into the place called in Hebrew Harmagedon. [17]And the seventh poured out its bowl upon the air and a great voice went out from the temple from the throne saying: It has happened. [18]And there occurred lightnings and voices and thunders and a great earthquake happened such as did not happen from when a human being happened on the earth such an earthquake so great. [19]And the Great City became into three parts, and the cities of the nations collapsed; and Baby-

lon the great was remembered before God to give it the cup of the wine of the anger of his wrath. [20]And every island fled, and mountains were not found. [21]And great hail like a talent (57 lb.) fell down from the sky upon human beings; and human beings blasphemed God on account of the injury of hail, because exceedingly great is that injury.

As we have seen, the opening cosmic scenario of Sector 3 quickly accounted for the presence on earth of the deceiving Dragon. Now John presents the consequences of this presence. The Dragon recruits subordinates, a pair of Beasts, to assist him in his treachery. These Beasts are first described as they carry out their task upon the earth. The first Beast is a constellation rising over the sea, hence the sea Beast. The second is a constellation rising over the land, the land Beast. In their configuration, they emerge as typically antediluvian beings that have impact on earth dwellers, as ch. 13 describes. In response to the presentation of these Beasts, the cosmic Lamb rises over Mount Zion with his entourage. Then seven sky servants perform tasks of judgment immediately before the presentation of the third sign of this sector: the seven injuries or plagues marking the restoration of God's honor. At the conclusion of this sector, we are told that the focus of these injuries had been the great city, Babylon (16:19), the first postdeluvian city on earth according to Israelite tradition.

Since the scenario in this sector begins with the period before the completion of creation and concludes with the period marking the outset of the human condition as we experience it, the prophet clearly has this pre-Babel period of the human story in mind. For John, as for any Israelite, this was not prehistory. Rather, it was a period marked by conditions qualitatively different from those after Babel, yet in some way continuing to impact on us. In that pre-present period, as we read in Genesis, our ancestors were created by God, interacted with the cosmic Dragon, were ejected from Eden, had sexual relations with angels, became increasingly wicked with very few exceptions, and were ultimately destroyed by God with a universal flood. After the Flood, the first common task of the survivors was to build a city, Babel, with the purpose of climbing beyond the vault of the sky! Such was history as known to John's tradition.

With his knowledge of this tradition, John now makes known the cosmic, celestial influences that account for what happened to our ancestors. Why bother describing this situation from the distant past? Obviously it is because what happened then in some way continues to impact the present.

9.1. THE TWO BEASTS

An attentive reading of the previous passage reveals how the author punctuates his narrative by marking off each new sight with the phrase "and I saw" (or a variant of it). If we take him at his word, the astral prophet saw nine distinctive scenes:

the Beast over the sea (13:1)
the Beast over the land (13:11)
the cosmic Lamb (14:1)
another sky servant at the center of the sky (14:6)
a sickle-wielding human-like being on a cloud (14:14)
another (the third) sign of this sector (15:1)
a sea of glass (15:2)
the sky temple (15:5)
and finally three unclean sky winds from the Dragon and Beasts (16:13).

The first two sights are two constellations, the first rising along the horizon of the sea (13:1), the second arising along the horizon of the land (13:11). The constellations are both designated as having the form of "Beasts." After each is presented, its relationship to the Dragon of the previous chapter is specified, and then the functions performed by each are listed. Since the relationship of these Beasts with the Dragon is significant, it is important to note once more that the location of this scenario is in the southern sky.

9.1.1. The Beast Rising Over the Sea

The author describes his first vision as that of "a Beast coming up from the sea." Of course, there is a sea monster in the southern sky. Manilius describes it as follows:

Then it was that Jupiter set up the constellation of the Altar, which of all altars shines brightest even now. Next to it Cetus undulates its scaly body; it rises aloft upon a spiral of coils and splashes with such a belly as drove the sea beyond its proper shores when it appeared from the waves to destroy the daughter of Cepheus exposed upon the cliffs (Manilius, *Astronomica* 1.431–437, LCL).

Commentators on Manilius are quick to point out that the constellation Cetus is located not next to the Altar, but on the other side of the sky (Goold, Lel, pp. xxx–xxxi and 38, note a). Yet the constellation rising over the horizon of the sea here best fits the traditional, celestial *Sea-monster* or Cetus (Babylonian: Tiamatu, Ugaritic: Yamm, Hebrew: Tehom, Berossos: Thauatth). In the ancient eastern Mediterranean, this celestial being represented the chaos before creation, "and secondarily, the reduplication of this in the dark and stormy sea whose tempests, clouds and gales form the brood of Tiamat, which in Euphratean myth were especially regarded as seven Evil Spirits of great and malignant potency" (Brown 1899: 1.89). Thus the being has seven heads. Brown summarizes the character of this constellation:

> Tiamat and her brood, as of course, come into conflict with the bright powers, Sun-god and Moon-god; and the victory of Merodakh over her forms one of the staple subjects of Euphratean Hymns, and is reduplicated in Syrian regions in the triumph of Perseus over the Sea-Dragon (Ketos), a contest localized at Joppa. The sickle-shaped scimitar of Marduk (crescent-moon) is also reproduced in the Semitic *khereb*, Greek: *harpe*, with which Barsav–Perseus is armed. This is ever a potent weapon against the darkness-powers. Tiamat is the head of the *tanninim* ("sea-monsters, whales"), and is called in Akkadian: *Bis-bis* ("Dragon"), Assyrian: *Mamlu*, and *Rahabu*, Hebrew: *Rahabh* ("sea-monster," hence "crocodile," and used symbolically for "Egypt"). . . . *Bis-bis* is "the Fiery-one," the Livyathan, who "maketh the deep to boil like a pot" (Job 41:31). And, as illustrated by the root *bis*, the idea of moral evil and wicked hostility to the gods and the good, is also inextricably connected with Tiamat and her brood. She is further reduplicated in *Hydra*, and the seven Evil Spirits appear to be reduplicated, to some extent, in certain southern constellations. . . . They habitually live "in the lower part of heaven" [= nocturnal southern sky] and devise evil "at sunset." One is like a Sea-monster (= *Cetus*), another a Scorpion (= *Scorpio*), a third a Leopard (= *Therion, Lupus*), a fourth a Serpent (= *Hydra*), a fifth a raging Dog (= *Canis Major*), an animal disliked by the Semite, a sixth, "the evil Wind," the "Storm-bird" (= *Corvus*) (Brown 1899: 1.89–90).

If we add to this listing the constellation depicting a person with a wounded and healed head (noted in 13:3), we have seven constellations replicating the traditional seven Evil Spirits of this Beast. In fact, in Babylonian texts, Orion is called "the (Star of the) One Cleft by the Weapon" (McKay 1973: 56) and the "Lord of the River Bank" (Brown 1899: 1.92). Interestingly, Orion "is slain (devoured) by the Monster of darkness and the deep (*Cetus*), at the Ocean-stream; and this is constellationally reduplicated in *Orion*, 'Lord of the River Bank,' on the margin of *Eridanus*, holding up his spear against the advancing *Sea-monster*, which touches the *Stream* on its further side" (Brown 1899: 1.93). It would seem that the Beast's wounded head here results from its having swallowed the "One Cleft by the Weapon," which then emerged at its head, to be revivified, to the amazement of "the whole earth"! On the other hand, Lehmann-Nitsche (1933: 223) believes that the seven heads are a round number, deriving from the tradition that a Dragon-related sea Beast must be many-headed. The ten horns refer to dorsal protuberances, like the protruding fins or bumps on the back of a crocodile. Each of these horns was crowned with a diadem. The Beast itself had seven heads inscribed with a word or words insulting to God—for that is what a blasphemy is.

This Beast is described by John as "similar to a leopard, and its feet like a bear, and its mouth like a lion's mouth" (13:2). In the rather stable Islamic tradition rooted in the Mesopotamian region, Cetus (*Al-Qitus*) was often depicted as an oriental winged Dragon. On the celestial globe described by Savage-Smith, Cetus "has a snarling dog's head, bird's feet, and a feathered fish tail" (Savage-Smith 1985: 187). Ancient Mesopotamian artifacts depict walking serpents with seven heads and rays or protuberances from their back (see Black and Green 1992: 64). Modern readers often find this combination of animal forms disconcerting. Yet in the first-century Mediterranean world, it was quite understandable. Specifically, the description is typical of the way animals were thought to have looked before the Flood. Consider now the perceptions of Philo of Byblos, born in the second half of the first century A.D.:

> Greatest Astarte and Zeus, called both Demarous and Adodos, kings of gods, were ruling over the land with the consent of Kronos. Astarte placed upon her own head a bull's head [= horns of Hathor] as an emblem of kingship. While traveling around the world, she discovered a star which had fallen from the sky. She took it up and consecrated it in Tyre, the holy island. The Phoenicians say that Astarte is Aphrodite.

> Also when Kronos was traveling around the world, he gave the kingdom of Attica to his own daughter, Athena. At the occurrence of a fatal plague, Kronos immolated his only son to his father Ouranos and circumcised himself, forcing the allies who were with him to do the same. And not long after this, when another of his children died, one born of Rhea and called Muth, he made him an object of worship. The Phoenicians call him Death and Pluto. In addition, Kronos gave the city Byblos to the goddess Baaltis, who is also Dione, and the city Beirut to Poseidon and to the Kabeiri, the Hunters and the Fishers, who made the relics of Ponto an object of worship in Beirut.

> Before this, the god Taautos, imitating the visages of his fellow gods, Kronos, Dagon and the rest, engraved the sacred forms of the letters. He also invented as royal emblems for Kronos four eyes, on the front and in the rear, two awake, and two closed restfully, and upon the shoulders, four wings, two as if fluttering, and two as if relaxed. This is a symbol since Kronos was watchful even when in repose, and was in repose even when awake; similarly the wings were symbolic because he flew while at rest and was at rest when flying. Each of the other gods had two wings protruding from his shoulders, since they in fact flew with Kronos. In addition, he also had two wings on his head, one for the mind, which is the supreme authority, and one for the faculty of perception (*The Phoenician History* Frag. 2 cited with alterations from Attridge and Oden, pp. 54–59).

Now consider Berossos of Babylon, an author who dates to the third century B.C. Brown (1899: 1.112) calls Berossos' description as relating to "the mythical and mystical Scorpion-and-Dragon period." This, of course, perfectly describes the situation that begins to unfold from Rev 12 on:

> There was a time, he said, in which everything was darkness and water, and at that time animate beings having strange and grotesque forms were bred. For two-winged human beings were born, as well as some with four wings and two faces. While they had a single body, they had two heads, male and female, along with double sexual organs, masculine and feminine. And other sorts of human beings were born, some having the legs and horns of goats, others with horses' hooves, some with bodies composed of horses' hind quarter and human being's from which are the shape of Centaurs.
>
> Bulls likewise were bred having the heads of human beings; and dogs with fourfold bodies, terminating in their extremities with the tails of fishes. And dog-headed horses and human beings and other living beings having the heads and even the bodies of horses, tails of fish and still other living beings having the shapes of every sort of Beast. In addition to this, there were fish and serpents and snakes and other living beings full of marvel and having the combined appearance of one another, whose likenesses (= icons) have been set up in the temple of Belos (*Babyloniaka* 6, translated from Jacoby 1958: Part III, C, 370–71).

Finally, for the Greek tradition, a passage from Nonnos' *Dionysiaca*:

> Now Typhoeus shifted to the rocks, leaving the air, to flog the sea. He grasped and shook the peak of Corycios (a rock of Asia Minor near Erythrai), and crushing the flood of the river that belongs to Cilicia, joined Tarsos and Cydnos (river through Tarsos) together in one hand; then hurled a volley of cliffs upon the mustered waves of the brine. As the Giant advanced with feet trailing in the briny Flood, his bare loins were seen dry through the water, which broke heavy against his mid-thigh crashing and booming; his serpents afloat sounded the charge with hissings from brine-beaten throats, and spitting poison led the attack upon the sea. There stood Typhon in the fish-giving sea, his feet firm in the depths of the weedy bottom, his belly in the air and crushed in clouds; hearing the terrible roar from the mane-bristling lions of his giant's head, the sea-lion lurked in the oozy gulf. There was no room in the deep for all its phalanx of leviathans, since the Earthborn monster covered a whole sea, larger than the land, with flanks that no sea could cover. The seals bleated; the dolphins hid in the deep water; the manyfooted squid, a master of craft, weaving his trailing web of crisscross knots, stuck fast on his familiar rock, making his limbs look like a pattern on the stone. All the world was a-tremble: the love maddened lamprey drawn by her passion for the serpent's bed, shivered under the god-desecrating breath of these seafaring serpents. The waters piled up and touched Olympos with precipitous seas; as the streams mounted on high, the bird never touched by rain found the

sea his neighbor and washed himself. Typhoeus, holding a counterfeit of the deep-sea trident, with one earthshaking flip from the enormous hand broke off an island at the edge of the continent which is the kerb of the brine, circled it round and round, and hurled the whole thing like a ball. And while the Giant waged his war, his hurtling arms drew near to the stars, and obscured the sun, as they attacked Olympos, and cast the precipitous crag (*Dionysiaca* 1.258–293, LCL).

The first Beast is clearly an antediluvian being. What of his cosmic role? John informs us that this Beast receives the Dragon's power, throne, and great authority. It thus functions as vice regent for the Dragon. Since we are in the pre-Flood period, it is the antediluvians of "the whole earth" who now pay homage to the Dragon for giving authority to the Beast, and to the Beast for its undoubted cosmic power. The rhetorical question "Who is like the Beast?" is like the question-name *Michael*, meaning "Who is like God?" The question-name recalls the previous sky battle and anticipates another one. Since John mentions this Beast's feet and mouth (13:2), he now tells about what the Beast is authorized to say (mouth) and do (feet). The passive voice "it was given" repeated four times points back to the authorizing agent, the Dragon, functioning (deceptively) as God since normally, passive voice statements among Israelites in our period have God as their implied subject. The Beast speaks, revealing wonders to astound his audience, and insults to dishonor God. It is to carry on in this way for three and a half years, as previously noted.

But its primary role is to do battle with the celestial "holy ones," with a view to conquering them (13:7), as well as to control the behavior of "the whole earth," here described as "every tribe and people and tongue and nation." Once more we are told of the homage paid to the Beast, so that the author might note the fact that those doing homage to the Beast are not written in the Lamb's scroll of life, the scroll containing God's decrees for humankind.

9.1.2. The Beast Rising Over the Land

John next sees a constellation rising over the land which he recognizes as another Beast, a land Beast. If the first Beast is the viceregent of the Dragon, this Beast is a sidekick of the sea Beast. It always accompanies the Beast from over the sea; eventually it assumes the role of a "false prophet" (see 16:13; 19:20). What of the sky situation of this personage?

There is a constellation in the southern sky called simply "The Beast" (Greek: θηρίον, *thērion*). For example, Aratus writes: "He (Centaur) ever seems to stretch his right hand toward the round Altar, but through his hand is drawn and firmly grasped another sign—the Beast, for so men of old have named it" (Aratus, *Phenomena* 439–441, LCL). In later times, this constellation came to be called the Wolf (*Lupus*).

Now as John sees it, this constellation that rises over the land has two lamb's horns. In order to figure out what sort of beast this might be, Boll begins with Gunkel's observation that these horns would point to some neutral ancient mythical tradition and not to some power of deception. To this he adds a citation referring to the Orphic Zeus, the full image of the supreme God (found in the famous great fragment 123 Abel, v. 16; Greek text in Boll 1914: 43): "On either side two golden horns like a bull's (horns), at the rising and at the setting, the pathways of the celestial deities, the eyes of the sun and the shining of the Moon." The mention of the "ways of the celestial deities" refers to the Orphic Milky Way, which in fact cuts the Zodiac into two opposing parts. While this might be far from what our astral prophet has in mind, it does allow us to come closer to the origin of his imagery. Because of its two horns which point to the place of rising and of setting, the Lamb can be designated as "first and last." In this regard, the lamb-like horns of this second Beast which rises over the land suggest the rising and setting of some earthly power.

Along with this reference to the places of rising and setting, the word "horn" (Greek κέρας, *keras*) has a range of meanings, for it can mean a "wing" in a military formation; from this usage it can refer to the "end" of the formation, hence conclusion. And in Greek educated circles the "wings" or "horns" could refer to what Latin speakers called *cornua* ("horns"), namely, the beginning and end of a scroll, including our astral prophet's sky, which was like a scroll (see Boll 1914: 43).

But a look at Dan. 8 points to the certainty of the previous line of interpretation. In that vision, a single-horned "he-goat of he-goats from the west" vanquishes the ram, "and the he-goat grew exceedingly great: and when he was strong, his great horn was broken; and four other horns rose up in its place toward the four winds of the sky. And out of one of them came forth one strong horn, and it grew very great toward the south and the east and the north" (Dan 8:8–9 LXX). The four horns in Daniel designated four kingdoms, according to the four directions of the sky. And like Daniel's Lamb, the Beast rising over the sea and its companion Beast ruled the whole inhabited world (cf. 13:12), the region from the rising and to the setting. In the original text of Daniel (8:4) the two horns of the ram butt against three sides: west, north, and south. This is rather confusing; hence the ancient Greek version (LXX) makes four heavenly directions out of the scene (and two at a time, that is east + north and west + south). Theodotion's Greek translation has "the sea and the north and the south," hence only two celestial directions, while some manuscripts add two more sky directions. It seems the ancient scribes who handed down Daniel felt the need to find some agreement between the horns and the heavenly directions (see Boll 1914: 42–43).

In John's narrative, the land Beast serves as a veritable surrogate of the sea Beast. And it coerces all the antediluvian inhabitants of the land to pay homage now to the sea Beast, just as the sea Beast had them pay homage to the Dragon. Further, this Beast is given the power (presumably from the Dragon) to perform great signs, specifically bringing fire from the sky. The land Beast's ability to perform signs make people think it is a prophet (see 16:13; 19:20). It thus convinces earthlings to make an icon for (one of the heads of) the sea Beast. Furthermore, this beast is empowered to brand the right hand and forehead of all earthlings, regardless of their status in order to control their buying and selling activity. While tattooing of humans for a variety of reasons was far more prevalent in Hellenism, religious branding on the forehead and hand was also known (see Jones 1987: 152). A well known instance of such branding is found in the third book of Maccabees. There we are told how Ptolemy Philopator forced all inhabitants of Alexandria, Judeans included, to be enrolled in a census and "that those who were enrolled should be branded by fire on their bodies with an ivy leaf, the emblem of Dionysius" (3 Macc 2:29, *OTP*).

Here in Revelation, the mark consists, we are told, of the name/numeral of the sea Beast. In Greek as well as in Semitic languages of the period, letters of the alphabet had to serve as numerals. Thus every name was a set of numerals, and every set of numerals could equal a name. And the numeral in question, equating to the name of the sea Beast was 666. It seems that all commentaries on this passage provide information about whose name in antiquity could equal to the sum of 666. For example, using Aramaic letters, CAESAR NERO would count out as follows: ק=100, ס=60, ר=200, נ=50, ר=200, ו=6, נ=50, with the grand total of 666 (see Ford 1975: 226–30). The author notes that the numeral was a human one, hence the commentators' quest for a name totaling the number in question. However, a "human number" might equally refer to a non-divine number, a non-revealed number, a number known to humans.

Perhaps it might be useful to note here that the study of numerals was basic to ancient astronomics. Astronomers were often called mathematicians (see Sextus Empiricus' essay: *Against Mathematicians*, LCL). For example, the handbook by Theon of Smyrna, entitled *Mathematics Useful for Understanding Plato*, has three parts: arithmetic, music, and astronomics. In the arithmetic section, numerals are rated by quality as odd, even, composite, oblong, triangular, square, circular, spherical and so forth (for the cosmological implications of these numbers, see Critchlow 1976: 57–73 who demonstrates how this traditional evaluation of numbers lay behind patterns of Islamic and later Gothic architecture). The numeral in question here, 666, is a triangular number. Theon writes:

By adding no longer just the evens alone or the odds alone, but the evens and the odds, we will obtain the triangular numbers. The series of the even and the odd numbers is 1, 2, 3, 4, 5, 6, 7, 8, 9, 10; in adding them together we form the triangular numbers. The first is unity or monad, because if it is not so in act it is so in power, being the principle of all numbers. If the number 2 is added to it, the result is the triangular number 3. If 3 is added to this triangular number, 6 is obtained, and by adding 4 to this, the result is 10. If 5 is added to this you will have 15, to this add 6 and you will have 21, to which if your add 7 you will have 28 which, augmented by 8 becomes 36. And 36 augmented by 9 becomes 45. Add 10 and you will have 55. And this continues to infinity. Now it is evident that these numbers are triangular according to the figure obtained by adding the successive gnomons [= natural series of numbers] to the first numbers. The triangular numbers obtained by addition will then be 3, 6, 10, 15, 21, 28, 36, 45, 55 and so forth (*Mathematics Useful for Understanding Plato* 1.19, trans. R. and D. Lawlor 22–23).

Now 666 is a triangular number; it is the sum of all numbers from 1 to 36. And 36 is itself a triangular number, the sum of all numbers from 1 to 8, the number of heavens and of totality.

If we remain in the sky and search for a figure that fits this triangular number, the obvious candidate is the constellation called Triangle (or Deltoton). Aratus writes:

There is also another sign, fashioned near, below Andromeda, Deltoton, drawn with three sides whereof two appear equal but the third is less, yet very easy to find, for beyond many is it endowed with stars. Southward a little from Deltoton are the stars of the Ram (*Phenomena* 233–237, LCL).

Image 5: This second-first century B.C. neo-Punic (= Phoenician) stele, now kept in the British Museum, depicting the celestial entities: Sun, Moon, and Deltoton (= Triangle) flanked by two stars, over the Goddess Tannit flanked by Caducei. By the Hellenistic period, Tannit was identified with Astarte and Aphrodite/Venus. Her symbol, the Triangle, was a regular Phoenician sky symbol, frequently depicted on votive steles and in the shape of the top of the votive steles themselves; see Berthier's essay in Berthier and Charlier 1955: 179–219.

As to the meaning of this triangle, Brown notes:

> Not without careful design has this Triangle been placed with the family group of Phoenician divinities. It is an exact celestial reproduction of the sacred pyramidal monoliths, specimens of which still exist in Kypros (Cyprus). . . . In all regions within the sphere of Phoenician influence the sacred Stone occupies a most prominent place, and actually represents both god and goddess (Brown 1900: 2.51).

He goes on to note how the Phoenicians spread their pyramidal stone and pillar cult to Greece. Both Tacitus and Maximus of Tyre speak of Aphrodite (i.e., Tannit) of Paphos as represented by a pyramidic stone, while Pausanius saw a similar stone near Sikyon, which stood for Zeus Meilichios. "Rock" (= Tsur or Tyre), standing for the pyramidal triangle, was a divine appellation in Syria and Israel (Brown, loc. cit.).

Now if we attempt to make a triangle of pyramidal form out of the numbers in question, it would have a characteristic kite shape composed of right- and left-handed constituent triangles (see Critchlow 1976: 36). And the resulting shape, deriving from two juxtaposed triangles to give a three-dimensional, pyramidal effect, very well fit Aratus' description of Deltoton as a triangle with two equal sides and narrower base:

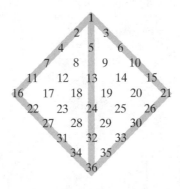

Now if we add the numbers along each side we get:

    1 + 2 + 4 + 7 + 11 + 16 = 41
    1 + 3 + 6 + 10 + 15 + 21 = 56
    16 + 22 + 27 + 31 + 34 + 36 = 166
    21 + 26 + 30 + 33 + 35 + 36 = 181

Now add the numbers down the center and across the middle:

    1 + 5 + 13 + 24 + 32 + 36 = 111
    16 + 17 + 18 + 19 + 20 + 21= 111

Giving the grand total of 666.

Hyginus states that "it is thought that Mercury situated the Triangle above the head of Aries so that the Triangle would by its brilliance signal the location of Aries, and so that forms the first letter of the name of Jupiter in Greek, Dios [Διός = gen. of Ζεύς]" (*Astronomia* 2.19 ed. A. Le Boeuffle, Belles Lettres 57).

This simple triangle consisting of eight numbers per side, totaling 666, looks as follows:

```
                        1
                     2     3
                  4     5     6
               7     8     9    10
            11    12    13    14    15
         16    17    18    19    20    21
      22    23    24    25    26    27    28
   29    30    31    32    33    34    35    36
```

The point is, whether we take the first shape of the pyramid (adjacent triangles) standing for traditional Phoenician deities or the second shape of the plain triangle standing for Zeus, the constellation in question would be an idolatrous sign. What makes these human numbers is that they are not infinite; rather they are limited and finite, used by people for their purposes.

If indeed the author is viewing the Triangle in the sky, he would find the cosmic Lamb quite at hand, as he does indeed turn to that being once more.

9.2. THE COSMIC LAMB ONCE MORE

Although the author does not note the point, it would seem that the Lamb is certainly the same one presented in the previous sector of our tour (5:6, 12). However, the scenario here is quite different from the earlier one. For we are not considering the throne of God and its attendant personnel. Rather we are regarding the situation in the sky early on in the process of God's creation of the universe, the antediluvian period. Furthermore, the Lamb is presented in a quite distinct way. For the first time in this work, this being is presented as "the Lamb slaughtered from the foundation of the world."

Again note the chronological reference to the period even before the Flood, to the time before creation itself. As noted in the tour of Sector 2, the cosmic Lamb refers to the constellation Aries, situated in the sky with its head twisted one-hundred-and-eighty degrees, looking back at Taurus. Only a slaughtered lamb with broken neck could turn its head in that fashion. Thus Manilius describes Aries in his poem: "Resplendent in his golden fleece, first place holder Aries looks backward admiringly at Taurus rising" (*Astronomica* 1.263–264, LCL). Here this cosmic Lamb contrasts with one of the seven heads of the Beast which was likewise slaughtered (13:3). Furthermore, given the preeminence of Aries in the zodiac sequence in vogue during Hellenistic times, it is not surprising that Mediterranean high gods (e.g., Anu, Zeus) were the special patron-divinities of Aries (Brown 1899: 1.336). So also with the God of Israel's traditions. He too singles out the cosmic Lamb, as we have previously seen. And since God created the sky before the earth, this Aries is the Lamb slaughtered from before the foundation of the world.

The scenario constituting our seer's third vision here is the cosmic Lamb situated over Mount Zion. The Lamb, as an honorable being, has a large entourage, here numbered at 144,000 beings. These beings are branded with the Lamb's name and that of his patron-Father, undoubtedly as a counterfoil to those branded with the name of the Beast in the previous scenario. John reports, for the first time in this sector, sky voices, described as a loud waterfall and very loud thunder. The sky voices turn out to be a choir of 144,000 voices in the sky, singing before the throne, the four living beings, and the decans round about the throne. This singing entourage of the Lamb is located in the sky. This detail, then, alerts us to the fact that the Lamb and Mount Zion are both located in the sky. The locale for the whole scenario, then, is the celestial Mount Zion.

Again, music in the sky is something to be expected, much like the Greek harmony of the spheres. In the Israelite tradition, "The skies declare the glory of God; the firmament proclaims the work of his hands. Day to day utters speech, and night to night proclaims knowledge. There are no speeches or words in which their voices are not heard. Their voice has gone out into all the earth, and their words to the ends of the inhabited world" (Psalm 19:1–4 LXX). That the singing sounds like thunder points to a contemporary interpretation of the phenomenon of thunder. For example, in the Gospel of Eve, "the sound of thunder" is the vehicle of articulate revelation "on a high mountain," from "a tall man" (Hennecke and Schneemelcher 1.241).

That "no one could learn that song . . . " perhaps intimates that only the 144,000 understood it, not unlike that visionary who "was caught up into Paradise and heard things which are not to be told, that no mortal is permitted to repeat" (2 Cor 12:4). As I mentioned previously, the ancients believed humans could not hear the music of the spheres, just as they cannot look directly on the sun. Furthermore, according to Pythagorean traditions, celestial music cannot be heard since humans are endowed with mortal ears, but it can be perceived by the pure souls wandering upon the light-filled heights of the sky, hence in altered states of awareness.

In the world of John, the personages who were known to have been "defiled with women" were sky servants. This tradition likewise recalls the antediluvian situation of humankind, as noted in Gen 6:1–4 and again articulated in 1 Enoch 7:1–6. In 1 Enoch 6 we are given the names of the twenty sky servants who head groups of ten sky servants (thus two-hundred in all), who descend to earth:

> Those two hundred and their leaders all took for themselves wives from all that they chose; and they began to go in to them, and to defile themselves with them and they began to teach them sorcery and spell-binding and the cutting of roots; and they showed them herbs. And they became pregnant by them and bore giants three thousand cubits high who were born and multiplied on the earth according to the kind of their childhood, and growing up according to the kind of their adolescence, and they were devouring the labor of all the sons of men and men were unable to supply them. But the giants conspired to slay men, and to devour them. And they began to sin and to . . . against all birds and Beasts of the earth, and reptiles which creep upon the earth and creatures in the waters, and in the heaven, and the fish of the sea, and to devour the flesh of one another, and they were drinking blood. Then the earth made the accusation against the wicked, concerning everything which was done upon it (cited from Milik 1976: 151).

We are further informed about these sky servants and their human wives, for example, in 1 Enoch 8:3–4:

> Shemichazah taught spell binding and the cutting of roots. Hermoni taught the loosing of spells, magic, sorcery, and skill. Baraqel taught the signs of thunders. Kokabel taught the signs of the stars. Zeqel taught the signs of lightning flashes. Artaqoph taught the signs of the earth. Shamshiel taught the signs of the sun. Shahriel taught the signs of the moon. And they all began to reveal secrets to their wives. And because part of humankind was perishing from the earth, their cry was going up to the sky (Milik 1976: 158).

What these sky servants did provoked a reaction from the four chief sky servants (archangels) in the sanctuary of the sky, "Michael, Shariel, Raphael, and Gabriel." These complain to God how one of their fellows "made known the eternal mysteries which were kept in the sky, so that the experts among the sons of man should practice them. And you see what Shemichazah has done, to whom you gave authority to be king over all his companions. And they have gone to the daughters of men of the earth, and slept with them, having defiled themselves by females . . . " (1 Enoch 9:6–8, cited from Milik 1976: 158).

The seer thus sees the Lamb's entourage consisting of those sky servants who did not cross cosmic boundaries to defile themselves with human females to produce offspring who are gigantic beings. But they did descend to earth at that time hence they were "bought from the earth," "from among human beings." Since they did not intermingle with humans, they were not like their deviant colleagues, who are trounced by Michael and his sky hosts.

9.3. Six Sky Servants Plus One

The seer's fourth vision in this sector begins with the first of a series of seven sky servants. This sky servant appears at the zenith of the sky with a message called "aeonic good news." An "aeon" is a cosmic time period. His audience includes both those seated over the earth and those dwelling on the earth. The former cosmically control the earth. The interest in celestial phenomena controlling human nations, tongues, tribes, and peoples resulted in celestial geography (see p. 103 above). Goold (1977: xci–xcii) offers a summary of Manilius' zodiacal geography (*Astronomica* 4.744–817) as follows:

> The Greek astrologers contradict one another to a degree one would have thought positively embarrassing. Manilius's arrangement is as follows, agreements with Dorotheus of Sidon (the only rival with whom he has much in common) being indicated by asterisks:

Aries:	Hellespont (*which it swam*); Propontis; Syria; Persia; Egypt.
Taurus:	Scythia; Asia (*because of Mount Taurus*); Arabia.
Gemini:	Euxine; Thrace; India.
Cancer:	Ethiopia.*
Leo:	Phrygia* (*because of Cybele's lion*); Cappadocia; Armenia; Bithynia*; Macedonia.*
Virgo:	Rhodes*; Ionia*; Greece*; Caria.
Libra:	Italy.*
Scorpius:	Carthage*; Libya* (*land of reptiles*); Hammonia*; Cyrene; Sardinia and other islands.
Sagittarius:	Crete*; Sicily; Magna Graecia.
Capricorn:	Spain; Gaul; Germany.
Aquarius:	Phoenicia; Tyre; Cilicia; Lycia.
Pisces:	Euphrates; Tigris; Red Ocean*; Parthia; Bactria; Asiatic Ethiopia; Babylon; Susa; Nineveh.

Earth's inhabitants are presented in the usual categories favored by our seer and deriving from the book of Daniel. The categories include: nation (based on birth), tribe (based on family of orientation), tongue (based on language group), people (based on shared customs). Thus the first two categories are rooted in the social interpretation of the procreative process, on ascribed status. The last two derive from the people among whom and with whom one lives, that is, the common social system that endows language and customs with meaning. The ancients believed that family and place of origin determined what sort of a person one was, and sky lore did much to emphasize this point.

The message proclaimed throughout the cosmos by this sky servant ran as follows: Because the hour of judgment has come, God should be shown reverence and honor. First of all, note that since we are in the realm of the sky, the reverence and honor to be shown God have nothing to do with Israel's history. The perspective is not particularistic, but universalistic. It is God as creator of all that exists who is the object of this respect. And if judgment is to take place, it will not be in terms of God's covenant, God's laws, God's revelation, or anything else of the sort most Bible readers are used to supplying. This is because we are still in the antediluvian period and its immediate consequences, namely, in the period from Eden to Babel.

The next sky servant indicates as much by making known the first phase of the proclaimed judgment: the fall of "Babylon the Great." This is the first mention of Babylon in the work. And like many of the features of the astral prophet's scenarios, this one is quite abrupt. It would seem to be of great importance to note that the Greek word translated "Babylon" is "Babel" in Hebrew. The words refer to identical realities. In Gen 11, immediately after the Flood, the first common project of humanity, of "all the nations," is the building of the city called Babel/Babylon, with an outstanding feature, a tower with its top in the sky (Gen 11:4). Since all the previous scenarios deal with antediluvians and their fate, Babylon/Babel points to the first tasks of human beings after the Flood. The seer will eventually report much more information about the quality of this Babylon/Babel. Here he simply notes its idolatry. Fornication in the Israelite tradition is a usual synonym for idolatry. Babylon the Great is accused of having "all the nations" drink of her intoxicating (= wine) and vindication provoking (= anger) idolatry.

A third sky servant appears, announcing a further dimension of the proclaimed judgment. The "if . . . then . . . " form is a usual one underscoring a tit for tat punishment. Literally, those who have drunk Babylon's wine of the anger of fornication will have to drink God's wine of anger from the cup of his wrath. Dishonoring God by idolatry demands recompense, if only so that God's honor be maintained. The idolatry is indicated in the "if" clause: those who have worshipped the

Beast and its icon and allowed themselves to be branded (the behavior noted in Rev 13). The satisfaction is the "cup of wrath," consisting in a destiny of torment by fire and sulphur.

Fire and sulphur (a synonym is brimstone) falling from the sky is the typical punishment for heinous criminals, beginning with the inhospitable inhabitants of Sodom and Gomorrah: "Then Yahweh rained on Sodom and Gomorrah brimstone and fire from Yahweh out of the sky" (Gen 19:24; see Ezek 38:20; Ps 11:6). Luke notes this tradition too: "but on the day when Lot went out from Sodom fire and sulphur rained from the sky and destroyed them all" (Luke 17:29).

However, Isaiah notes another tradition according to which such criminals have a special location set apart for their punishment: "For a burning place has long been prepared; yea, for the king it is made ready, its pyre made deep and wide, with fire and wood in abundance; the breath of Yahweh, like a stream of brimstone, kindles it" (Isa 30:33). As we shall see, our astral prophet forecasts punishment by fire and sulphur as the fate of the cosmic leaders in evil, the Dragon and the two Beasts (19:20; 20:10), as well as wicked human beings (21:8).

The dishonor of this torment is underscored by the fact that it will take place in public: before the holy ones and the Lamb, both mentioned at the beginning of this segment so as to still be on the author's mind. The duration of the punishment of the idolaters, lasting through cosmic ages, points to some stable feature of the cosmos that allows for such endless duration. And this, as we shall see, is the vault of the sky where the Abyss is to be found.

Before the next sky servant in the series appears, the statement in 14:12–13 interrupts the flow of the narrative. While verse 12 notes the basic value of endurance for early Christian groups, it describes the holy ones as those who keep the commandments of God and Jesus' faithful witness. This statement, of course, can make sense even if applied to the holy ones in the cosmic Lamb's entourage, the undefiled sky servants. However, the next verse with a voice from the sky indicates a reapplication of the seer's vision of the holy ones to Christians who keep God's commandments. Proof of their having died in the Lord is their works. That the seer gets a command to write is not disturbing. What is disturbing is that he sets down this information here. Now back to the sky.

The seer now sees something like a sickle-wielding, crowned human being seated on a white cloud. This human-like entity is the central personage in the sequence consisting of seven characters: three sky servants, one human-like being, three sky servants. And this vision is likewise the central vision (the fifth) in a series of nine visions. Hence as central personage in the central vision, his action is what is underscored in this presentation. Clearly what is to happen is some cosmically controlled harvesting. The word "sickle" is much repeated in the next few verses. What does the seer see here? There are many constellations that wield sickle-shaped swords or scimitars. However, among the comets, there is one called "the Whirlwind" that has a sickle shape, as reported by the legendary astrologer-priest, Petosiris who writes for the worthy Pharaoh Nechepso (the document is from ca. first century B.C.):

> The comet Whirlwind. This arises from a reflection of light in the sky. It is sickle-shaped, dusky, gloomy, and wherever it faces the consequences will be universally bad. There will be foreign and serious civil wars, popular seditions and dearth of necessities. Famous leaders will die in battle, especially if the comet appears for three or four days. If it appears longer it threatens total destruction and ruin, and ills without end. Many in the Roman army will die in battle, and camps and forts belonging to the Romans will be captured. The plebes in sedition will attack the very consuls. There will be plague, and no one's prayers will be heard. Successions of consuls will result from the fatuity of the powerful. Extraordinarily violent and deadly fires will burn whole cities to ashes. Irresistible woes will be general, but worse for western peoples. For a mighty war will strike them from the east, but because of discord among the attackers from the east the bulk of the army will perish. Sedition will arise in the armies and the armies will rain punishments upon one another. But not long afterwards the victors in turn will fare ill and be sorely vexed, and quite simply there will be troubles for people everywhere for as many years as the number of days this sign appears in the heavens (Nechepso-Petosiris Frag. 9, trans. Lewis 1976: 146–47).

Now a fourth sky servant emerges from God's celestial temple and shouts a command to the humanoid. Harvesting symbolizes judgment, the previously announced theme of this text-segment. The command to harvest, based on the fact that it is time to harvest, is followed by obedient fulfillment of the command. The earth is quickly harvested.

A fifth sky servant, with sharp sickle in hand, now appears from God's celestial temple. He is immediately followed by a sixth sky servant, this time from the sacred Altar before the temple, where this sky servant has charge of the Altar fire. He too gives the command to harvest to the sickle-wielding sky servant, based on the fact that the grapes are ripe. The command is immediately followed by its fulfillment. The vines of the earth are gathered and placed in "the great wine-press of the anger of God." The action of the wine-press then symbolizes satisfaction for the dishonor done to God through idolatry, hence it predictably yields blood, the life of idolaters. This pressing occurs outside the city. So far the only city mentioned is Babylon/Babel, which must serve as the city in question.

The yield effected by this cosmic judgment is quite phenomenal, of course: a torrent of blood about five feet deep and one-hundred-ninety miles long. Pliny notes: "A Greek stadion equals one-hundred twenty-five of our Roman paces (that is six-hundred twenty-five feet)." A stadion, then, was about 200 yards or 190 meters; see Pliny, *Natural History* 2.85, LCL). (Pliny likewise mentions that the total number of stars is 1,600; *Natural History* 2.110, LCL).

9.4. THE THIRD SIGN: INTRODUCTION

The author began this sector by telling his readers that the Pregnant Woman and the Dragon were signs. Now we come to another sign, the third one, consisting of the set of seven injuries or afflictions to be dropped on the earth. While in the book as a whole (consisting of five sectors) this is the final set of seven injuries, yet in this third sector it is the only set of seven. The injuries described in Sector 2 were aimed at provoking repentance in Israel ("the land") and Jerusalem. These injuries, on the other hand, are directed at the repentance of the antediluvian generation whose offspring built Babel.

In introducing this sign, John describes three visions. In the first the seer presents us with a final septet of sky servants, about to perform a final task (15:1). In the second he describes victors singing at a celestial sea (15:2–4). And in the final vision, he sees the sky temple opened and describes the incipient activity going on there as he watches (15:5–8).

The first vision catches a glimpse of the sign in the sky, which the seer characterizes as great and astonishing, presumably because everything takes place in an atmosphere of finality, of the absolute last chance, for the seer witnesses the final set of seven sky servants about to afflict the earth with a final set of injuries. These are the final ones, we are told, because these will suffice to restore God's honor to the universe.

The next vision depicts those who did not submit to the demands of the Beast by worshipping his icon and obtaining his mark. These victors are in the sky now, not at some future date. Outfitted with the lyres of God, they join in the music of the celestial spheres by adding the Mosaic song of the cosmic Lamb. The opening words of the song ("Great and astonishing") underscore the quality of the first sign in the sky: seven sky servants with the seven final injuries.

The description of victors at the shore of a celestial sea of glass mixed with fire presents another scenario that would be well known to the contemporaries of the seer. They are located in the fiery region of the starry sky. As previously noted, the Mesopotamian tradition relates the existence of numerous celestial starry "bodies of water," usually connected with a varied listing of seven starry sky rivers (Brown 1900: 2.203–5). As for Egyptian and Greek models available in the first century, Boll writes:

There is the conception of the heavenly ocean, current among the Egyptians and not entirely foreign to the Greeks. This ocean is traveled by Helios and makes the course of the sun into a heavenly sea; but the Milky Way too (the presumably older course of the sun) was such a sea, at least for the Egyptians (poorly attested to for Romans and Greeks). There was a widespread scenario among the ancients (and many peoples at that) that the Milky Way was the path followed by the freed souls of the dead on their way to "heaven," or found their eternal homeland on it. The Milky Way is "the path of the souls making their way to the Hades in the sky" (Heraclides of Pontos, see Rohde, *Psyche* II, 213,2). This is Pythagorean doctrine, maintained even at later periods. The doctrine was at home in popular consciousness because it was patently supported by the visible phenomenon of an endless fullness of shining stars in the sky. Thus the scenario in Revelation of the resting place of the praising souls of the "victors" would have readily been suggested by such images (Boll 1914: 32–33).

As previously noted, the belief that the righteous person will be glorified by God and shine as brilliantly as the stars of the sky was generally held among Israelite seers with a penchant for astral prophecy. For example, 2 Baruch 51:10 professes: "For in the heights of that world shall they (the righteous) dwell, and they shall be made like unto the angels, and made equal to the stars." In turn we find in 4 Ezra 7:97: "The sixth order, when it is shown to them how their face is to shine like the sun, and how they are to be made like the light of the stars, being incorruptible from then on." And of course the well known passage from Dan 12:3 states: "And those who are wise shall shine like the brightness of the firmament; and those who turn many to righteousness, like the stars for ever and ever."

The final vision here is that of "the temple of the Tent of Witness." This elaborate phrasing recalls the conclusion of the book of Exodus (Exod 39:32; 40:2, 6, 28). Of course there must be a "Tent of Witness" in the sky with God since Moses simply followed a celestial prototype in his construction plans "in accordance with all that the Lord has commanded" (Exod 36:1). The Ark of the Covenant, whose appearance marked the end of Sector 2, was housed in this Tent of Witness (Exod 40:21). Hence the scene here is much like the one at the close of the previous sector (11:19).

The reason why this open sky temple is mentioned at this juncture is to situate the action that follows. The first action is the exiting of the seven sky servants from the sky temple; they are dressed for some solemn action, it seems (normally the clothing of the sky servants is not mentioned). One of the four living beings on the horizon of the cosmos (which one is not specified), gives each of the sky servants a comet to hurl on the earth: golden bowls full of God's honor-restoring wrath. God's title, "the one living unto the aeons of aeons," is the same as that at the opening of the book. As when Isaiah had his inaugural vision in the temple of Jerusalem (Isa 6), so too in the sky temple, the edifice is filled with smoke. But in the sky the smoke is a concrete expression of God's honor and power. The fact that the temple is now honor and power filled, as though full of dense smoke, thus prevents anyone else from entering it for the time being. Specifically this interval is the time it takes for the sky servants to carry out their tasks.

The point behind the whole scenario is the close correlation between the afflictions sent upon humankind from the realm of God and the level of disrespect and dishonor shown God. The whole scenario is an honor/shame scenario.

9.5. The Third Sign: Seven Bowl Comets

The actual event of the third sign now takes place, marked off at its beginning and end by means of "a loud voice from the sky temple" (16:1, 17), a voice from the throne. After God's command, the first three bowl-shaped comets are hurled from the sky by God's sky servants. During the ensuing pause, two sky beings affirm the rightness of God's commanded action. Then four more comets come, each followed by a reaction. In three cases people disaffirm God's doing, that is, they blaspheme, while in one instance the hostile cosmic trio of chs. 12–13 open their mouth in opposition. The series of injuries follow the sequence noted in ch. 8: earth, salt water, fresh water, sun, stone/bones, clouds/vapor and air.

The first comet aimed at the earth afflicts the idolatrous who showed allegiance to the Beast and his cronies with ulcers. For a like effect caused by celestial disturbances, see John Lydus (*De ostentis* p. 73, 13): "(October) 20th: if it thunders, strange ulcers threaten, for the greater part ultimate misfortune due to discord."

The second comet is aimed at the sea, turning it to blood so that a basic human food supply is cut off, i.e., fish. Boll (1914: 144) lists passages in CCAG noting the destruction of fish in conjunction with celestial phenomena. In turn John Lydus (*De ostentis* p. 76, 6): "(December) third, if it thunders, human beings will use up (other) creatures because of lack of fish." However, the blood is characterized as a dead person's blood. Life is in the blood. With all the ocean's waters turning to dead person's blood, every living being in the sea must die in a sort of reverse cause and effect sequence. Furthermore, all land is now marked off by blood, hence unclean. This is further underscored in the next scene.

The third comet, aimed at fresh water supplies, likewise turns them to blood, making the water unpotable. Now all the water supplies are filled with the fluid of life outside its proper place; hence all regions are unclean.

After the first three comets produce their effects, the seer hears the sky servant in charge of the waters affirm God's choices. It is this sky servant who is to protect the waters as guardian being. The specifics of God's decision here derive from the fact that those afflicted shed the blood of both the ancient holy ones and of the prophets. Thus they are "worthy," i.e., they deserve it. Even the cosmic Altar, the constellation marking the location of traditional cosmic oath taking and covenant making, affirms God's decision to be "truthful and just."

The fourth comet is directed at the sun to direct intense heat upon human beings only. Instead of having a change of heart, the afflicted humans respond by insulting God's honor in speech and in their activity.

The fifth comet strikes the location of the enthroned Beast and its kingdom. This is the constellational Beast presented in 13:11, the Beast rising over the land, with horns like the Lamb and a voice like the Dragon. It could bring fire down from the sky (13:12), but now its kingdom is in darkness. And this is the land Beast who had the power of the sea Beast, who in turn had the power of the Dragon. Yet the Beast could do nothing to assuage the pain of those under its dominion. Its followers who have been insulting God now chew their tongues in pain. Incredibly, in face of accumulating affliction, the followers of the Beast continue insulting God with no thought to a change of heart.

The sixth comet dries up the Euphrates River. The Euphrates was the water source of the great city, Babel. It was the traditional eastern point of passage for invading easterly armies. Thus a dry path for eastern kings is made ready.

With the preparation of a pathway from the east, right before the final affliction, the cosmic trio reacts. The seer sees this reaction in three unclean sky winds, like frogs, issuing from the mouths of the cosmic Dragon, the cosmic sea Beast and the cosmic land Beast, now identified as a false prophet. After all, the task of these constellational creatures was always to deceive those on earth (13:14). In the astronomic traditions of Arab bedouin, there are two well known stars called the Frogs. "The First Frog" (*al-dafdaʿ al-awwal*) is in the mouth of the southern Fish (*Piscis Austrini*) and still bears an Arabic name, "Fomalhaut" (meaning "mouth of the fish"). "The Second Frog" (*al-dafdaʿ al-thani*), likewise still with the Arabic name, "Diphda" (meaning "frog") is located on the tail of "the hated sea-monster," Cetus. Aratus singles out these two stars as "two of more lustrous form" but does not call them frogs (*Phenomena* 395–398, LCL).

Why do the sky winds, like starry Frogs, issue from the mouth? The mouth is the zone of self-revelation and self-communication, of confessing and commanding. Sky winds, on the other hand, essentially do things, they act (like hands and feet). Now the sky winds perform cosmic signs which get all earthly kings to assemble. The seer tells us the purpose, time and place: "to do battle," "on the great day of God the Almighty," and "at the hill of Megiddo."

Rev 16:15 is an insertion into the flow of the action. It cites a word of God, qualifying the time of the final scene: suddenly ("like a thief"). The honorable line of conduct is then underscored: to be alert and be ever prepared so as not to be shamed.

Once all the kings have been assembled, the seventh comet strikes the air. The voice from the throne in the sky temple now states: "It has happened," equivalent to "It's all over now." The final bowl-shaped comet impacting the realm of the air produces the usual sky phenomena (lightning, sounds, thunder, and earthquake), yet to an unusual degree. The formula "such as had never been before (or since the creation of the world)" signifies simply the events's extreme character. Astral prophets, it seems, never describe the average or use ordinary terms. The formula thus is also used to describe the extreme quality of the event in question (Berger 1976: 74). Berger describes sixty instances of this formula, beginning with biblical ones such as (all LXX): Exod 10:6; 10:14; Joel 1:2; Dan 9:12; 12:1 (Theod); Mark 13:19; Matt 24:21; the other 52 are in non-biblical ancient writings. To appreciate the ancient sensitivity to earthquakes, consider the description of what happened in Antioch at the time of Emperor Trajan (reigned A.D. 98–117) in Appendix D: On Earthquakes.

The extremely unusual intensity of the earthquake is noted by the fact that the Great City falls into three parts. What does this refer to? Instead of beginning with the "Great City," consider the three parts. It was well known in antiquity that the inhabited earth consisted of three parts: Europe, Asia, and Libya (Africa). Hyginus notes that the constellation Deltoton (Triangle) is an image of the world, divided by the ancients into three parts (*Astronomia* 2.19, Belles Lettres). If at the outset, as Genesis indicates, God made the heavens and a single inhabited earth, then why is the inhabited earth divided into three segments or pieces? It would seem that John here refers to the inhabited world, the οἰκουμένη, *oikoumenē*, as a Great City, the place where humans dwell. This habitation was split into three parts due to the final bowl-shaped comet of antediluvian times, cast upon the once unified earth due to mounting evil, insults to God, and the people's refusal to have a change of heart. The result is a collapse of all antediluvian civilizations, a fate foreboding what would happen after the Flood to Babylon when that city too will have to drink up its "cup."

The scenario concludes with emphasis on the earthquake's intensity. While there is no mention of rain, the Flood of Genesis likewise resulted in islands fleeing and mountains disappearing. Perhaps the high context author expects his readers to supply this information. Be that as it may, the final item to be noted are the unbelievably gigantic hail stones the size of a talent, fifty-seven pounds. These drop from the sky upon those who continue to insult God because of the atmospheric havoc they suffer.

With this sequence of events, we come to the close of the third sector of the book of Revelation. With the author's reference to Babel, we should expect the seer to tell us about how that great city fared. This he does in the next sector of our tour.

In sum, the third sector of the book of Revelation does indeed reveal. Its focus is not on the future but on cosmic and human prehistory. Both the distant past and the distant future (not the forthcoming) are unknown to humans. To learn about them requires God's assistance. The past, of course, is quite significant since it explains the present. And it is forces unleashed in the past that continue to affect the present. Like the author of Enoch before him, our astral prophet John learns about this past through his cosmic travels. And he recounts it all to his fellow Christians so that they might be fully aware of what happened in the distant past that explains what going on all around them as they endure.

10 SECTOR 4: THE FIRST POSTDELUVIAN CITY OF HUMANKIND

17¹And one of the seven sky servants of those having the seven bowls came, and he spoke with me saying: "Over here, I will show you the judgment of the Great Harlot seated upon many waters. ²With whom the kings of the earth have fornicated, and those who inhabit the earth have become drunk with the wine of her fornication." ³And he took me away into the wilderness in a sky wind. And I saw a Woman seated on a scarlet Beast, full of names of blasphemy, having seven heads and ten horns. ⁴And the Woman was clothed in purple and scarlet, and gilded with gold and precious stone and pearls, having a golden cup in her hand filled with abominations and unclean things of her fornication. ⁵And on her forehead a name written, a mystery, Babylon the Great, the mother of harlots and of the abominations of the earth. ⁶And I saw the Woman drunk from the blood of the holy ones and from the blood of the witnesses of Jesus. And I was astonished seeing this great astonishing thing. ⁷And the sky servant said to me: "Why were you astonished? I will tell you the mystery of the Woman and of the Beast carrying her, the one having the seven heads and the ten horns. ⁸The Beast which you saw was and is not and is going to come up from the Abyss, and goes into destruction. And those who inhabit the earth will be astonished, whose name is not written on the scroll of life from the foundation of the world, seeing the Beast because it was, and is not, and will be present. ⁹At this point, understanding, O one having wisdom: The seven heads are seven mountains, where the Woman is seated upon them; and there are seven kings. ¹⁰Five fell, the one is, and the other has not yet come, and when he will come he must stay for a little [while]. ¹¹And the Beast who was and is not, he too is the eighth and is one of the seven, and goes into destruction. ¹²And the ten horns which you see are ten kings, who did not yet receive kingdom, but who receive authority as king for one hour with the Beast. ¹³These have one intention, and they give their power and authority to the Beast. ¹⁴These do battle with the Lamb, and the Lamb will conquer them, because he is Lord of lords and King of kings and those with him [are] the called and the chosen and the trustworthy. ¹⁵And he says to me: the waters which you see, where the harlot is seated, are peoples and crowds, and nations and tongues. ¹⁶And the ten horns which you see and the Beast, these will hate the harlot, and they will make her desolate and naked and they will eat her flesh and they will burn her up in fire. ¹⁷For God gave it into their heart to do his intention, and to do one intention and to give their kingdom to the Beast until the utterances of God will be fulfilled. ¹⁸And the Woman whom you see is the great city having dominion over the kings of the earth.

18 [1]After these things I saw another sky servant coming down from the sky, having great authority, and the earth was lit up because of his glory. [2]And he shouted with a mighty voice saying:

> "She fell, she fell, Babylon the great,
> and she has become a dwelling place of demons,
> and a prison of every unclean sky wind,
> and a prison of every unclean and hated bird,
>
> [3]"Because all the nations have drunk
> from the wine of the anger of her fornication.
> And the kings of the earth fornicated with her,
> and the merchants of the earth grew rich from the power of her luxury."

[4]And I heard another voice from the sky saying:

> "My people go out of her,
> so that you may not be associated with her sins,
> and so that you may not receive of her injuries.
>
> [5]"Because her sins have attained to the sky,
> and God did not forget her crimes,
>
> [6]"Repay her just as she paid out,
> and pay back double, a double amount according to her works,
> in the cup which she mixed, mix a double amount for her.
>
> [7]"To the extent that she glorified herself and lived luxuriously,
> so give her that much torment and grief.
> because in her heart she says that
> 'I sit [as] a queen,
> and I am not a widow,
> and I shall not see grief.'
>
> [8]"Because of this her injuries will come in one day,
> death and grief and famine,
> and she will be burned up in fire
> because mighty [is] the lord God, the one who is judging her."

[9]And the kings of the earth, those who fornicated with her and lived luxuriously, are going to weep and wail over her, as they see the smoke of her burning, [10]Standing from afar on account of fear of her torment, saying,

> "Woe, Woe, the great city
> Babylon the mighty city,
> because your judgment came in one hour."

[11]And the merchants of the earth weep and grieve over her, because no one buys their merchandise any longer, [12]merchandise of gold and silver and precious stone and pearls and linen and purple and silk and scarlet and every sort of aromatic wood and every sort of ivory utensil, and every sort of utensil of more precious wood and copper and iron and marble. [13]And cinnamon and amomum and incenses

and myrrh and frankincense and wine and oil and semolina and wheat and cattle and sheep and horses
and chariots and slaves and human souls.

[14]And the late summer fruit your soul's desire
> was taken from you,
> and all polished and resplendent things
> perish from you
> and they will surely no longer be found.

[15]And those merchants, those growing wealthy from her, will stand from afar because of fear of her torment, weeping and grieving,
[16]saying:

> "Woe, woe, the great city.
> Clothed in linen and purple and scarlet,
> And gilded with gold and precious stone and pearl,

> [17]"because in one hour so much wealth was ravaged.
> And every pilot and everyone sailing to port and sailors and those working the sea stood
> from afar."

[18]And they shouted, seeing the smoke of her burning, saying: "What is there like the great city?"
[19]And they threw dust upon their heads and shouted, weeping and grieving, saying:

> "Woe, woe, the great city,
> by means of which all having ships grew wealthy,
> by means of the sea, from her abundance.
> Because she was ravaged in one hour."

> [20]"Be glad over her, O sky,
> And the Holy Ones and the apostles, and the prophets,
> because God has judged your case against her."

[21]And one mighty sky servant took up a great milling stone and threw it into the sea saying:

> "With such impetus will be thrown
> Babylon the great city,
> and it will no longer be found.

> [22]"And the voice of harp-singers and musicians
> and flutists and trumpeters
> will no longer be heard in you,
> and every craftsman of every craft
> will no longer be found in you.
> And the voice of the mill
> will no longer be heard in you,

> [23]"And the light of a lamp
> will no longer shine in you.
> and the voice of a bridegroom and bride,
> will no longer be heard in you.
> Because your merchants were the great ones of the earth,
> because all the nations were deceived by means of your magical arts."

[24]And in it were found the blood of prophets and holy ones,
and of all those slaughtered upon the earth.

19[1]After these things I heard as though the great voice of a numerous crowd in the sky saying:
  "Alleluia!
  The rescue and the glory and the power of our God.

  [2]"Because his judgments are truthful and just,
  because he judged the great harlot,
  who corrupted the earth with her fornication,
  and vindicated the blood of his slaves from her hand."

[3]And a second time they said: "Alleluia." And her smoke went up into the aeons of aeons. [4]And the
twenty-four elders and the four living beings fell down and prostrated themselves to God seated upon
the throne, saying:
  "Amen. Alleluia."

[5]And a voice came from the throne saying:
  "Give praise to our God,
  all his slaves,
  [and] those who fear him,
  the small and the great."

[6]And I heard like the voice of a numerous crowd and like the voice of many waters and like the voice
of mighty thunders saying:
  "Alleluia.
  Because the Lord has reigned [as king],
  [our] God, the Almighty,

  [7]"Let us rejoice and exult,
  and let us give glory to him,
  because the wedding of the Lamb came,
  and his Woman prepared herself,

  [8]"And it was given to her so that she be clothed
  with pure, resplendent, linen,
  for the linen is the just deeds of the holy ones."

[9]And he says to me: "Write: How honorable are those called to the supper of the wedding of the
Lamb"; and he says to me: "These are the truthful utterances of God." [10]And I fell down before his feet
to prostrate myself to him; and he says to me: "No, look! I am a fellow slave of yours and your brothers, those having the witness of Jesus; prostrate yourself to God. For the witness of Jesus is the sky
wind of prophecy." [11]And I saw the sky opened, and behold a White Horse, and the one seated upon it
[called] trustworthy and truthful and he judges with justice and does battle. [12]Now his eyes [like] a
flame of fire, and upon his head many diadems, having a name written which no one knows but he.
[13]And clothed with a garment soaked with blood, and his name is called the utterance of God. [14]And
the army in the sky followed him upon White Horses, clothed in pure white linen. [15]And from his
mouth proceeds a sharp sword, so that with it he might strike the nations, and he will shepherd them
with an iron rod; and he trods the winepress of the wine of the anger of the wrath of God the

Almighty. [16]And he has written on his garment and on his thigh: King of kings and Lord of lords. [17]And I saw one sky servant standing in the sun, and he shouted with a loud voice saying to all the birds flying at the height of the sky: "Come and gather unto the great supper of God, [18]so that you might eat the flesh of kings and the flesh of tribunes and the flesh of the mighty and the flesh of horses and of those seated on them and the flesh of all free men as well as of slaves, and of the small and of the great." [19]And I saw the Beast and the kings of the earth and their armies gathered together to do battle with the one seated on the horse and with his army. [20]And the Beast was apprehended and with him the false prophet who did signs before him, by means of which he deceived those accepting the seal of the Beast, and those prostrating themselves to his icon; the two were thrown alive into the pool of fire which burned with sulphur. [21]And the remainder were killed by the sword of the one sitting on the horse, the one that proceeded from his mouth, and all the birds were sated from their flesh.

20[1]And I saw a sky servant descending from the sky, having the key of the Abyss and a great chain on his hand. [2]And he seized the Dragon, the ancient serpent, which is the Devil and Satan, and bound him for one thousand years. [3]And he cast him into the Abyss and locked [it] and sealed over it so that the nations might no longer be deceived until the thousand years be completed; after these things it is necessary to set him loose for a short time. [4]And I saw thrones, and they sat upon them and judgment was given to them and the souls of those beheaded on account of the witness of Jesus and on account of the utterance of God and whoever did not prostrate themselves to the Beast or to his icon and did not accept the seal upon the forehead and upon their hand; and they lived and reigned with the Christ for a thousand years. [5]The rest of the dead did not live until the thousand years were completed; this [is] the first resurrection. [6]How honorable and holy is the one who has a share in the first resurrection; upon them the second death does not have authority, but they will be priests of God and of the Messiah, and they will reign with him [the] thousand years. [7]And when the thousand years were completed Satan will be loosed from his prison. [8]And he will go out to deceive the nations in the four corners of the world, Gog and Magog, to gather them together into battle, whose number [will be] like the sand of the sea. [9]And they ascended along the latitudinal line of the earth and encircled the array of the holy ones and the Beloved City; but then fire descended from the sky and devoured them. [10]And the Devil who was deceiving them was thrown into the Pit of Fire and of sulphur, where also the Beast and the false prophet, and they will be tormented day and night into the aeons of aeons. [11]And I saw a great white throne and the one sitting upon it, from whose face fled the earth and the sky and a place was not found for them. [12]And I saw the dead, the great and the small, standing before the throne, and scrolls were opened; and another scroll was opened, which is that of life; and the dead were judged from what was written in the scrolls according to their works. [13]And the sea gave the dead in it, and Death and Hades gave the dead in them; and they were judged, each according to their works. [14]And Death and Hades were thrown into the Pit of Fire; this is the second death, the Pit of Fire. [15]And if anyone were not found written in the scroll of life, he was cast into the fire.

Our tour through the book of Revelation comes to Sector 4. Here the astral prophet, John, describes his vision of what happened with the very first instance of human civilization after the Flood, the city of Babel. The destruction of Babel marks the end of remnants of the antediluvian way of life and the inauguration of the human condition as we now experience it. In his altered state of awareness, John is brought back to the situation of humankind immediately after the Flood, "when the earth had one language and few words" (Gen 11:1).

The tour of Sector 4 begins with a sky servant from the previous scenario offering to show John what happened to "The Harlot Seated Upon Many Waters." The seer is soon told that this harlot is Babylon. The Greek *Babylon* (Βαβυλών) is, of course, identical to the Hebrew and Aramaic *Babel* (בבל). As John would know from Israelite lore, Babylon was the first postdeluvian city. The city is personified as a female simply because this was customary in the Hellenistic period and perhaps earlier. Interestingly, Babylon's protecting star at that period was Aphrodite Anaitis. This same personage was known as Venus, Isis, Ishtar, Anatu, or Dilbat, depending on one's location. The sky servant then carries the seer off to see the personified city. At this point in the narrative there is a long interlude, of an allegorical sort, during which a sky servant explains the meaning of the elements of the vision—the Beast, the many waters—and finally offers a single sentence on the woman.

If we are not detoured by this interlude, we immediately hear another sky servant announcing the fall of Babylon, and still another inviting his protégés to leave the city. Finally, we overhear with the seer a set of persons who regularly interacted with the city: kings of the earth, merchants of the earth, seamen. At the close of this chorus of voices, another "mighty" sky servant performs an action symbolizing the fate of crushed Babylon.

Next an even more impressive cosmic chorus lauds God's just judgment on the city. The seer is abruptly directed to write, and hence announces the supper of the Wedding of the Lamb (19:9). But before that takes place, another supper takes place. The mounted "King of kings and Lord of lords," along with his army, vanquishes that antediluvian force, the sea Beast with its kings, tribunes, the mighty and their horses, freemen and slaves, small and great. All of these cadavers serve as the supper of the birds of the sky. But the sea Beast and its false prophet (the land Beast) are thrown into the burning sulphurous pool. Thus the fall of Babel entails the fall of the antediluvian forces to evil personified in the cosmic Beasts.

With the two Beasts vanquished, it is finally the Dragon's turn. The seer sees a sky servant bind the Dragon with a chain for one thousand years (20:1–3), that is, for a "day" in the sight of the Lord ("But do not ignore this one fact, beloved, that with the Lord one day is as a thousand years, and a thousand years as one day" [2 Pet 3:8]). During this period, those who witness to Jesus live and reign with him (20:4–6). Then, a final period is ushered in with the release of Satan for destruction with the Beasts (20:7–10) and with God's judgment of humankind (20:11–15).

An attentive reading of the previous passage once again reveals how the author punctuates his narrative by marking off each new sight with the phrase "and I saw" (or a variant of it). If we take him at his word, the astral prophet again saw nine distinctive scenes:

the Woman on the Beast (17:3)
the Woman drunk with blood (17:6)
a descending sky servant (18:1)
the open sky and White Horse (19:11)
a sky servant in the sun (19:17)
battle with Beast and kings (19:19)
a descending sky servant (20:1)
thrones (20:4)
a Great White Throne plus the dead before it (20:12).

The first two scenes of the seated Woman are matched by the final two scenes of thrones. Next the descending sky servants balance in the picture. The central scene is the set of three sights of destruction marked by the opened sky with the rider on the White Horse, the sky servant in the sun, and the final sky battle between the White Horse Rider and the Beast and its followers. Our tour through this sector will consider these sights.

10.1. THE FIRST TWO SIGHTS

This sector opens with the seer being offered the opportunity to see the outcome of the negative judgment on "the Great Harlot seated upon many waters." He obviously takes the offer, since the vision follows. In order to show "the Great Harlot" to the seer, the sky servant takes him to the realm of chaos, the wilderness, through the controlling power of a sky wind, hence in an altered state of awareness.

10.1.1. The City Babylon

In the Genesis account, Babel/Babylon marked a new start for humankind after the first total flooding of the earth. It was a new creation, a new city. And, we are told, Babel was the only city in the world into which God ever descended for a look around (Gen 11:5). Yet as everyone in the Israelite tradition knew, with the fresh beginning of humanity after the Flood, people were:

. . . incited to this insolent contempt of God by Nebrodes (= Nimrod), grandson of Ham the son of Noah, an audacious man of doughty vigor. He persuaded them to attribute their prosperity not to God but to their own valor, and little by little transformed the state of affairs into a tyranny, holding that the only way to detach men from the fear of God was by making them continuously dependent upon his own power. He threatened to have his revenge on God if he wished to inundate the earth again; for he would build a tower higher than the water could reach and avenge the destruction of their forefathers (Josephus, *Antiquities* 1.113–114, LCL).

This tradition derives from the fact that Nimrod was "the first on earth to be a mighty man" (Gen 10:8). Philo of Alexandria notes that he was first to desert God after the Flood. "It was Nimrod who began this desertion. For the lawgiver says, 'he began to be a giant [*gigas*, γίγας] on the earth' (Gen. x.8), and his name means 'desertion' . . . And therefore to Nimrod Moses ascribes Babylon as the beginning of his kingdom" (*On the Giants* 66, LCL). The people of Babylon wished to build "a tower with its top in the sky" (Gen. 11:4), that is a tower reaching right into the very realm of God. The early third-century Christian author, Hippolytus, wished that Ptolemy, the astronomer, would have lived then to warn people of the impossibility of the venture:

> This Ptolemy, however,—a careful investigator of these matters—does not seem to me to be useless; but only this grieves (one), that being recently born, he could not be of service to the sons of the giants, who, being ignorant of these measures [distances of planetary bodies from each other and vault of the sky], and supposing that the heights of the sky were near, endeavored in vain to construct a tower (Hippolytus, *Refutation of All Heresies* 4.12, *ANF*).

The name, "Babel" (*Bab-ili*), means the "Gate of God," the place of access to the sphere of the deity for humans and to the sphere of the human for the deity. As a matter of fact, in the Genesis account we are told "And Yahweh came down to see the city and the tower, which the sons of men had built" (Gen 11:5). The technology worked. But the tower that was to maintain human unity (Gen 11:4) instead resulted in human disharmony. The Genesis story does not explain exactly why this happened, but Israel's later traditions do: the person with the gigantic antediluvian features and attitudes, Nimrod, acted in contempt of God! And thus began Babel's harlotry, a code word for blasphemous idolatry.

> But when the threats of the great God are fulfilled with which he once threatened men when they built the tower in the land of Assyria . . . They were all of one language and they wanted to go up to the starry heaven. But immediately the immortal one imposed a great compulsion on the winds. Then the winds cast down the great tower from on high, and stirred up strife for mortals among themselves. Therefore humans gave the city the name Babylon. But when the tower fell, the tongues of men were diversified by various sounds, the whole earth of humans was filled with fragmenting kingdoms. Then was the tenth generation of articulate men, from the time when the Flood came upon the men of old (*Sibylline Oracles* 3.97–109, *OTP*).

Along with the title "Gate of the Gods," the city of Babylon was known as "the Place of Heavenly Power," and "the Place of the Tree of Life." In history, it was during Babylon's political ascendancy that Judean elites were evicted from the kingdom of Judah and forced into exile. Jeremiah could see this exile as punishment from God. For example: "For thus says Yahweh: 'Behold, I will make you a terror to yourself and to all your friends. They shall fall by the sword of their enemies while you look on. And I will give all Judah into the hand of the king of Babylon; he shall carry them captive to Babylon, and shall slay them with the sword'" (Jer 20:4). And yet for its behavior Babylon would be totally destroyed; Isaiah 13–14 spells out the details, ending with the powerful statement: "'I will rise up against them,' says Yahweh of the sky armies, 'and will cut off from Babylon name and remnant, offspring and posterity,' says Yahweh" (Isa 14:22). In another part of that prophet's tradition, we have him describing a pair of riders who report: "Fallen, fallen is Babylon; and all the images of her gods he has shattered to the ground" (Isa 21:9).

After Alexander the Great conquered Persia, he planned to make Babylon the center and capital of his worldwide empire. But his Seleucid successors abandoned both the venture and the once great city. We are rather well informed about Babylon in the first century. Quite in agreement with our astral prophet, the geographer Strabo (d. A.D. 14), tells us: "The greater part of Babylon is so deserted that one would not hesitate to say what one of the comic poets said in reference to the Megalopolitans in Arcadia: 'The Great City is a great desert' " (Strabo, *Geography* 1.738E, LCL). And Dio Cassius, describing Trajan's visit to Babylon in 116 A.D., reports: "Trajan learned of this at Babylon; for he had gone there both because of its fame—though he saw nothing but mounds and stones and ruins to justify this—and because of Alexander, to whose spirit he offered sacrifice in the room where he had died" (Dio Cassius, *Roman History*, 68.30, 1, LCL). Curiously enough, even today Babylon consists of seven hills or mounds:

> The present site, an extensive field of ruins, contains several prominent mounds. The main mounds are (1) Babil, the remains of Nebuchadrezzar's palace in the northern corner of the outer rampart; (2) Qasr, comprising the palace complex (with a building added in Persian times), the Ishtar Gate, and the Emakh temple; (3) Amran ibn Ali, the ruins of Esagila; (4) Merkez, marking the ancient residential area east of Esagila; (5) Humra, containing rubble removed by Alexander from the ziggurat in preparation for rebuilding, and a theater he built with material from the ziggurat; and (6) Ishin Aswad, where there are two further temples. A depression called Sahn marks the former site of the ziggurat Etemenanki (Henry W. F. Saggs, "Babylon," *The New Encyclopaedia Britannica: Macropaedia* 2:556).

Of course this situation contrasts starkly with the glory that once was Babylon. But it is much like Babylon during the seer's time. While this sort of information is interesting, and commentaries are replete with it, it really does not bring us close to really understanding John. For that we have to get back to the sky.

10.1.2. The Star Babylon

To see the reality John observed, we must set the opening sight of Babylon seated on the crimson covered Beast within an astronomical register. The first sight involves two astral bodies, the planet Venus setting over the constellation of the Beast. The second sight is Venus alone. Initially Venus is viewed as setting in a crimson sky over the constellation previously described as the sea Beast. Interestingly, the Aramaic version of Isaiah states concerning Babylon: "How have you been thrown down from the heights (of the sky), you who were resplendent among the sons of men as the star of the evening (= Venus) among the stars . . . " (Tg. Isa. 14:12). But why the connection between Venus and Babylon?

To begin with, from time immemorial, each Mesopotamian city, town and district had its own special and peculiar patron stellar divinity. Thus Dilgan (the star Capella) was the patron star of ancient Mesopotamian Bab-ili (Brown 1900: 2.136). Furthermore, each star or constellation itself was equally a divinity (Brown 1900: 2.97). There is abundant information about Dilgan (= Capella) and the divinities of ancient Babylon (see Brown 1900 2.86–87, 184 and passim). This information is of little use, however, for understanding our seer, for right before Alexander's conquest of Persia, Anahita (Undefiled one), an Avestic goddess, was given central place in Babylon. The star (planet) Venus took the place of traditional Dilgan/Capella. Clement of Alexandria reports:

> Berossos, in the third book of his *Chaldaica*, describes them (the Babylonians) as venerating a statue in human shape, after Artaxerxes, son of Darius Ochos, introduced the usage there. He erected the first statue of Aphrodite Anaitis in Babylon, Susa, Ecbatana and egged on the Persians, Bactrians, Damascenes and Sardians to venerate it (*Protreptikos* V, 65 ed. Mondesert SC 2.130).

Thus from Hellenistic times on, Aphrodite was known to be the divinity over Babylon. Moore observes:

> In the previous verse (22:15) the writer speaks of several groups of people who, because of their wickedness, are left outside the gates of the new Jerusalem, the pure city that replaces the wicked city, Babylon, after the warrior King conquers her. Of that group, sorcerers, fornicators, and idolaters are mentioned: frequently used terms in the Apocalypse (cf. Rev 2:14.20; 17:1, 2, 5, 15, 16; 18:3, 9; 19:2; 21:8). These activities, of course, were essential elements in the worship of the female goddess Ishtar (Babylon);

Ashtarte (Northwest Semitic); Kwkbt' (Syria, Northern Arabia); Aphrodite (Greece); Venus (Rome) (Moore 1982: 90).

To these we may add the Egyptian Isis or the ancient Canaanite 'Anatu or Athtartu (= Ashtarte). In other words, the Greek Aphrodite under any of her various equivalent names was a well-known figure throughout the region from Spain to Persia. In the Middle East and the Mediterranean as well, this divine personage was always identified with the planet we call Venus. There are countless instances of ancient Middle Eastern steles inscribed with the stars Sun, Moon and Venus located over some royal personage or some significant event. It was the God/Goddess sun, the God/Goddess moon and the God/Goddess Venus that were equally significant in the stories deriving from ancient Canaanite lore, and frequently alluded to in Israel's sacred books.

In sum, at the time of our author Babylon had as its patron and protector Aphrodite/Venus. Under any and all of her names, she was the planet/star who bore the same name. Now non-fixed stars such as planets that are observed one time rising and another time setting have two gender aspects. Ptolemy explains:

> They say too that the stars become masculine or feminine according to their aspects to the sun, for when they are morning stars [lit. "being of the dawn"] and precede the sun they become masculine, and feminine when they are evening stars and follow the sun. Furthermore this happens also according to their positions with respect to the horizon; for when they are in positions from the east to Mid-Heaven, or again, from the west to lower Mid-Heaven, they become masculine because they are eastern, but in the other two quadrants, as western stars, they become feminine (Ptolemy, *Tetrabiblos* 1.20, LCL).

The point here is that Venus as female is a setting star, an evening star, in the west, a western star. The question now is what was some of the traditional lore that attached to Aphrodite?

10.1.3. The Hellenistic Patron Deity of Babylon

The seer tells us that the item that interests the sky servant who starts him on this leg of his stellar adventure is "the judgment of the Great Harlot seated upon many waters." Titles equivalent to "Great Harlot" were borne with honor by a number of ancient Middle Eastern celestial beings. From a tradition close to Israel, we know of the Canaanite goddess 'Anatu as early as the eastern Mediterranean Late Bronze Age. Such titles are attested by Ugaritic documents which date between 1400 and 1200 B.C. While these documents antedate the book of Revelation by more than a millennium, they witness to a regional tradition still in vogue in Israel's traditions well into New Testament times.

'Anatu's invariable epithet is "virgin" (*btlt*). Yet the virginal status of 'Anatu is not to be confused with our contemporary usage, for we are told how "the orifice of the Virgin 'Anatu was deflowered, yes, the orifice of the most graceful of the sisters (= wives) of Ba'alu" as the divine couple has sexual intercourse (Loves II.iii, 9–10, de Moor 1987: 114). Thus virginity is not dependent on the lack of sexual intercourse. Rather, the behavior of 'Anatu in the various Ugaritic text-segments indicates that "virgin" can mean only "a young woman who did not yet bring forth male offspring" (de Moor 1987: 7, n. 33). Furthermore, the Virgin 'Anatu is regularly called *ybmt l'imm*, translated by de Moor as "the Wanton Widow of the Nations" (de Moor 1987: 7, 9, passim). The title "Wanton Widow of the Nations" describes this celestial goddess of love as the harlot of the world, just like Aphrodite in Babylon. De Moor explains:

> 'Anatu received this epithet because she became a nubile widow when Ba'lu had died, cf. Baal VI (KTU 1.6):i.30f. The nearest male kin of her husband had to marry her according to the custom of the time. We know from the Bible that men obliged to marry such a young widow were often unwilling to fulfill their duty (Gen. 38:9; Deut. 25:7–10; Ruth 4:6). Women in this position had to go pretty far in trying to seduce the man (Gen 38:14ff: Ruth 3). As a result the *ybmt* acquired a reputation of lewdness. This is why 'Anatu is the patroness of wanton love, the harlot of the world, who virtually denies her widowhood (cf. Ezek. 23:8, 21; Isa. 60:16; Rev. 17:2, 15; 18:3, 7, all patterned after the Canaanite goddess of love) (de Moor 1987: 7, n. 34).

Finally, 'Anatu has another significant title: "The Breast of the Nations." Again, de Moor (139, n. 28) explains this title as an epithet of 'Anatu referring to her role as the harlot of the world.

In the Ugaritic documents, 'Anatu regularly decks herself out in the color of the murex, the snail used to make the famous dye or paint called "purple," a color ranging from red through crimson to purple (Edgeworth 1992: 215–26). Hence to connect the celestial Harlot with the color crimson would be quite expected.

From Israel's scriptures alone we can trace how the attributes of ancient 'Anatu remained with her in her more recent avatars or equivalents: Ashtarte, Ishtar, Isis, Aphrodite, Venus, and the like. As a celestial being, 'Anatu, by whatever name, was identified as the deity who was or who controlled the planet Venus. As for the significance of Venus in the first century, Pliny reports as follows:

> Below the sun revolves a very large star named Venus, which varies its course alternately, and whose alternative names in themselves indicate its rivalry with the sun and moon—when in advance and rising before dawn it receives the name of Lucifer, as being another sun and bringing the dawn, whereas when it shines after sunset it is named Vesper, as prolonging the

daylight, or as being a deputy for the moon. This property of Venus was first discovered by Pythagoras on Samos, about the 42nd Olympiad, 142 years after the foundation of Rome. Further it surpasses all the other stars in magnitude, and is so brilliant that alone among stars it casts a shadow by its rays. Consequently there is a great competition to give it a name, some having called it Juno, others Isis, others the Mother of the Gods. Its influence is the cause of the birth of all things upon earth; at both of its risings it scatters a genital dew with which it not only fills the conceptive organs of the earth but also stimulates those of all animals. It completes the circuit of the zodiac every 348 days, and according to Timaeus is never more than 46 degrees distant from the sun (*Natural History* 2.36–38, LCL).

Again, Ptolemy underscores Venus' impact as feminine, evening star, with ever greater clarity:

But on the other hand, when the luminaries in the aforesaid configuration are unattended in feminine signs, the females exceed in the natural, and the males in unnatural practice, with the result that their souls become soft and effeminate. If Venus too is made feminine, the women become depraved, adulterous, and lustful, with the result that they may be dealt with in the natural manner on any occasion and by any one so-ever, and so that they refuse absolutely no sexual act, though it be base or unlawful. The men, on the contrary, become effeminate and unsound with respect to unnatural congresses and the functions of women, and are dealt with as pathics, though privately and secretly. But if Mars also is constituted in a feminine manner, their shamelessness is outright and frank and they perform the aforesaid acts of either kind, assuming the guise of common bawds who submit to general abuse and to every baseness until they are stamped with the reproach and insult that attend such usages. And the rising and morning positions of both Mars and Venus have a contributory effect, to make them more virile and notorious, while setting and evening positions increase femininity and sedateness. Similarly, if Saturn is present, his influence joins with each of the foregoing to produce more licentiousness, impurity, and disgrace, while Jupiter aids in the direction of greater decorum, restraint, and modesty, and Mercury tends to increase notoriety, instability of the emotions, versatility, and foresight (*Tetrabiblos* 3.14, LCL).

In sum, there can be little doubt that the seer is referring to Venus. There really is no other female celestial body that the name "Babylon" might conjure up.

As for the star that rises along the desert horizon under Venus, the seer tells us that this astral configuration has seven heads and ten horns, that is a seven-headed beast with ten dorsal protuberances. This, of course, is the way the previously mentioned Dragon (12:3) and the sea Beast (13:1) looked. And as noted earlier, such seven-headed beasts were not uncommon in the cosmological lore of Mediterranean antiquity (e.g., Mesopotamian cylinder seals, the Greek Hydra, the Canaanite Lotan, the Hebrew Rahab).

7-headed beast

In this context, however, since the seer says nothing about the Dragon, it seems clear that this constellation is the previously described surrogate of the Dragon, the sea Beast with a blasphemous name. And yet here there is no Beast with a single blasphemous name, but a Beast full of such names insulting to God. Hence along with the sea Beast, there would have been a star that habitually bore a string of blasphemous names. This last feature points to the custom in vogue in our seer's age of collecting various lists of deity names to help people control deities or their sky servants. By means of such control, people could find rescue and relief in difficult situations. They thus could obtain what they needed or desired. Such a list of blasphemous names can be easily imagined from the endless lists of various divine names in so-called magical papyri (see Betz 1986). For example, consider the divine names in the following third-century A.D. amulet inscription from the Getty Museum (cited from Llewelyn 1992: 192–93):

> The God of Abraham, the God of Isaac, the God of Jacob, the God of us, rescue Aurelia from every evil spirit, and from every epileptic fit and seizure. I implore you Lord Iao, Sabaoth, Eloaion, Ouriel, Misichael, Raphael, Gabriel, Sariel, Rasochel, Ablanathanalba, Abrasax, xxxxxx, nnnnnnna, oaaiiiiiiiiiiiixouuuuu, uuaaoooooooono . . . Sesengenbarpharanges, protect, ephin, io Erbeth . . . protect Aurelia from every seizure, from every seizure, Iao, Ieou, Ieolammo, Iao, charakoopou, Sesengenbarpharanges Iao aieiuai Ieou Iao, Sabath, Adonaie, Eleleth, Iako . . .

Such a list of "blasphemous" divine names was quite common in amulets and papyri used for protective and/or controlling purposes. Here they are characteristic of the Beast supporting Venus. The Beast in question here, then, relates to a celestial body that bears a range of titles that should belong to the God of Israel alone. The best candidate for this role is not the sea Beast, but rather the planet Jupiter, presumably accompanying the sea Beast here. First of all, note Jupiter's aliases:

The Greek divinities respectively connected with the five planets are Kronos, Zeus, Ares, Aphrodite and Hermes, the reason being that they were considered the analogues of Ninip, Marduk, Nirgal, Istar, and Nabu, who were similarly connected with the planets in the Babylonian scheme. The Romans in turn acting on the same principle with respect to the Greeks, made Saturnus, Jupiter, Mars, Venus and Mercurius their planetary gods, whence our modern name for the planets (Brown 1899: 1.335).

For our prophet, the planet Jupiter was known in Greek as Zeus, Semitic: Ba'al, Ba'alu, Belu, Belos, Bel. In ancient Mesopotamia, it was known as Marduk. In the sky, the "River of Marduk" was the Milky Way as it flows past the ancient star of Babel, Capella, and southwards to Orion (Brown 1900: 2.205).

Interestingly, Belu Marduk was the protecting patron deity of Babylon before the Persians put in Aphrodite. The famous Tower of Babel was what Babylonians called the "Holy Hill" of the sky. It allowed for access to the protecting deity of the city, the very ancient Mul-illi, later identified with Bel-Marduk. There was also a temple to Bel-Marduk.

The shrine of the temple possessed a copy in miniature of the Holy Mound itself; and it seems, on the whole sufficiently probable that the temple and its arrangements were intended to be a pattern of "things in the heavens," and that, to the initiated votary, it occultly typified the Holy Hill of heaven "in the sides of the north" (Isa 14:13) (Brown 1900: 2.189).

The first-century B.C. temple to Bel in Palmyra was also situated on a great mound, a holy hill. For our purposes, it is interesting to note that there is a constellation called "Kakkab Belit," that is, constellation of the Lady of Babylon, the Might of the Grove-of-life. In the sky it consists of the stars alpha and beta Librae. Moreover, the constellation of the zodiac called by Babylonians the "Temple Tower Altar" held in the claws of Scorpio, is particularly connected with Babilu, the Gate of the gods.

The connection between the famous Tower, Babylon, and the autumnal season, the 7th month, explains the position of this asterism at the base of the constellation Chelai–Libra [the name of the constellation is Lord of the foundation of brickwork, the god the Creator]; and further light is thrown upon the matter by the name of the 16th Chinese lunar asterism consisting of alpha, beta, gamma, zeta Librae and the archaic name of which is I-shi (the Foundation). Entenamasluv was called (Semitic) Siru-etsen-tsiri, "the Limb Tip-of-the-Tail." This is not a translation of the Akkadian name but an explanation of the position of the Asterism, as being at the end of the tail of Hydra. . . . This double or triple aspect of Entenamasluv gives rise to various statements concerning it which except under most careful investigation, appear to be contradictory. Thus, we are told that in the month Tammuz, with which it is specially connected, at its rising it raises the waves of the sea. This idea is connected with Hydra, as 'the strong serpent of the sea.' As an ecliptic asterism it "holds" Jupiter; and is particularly connected with Tisri, the 7th month. Its connection with Tammuz, the 4th month, is illustrated by the fact that as Hydra, it extends right up to Cancer (= Allab). The patron divinity of this Asterism is the god 'Ip. 'Ip and Nin-ip were two primeval deities who in Akkadian cosmology represented the male and female principles but the genderless character of the Akkadian Nin "lord" or "lady," caused the Semites to change NIN-IP into a god and identify him with IP, that is, "Anu who listens to prayer" (Sayce, cited by Brown 1900: 2.86–87).

While this passage illustrates the fluidity of astronomic identifications, it does underscore the connection of Babel's Holy Hill with the sea Beast of our seer and the planet Jupiter/Zeus/Bel. Strabo recalls the temple of this deity when he describes the city of Babylon. He tells us that the circuit of Babylon's walls was 385 stadia, the walls being thirty-two cubits thick and fifty cubits high, with room for four horse chariots to easily pass each other on the wall. The towers were sixty cubits.

> And it is on this account that this and the hanging garden are called one of the Seven Wonders of the World. The garden is quadrangular in shape, and each side is four plethra in length. It consists of arched vaults which are situated one after another on checkered, cube-like foundations. The checkered foundations which are hollowed out, are covered so deep with earth that they admit of the largest of trees, having been constructed of baked brick and asphalt—the foundations themselves and the vaults and the arches. The ascent to the uppermost terrace-roofs is made by a stairway; and alongside these stairs there were screws, through which the water was continually conducted up into the garden from the Euphrates by those appointed for this purpose. For the river, a stadium in width, flows through the middle of the city; and the garden is on the bank of the river. Here too is the tomb of Belus, now in ruins, having been demolished by Xerxes, as it is said. It was a quadrangular pyramid of baked brick, not only being a stadium in height, but also having sides a stadium in length (Strabo, *Geography* 738C, LCL).

Alexander the Great was remodeling this "tomb of Belus" when he died.

The point here is that historically the deity signaled by Jupiter/Zeus/Baal preceded the deity signaled by Venus/Aphrodite/Istar as protector of Babylon. In this sense Venus can be said to be seated on Jupiter. The conjunction thus makes good astronomic sense.

Further, what John sees is the Great Harlot with a cup of blood. Images of gods and goddess with a cup in one hand, with the other raised, generally depict a posture of blessing. The "cup of blessing" of 1 Cor 10:16 is based on this traditional gesture, already witnessed in the Ugaritic texts, where Ilu (El, that is "god") thus blesses. The cup is the "cup of destiny," the expected outcome of the blessing (see de Moor 1987: 205, n. 49), the "destiny" or outcome of associating with her. The

seer describes the woman as clothed in royal garments, yet her royal
"cup" is full of unbefitting contents—idolatry.

Finally we are given her name (17:5) written over her forehead:
"Babylon the Great." In Mediterranean antiquity it was quite normal to
depict cities as women. There are many coins depicting cities, such as
Alexandria, Rome, Antioch and the like, as women enthroned. And
these female personifications usually wear images of the city walls as a
crown on their heads. We are then told the woman was drunk with
blood, a figure of speech applied to conquerors (e.g., in the Greek
version of Isa 34:5: God's sword, 34:7: the land; Jer 26:10: God himself
is drunk with the blood of his enemies; the idiom is otherwise well
known; see Charles 1920: 2.66). It was the blood of the holy ones, those
antediluvian sons of God of Gen 6, again. Babylon is thus accused of
having exterminated the remaining antediluvians who once descended
from the sky.

The Great Harlot, "the mother of harlots and of the abominations
of the earth," was the source of all subsequent cities with their insistence upon idolatry. After all, Babel was the first city after the Flood.
Furthermore, as manifestation of its protecting deity, Aphrodite/'Anatu,
Babylon obviously gets intoxicated by drinking blood. Consider the
following Canaanite description of 'Anat (and her replications), as goddess of battle:

> And look! 'Anatu fought in the plain, she slaughtered between the two
> cities.
>
> She smote the people of the sea-shore, silenced the men of the East.
>
> Heads were under her (feet) like clods of earth, on her were hands, like
> locusts, like scales of a plane tree the lands of the warriors.
>
> She attached the heads to her chest, tied up the hands with her girdle.
>
> She plunged her knees in the blood of the guards, her buttocks in the gore
> of the warriors.
>
> With a staff she chased the old men, with the stave of her bow the
> veterans. . . .
>
> The Virgin 'Anatu washed her hands, the Wanton Widow of the Nations
> her fingers.
>
> She washed her hands of the blood of the guards, her fingers of the gore
> of the warriors (Baal I.2, 2–31, de Moor 1987: 5–7).

She also drinks blood: "She ate his flesh without a knife, she drank
his blood without a cup" (Loves of Baal and Anath I, de Moor 1987:
109; concerning 'Anatu's sexual desire for Ba'lu). In the previous chapter of Revelation (16:6), blood drinking was far more noxious to its
consumers; but they were not deities. Here the seer sees that this

celestial deity gets intoxicated by drinking the blood of the holy ones and of the witnesses of Jesus (see Hanson 1993). She stands in conflict, then, both with the antediluvian celestial beings who refused the enticements of human sexual union as well as with those who witness to Jesus, now on the same footing as the holy ones. These first two sights conclude with the seer expressing his astonishment at the scenario.

10.1.4. Appropriations of the Vision

We would expect John to continue describing the sights that unfolded before him. But the series is now interrupted by an allegorical explanation of the personages of these first two sights. Such explanatory interruptions are rare in the book. Perhaps the most significant one occurred in Sector 1, when the cosmic Jesus, whom the seer regards in the first chapter, explains: "As to the hidden meaning of the seven stars which you saw in my right hand, and of the seven golden lamp stands: the seven stars are the sky servants of the seven churches, and the seven lamp stands are the churches" (1:20). Now we are in for more hidden meanings in 17:7–18. It is the allegorical explanation inserted here that has provoked endless commentators, perhaps following 4 Ezra, to apply this book to first-century Rome. In this set of clarifications, the sky servant is little concerned with the Great Harlot. Rather, his focus is on the Beast (vv. 8–14), with a sentence about the waters, and finally a sentence about the Woman. Obviously this is a curious procedure. Now if we take the sky servant's explanation as referring to celestial features, they will make good literal sense.

First of all, the sea Beast of the vision is described as one who "was and is not and is going to come up from the Abyss" before being totally destroyed. Now the chief celestial being who can readily be characterized as one who "was and is not and is going to come up from the Abyss" is Canaanite deity Ba'lu or Baal, the Syrian Adon or Adonis. In the cosmological theology of the region, Baal/Adonis (Roman Jupiter, Greek Zeus) is the spouse of 'Anat/Atargatis (Venus). As giver of fertility to humankind, Baal controls celestial phenomena such as rain, dew, lightning, thunder, and earthquakes. He annually disappears during the dry season, only to emerge with the autumn rains. All of this is indicated in the sky with the transit of respective constellations and planets. In other words, if any sky being "was, and is not, and is going to come up from the Abyss," it is Baal/Jupiter. The reemergence of this deity annually astonishes his devotees, that is, those persons not listed in the scroll of life "from the foundation of the world." Those listed in the scroll of life are not astonished since they know the unique God is in charge. This book of positive cosmic destiny is in possession of the cosmic Lamb, itself "from the foundation of the world" (13:8).

As the account proceeds, the sky servant provides the seer with even more specific applications of the Venus vision. The seven heads of the astral sea monster in fact stand for the seven mountains upon which the woman is seated. As previously noted, first-century Babylon lay in ruins; all that remained of the glory of the past was seven hills.

Yet we are told that the seven hills stand for seven kings. Of these kings, five have completed their kingship, one is now in power, while another is going to come. But after that next king, the cosmic sea Beast (Baal/Jupiter) will take over. That beast is "the eighth," or "an eighth," who is "one of the seven, and goes into destruction" (17:11). Of course the seven rulers of the cosmos are those stars called planets. In the Israelite tradition, God created in six days and rests on the seventh. For the seer, we are obviously at a period when the first five day-controlling planets have completed their rule; the sixth day planet is in power now (Venus), while another is going to come. Then comes the eighth, the cosmic Beast. In cosmic lore, this is the Ogdoad (literally in Greek: "the Eighth One") that marks completion, fullness, totality. Thus the destruction of the cosmic sea Beast marks the end of whatever is going on.

And what of the ten horns or dorsal fins of the cosmic sea Beast (17:12–13)? These stand for ten other kings who have no kingship of their own but function as king at the behest or under the control of the ruling sea Beast (itself, we learned, surrogate of the Dragon). What characterizes these kings is their harmony, unity, and agreement; they all agree to serve as client-kings of the cosmic sea Beast. Such harmony is pre-Babel, for since the destruction of the Tower of Babel the human condition is one of confusion and disharmony unleashed by God at Babel. Hence it would seem the seer is being told that once the cosmic sea Beast takes over as "the Eighth," it will appoint ten surrogate kings to rule in its stead. This is not unlike the situation of the meeting out of power to ten of the cosmic fallen Watchers, formerly holy ones, by their leader in Enoch:

> Then they all swore together and bound one another by a curse. And they were altogether two hundred; and they descended into 'Ardos, which is the summit of Hermon. And they called the mount Armon, for they swore and bound one another by a curse. And their names are as follows: Semyaz, the leader of Arakeb, Rame'el, Tam'el, Dan'el, Ezeqel, Baraqyal, As'el, Armaros, Batar'el, Anan'el, Zaqa'el, Sasomaspwe'el, Kestar'el, Tur'el, Yamayol, and Arazyal. These are the chiefs of tens and of all the others with them (1 Enoch 6:5–8, OTP).

Thus if Babylon is 'Anat/Venus and if the sea Beast is Baal/Jupiter, then this sea Beast stands in the same relationship to God as Baal to Ilu (Jupiter/Zeus to Saturn/Kronos is not as good a fit). In Canaanite and later Mediterranean theology, God (and Ilu) is the ultimate, the creator of all. The seer does not deny the power of Babylon or of the sea Beast (Baal or Jupiter), but sees their destruction "in the stars." For all that they stand for will do battle with the cosmic Lamb, "who will conquer them because he is Lord of lords and King of kings"; and the Lamb's celestial entourage are "the called and the chosen and the trustworthy" (17:14). In other words, believers can count on the Lamb and his entourage.

But that is not all that the seer has to say. With the phrase: "and he says to me," (17:15), the prophet presents another set of interpretations. The sky servant further clarifies that the many waters on which the Great Harlot is seated are actually a large population of varied peoples: "peoples, and crowds, and nations, and tongues," just as in Babel of old. Furthermore, the sea Beast itself along with its ten surrogate kings, will turn against Venus' city and utterly destroy it, for God has already directed those entities to do it when the utterances of God are fulfilled (17:17). In other words, the cosmic sea Beast along with its client-kings will detach themselves from the Harlot City. That they have detached themselves is demonstrated by their actions. They shame the city, devour it, and burn up what is left. In turning on the Harlot City, the client-kings serve as unwitting tools of God's plan, submitting themselves to the cosmic sea Beast until God's revealed will is carried out.

Finally, the seer is given a last interpretation of the meaning of the Woman. She is the "Great City" dominating the kings of the earth. We, of course, already know this, for her name is Babylon the Great. The question most interpreters presume to answer is: to which city during the author's day is the sky servant referring? Most would say Rome. But there is no hint of this at all in this document. Hence most interpreters have to explain the silence surrounding the answer to the question they alone have created. In line with the book as a whole, I believe we should look for our answer in the sky. Just as the cosmic Jesus of ch. 1 has John give messages to sky servants about the churches they controlled, perhaps the reference here is to an earthly Great City controlled by and in counterbalance to some celestial city.

Now the only sky city in the work is Jerusalem. There is a passage in Israel's scriptures that would suggest the sky and Jerusalem to our seer. The book of Lamentations aptly describes how God himself has cast down the splendor of Israel from "the sky to earth" (Lam 2:1):

How the Lord in his anger has set the daughter of Zion under a cloud!

He has cast down from the sky to the earth the splendor of Israel; he has not remembered his footstool in the days of his anger.

The Lord has destroyed without mercy all the habitations of Jacob; in his wrath he has broken down the strongholds of the daughter of Judah; he has brought down to the ground in dishonor the kingdom and its rulers (Lam 2:1–2).

Furthermore, that same book underscores:

> How lonely sits the city that was full of people!
> How like a widow has she become, she that was great among the nations!
> She that was a princess among the cities has become a vassal (Lam 1:1).

People view the destroyed city and ask:

> Is this the city which was called the perfection of beauty, the joy of all the earth? (Lam 2:15).

Jerusalem's iniquities outpaced Sodom, which also "was overthrown in a moment, no hand being laid on it" (Lam 4:6). And it was a truly great city since: "The kings of the earth did not believe or any of the inhabitants of the world, that foe or enemy could enter the gates of Jerusalem" (Lam 4:12). And why was it destroyed? "This was for the sins of her prophets and the iniquities of her priests, who shed in the midst of her the blood of the righteous" (Lam 4:13). Of course these are so many themes and ideas that resonate in the scenarios of Revelation.

In sum, the last sky servant's interpretation of fallen Babylon would seem to point to historical Jerusalem, the earthly counterpart of the celestial Jerusalem. For the protohistoric Great Harlot is the celestial Jerusalem's counterpart, just as the starry sky servants of ch. 1 were the celestial counterparts (as patrons) of the seven Christian communities. Previous mention of the "great city" in Revelation points in the direction of Jerusalem. The seer mentions "the great city . . . where their Lord was crucified" (11:8). Otherwise, the phrase is synonymous with Babylon, "the great city" so connected with other kingdoms that they too collapse with the demise of the great city (see 16:19; 18:10, 16, 18, 19, 21). Furthermore, that subsequent chapters of this work lavish so many indications to underscore that this city was central to God's concern further points to Jerusalem. If indeed the Great Harlot is Jerusalem, that would again explain its destruction. On the other hand, the vague description equally fits any city that expands into imperial dimensions as did Nineveh or Babylon or Persepolis or Hellenistic Antioch and Alexandria. Yet none of these have sky counterparts in Israel's traditional lore. From the perspective of Israelite tradition, none of these warrant God's attention. Their destruction requires neither explanation nor concern. But Jerusalem is another matter, for just as God descended to Babel of old, so Jerusalem was the place where God once made his name to dwell. But never again!

10.2. THE THIRD SIGHT: THE FIRST DESCENDING SKY SERVANT

The third sight the seer observes "after these things" is the first of a balancing pair of sky servants (the other appears in 20:1). This first one descends from the sky and is seen to be extremely powerful and extremely radiant. He announces the demise of the Harlot/City and the reasons for its collapse—idolatry, especially as revealed in social relations with kings and merchants. The focus is thus on the elites of the city, their international contacts, and their luxurious life-style bound up with "fornication," the idolatry typical of 'Anat or Venus.

After this the seer reports a sequence of statements that he overhears. To begin with he overhears a second voice emerging from the sky that speaks of the city dwellers as "my people," yet refers to God in the third person. Hence the speaker is not God. On the other hand, non-Judean cities would have a number of deities equally concerned about city populations. But since such deities are not mentioned, it would seem the city in question is Jerusalem, for apart from God, the other celestial personage connected with a city's population would be the city's guardian sky servant. Here that being urges "my people" to leave the city. To motivate them, this concerned sky being notes that (1) these people were not associated in the sins of the harlot/city; they were non-elite; (2) the elite's transgressions are against God (18:5); (3) the elites will be given double retribution, a "cup" with a double amount (v. 6); (4) elite claims to extreme honor will be reversed to extreme shame in torment and grief because the heart is perverse (v. 7). And most significantly, (5) retribution (death, grief, famine, fire) comes quickly and irreversibly, in "one day." The reason for all this is that God is the judge here.

The population of Babel sought to reach the sky (Gen 11:4), but here it is the sins of the elites that have reached the sky (18:5). Ancient Babel sought "to make a name for ourselves" (Gen 11:4), just as here, "she glorified herself and lived luxuriously" (18:7). And as Babel's patroness sought to sit "as a queen and not a widow" so too the city (18:7).

The former allies of the Great City serve as the major witnesses to her destruction. First are the kings of the earth who shared in idolatry; these fall into mourning at the sight of the smoke of destruction, and standing far off, sing their lament over Babylon, for judgment came in "one hour" (18:9–10).

Next merchants of the earth who shared in idolatry complain of loss of business in temple and luxury items; these too fall into mourning, and standing far off sing their lament because great wealth was ravaged in "one hour" (18:11–17a).

Finally, those who have grown wealthy shout at the sight of the smoke of destruction. They publicly mourn and sing their lament, for the city was ravaged in "one hour" (18:17b–19).

It seems that 18:20 is a later insertion, urging the sky to be glad over the destruction. Rejoicing is also fitting because God gives the holy ones, apostles and prophets justice by condemning the Great City that has done injustice to them. Mention of apostles and prophets again points to Jerusalem.

The next report concerns the laments of those who collaborated with the Harlot/City: kings, merchants, merchant marine. Their lament concludes with a reference that puts us back in the sky: "Be glad over her, O sky! And the Holy Ones and the apostles, and the prophets, because God has judged your case against her" (19:20; the "apostles" is an abrupt element here).

Then a final, "mighty" sky servant performs a prophetic act to depict the utterly annihilated condition of the Harlot/City. He takes up a great millstone only to throw it into the sea. This being, then, explains his action in terms of a number of images that exemplify how and to what extent the Great City will be cast away once and for all. This sky servant describes a truly dead city: no sounds, either of merriment or labor (18:22), no light, no family chatter (18:23). The reasons for the total desolation include the exclusivity of elites, the magical deception of the (other) nations, the murder of prophets and holy ones, and the slaughter in the land (see Elliott 1993). The mention here of "Gentiles," that is, other nations, underscoring Judean exclusivity, plus the murder of prophets, and slaughter in the land, indicates some accusing hand against Jerusalem.

Enoch likewise complains against the elites of the land of Israel, locating John in the same tradition:

> Thus the Lord commanded the kings, the governors, the high officials and the landlords and said: "Open your eyes and lift up your eyebrows—if you are able to recognize the Elect One! . . . Their faces shall be filled with shame and their countenances shall be crowned with darkness. So he will deliver them to the angels for punishments in order that vengeance shall be executed on them—oppressors of his children and his elect ones. They shall rejoice over the kings, the governors, the high officials and the landlords because the wrath of the Lord of the Spirits shall rest upon them and his sword shall obtain from them a sacrifice. The righteous and elect ones shall be saved on that day; and from thenceforth they shall never see the faces of the sinners and oppressors (1 Enoch 62:1–2, 10–13, *OTP*).

> Furthermore, at that time, you shall say: "Our souls are satiated with exploitation money which could not save us from being cast into the oppressive Sheol." After that, their faces shall be filled with shame before the Son of Man; and from before his face they shall be driven out. And the sword shall abide in their midst, before his face. Thus says the Lord of the Spirits, "This is the ordinance and the judgment, before the Lord of the Spirits, prepared for the governors, kings, high officials, and landlords" (1 Enoch 63:10–12, *OTP*).

10.2.1. The Celestial Response to Babylon's Fall

The final sequence of items that the seer overhears is the celestial response to the fall of Babylon the Great. It is overwhelming. He begins by describing the reaction of God's celestial entourage. The seer first notes a countless crowd praising God for the destruction of the Great City. Its destruction vindicates God's slaves. With another "Alleluia" (= Praise Yahweh!), the chant is taken up again, further underscoring the lasting destruction of the Great City. The innumerable celestial crowd yields to God's inner circle, the twenty-four elders and the four living creatures. These twenty-eight beings along the sky equator add their "Alleluia."

Subsequently, a voice comes from the throne. This is not God speaking since the voice urges praise to "our God." Hence the voice is that of a major-domo in this cosmic liturgy. Here we find that God's slaves are all who respect God, small and great. Finally, after the urging of this cosmic major domo, a truly countless crowd resumes its singing. The magnitude of the sound is compared in three ways. It is like the voice of a countless crowd, like the voice of many waters, and like the voice of mighty thunders. For the seer, magnitude of sound means an experience so loud that a person simply cannot conceive of anything louder. And this praise ringing out in the cosmos is rooted in two motives: because God finally rules as king (19:6) and because of the wedding of the Lamb (19:7).

10.2.2. Hinting at a New Jerusalem

The first motivation behind the cosmic jubilation is "because the Lord has begun to reign as king, our God, the Almighty." This indicates that from creation to this instance, God has refrained from asserting his kingship. Only with the total destruction of Babylon the Great does God's manifest rule begin. Now according to Israel's Scriptures, the only earthly location of God's rule is Jerusalem. The ushering in of God's rule with the destruction of Babylon the Great points to Jerusalem as the successor city to Babylon the Great; of course this occurs only after the destruction of present Jerusalem. God's incipient rule, then, alludes to some new Jerusalem in place of the old.

10.2.3. Announcing the Wedding of the Lamb

Next, the celestial sonic booming gives honor to God for the Wedding of the Lamb. The Wedding of the Lamb is a rather surprising development since nothing was previously said about such a wedding or about its participants. Why such a wedding? There are perhaps two reasons. The first has to do with 'Anat or Ishtar or Venus—a celestial being—ever a virgin and constantly sexually active. This cosmic being was viewed by one and all as patroness of marriage. The demise of the Great Babylon marks the demise of the influence of the celestial patroness of marriage. Who or what will now take the place of 'Anat in all her guises to hallow the primal symbol of kinship? To succeed the defunct goddess, it seems our seer had his sights turned to a constellation called "Wedding of the Gods." He is led to appropriate this constellation within the framework of the unfolding drama he witnesses. The constellation becomes "Wedding of the Lamb" (for more details, see the discussion in Sector 5).

After mentioning this Wedding of the Lamb, yet without identifying the bride (reserved for later 21:10ff.), the seer describes the bride's outfit, woven of "the just deeds of the Holy Ones," those cosmic sky servants who descended to the earth in antediluvian times and who now serve in the Lamb's entourage. The seer now leaves this scenario rather abruptly due to new orders from the sky servant. Specifically, John is to note the honorable estate of those called to take part in the Lamb's wedding supper. This statement is qualified as "truthful utterances of God," a sort of word of honor underscoring the veracity of the statement.

Even though John had previously interacted with sky servants, he suddenly falls prostrate before this one. This, of course, seems to have been customary, proper behavior for astral prophets in their interaction with these celestial beings. Consider the advice of the proverbial Solomon to his son Roboam in a first-century B.C. document. The document opens with a "Prayer for Sky Servants (Angels)":

> Whenever you might wish to adjure a sky servant and a demon at the hour when they exercise lordly power, adjure them thus: "I adjure you, O given sky servant, who exercises lordly power over this hour and who are appointed for the providence and service of the human race, O such a one, ever willing, capable and courageous and dazzling, I adjure you by the god who assigned you to watch over this hour, that you be my assistant with the given demon subject to you, who has been determined to be slave for this hour and hasten please to assist me and perform this service, and please be genuine, good and true.

Now instructions follow:

> Know, O most careful son Roboam, that whenever you intend to undertake some work, you should happen to know the planet and the hour in question. And first say the prayers, then adjure the sky servant and the demon of that hour; and in order that he be your assistant in the task which you wish to do then make the signs of the planet with the ink and incense for each respectively. And having the power of it, the lord of the hour is at your disposal (CCAG VIII, 2, 157, 20–158, 4).

Yet this messenger underscores the basic equality between God's sky servants and the followers of Jesus—all are slaves of God. Hence the sky servant urges the seer to fall prostrate before God because Jesus' witness (v. 1) is in fact prophetic power. For an identical scenario, but with different motivations, see 22:8–9.

10.3. The Central Scenario: Destruction of Enemies

In the central scenario of this sector the seer beholds three more sights: the fourth sight—that of the White Horse Rider; the fifth sight—that of the gathering for the Great Supper of God, and the sixth sight—the Final Battle.

10.3.1. Fourth Sight: The White Horse Rider

With the seer's fourth vision, we come to the central scenario of this sector. Meanwhile, back in the atmosphere, the sky vault opens and the seer sees a white horse and over/on it a being called Trustworthy and Truthful, whose function is to judge and to do battle. Riders in the sky were well-known at this time in the Mediterranean (see Johnston 1992). Among the various comet names previously indicated, one is called the "Horseman." Consider the description offered by the legendary astrologer-priest, Petosiris, who provided the fictional Pharaoh Nechepso with celestial revelation:

> The comet Horseman. The so-called Horseman is Venus, so named because of its quick movement. It trails a broad fiery tail, spreads into a swath of light and then contracts to a tight ball. . . . When it rises fiery and flashes its tail toward the east, it carries the threat of an uprising by the Persians requiring the concentration of many army units in the east: Syria will be filled with soldiery dispatched to every point and, as the standing army will be inadequate against the enemy movement, a new conscription will be held. A plague will come first and will fall especially on the horses, not those of the Persians but those brought from Europe against them. This will be a first defeat for the plague-struck. But fortune will not favor the Persian side all the way; a great array of forces will encounter them, they will flee for their lives, the cities taken from them will be set free, and their king will lose his life during the flight. Then the wealth of the Persians will be seized as booty. the crops of the farmers killed in the war or by the plague will become useless. However, the invaders from Europe will not stay on or tarry in the Persians' lands but, just as if the battle had been decided, the people on each side will return home. All of the above is what the comet threatens when it rises fiery. If it is pale it still portends war. but not against the Persians; also people will be overwhelmed by earthquakes and grief, a plague will attack the cattle and there will be an extremely severe famine . . . (Nechepso-Petosiris frag. 9, trans. N. Lewis 1976: 145–46).

The fact that this comet is related to Venus poses no inconsistency, for Venus has a male aspect, specifically when it rises in the east in the morning. Then it is a morning star, an eastern star. As we shall see, Jesus himself is identified with Venus as morning star 22:16 (see also in

2 Pet 1:19). Consider some more of the lore in this tradition in Appendix E: On Comets.

Here the seer interprets the meaning of the White Horse comet, specifically by further characterizing the rider (19:12–13, 15–16). This new sky being has fiery eyes, a multicrowned head, with a secret name on the head, and clothed in a blood-soaked garment. Now we are told his name is "God's Utterance." Furthermore, a sharp sword protrudes from his mouth, and with this sword he shepherds the nations. And he trods the winepress of God's vengeful wrath (hence the blood-soaked garment). On his garments he has further names: "King of kings and Lord of lords," or in more proper English, "the most eminent king and the most eminent lord." This, of course, is the title of the cosmic Lamb in 17:14. This sky being wages war in the sky.

The Maccabees once experienced help from the sky during one of their battles:

> Just as dawn was breaking, the two armies joined battle, the one having as pledge of success and victory not only their valor but their reliance upon the Lord, while the other made rage their leader in the fight. When the battle became fierce, there appeared to the enemy from heaven five resplendent men on horses with golden bridles, and they were leading the Judeans. Surrounding Maccabeus and protecting him with their own armor and weapons, they kept him from being wounded. And they showered arrows and thunderbolts upon the enemy, so that, confused and blinded, they were thrown into disorder and cut to pieces (2 Macc 10:28–30).

However, the present scenario is not quite like that reflected in 2 Maccabbees, for there is no action or help given to anyone on earth. Rather, all the action stays in the sky. To make this clear, the seer interrupts his focus on the Rider to say a word about the Rider's following. What accompanies him is none other than God's sky army, clothed in pure white linen. This interruption keeps the scenario in the sky.

10.3.2. Fifth Sight: The Great Supper of God

This vision is also part of the central portion of this sector. It explains how the enemies vanquished by the White Horse Rider are disposed of. Now the seer sees another sky servant in midsky, standing in the sun. He takes up that position in order to summon the birds that fly in midsky. The reason for this is that in the Middle East (e.g., Syria) the sun is the proper locus of the eagle, "the messenger of the sun" and king of birds (see Boll 1914: 38–39). These carnivores are invited to "the Great Supper of God," like vultures to vast carnage. The carnage to which the carnivorous birds are invited includes every social category, listed by rank: kings, tribunes, aristocrats, equestrians (knights), free men, slaves. In sum, the victims are "the small and the great," that is, everyone. Why the summons to the birds? It is simply preparation for the impending battle.

10.3.3. Sixth Sight: The Final Battle

The seer next sees the sea Beast (introduced in 13:1) allied with the kings of earth and their armies, ready to do battle with the sky judge-warrior and his sky army. We are not told where this battle is taking place; however, given the major participants, it would seem to be all taking place in the sky. The opposition consists of the constellational sea Beast (with the planet Jupiter/Baal), the land Beast who appears as false prophet; and the kings allied to the Beast (from 17:14), undoubtedly controlled by appropriate demons or sky servants. While the battle is not described, we learn about its outcome at the close of the scenario. The sky Beasts are thrown alive into the cosmic pool of sulphur fire, while followers are slain by the mouth-sword of the judge warrior and eaten by the carnivorous birds.

Thus God's Great Supper contrasts with the Wedding Supper of the Lamb. This latter, simply mentioned in the context of the praise of God for the downfall of Babylon, still awaits realization in the narrative. But before that final cosmic supper is introduced, the seer has several other matters to dispose of, specifically the fate of the cosmic Dragon, whose cohort has been consigned to the pool of sulphur fire, presumably in the cosmic Abyss.

10.4. SEVENTH SIGHT:
THE SECOND DESCENDING SKY SERVANT

In the seventh of this series of visions, the seer regards the second of a balanced pair of sky servants. The first descended from the sky to announce the collapse of Babylon the Great. The second now descends to restrain the cosmic Dragon. It is interesting to note that God's sky servant is more powerful than the cosmic Dragon. This sky servant, equipped with the key to the cosmic Abyss and a great chain, seizes the Dragon with impunity, binds him, and casts him into the cosmic Abyss where the Dragon's collaborators, the sea Beast and the land Beast already are. The description of the Dragon here as "the ancient serpent, the Devil and Satan" confirms that we are dealing with the same character as the one introduced in 12:9. But curiously, the Dragon is to be incapacitated for only a limited time, one thousand years. Then, for some cosmic reason, "it is necessary" that he be released briefly before his final destruction. Perhaps the seer is referring to some astronomic calculation that would have old Scorpio disappear to the south, below the horizon, only to emerge later at some predictable cosmic period. With this constellation ensconced below the horizon, the cosmic Abyss is now firmly closed and sealed. This allows the (other) nations a thousand-year respite from deception, the output of the Dragon.

10.5. EIGHTH SIGHT: THE TEMPORARY RULE OF THE JUST AND THE DEMISE OF SATAN

The incapacitation of the Dragon is followed by a scene of thrones on which those who did not succumb to idolatry were enthroned to rule along with the Messiah—for a thousand years. Those persons who did succumb remain dead—for a thousand years. This period during which the non-idolaters are honored with the Messiah is called "the first resurrection." Of course the scenario is located in the sky since we are dealing with countless thrones, the souls of the just, the reigning Messiah, and an extremely long life-span. Thus the "first resurrection," for John, is the presence of the just with the Messiah immediately upon their death.

The author (or someone else) acknowledges the honor of being included in the first resurrection. These persons are exempt from "the second death" (described in 20:14), have the status of "priests" of God and the Messiah, and remain enthroned—for a thousand years.

But this intervening period of bliss comes to a close, presumably for a new and better situation, if that is imaginable. What marks its close is the final cosmic battle. Upon completion of the thousand years, the cosmic Dragon, now called "Satan," is loosed from the Abyss to rise in the sky once more. His task is to practice his craft—deception. Perhaps it is important to note that the word for "to deceive" in Greek (*planaō*, πλανάω) serves to pun on the Greek word for "planet" (*planētēs*, πλανήτης). For in this context, the cosmic Dragon is to gather countless nations into battle *by means of* (grammatically, an accusative of agency in Greek) Gog and Magog. The opposing combatants in this war are to be the holy ones and the Beloved City.

It would seem that the pivotal characters are Gog and Magog. Who or what are Gog and Magog? Magog is mentioned as a son of Japheth in Gen 10:2. Thanks to this notice, "Magog" is taken as a place name designating the residence of Gog, hence Gog from Magog. This is how Gog is referred to in Ezek 38–39. This Gog "will come against the land of Israel" says Ezekiel (38:18); there he will fall and be buried with his horde from the uttermost north (Ezek 39:11).

However, this Ezekiel Gog from Magog tradition has little to do with Revelation, for our seer presents two entities, Gog and Magog. Now what is the significance of these two in a book of astral prophecy such as Revelation? To begin with, the word "Gog" in Sumerian means "Darkness." "[T]hus Magog = the land of darkness and Gog = the personification of darkness" (Benedikt Otzen, *sub verbo*, *TDOT* 2.422, citing Van Hoonacker). While this usage surely antedates our book by too many centuries, perhaps the Mesopotamian tradition lived on, for the fact is, in the Sibylline Oracles (3:319–322), Gog and Magog are taken to be black. Now this meaning cannot underlay the Gog of Magog in Ezek 38:2 since Gog is likewise chief prince of Meshech and Tubal— all descendants of Japheth in Gen 10:2. While Ezekiel does mention Persia, Cush (Ethiopia) and Put joining Gog's forces (Ezek 38:5), this does not explain the woe in the Sibylline Oracles 3:319–322:

> Woe to you, land of Gog and Magog, situated in the midst of Ethiopian rivers. How great an effusion of blood you will receive and you will be called a habitation of judgment among men, and your dewy earth will drink black blood (1.364 *OTP*).

The point is, by the first century A.D. Gog and Magog, two entities, are clearly associated with being black. Black what? Consider the reference to the black celestial body, *Ugaga*, in Babylonian literatures. Brown notes that Ugaga is the Raven (Corvus) in the Field of Anu. Ravens ranked among the evil brood of Tiamat; they were ill-omened birds. Now what sort of celestial body was it? Brown refers the reader to the contention that this Ugaga must be a comet. First of all, it is ill-omened; "a comet might similarly be looked upon as an ill-omened bird of the sky. . . . It faces Sulpa-uddua (Mercury), it has a halo round it, at times it is misty and again is not misty, and it is said to be sizi–color" (the Sizi bird, Sem. *rakraku*, is the Black Stork). Further, we find that the star of the Raven attained the path of the sun. Hence it is not a fixed star but a type of planet unlike the others that are always in the ecliptic region (Brown 1900: 2.171–73). In sum, Ugaga is a dark planet, and this from ancient times. By Hellenistic times, as we shall see, Mediterraneans knew of two such planets that emanated dark instead of light.

And it would seem John has these in mind here. The first clue is in verse 9, which begins with the Greek verb: ἀναβαίνω, *anabainō*. In fact the verse with its plural reference reads like an astronomical observation: "they ascended along the latitudinal line of the earth, then circled the array of the Holy Ones and the Beloved City, but then fire descended and devoured them." What would such an observation mean in terms of a sky scenario? To begin with, there were two planets in the ancient world described as dark planets. These were named the "Ascender" and the "Descender." Much later the Manichees would call both of them "Ascenders" (ἀναβιβάζοντες, *anabibazontes*), but the practice was much earlier. Just as the sun, for example, emanated light, these planets emanated dark. In this they worked just like the eyes of a blind person, which radiated dark. These dark planets are referred to in Jude 13 as "wandering stars for whom the gloomy darkness is forever kept" (see Merkelbach 1991; in Sanskrit, Indians knew them as *Rahu*, the Ascender, and *Ketu*, the Descender, see Balfour 1976).

These planets have their origin in an explanation of what causes a lunar eclipse or of what accounts for the "horns" of the moon in its first and final phases (see Stegemann 1938; Beck 1987). What is it that blocks the moon? Before the Hellenistic period, to introduce the concept of the earth's circular shadow is equivalent to postulating the sphericity of the earth. This conception was completely lacking in ancient Mesopotamian astronomy. Ancient Indian astronomers "discovered" the existence of special celestial entities, dark planets that obscured the moon moving always at 180 degrees elongation from the sun. These were the so-called Head and Tail of the Indian sky Dragon that moved in computable fashion as members of the planetary family (see Neugebauer 1975: 550).

In Mediterranean Hellenistic circles, the position of these planets was first recorded in a horoscope of 43 B.C. (Neugebauer and Van Hoesen 1959: L42). About a century later, Dorotheus of Sidon explains them as follows in his chapter on clarifying the phases of the moon and the head of the Dragon and its tail, which indicate selling and buying and cheapness and costliness:

> The head is called "ascending" and its tail "descending" and the signs which those learned in the stars call "obscured" are from Leo to Capricorn, which is the region of descent, while from Aquarius to Cancer is the region of ascent. Look, and if the moon is in the region of ascent increasing in computation, then he who buys at this time will buy dearly and at an increase in its price over what is right. If the moon is in the region of descent and is diminishing in computation, then he who buys at this time will buy cheaply and at a price less than what is right (Dorotheos of Sidon V, 43, trans. D. Pingree, 1976: 322).

And in a passage from Hephaestio, citing Dorotheus, we read:

> When the moon is full and is favorable in longitude and latitude with the Ascendant [ἀναβιβάζων, *anabibazōn*], the one doing business in the market will offer a greater price, but when it is waning and diminishing in computation in the Descendant [καταβιβάζων, *katabibazōn*], the one doing business in the market place will give a lesser price. For Dorotheos says thus:

> "When the moon is in conjunction with the Ascendant [ἀνάγων, *anagōn*], if waxing in its course increasing in computation, should you buy you will give more than is necessary to give, but when by pathways by which it will prove to be with the Descendant [κατάγων, *katagōn*], when it comes dimin-

ishing, buying will be easy. And should you behold the appearance of the moon, when it moves from a conjunction passing over to the side of the first quarter of fiery Helios, it is better for those dealing justly; for you will give money the value of which was fair for selling, and the better thing will be to put down neither too little nor too much over what is usual. When it moves into opposition, it will be advantageous to seller and initiator of litigation. When the Quick-glancing travels to the third quartile, then it is good for the one intending to buy or to save by stealth. But when it travels, moving from the fourth quartile a little, of the many, you ought give to the one who intends what is better" (cited from Stegemann's edition of Hephaestio in the appendix to Dorotheus of Sidon, Pingree 1976: 388).

The ascending planet is likewise mentioned in three horoscopes of A.D. 74, 75 and 115 recorded by the second-century astrologer Vettius Valens (see Neugebauer and Van Hoesen 1959: L74.IV, L75.1, L115.II). In his work *Against Marcion* (1,18,1 *CCSL* I, 459), Tertullian belittles presumed stellar influences, stating, "Perhaps Anabibazon (sic) was in the way, or some other evil-doing star, Saturn in quadrature or Mars in trine." As Beck notes (1987: 194), Tertullian here ranks the dark Ascender on par with Saturn and Mars. The fact is that from the Hellenistic period on, sky calculations such as horoscopes entailed the reckoning of the positions of nine planets: Moon, Sun, Mars, Mercury, Jupiter, Venus, Saturn, the Ascender, and the Descender (see Kunitzsch 28.108 and n. 55; further details can be found in Abu Ma'shar *De Revolutionibus Nativitatum* 1,4–5 4,1. 7; Appendix 3, ed. David Pingree 1968: 14–15; 181–82; 205–6; 274ff.). Finally note the report from Hippolytus of Rome about these planets in the teaching of the Elchasites:

> These are evil stars of godlessness. This now is spoken to you, you pious and disciples: Beware of the power of the days of their dominion, and do not make a start to your works in their days! Baptize neither man nor woman in the days of their authority, when the moon passes through from them and travels with them. Await the day when it departs from them, and then baptize and make a beginning with all your works! Moreover, honor the day of the Sabbath, for it is one of these days! But beware also not to begin anything on the third day of the week, for again when three years of the emperor Trajan are complete, from the time when he subjected the Parthians to his own authority, when these three years are fulfilled, the war between the godless angels of the north will break out; because of this all kingdoms of godlessness are in disorder (Hippolytus, *Refutation of All Heresies*, 9.11, also cited as part of the book of Elchasai, ed. Johannes Irmscher, in Hennecke, Schneemelcher, Wilson (eds.), *New Testament Apocrypha* rev. 1992: 2.689).

Hence the scenario, I submit, is a celestial one. The battle is to take place in the sky, set under way by the dark planets and their cohort, who ascend to attack the array of holy ones and the Beloved City, located in the sky before its descent. But the battle does not materialize since sky fire devours the enemies, much like the Flood devoured the enemies of God previously. This, of course was to be expected since the father of humankind knew it and passed it on. Thus Josephus writes of the immediate descendants of Seth, Adam's son:

> These, being all of virtuous character, inhabited the same country without dissension and in prosperity, meeting with no untoward incident to the day of their death; they also discovered the science of the heavenly bodies and their orderly array. Moreover, to prevent their discoveries from being lost to mankind, and perishing before they became known—Adam having predicted a destruction of the universe, at one time by a violent fire and at another by a mighty deluge of water—they erected two pillars, one of brick and the other of stone, and inscribed these discoveries on both; so that if the pillar of brick disappeared in the deluge, that of stone would remain to teach men what was graven thereon and to inform them that they had also erected one of brick (*Antiquities* 1.68–71, LCL).

And finally, the Dragon, now called "The Devil," meets the same fate as its collaborators, the sea Beast and the False Prophet (the land Beast), for endless time. The Dragon is confined to the lowest point of the cosmos, the cosmic Abyss.

10.6. NINTH SIGHT: BEFORE THE GREAT WHITE THRONE

In the final vision of this sector our seer observes the highest point conceivable, the Great White Throne, the throne of God. We are beyond the vault of the sky now, where there is no place for the earth and sky. At this location the visionary sees how all that is left is the dead, including those who disappeared at sea and those with the celestial twins, Death-and-Hades (v. 13). Now is the time for all to be judged by what was recorded of them in the sky scroll of life.

Those twins, Death-and-Hades, were ostensibly the abode of the dead. Previously the seer informed us that the one like a human in his initial vision had the keys to Death-and-Hades (1:18), and he saw Death-and-Hades mounted over/on the pale horse (6:8). Now Death-and-Hades are thrown into the abysmal Pit of Fire (like the Dragon, sea Beast and land Beast previously v. 10), along with those not listed in the scroll of life. This Pit of Fire is "the second death."

With this scenario embracing the highest and lowest regions of the cosmos, Sector 4 of the book of Revelation closes. The seer's reading of the sky has informed us of the antediluvian situation and its immediate aftermath. What struck the seer about this situation were both its evils and the way God disposed of that situation. God's decree included Babel's fate as well as the final disposition of the Dragon, of its client

Beasts, of celestial Gog and Magog and finally Death-and-Hades. At the conclusion of all this cosmic activity, the seer leaves his readers with the vision of a vacuous earth in a cosmic void between the central throne on the other side of a vault of fixed stars and the cosmic Abyss lost in the profundity of creation. However, the readers have been equally alerted to the proximate presentation of the Wedding of the Lamb, soon to emerge at the cosmic center stage.

11 SECTOR 5: THE FINAL CITY OF HUMANKIND

21 [1]And I saw a new sky and a new earth; for the first sky and the first earth went away, and the sea no longer is. [2]And I saw the holy city, the new Jerusalem, coming down from the sky from God, prepared as a bride adorned for her husband. [3]And I heard a loud voice from the throne saying, "Behold the tent of God with men, and he will tent with them, and they will be his people, and he will be God with them, [their God]. [4]And he will wipe away every tear from their eyes, and death will be no longer, nor grief, nor wailing, nor will pain be any longer; [because] the first things went away." [5]And the one seated on the throne said: "Behold I make all things new"; and he said: "Write that: These are trustworthy and truthful utterances." [6]And he said to me: "It has happened. I [am] the Alpha and the O[mega], the beginning and the end. I will give the one thirsting from the source of living water for free. [7]The one conquering will inherit these things, and I will be God to him and he will be to me a son. [8]But to the timid and untrustworthy and filthy and murderers and fornicators and magic-practitioners and idolaters and all liars, their share [is] in the pit burning with fire and sulphur; this is the second death." [9]And one of the seven sky servants having the seven bowls filled with the seven last injuries came and spoke with me saying: "Come here! I will show you the Bride, the Wife of the Lamb." [10]And he carried me up in sky wind over a great and high mountain, and he showed me the holy city Jerusalem coming down out of the sky from God, [11]having the glory of God; her brilliance like a most precious stone, as a crystalline jasper stone, [12]having a great and high wall, having twelve gates, and over the gates twelve sky servants, and names inscribed which are the twelve tribes of the sons of Israel. [13]From the east three gates, and from the north three gates, and from the south three gates and from the west three gates. [14]And the wall of the city having twelve foundations, and upon these twelve the names of the twelve apostles of the Lamb. [15]And the one speaking with me had a golden measuring reed, so that he might measure the city and her gates and her walls. [16]The city was a quadrangle, and her length as much as her breadth. And he measured the city with the reed, twelve thousand stadia; her length and breadth and height were equal. [17]And he measured her wall, one hundred forty four cubits in human measure, that is sky servant (dimensions). [18]And the construction of her wall [was] jasper, and the city [was] pure gold like clear glass. [19]The foundations of the wall of the city [were] adorned all with precious stone; the first foundation jasper, the second sapphire, the third chalcedony, the fourth emerald, [20]the fifth sardonyx, the sixth sard, the seventh chrysolite, the eighth beryl, the ninth topaz, the tenth chrysoprasos, the eleventh hyacinth, the twelfth amethyst. [21]And the twelve gates twelve pearls, each of the

gates was of one pearl. And the square of the city [was] pure gold, as lucid glass. [22]And I did not see a temple in her, for the Lord God, the Almighty, is her temple, and the Lamb. [23]And the city has no need of the sun or the moon to illuminate her, for the glory of God lit her up, and the Lamb was her lamp. [24]And the nations walked about on account of her light; and the kings of the earth brought their glory into her. [25]And her gates surely would not be closed by day, for there was no night there. [26]And they will bring the glory and the honor of the nations into her. [27]And surely anything unclean and making an abomination or a lie would not enter into her, but only those written in the scroll of life of the Lamb.

22[1]And he showed me a river of water of life, resplendent as crystal, come out of the throne of God and of the Lamb. [2]In the middle of her square and of the river on the one side and the other a tree of life making twelve fruits, according to the month each giving its fruit, and the leaves of the tree for healing the nations. [3]And every curse will be no longer. And the throne of God and of the Lamb will be in her, and his slaves will worship him. [4]And they shall look upon his face and his name [will be] on their forehead. [5]And night will be no longer, and they will have no need of the light of a lamp and the light of the sun, because the Lord God will shine upon them and will reign into the aeons of aeons. [6]And he said to me: These are trustworthy and truthful utterances, and the Lord, the God of the sky winds of the prophets, sent his sky servant to give to his slaves what must happen quickly. [7]And behold I am coming quickly. How honorable is the one who holds the utterances of the prophecy of this scroll. [8]And I, John, [was] the one hearing and seeing these things. And when I heard and saw, I fell to prostrate myself before the feet of the sky servant showing me these things. [9]And he says to me: "Look, no! I am a fellow slave of yours and of your brothers the prophets and of those holding the utterances of this scroll. Prostrate yourself to God." [10]And he says to me: "Do not seal up the utterances of the prophecy of this scroll, for the time is near. [11]Let the unjust behave unjustly still, and let the filthy practice filth still, and the just do justice still, and let the holy practice holiness still. [12]Behold I am coming quickly, and my reward [is] with me, to pay back each one according as his/her work is. [13]I am the Alpha and the O[mega], the first and the last, the beginning and the end." [14]How honorable are those washing their garments so that their authority will be over the tree of life and [so that] they enter through the gates into the city. [15]Outside are the dogs and the magicians and the fornicators and the murderers and the idolaters and everyone loving and doing the lie. [16]"I, Jesus, sent my sky servant to witness to you concerning the churches. I am the root and the offspring of David, the brilliant Morning Star." [17]And the Sky Wind and the Bridegroom say: "Come." And let the one hearing say: "Come." And let the one thirsting come, let the one wishing the water of life take for free. [18]I witness to each one hearing the utterances of the prophecy of this book. If anyone adds to them, God will add to him the injuries written in this scroll. [19]And if anyone takes away from the utterances of the scroll of this prophecy, God will take away his share of the tree of life and of the holy city written in this scroll. [20]The one witnessing to these things says: "Indeed, I am coming quickly." Amen. Come, Lord Jesus. [21]The grace of the Lord Jesus [be] with all.

Sector 4 concluded with the seer's vision of a cosmic void. Now, in the final sector we find John describing what fills that cosmic void. He sees a new sky and a new, sealess earth; these serve as the broader environment for a new Jerusalem that is in the process of descending from the realm of God. This final city of humankind, a truly "holy city,"

to use John's designation, not only looks as radiant as a bride adorned for her husband to be, but in fact, as we soon learn, is the bride of the cosmic Lamb. And thanks to the vision of the seer, we too are privileged to marvel at the beauty of the Lamb's bride.

After the description of the city, the work comes to a conclusion with multiple attestations. First, there is John, who upon seeing/hearing all of this (see 19:10), attempts again to worship the sky servant; again he is repulsed. Then, we have an attestation by God, and finally by Jesus. The author wraps up the whole work with a typical letter ending.

This sector consists of four visions. It opens with John quickly seeing a new heaven and earth and a new Jerusalem. While John hears several things about who does and does not share in this forthcoming restoration, as yet no descriptions accompany these two sightings (21:1–2). However, he is soon shown a close-up of the descending new Jerusalem (21:10–27) and of the throne of God and the Lamb (22:1–5). At the close, the city still remains in the process of descending.

11.1. THE FIRST TWO SIGHTS: THE RENOVATED WORLD IN GENERAL

The theme of the transformation of the cosmos was traditional in Israelite lore. For example, in 1 Enoch 91:16, the seer states: "And the first heaven in it (the end of the Tenth Week) shall pass away, and a new heaven shall appear and all the powers of heaven shall rise for all eternity with sevenfold brightness" (Milik 1976: 267). One reason why the seer could see the new sky and new earth already is that these realities are already present in the sky with God. In the Israelite tradition, God completed creating everything by the end of creation week (Gen 1). Hence anything that subsequently emerges in the universe in the course of time was already with God by the close of the first and only creation week.

Thus, other seers in this tradition might see similar realities. For example, the oracles ascribed to the ancient Sibyl relate:

> For a blessed man came from the expanses of heaven with a scepter in his hands which God gave him. And he gained sway over all things well, and gave back the wealth to all the good, which previous men had taken. He destroyed every city from its foundations with much fire and burned nations of mortals who were formerly evildoers. And the city which God desired, this he made more brilliant than stars and sun and moon, and he provided ornament and made a holy temple, exceedingly beautiful in its fair shrine, and he fashioned a great and immense tower

over many stadia touching even the clouds and visible to all, so that all faithful and all righteous people could see the glory of eternal God, a form desired. East and west sang out the glory of God. For terrible things no longer happen to wretched mortals, no adulteries or illicit love of boys, no murder or din of battle, but competition is fair among all. It is the last time of holy people when God, who thunders on high, founder of the greatest temple, accomplishes these things (*Sibylline Oracles* 5.414–433, *OTP*).

Apart from John's insistence that there was no temple in this celestial city, the sequence of scenes in this Sibylline passage is similar to our seer's concluding Sectors 4 and 5. This indicates that both seers, John and the Sibylline oraclist, brought the same story to their altered states of awareness experiences. John, however, was an astral prophet not an oraclist. His concerns move in a different direction. He notes, for example, that the new earth has no sea. One reason for this is that the sea is the traditional symbol of chaos. If there is no chaos or possibility of chaos in the transformed cosmos, then there can be no sea either.

Now along with the new cosmos comes a new center to the cosmos, that is, a genuine "holy city," the new Jerusalem. The celestial city looks like a bride. The female imagery derives, of course, from the fact that Mediterranean cities in antiquity were invariably depicted as women. This reference, however, is our first hint as to the identity of the previously mentioned celestial bride of the cosmic Lamb. The major-domo at God's throne now announces the new Jerusalem as the place of God's dwelling with his people. In the new cosmos and the new Jerusalem, anything thwarting human well-being, from pain to death, will cease to be, passing away with "the first things." Such a statement serves as moral encouragement for John's audience, as does the listing of participants in these realities.

Now the enthroned God himself, the Alpha and Omega, the beginning and end, announces that he personally transforms everything. Then he addresses the seer on two counts: first to make a record of the veracity of these utterances, and then to announce the finality of the transformation. This final sector is closely related to Sectors 3 and 4 of this work. God's emphatic "It has happened" here (21:6) is just like the "It has happened" in 16:17, when "the seventh sky servant poured out his bowl upon the air." And just as God's statement, "It has happened," recalls the seventh and final bowl of the final seven in ch. 16, so too, the sky servant transporting the seer in his altered state of awareness comes from that previous scenario. Further, just as one of that same group of sky servants showed the seer the fate of the Great Babylon, the first postdeluvian city of humankind, so too another of that group now shows the seer the final city of humankind.

11.2. SIGHT THREE: THE NEW JERUSALEM

In order to see the descending new Jerusalem, John needs to be placed on a great and high mountain. The mountain in Mediterranean culture was a height outside inhabited and cultivated space, that is, outside the city, village, or town. A mountain top was a well attested place for observing the sky (Buxton 1992: 5, n. 39). There were two well known great and high mountains, actually called the Twins, located at the western and eastern ends of the earth. They are attested to in Mesopotamian, Phoenician, Israelite, and Greek tradition (see Grelot 1958 and Figure 5, above). Among other things, these mountains mark the place of the setting and rising of the sun and other celestial bodies. On his first sky journey, for example, Enoch saw the western mountain, "the top of its summit reaches into the sky" (1 Enoch 17:2, *OTP*). It was from such a summit that John observed the descent of the Great City from the sky. However, reports of sightings of this celestial phenomenon were not confined to our seer. For example, the second-century Christian, Tertullian, recounts:

> This both Ezekiel had knowledge of [48:30–35] and the Apostle John beheld [Rev 21:2]. And the word of the new prophecy [Montanism] which is part of our belief, attests how it foretold that there would be for a sign a picture of this very city exhibited to view previous to its manifestation. This prophecy, indeed, has been very lately fulfilled in an expedition to the east [Emperor Severus against the Parthians]. For it is evident from the testimony of even heathen witnesses, that in Judea there was suspended in the sky a city early every morning for forty days. As the day advanced, the entire figure of its walls would wane gradually, and sometimes it would vanish instantly. We say that this city has been provided by God for receiving the saints on their resurrection . . . (*Against Marcion* 3,24,4, *CCSL* I: 542 and for the version *ANF* 3.342–43).

In the same context, Tertullian attests that he believed Paul is speaking of this descending celestial reality in Gal 4:26 when he refers to the Jerusalem that comes down from the sky, "the Jerusalem above (that) is free, (that) is our mother!" This is the city in which the followers of Christ have their citizenship (the Latin-speaking Tertullian cites the Greek word *politeuma,* πολίτευμα; see Phil 3:20).

Mention of a new Jerusalem naturally presupposes the destruction of the old Jerusalem, something the seer does not explicitly report, although he alludes to it at the close of Sector 2 (11:13) and variously in Sector 4. As a matter of fact, if anything was certain to trigger speculation concerning the descent and forthcoming arrival of the new Jerusalem, it surely was the destruction of its anti–type. As previously noted, "For all persons in the Israelite tradition, the uncontested and uncontestable principle, since it was affirmed by Daniel (9:26), was that the destruction of Jerusalem indicated the beginning of the end" (Gry 1939: 355, n. 1).

Be that as it may, now the sky servant in question shows the seer the bride, the spouse of the Lamb, mentioned first in 19:7–9. Why the reference to a descending, celestial city married to a cosmic zodiacal Lamb? Note that there is a constellation called "The Wedding of the Gods," located in the vicinity of Cancer. "The Wedding of the Gods" was part of traditional Egyptian sky perception and is duly noted in a book called *The Book of Hermes Trismegistus*, published by Gundel (1936b). The present document is a sixth century A.D. Latin version of a work deriving from an original Egyptian writing from the Ptolemaic period (see Festugière 1950: 112–23). The constellation is likewise mentioned in a Greek text published by Franz Cumont where it is bears the Greek name θεῶν γάμος, *theon gamos*, that is Wedding of the Gods (CCAG VIII, 4, 119, 16, corrected by Cumont as noted by Gundel 1936b: 259).

In *The Book of Hermes Trismegistus* this constellation is mentioned twice. First of all, its author lists all the stars and/or constellations that accompany the rising of the twelve zodiacal signs, noting at which of the thirty degrees assigned to each sign the given star or constellation is found. Thus under Cancer we read: "The twenty-ninth degree (of Cancer) is called the Wedding of the Gods" (*Vicesimus nonus gradus vocatur deorum nuptiae*; Gundel 1936b: 60, 1). We are further told that this location in the sky ranks as "vacant," hence neither negative nor positive in its influence on the earth and its inhabitants.

This agrees with a prior mention of this constellation in a general section explaining how to interpret the sky. There the compiler writes: "The final degrees of the zodiacal signs generally signify dishonorable qualities in one's mother except for the final degrees of Libra and Cancer. For the final degrees (of Libra) are called 'Increase,' and of Cancer, 'The Wedding of the Gods'" (Gundel 1936b: 41, 10–11). The lore behind this constellation derives from Egyptian tradition. Gundel suggests that it would have been something like what can be found in Plutarch's work on Isis and Osiris:

> Here follows the story related in the briefest possible words with the omission of everything that is merely unprofitable or superfluous:

> They say that the sun, when he became aware of Rhea's intercourse with Cronus, invoked a curse upon her that she should not give birth to a child in any month or any year; but Hermes, being enamored of the goddess, consorted with her. Later, playing at draughts with the moon, he won from her the seventieth part of each of her periods of illumination, and from all the winnings he composed five days, and intercalated

them as an addition to the three hundred and sixty days. The Egyptians even now call these five days intercalated and celebrated them as the birthdays of the gods. They relate that on the first of these days Osiris was born, and at the hour of his birth a voice issued forth saying, "The Lord of All advances to the light." But some relate that a certain Pamyles, while he was drawing water in Thebes, heard a voice issuing from the shrine of Zeus, which bade him proclaim with a loud voice that a mighty and beneficent king, Osiris, had been born; and for this Cronus entrusted to him the child Osiris, which he brought up. It is in his honor that the festival of Pamylia is celebrated, a festival which resembles the phallic processions. On the second of these days Arueris was born whom they call Apollo, and some call him also the elder Horus. On the third day Typhon was born, but not in due season or manner, but with a blow he broke through his mother's side and leapt forth. On the fourth day Isis was born in the regions that are ever moist; and on the fifth Nephthys, to whom they give the name of Finality and the name of Aphrodite, and some also the name of Victory. There is also a tradition that Osiris and Arueris were sprung from the sun, Isis from Hermes, and Typhon and Nephthys from Cronus. For this reason the kings considered the third of the intercalated days as inauspicious and transacted no business on that day, nor did they give any attention to their bodies until nightfall. They relate, moreover, that Nephthys became the wife of Typhon; but Isis and Osiris were enamored of each other and consorted together in the darkness of the womb before their birth. Some say that Arueris came from this union and was called the elder Horus by the Egyptians, but Apollo by the Greeks (*Isis and Osiris* 355D–356A, LCL).

These quotations are not intended to demonstrate the sources of John's description. Rather their value as regards the book of Revelation is that they prove that there was in fact a constellation in the sky referred to as a divine Wedding. Hence a wedding of two celestial entities such as a sky city and a cosmic Lamb would not be unusual. Such a celestial configuration was available for first-century eastern Mediterranean prophets to appropriate into their traditions. The significant feature here, though, is that this Wedding of the Lamb takes place, it would seem, in the location of the zodiacal Aries, the cosmic Lamb. This, of course, fits the theme of newness very well, since Aries stands at the beginning of things. When the vault of the sky returns to the position it had at the very time of creation, it will be with Aries at the point of preeminence, the head of the cosmos. And such a return to beginnings was expected.

For people commonly measure the year by the circuit of the sun, that is, of a single star alone; but when all the stars return to the place from which they at first set forth, and, at long intervals, restore the original configuration of the whole heaven, then that can truly be called a revolving year . . . I hardly dare to say how many generations of men are contained within such a year; for as once the sun appeared to men to be eclipsed and blotted out, at the time when the soul of Romulus entered these regions, so when the sun shall again be eclipsed at the same point and in the same season, you may believe that all the planets and stars have returned to their original positions, and that a year has actually elapsed. But be sure that a twentieth part of such a year has not yet passed (Cicero, *The Republic* 6.24, LCL).

For our author, that year is already here, with the Wedding of the Lamb.

Upon beholding the descending celestial city from his vantage point over a great, high mountain, the seer proceeds to describe the city. First of all, he notes that the city's structure itself reveals God's honorable status. The city's plan is related to the twelve tribes of the sons of Israel (gate names) as well as to the twelve apostles of the Lamb (foundation names). As for the gate names, Ezekiel 48:30–34 forecasts: "these shall be the exits of the city"; he then names the north gates after Reuben, Judah, and Levi, the east after Joseph, Benjamin, and Dan, the south after Simeon, Issachar, and Zebulon, and the west after Gad, Asher, and Naphtali. This city, called the "Lord Is There," was likewise a square, like Babylon which "is in shape a square" (according to Herodotus, *Histories* 1.178 LCL).

Now it seems quite apparent that the new Jerusalem descending from the sky is an astral construction. It is laid out in the four directions of the sky just as the twelve signs of the zodiac are. The fact that it has no temple and no sun or moon for light points to a celestial arrangement above the earth, sun, and moon. That twelve sky servants stand over its twelve gates is not unlike the twelve gates at the four corners of the cosmos through which winds and stars emerge (e.g., 1 Enoch 33–35). The sky servants control the gates.

Furthermore, the mention of twelve foundations is highly significant since "foundation" (θεμέλιος, *themelios*) is a synonym of the word for "element," "basic constituent," and the like (στοιχεῖον, *stoicheion*). There is little difference in first-century Mediterranean Greek between foundations of the cosmos and elements of the cosmos (see Boll 1914: 39). And either of the terms can stand for the signs of the zodiac. Thus, for example, we are told by Diogenes Laertius, a first-century witness, that Menedemos, the philosopher of Eretria, wore "an Arcadian hat on his head with the twelve signs of the zodiac (τὰ δωδέκα στοιχεῖα, *ta dōdeka stoicheia*) inwrought in it" (Diogenes Laertius 6.102, LCL). Similarly, Philo of Byblos reports:

[The Phoenicians] assigned names chosen especially from those of their kings to the cosmic constellations [τοῖς κοσμικοῖς στοιχείοις, *tois kosmikois stoicheiois*] and to some of the recognized deities. Among things of nature they acknowledge as gods only the sun, the moon, the other planets and τὰ στοιχεῖα, *ta stoicheia* (zodiacal constellations) and their conjunctions, so that for them some gods were mortal (e.g., kings) and some immortal (*Phoenician History* Frag. I, Attridge and Oden, 1981: 32, 10–17; see also Epiphanius, *Adversus haereses* 1.1.16 "Against the Pharisees," § II calls the zodiacal constellations *stoicheia* [PG 41: 251–2]).

Furthermore, it is obvious that the 12,000 stadia is an astral measurement (Pliny notes: "A Greek stadion equals one-hundred twenty-five of our Roman paces, that is six–hundred twenty-five feet." This is about 200 yards or 190 meters; *Natural History* 2.85, LCL) Furthermore, the reference to the three dimensions, the 144 (12 by 12) ells for the wall, the twelve gates and their twelve star servants, and then the twelve gem stones for the foundations, exactly fits this scenario of the twelve zodiacal constellations. The same holds for the "gold like pure crystal" of which the city and its central place, the city square (21:21) is constituted, a reference to the Milky Way. That the city is square (21:16) is not a point against the scenario of the zodiac, as one might think. Rather, it fits the fundamental doctrine of astrology concerning the regular figures in the zodiac, of which the square designates the four "corners of the world" or the four directions of the sky.

Furthermore, this equally ties in with the gem stones. In the Israelite tradition in Exod 28:17–20, we learn of such gem stones laid out in a square on the breastplate of the highpriest of Israel. There each stone was inscribed with the name of a tribe. And the whole layout stood for the zodiac, as Josephus relates: "As for the twelve stones, whether one would prefer to read in them the months or the constellations of like number, which the Greeks call the circle of the zodiac, he will not mistake the lawgiver's intention" (*Antiquities* 3.186, LCL). That a new Jerusalem might have such a gem stone substructure is equally known in Israelite tradition: "For Jerusalem will be built with sapphires and emeralds, her walls with precious stones, and her towers and battlements with pure gold. The streets of Jerusalem will be paved with beryl and ruby and stones of Ophir; all her lanes will cry 'Hallelujah!' " (Tobit 13:16–18). What is distinctive in John's vision is that now the gemstones form the twelve foundations of the city, inscribed with the names of the twelve apostles of the Lamb.

Concerning such gem stones, Martianus Capella (1.75 ed. Dick 1925: 34–35) notes the following for the crown of Juno, probably a crown looking like a city wall protected by the goddess, as so many of such crowns were. This crown description alludes to the seasons of the year as well. It is arranged as follows:

CROWN SIDES	ZODIAC SIGNS	GEMSTONES	SEASONS
Front	Gemini	keraunos	summer
	Cancer	lychnis	
	Leo	asterites	
First Side	Virgo	hyakinthos	autumn
	Libra	dendrites	
	Scorpio	heliotrope	
Back	Sagittartius	hydatis	winter
	Capricorn	diamond	
	Aquarius	crystal	
Second Side	Pisces	emerald	spring
	Aries	scythis	
	Taurus	jasper	

Some of these names defy translation, others are rather well known: keraunos = thunderstone (Pliny, *Natural History* 37.134, LCL); lithos = heliotrope (ibid., 37.165); lychnis = precious stone of white color (ibid., 36.14); asterites = star stone (ibid., 37.133); hyakinthos = precious stone of blue color, perhaps aquamarine (ibid., 37.125); dendrites = ?; heliotrope = green stone streaked with red, blood stone (ibid., 37.165); hydatis = ?; skythis = light brown haematite (ibid., 37.169; cf. 36.144–146). Throughout his work, Pliny records the uses of these stones for healing and other purposes. A number of other documents describe instances of precious stones, plants, and heavenly bodies having correspondences (see Boll 1914: 39–42; Festugière 1951: 160-7). However, there is no evidence to indicate any fixed relationship between specific stones and constellations (as Charles 1920: 2.167–68 presupposes).

All in all, then, one would have to agree with Charles "that our author is acquainted with the[se] current beliefs as to the connection of the twelve precious stones with the signs of the Zodiac, and the sun's progress through the signs of the Zodiac cannot in the face of the above facts be questioned . . . " (1920: 2.168). Yet it is essentially because John understands his visionary experience in terms of Israel's traditions as prismed through his Christian loyalties that he regards the celestial city as the new Jerusalem related to ancient Israel, but now firmly founded on the Lamb's twelve apostles.

The sky servant serving as the prophet's interlocutor proceeded to "measure" the city, if only to show how astronomically great it was. Twelve-thousand stadia is 1,500 miles. And a city with a 6000-mile circumference and a height of 1,500 miles is simply astronomic. Then we are informed that in its plan, the city has a forum (city square), but no temple, for God himself is the city's temple. God's honor supplies light to the city, with the Lamb as its lamp. And this light supply suffices for the whole earth (as expected from Isa 60:19–20). In turn the rest of the earth's dwellers bestow signs of honor (gifts) to the city. The continuous presence of light points to abiding security—the gates need not be closed since there is no night. Finally, deviance of any sort is excluded from the city, since only those enrolled in the Lamb's scroll of life can enter (on the scroll, see 13:8; 17:8; 20:12, 15).

11.3. SIGHT FOUR: THE THRONE OF GOD AND THE LAMB

The fourth sight describes the throne of God and of the Lamb out of which flows a river of the water of life (expected from Ezek 47:1–12). This river flows to the city square where it is bifurcated by an island on which the tree of life grows, as formerly in Paradise (Gen 2:9). These items belong to the last mentioned appurtenances of the new Jerusalem. The stream of the water of life, "white like crystal," again recalls the Milky Way, that "Band of Heaven" according to Plato (*Republic* 616C, LCL). For Empedocles the fixed stars taken together are crystal. Finally, we previously noted the various rivers in the sky observed in Babylonian lore; all these were part of the Milky Way (see Brown 1900: 2.203–5). These references should clarify the celestial context of this scenario.

Further, a feature of the cosmic landscape prepared by God for those faithful to him includes the tree of life. The tree of life is one of the many ancient Mesopotamian symbols taken up into the Israelite tradition. It was an imperial symbol, a symbol of the divine world order centered in God's chosen central place (Parpola 1993: 168–69). This tree was to be found in the original park or paradise made by God for humans (Gen 2:4ff.). Consider the listing of items in 4 Ezra 8:51–52: "But think of your own case, and inquire concerning the glory of those who are like yourself, because it is for you that paradise is opened, the tree of life is planted, the age to come is prepared, plenty is provided, a city is built, rest is appointed, goodness is established, and wisdom perfected beforehand" (NRSV). Interestingly enough, the seven-branched lamp stand of the first vision in this book was itself a stylized version of the tree of life (see Parpola 1993: 177 nn. 68–69 and 205).

The twelve fruits of the tree of life "according to the month" likewise readily fit the twelve zodiac signs. Hellenistic Greek names for the months of the year derived from the zodiac sign through which the sun was currently passing. Concerning this tree and the general themes of the conclusion of this revelation, 1 Enoch 25:1–5 is informative:

> And he (Michael) said to me, Enoch, "What is it that you are asking me concerning the fragrance of this tree and you are so inquisitive about?" At that moment, I answered saying, "I am desirous of knowing everything, but specially about this thing." He answered, saying: "This tall mountain which you saw whose summit resembles the throne of God is indeed his throne, on which the Holy and Great Lord of Glory, the Eternal King, will sit when he descends to visit the earth with goodness. And as for this fragrant tree, not a single human being has the authority to touch it until the great judgment, when he shall take vengeance on all and conclude (everything) forever. This is for the righteous and the pious. And the elect will be presented with its fruit for life. He will plant it in the direction of the northeast, upon the holy place—in the direction of the house of the Lord, the Eternal Kings" (*OTP* 1.26).

The idea of eating a different fruit each month has curious parallels. One of Plutarch's interlocutors mentions a man who meets humans once a year, but "the other days of his life, according to his statement, he spends in association with roving nymphs and demons. He was the handsomest man I ever saw in personal appearance, and he never suffered from any disease, inasmuch as once each month he partook of the medicinal and bitter fruit of a certain herb" (Plutarch, *On the Obsolescence of Oracles*, 421A–B, LCL).

In this scenario of restored tranquillity the seer mentions the elimination of curses and their threat. This is part of the elimination of whatever thwarts human well-being, mentioned in 21:4. The worshipers of God will bear his name on their forehead, as slaves of God (a feature previously noted in 7:1; 9:4 and 14:1). It seems that for the seer, everyone has a name of allegiance inscribed on their forehead. Here it is the name of God. Previously we learned of the followers of the sea Beast and the land Beast required marks on hand and forehead (13:16; 14:9; 20:4). Babylon wore her own name on her forehead (17:5). Finally, the assurance of the security of permanent light provided by God's presence "into the aeons of aeons" brings this scenario to a close.

11.4. A RATHER COMPLEX POSTSCRIPT

The tour through the book of Revelation is over. The final sector closes at 22:5, but before the author lets us go, he has several somewhat bewildering items to add. They consist of a series of statements at times without clear indication of who the speaker might be.

First of all, the sky servant who showed John the last sight reasserts the reliability of the utterances of God through his prophets: "These are trustworthy and truthful utterances." This is the same insistence that came from the throne at the opening of this sector (21:5). The whole book is sprinkled with the requirement of trustworthiness, something characteristic of Jesus the Messiah from the outset (1:5). Why this insistence? There are two main reasons. First, persons enculturated in the Mediterranean were fully aware that the level of permissible deception common in their society was very high. Given the antagonistic quality of group relations, only fellow in-group members were owed the truth because of what outsiders might do with insider information (see Pilch 1992). And a second reason is the fact that there were articulate critics of astral prophecy. Consider Lucian in the second century who lambastes authors who:

> wrote much that was strange about the countries in the great sea: he made up a falsehood that is patent to everybody, but wrote a story that is not uninteresting for all that. Many others, with the same intent, have written about imaginary travels and journeys of theirs, telling of huge beasts, cruel men and strange ways of living. Their guide and instructor in this sort of charlatanry is Homer's Odysseus, who tells Alcinous and his court about winds in bondage, one-eyed men, cannibals and savages; also about animals with many heads, and transformations of his comrades wrought with drugs. This stuff, and much more like it, is what our friend humbugged the illiterate Phaeacians with! Well, on reading all these authors, I did not find much fault with them for their lying, as I saw that this was already a common practice even among men who profess philosophy. I did wonder, though, that they thought that they could write untruths and not get caught at it (*A True Story* 1, LCL).

Lucian's criteria for a credible and reliable account are the following. The account must be based on a report about what persons actually saw themselves. Or secondly, the account must be based on what persons heard from others with a reputation for truthfulness. So he mocks by name a certain "Ctesias, son of Ctesiochus, of Cnidos, who wrote a great deal about India and its characteristics that he had never seen himself nor heard from anyone else with a reputation for truthfulness" (*A True Story* 1, LCL). Consequently, it is within a culture in which deception was common that we find our prophet, John, insisting upon the reliability of his own experiences in an altered state of awareness. Further, he appeals to the trustworthiness of those who witness what he beheld, as extraordinary as the events might seem.

The new feature here is the emphasis on the "quick" realization of everything described previously. The very first sentence of the work presents it as unfolding what is to happen soon (1:1). And Jesus' new title here could easily be "The One Who is Coming Quickly," since "I am coming quickly" is almost the motto of Jesus Messiah in this work (2:16; 3:11; and in this final text-segment three times: 22:7, 12, 20). Observing the prophecies in the scroll will result in the bestowal of honor.

Given the customary behavior of astral prophets with regard to the sky servants (see above relative to the scene reported in 19:10), John again feels moved to fall down at the feet of the sky servant to do homage. But once more, the sky servant insists that he ranks on the same level as the prophet and his brother prophets and is worthy of no special honor.

The final direct order from the sky servant is: "Do not seal up the utterances of the prophecy of this scroll, for the time is near" (22:11). This, too, is distinctive since in the tradition of Israel, astral prophecies usually were to be sealed up for some unspecified future date. For example, consider Daniel:

> The vision of the evenings and the mornings which has been told is true; but seal up the vision, for it pertains to many days hence (Dan 8:26).

> But you, Daniel, shut up the words, and seal the book, until the time of the end. . . . Go your way, Daniel, for the words are shut up and sealed until the time of the end (Dan 12:4, 9).

The same can be found in 1 Enoch 1:2:

> This is a holy vision from the heavens which the angels showed me: and I heard from them everything and I understood. I look not for this generation but for the distant one that is coming. I speak about the elect ones and concerning them (*OTP;* see also 1 Enoch 93:10; 104:12).

While it is historically accurate, as Charles (1920 2.221) notes, that Israel's astral prophecies "were referred to as sealed . . . in order to explain the withholding of their publication till the actual time of their author," it was nonetheless customary to stamp them with an aura of concealment. And it was this aura of concealed information from the past that gave the works a future-oriented quality. This is a quality which they in fact never had. Our seer leaves no ambiguity about the matter. John's astral prophecy, in contrast, is both readily available and to be realized quickly now, as somehow present and forthcoming for his audience.

A sequence of juxtaposed statements now follows. The first is a sort of proverb about ongoing, habitual, present behavior: let things continue as they are (v. 11). Then a statement by Jesus Messiah about coming quickly (v. 12). This is followed by a statement by God, with titles presented in the opening of the book. These are worth some attention here.

11.4.1. God, the Beginning and End of All

At the conclusion of the work (22:13), the prophet once more reports the titles of God from 1:8 and 21:6. Of course "the first and last" was initially attributed to the humanoid constellation 1:17 and 2:8. These titles fit here since they emphasize the O(mega), last and end quality of what is going on.

However, while moderns might be used to seeing the Greek letters Alpha and Omega written in various places, from churches to license plates to sorority and fraternity houses, the fact is that in a first-century setting, for God to designate himself in terms of these letters entails something more than simple labeling. Divining hidden meanings by means of letters is often called "alphabet mysticism" or "grammatology" (from the Greek word γράμμα, gramma, meaning "syllable" or "letter" of the alphabet). Grammatology was common in Hellenism. If it were not, this description of the Almighty as identical with the first and last letters of the Greek alphabet would be quite bizarre and wholly incomprehensible. In grammatology the letters of the alphabet are believed to have cosmic character. The twenty-four letters of the Greek alphabet are directly related to the zodiac and the course of the moon. In fact there is a name of God in every letter and syllable. Hence all demonic and divine powers of the world, animated and penetrated by the astral forces, are captured and enclosed in these twenty-four letters.

Furthermore, there is a related process, mentioned previously relative to 666, of taking letters to refer to numerals, called "numerology" or "gematria." In Greek (and Hebrew) there were no written numeric signs (such as our Hindu-Arabic numbers) apart from the letters of the alphabet. Thus each letter served as a number and each number served as a letter. To count up the letters/numbers in a person's name, for example, was believed to indicate something about that person.

The seven Greek vowels were related to the seven planets, the twenty-four letters to the zodiac. Along with astral entities the term "element," as in "elements of the world" (στοιχεῖα, stoicheia), means both the letters of the alphabet and elements constituting the world, such as air, earth, fire, and water in varying proportions. The hidden meaning of the series of letters meant to serve as a revelation of God ("I am = Alpha and Omega") is part and parcel of the real meaning of God's name, for God's name really tells us who God really is. God's name then is a full disclosure of God's essence. Thus a person who knows that name has power over God.

God's title of "Beginning and End" was common in the first-century Mediterranean. It is mentioned as early as Plato, as an ancient

Orphic saying (*Laws* 4.716A): "However, God (as the ancient utterance has it) is the beginning and the end and the middle of everything that is." Charles (1920 2.220) quotes an ancient scholiast on Plato who gives the context of the statement: "For he cites the ancient Orphic adage clearly referring to God the demiurge: God is the beginning, God is the middle and from God has everything been wrought; God is the foundation of the earth and of the starry sky; and he is the beginning as efficient cause, end as final, and middle insofar as equally present to all." This adage subsequently became Mediterranean common knowledge.

A little scene now marks off in-group and out-group. It begins with the work's seventh "blessing," directed to those who wash their garments. The phrasing indicates that they have "authority over the tree of life," a phrase likewise found in 1 Enoch 25 and indicating those who can eat of the tree. Those with washed garments likewise have ready access to the city. They form the in-group in this scene. The out-group is listed once more, as in 21:8 (where they are worthy of the second death): "Outside are the dogs and the magicians and the fornicators and the murderers and the idolaters and everyone loving and doing the lie" (see Elliott 1993).

11.4.2. A Word of Jesus: the Brilliant Morning Star

The seer now quotes the very words of Jesus, undoubtedly heard during his altered state of awareness experience. The words he quotes (22:16) restate the principle presented at the outset of the book—that the revelation in the book comes from Jesus through his sky servant to John. Jesus presents two titles here. The first, the "Root and Offspring of David," occurs at the beginning of the work and refers to the cosmic Lamb. The second is a new title; Jesus is the "brilliant, Morning Star" (see 2 Pet 1:19). Linking Jesus the Morning Star with the Davidic line suggests a fusion of two perspectives. First, there is the star of Jacob in Num 24:17; this popular star was interpreted as heralding an anointed king (T. Levi 18:3; T. Judah 24:1; CD 7:18–20). The Morning Star is a "light bringer" (meaning of the Greek for "morning star," *phōsphoros*, φωσφόρος), herald of the dawn of God's rule.

To call Jesus the "Morning Star" is to identify him with the planet Aphrodite/Venus. In the Middle East, from time immemorial, Venus along with the sun and the moon, was considered the greatest of all celestial bodies. As previously noted, of all the stars only the Morning Star had an imposing presence, for only Venus among all stars casts a shadow by its rays.

There would be little difficulty in identifying Jesus, a male, with the planet Aphrodite/Venus, a female. The reason for this is that Venus, as our informants tell us, was both a morning and evening star. Depending on the cosmic disposition of the star, it could be masculine or feminine, thus serve in male or female roles. Henninger, for example, concludes his study of Venus among the Semites as follows: The various Semitic names for Venus ('Ishtar, Attar, etc. all derived from a common root. But in northern and southern Arabia, there was a male Venus star worshipped as Morning Star and Evening Star. The morning star called Eastern Attar, was considered a mighty, war-like protecting God. As Evening Star Attar was the fount of life-giving water. Two personifications of a male Venus star occur in the Palmyrene pantheon as Azizu and Artsu, and in northern Syria as Azizos and Monimos, clearly replicating the ancient Ugaritic Shahr and Shalim (Dawn and Dusk; culled from Moore 1982: 86). The point is that this deity, as male at one time, female at another, was common to the cultural region. Ptolemy gives his scientific reason for assessing the matter as follows:

> They say too that the stars become masculine or feminine according to their aspects to the sun, for when they are morning stars (lit. "being of the dawn") and precede the sun they become masculine, and feminine when they are evening stars and follow the sun. Furthermore this happens also according to their positions with respect to the horizon; for when they are in positions from the east to Mid-Heaven, or again, from the West to lower Mid-Heaven, they become masculine because they are eastern, but in the other two quadrants, as western stars, they become feminine (*Tetrabiblos* 1.6.20, LCL).

This sort of identification is not unlike identifying Jesus with other celestial bodies. For example, in Zechariah's song in Luke 1:68–79, Jesus is called "the Dawn" or "Rising One" (Greek: ἀνατολή, *anatolē*) from the height of the sky (v. 78). Boll (1914: 47–48) notes that Melito of Sardis in the second century calls him the eastern or Rising sun (Greek: ἥλιος ἀνατολῆς, *hēlios anatolēs*); and further, that according to Tertullian and Origen, many pagans thought the sun was the God of the Christians because they referred to Jesus as the sun of Justice (after Mal 4:2).

The specific function of this particular star, however, underscores its characteristic name of "Light Bringer." Cicero notes: "Lowest of the five planets and nearest to the earth is the star of Venus, called in Greek *Phosphōros* and in Latin *Lucifer* when it precedes the sun (*On the Nature of the Gods* 2.53, LCL). The Morning Star ushers in the light; Messiah Jesus ushers in the Lord God. Similarly, in 2 Pet 1:19 the context of mentioning the Morning Star has to do with our looking to prophecies about the arrival of Jesus, the Morning Star, as one uses a lamp to illumine darkness. Moore concludes that if John had Venus in mind, in line with previous well-worn Semitic categories, he would have Jesus:

[As] (a) the Morning star Attar Shariqan = the Eastern Attar sometimes also known as Attar Azizan = the Strong Attar, the warlike protecting god who may have even been a model for much of the warlike imagery in Rev. 19:11–16; and (b) as Evening Star Attar was the god of the life-giving water in certain Semitic circles, the very imagery employed in Rev. 22:17, and alluded to in 7:17; 8:11 (where another interesting "star" is mentioned); 16:5; 21:6; and 22:1 (Moore 1982: 99).

In the same vein, early Christians knew a hymn about Jesus as a star. It is quoted by Ignatius of Antioch (d. A.D. 106) in his letter to the Ephesians (19:23) to explain how Jesus was made manifest to the cosmos:

A star shone forth in the sky
brighter than all the stars
and its like was unspeakable
and its newness caused astonishment.

All the other stars
with the sun and moon
gathered in chorus around this star,
and it far exceeded them all in its light.
There was perplexity, whence came this new thing so unlike them.

By this all magic was dissolved
and every bond of wickedness disappeared
ignorance was removed
and the old kingdom was destroyed,
when God was humanly revealed
for the newness of endless life.

What had been prepared by God took its beginning
hence all things were disturbed
because the abolition of death was being planned (after the text of Stander 1989: 210).

In this hymn, there are four stanzas. The first speaks of the appearance of Jesus as a star; the second, of the reaction of other celestial bodies; the third of what Jesus as star does, and the last stanza offers a theological insight (see Stander 1989: 209–14). The hymn clearly resonates with the work of early Christian astral prophecy.

11.5. CONCLUSION

The work concludes with various formal features that relate it to its opening letter form. Thus we have an invitation (as in 21:6) to drink of the water of life, noted in verse 1 above. Verses 18–19 present a usual "curse" found in revelational material warning against tampering. For example, the prophet Moses tells the Israelites: "You shall not add to the word which I command you, nor take from it; that you may keep the commandments of the LORD your God which I command you" (Deut 4:2; see Charles 1920: 2.223 for other instances). And verse 20 offers a final assurance from Jesus, answered by an "Amen. Come Lord Jesus," completed with a concluding formula typical of the letter form: "The favor of the Lord Jesus be with all."

12 THE THEOLOGY AND MESSAGE OF REVELATION

Throughout our tour we stayed with John, the astral prophet, who in his cosmic trips and visions never really touches down on the earth we know. Everything takes place in the sky, even though at times he views prehistoric earth events from a nameless desert or mountain. In Sector 1 we viewed with the seer the magnificent vision of Jesus Messiah in control of the cosmic pole, the power source behind the entire universe. Then in Sector 2 we beheld the throne of God, with the single and sole God enthroned above and beyond the universe he created. From this throne come the directives that govern all existence and all life in the cosmos. We further saw in Sector 2 how God, through the cosmic Lamb, passed judgment on the land of his concern, presumably Judea, and its central city, presumably Jerusalem. The sector ended with a vision of the cosmic temple of God, locating us beyond any land or any land-based temple. The prophet's experience reveals that God is in control and explains how he exercises that control.

While Sector 3 clearly notes the presence of a cosmic Child, the latter Messiah, enthroned with God, its overwhelming purpose is to expose the cosmic sources of deception in creation and how those sky sources deceived the generations of antediluvians. Still in the sky, we are led on to Sector 4 which tells of the fate of the first postdeluvian city of humankind, the great Babylon. Sector 5 reveals the forthcoming presence of the final city of humankind, the new Jerusalem, which is descending already now.

This astral prophecy in the Israelite tradition underscored the fact that what triggers negative outcomes in the cosmos is the dishonoring of the Lord God. This dishonoring is called idolatry. First, the inhabitants of the land of God's concern reject God's Messiah. This obviously dishonors God. The inhabitants of the land reject any idea of repentance; hence God must vindicate his honor (Sector 2). Second, the cosmic Dragon deceives antediluvians (Sector 3), and deception is institutionalized in the first city of post Flood humankind (Sector 4). These ultimately account for the range of miseries afflicting God's creation. If there is a message in Revelation, it is: "Don't be deceived! And if you have been deceived, repent!" So it seems human beings cooperate in their own deception, let themselves be taken in, succumb to the allure that encases the deception. John's astral prophecy removes the veil and reveals the cosmic underpinnings behind the prevailing deceptions. It also manifests the gloriously reigning Lord God and his Messiah Lamb who provide the energy for endurance in face of deceit and duplicity. What remains is for the deceived to change their heart (to Christians: 2:5[twice], 16, 21[twice], 22; 3:3, 19; to Judeans: 9:20–21; to antediluvians: 16:9, 11).

Before dealing with the theology of John the astral prophet, it might be useful to take a look at the Christian churches with which he seems to have been affiliated.

12.1. THE EDICTS TO THE SEVEN CHURCHES

At the close of the opening vision of Revelation there were the seven dispatches from the celestial Jesus (chs. 2–3 in Sector 1). As befits one who controls the cosmic pole, the communications that John writes down have the literary form or pattern of an edict. There is a Roman edict from early second century Egypt that will help explain the structure of these dispatches.

> Copy of an Edict. Titus Haterius Nepos, prefect of Egypt says: our Lord and God most manifest Imperator Caesar Trajan Hadrian Augustus having appointed, as you know [XX] as high priest of the gods Augusti and of great Sarapis and in charge of the cults in Alexandria and in Egypt . . . (from Horsley 1982: 33).

In the book of Revelation, of the twenty-one times "Lord" is used, eleven times it is accompanied with "God," just as in this edict. Note too how in 11:17; 15:3; 16:7; 19:6; 21:22 the title "almighty" (Greek: παντοκράτωρ, *pantokratōr*) is further found with "Lord" and "God" (here it is the Greek: *autokratōr,* translated "Imperator"). The first Roman Caesars were regularly called "God." However, after his death, so was the first "Christian" emperor, Constantine. An inscription from A.D. 337 refers to "the deified Flavius Valerius Constantinus Augustus" (Horsley 1982: 192). E. A. Judge notes in this regard:

[T]he establishment of Christendom had by no means done away with the imperial cult; rather had it clarified some of its ambiguities. The Caesars had mostly insisted on their own humanity, at the same time as they accepted or encouraged the cult as an expression of gratitude and loyalty. The reaction against Gaius and others who explicitly claimed divinity shows that most people could not take it literally. . . . The conversion of Constantine helped define the difference. He promoted his own family's temple and cult 'provided it is not polluted by the deceits of any contagious superstition'; sacrifices were presumably stopped. But as one chosen by God he could both revive the traditional disclaimers of divinity and anticipate his own apotheosis in the form of a personal reception into heaven at death. . . . Paradoxically, the Christianization of the cult may actually have opened the way for people seriously to pray to their rulers for the first time. Their divine calling and sanctity ranked them with the saints in this respect (in Horsley 1982: 192).

If Roman emperors could be ranked as Lord and God and could wield untold power, so could the one raised by God from the dead, designated Messiah to come (Rom 1:1). As one wielding control of the cosmos, Jesus too gives edicts.[1]

Edict 1

2[1]To the sky servant of the church in Ephesus, write:
These things says the one holding the seven stars in his right hand, the one walking about in the middle of the seven golden lampstands:
[2]I know your works and fatigue and your perseverance, and that you cannot stand wicked persons, and that you examined those who said they [are] apostles and are not, and you found them [to be] false. [3]And you have perseverance, and you withstood because of my name, and you have not grown weary.[4]But I have [it] against you that you have abandoned your initial loyalty. [5]Therefore remember from where you have been falling and change [your heart] and take up doing your previous works. But if not, I am coming to you and I will move your lampstand from its place, unless you change [your heart]. [6]But this you have [in your favor], that you hate the works of the Nicolaitans, which I too hate. [7]Let the one who has ears listen to what the controlling sky wind says to the churches. To the one who overcomes I will give to eat of the tree of life which is in the paradise of God.

Edict 2

[8]And to the sky servant of the church in Smyrna, write:
These things says the First and the Last, he who was dead and lives on:

[9]I know your distress and poverty, but you are wealthy, and the blasphemy from those calling themselves Judeans while they are not, rather [they are] a synagogue of Satan.

---

[1] For an explanation of the pattern in these edicts, see Aune 1983; and for the interpretation of the passages, see Charles 1920; Ford 1975.

[10]Now stop being afraid about what you are going to suffer. Behold the Accuser is going to throw some of you into prison so that you might be tested, and you will have distress for ten days. Stay trustworthy unto death, and I will give you the wreath of life. [11]Let the one having ears listen to what the controlling sky wind says to the churches. The one who overcomes will surely not suffer from the second death.

Edict 3

[12]And to the sky servant of the church of Pergamum, write:
These things says the one who has the sharp two-edged sword:

[13]I know where you dwell, where the throne of Satan [is], and you hold fast to my name and you did not disavow allegiance to me even in the days of Antipas, my trustworthy witness, who was killed among you, where Satan dwells. [14]But I have a few things against you, that you have there those holding the teaching of Balaam, who taught Balak to set a trap before the sons of Israel, to eat food offered to idols and to commit fornication. [15]Thus you even have those holding on to teaching like that of the Nicolaitans. [16]So then have a change [of heart]. But if not, I am coming to you quickly, and I will wage war with them with the utterance of my mouth. [17]Let the one having ears listen to what the controlling sky wind says to the churches. To the one who overcomes I will give the hidden manna and I will give a white pebble and on the pebble is inscribed a new name which no one but the recipient knows.

Edict 4

[18]And to the sky servant of the church of Thyatira, write:
These things says the son of God, the one who has eyes like flames of fire, and whose feet are like brass.

[19]I know your works and your group-loyalty and allegiance and service and perseverance, and your recent works are more abundant than previous ones. [20]But I hold [it] against you that you exonerate the woman Jezebel, who calls herself a prophetess and she teaches and leads my slaves astray to fornicate and to eat food offered to idols. [21]And I gave her time to have a change [of heart], but she does not want to change away from her fornication. [22]Behold I am casting her down upon a [sick] bed, and those committing adultery with her [I am casting] into great distress, unless they change away from their works. [23]And I shall kill her children with death; and all the churches will know that I am the one who scrutinizes the kidneys and hearts, and I will give you each according to your works. [24]Now I say to the rest of you in Thyatira who do not hold to that teaching, who have not known "the deep things of Satan," as they say, I do not cast upon you any other burden; [25]but hold on to what you have until I shall come. [26]And to the one who overcomes and who keeps my works until the end,
I shall give him authority over the nations,

[27]and he shall shepherd them with an iron rod,
like ceramic vessels they shall be shattered.

[28]Just as I too have received from my father, so I shall give him the morning star. [29]Let him who has ears listen to what the controlling sky wind says to the churches.

Edict 5

3[1]And to the sky servant of the church in Sardis, write: These things says the one having the seven controlling sky winds of God and the seven stars:

I know your works, that your name indicates you are alive but you are dead.

[2]Be vigilant, and support the remainder that was going to die. For I have not found your works perfected before my God. [3]Remember therefore how you have received and heard; [now] be observant and have a change [of heart]. If therefore you do not stay vigilant, I shall come like a thief, and you will certainly not know at what hour I shall come to you. [4]But you have several names in Sardis who have not sullied their garments; and they shall walk about with me in white, because they are worthy. [5]The one who overcomes will thus be clothed in white garments, and I shall not erase his name from the scroll of life, and I shall profess his name before my father and before his sky servants. [6]Let the one who has ears listen to what the controlling sky wind says to the churches.

Edict 6

[7]And to the sky servant of the church in Philadelphia, write:
These things says the holy one, the truthful one,
the one having the key of David,
who opens and no one will close,
and who closes and no one will open.

[8]I know your works—behold I have given before you an open door which no one can close—because you have little power and you observed my utterance and you did not disavow my name. [9]Behold I give [some] of the synagogue of Satan, of those claiming to be Judeans, and they are not, rather they lie. Behold I make them so that they will come and bow down before your feet and so that they may know that I have remained loyal to you. [10]Because you have kept my enduring utterance, I too shall keep you from the coming hour of testing to come upon the whole inhabited world to test those dwelling upon the earth. [11]I am coming quickly. Hold on to what you have, so that no one take your crown. [12]The one who overcomes—I shall make him a pillar in the temple of my God, and he shall certainly no longer depart outside, and I shall write upon it [him] the name of my God and the name of the city of my God, the new Jerusalem which descends out of the sky from my God, and my new name. [13]Let him who has hears listen to what the controlling sky wind says to the churches.

Edict 7

[14]And to the sky servant of the church in Laodicea, write:
These things says the Amen, the trustworthy and truthful witness, the beginning of God's creation:

[15]I know your works, that you are neither cold nor hot. Would that you were hot or cold. [16]Thus because you are lukewarm and neither hot nor cold, I am going to vomit you out of my mouth. [17]Because you say: "I am rich" and "I have become wealthy" and "I have no need of anything" and you do not know that it is you who are the wretched

one, and pitiable and impoverished and blind and naked. [18]I counsel you to buy from me gold smelted in fire so that you might become rich, and a white garment so that you might be clothed and so that the shame of your nakedness not be manifest, and ointment to apply to your eyes so that you might see. [19]Those whom I love I admonish and chastise. Therefore be zealous and have a change [of heart]. [20]Behold I stand at the door and knock; should anyone hear my voice and open the door, I shall enter into his place and I shall dine with him and he with me. [21]The one who overcomes—I shall give him to be seated with me on my throne, just as I too have overcome and have been seated with my father on his throne. [22]Let him who has ears listen to what the controlling sky wind says to the churches.

Perhaps the most significant feature about these edicts is that the seer, John, mediates the communication from Jesus Messiah to a set of sky servants. These sky servants were the Israelite and Christian equivalent of lesser astral deities guarding and directing the Christian churches, assemblies of those loyal to Jesus Messiah in Asia Minor. In the Israelite and later Christian tradition these sky servants become known as "guardian angels" (see Tob 5:4ff.; Matt 18:10). The Greek equivalent of such sky servants is δαιμόνιον, *daimonion* or demon. "Now demons are judged to be servants of the gods and guardians of human beings as well as interpreters should people wish anything from the gods . . . " (Apuleius, *Concerning Plato* 1.12, cited in *Corpus Hermeticum,* ed. A. D. Nock and A. J. Festugière, 2.361, n. 41). Romans treated the sky being that accompanied persons from birth (called a *genius* for males, *iuno* for females, in Latin) in the same way, as guardian beings. Not only individuals, but groups of people such as cities and nations as well as localities and territories, had guardian sky beings (see Schilling 1979). The same was true for stars and constellations since they were themselves regarded as intelligent beings. Specific cities and nations, localities and territories, were directly influenced by certain stars and constellations, for good or ill.

12.1.1. The Problem Facing the Seven Churches

A close reading of Sector 1 as well as the rest of the book indicates that John addresses the "seven churches of the Apocalypse" only indirectly. Rather, it is Jesus Messiah, the one who wields control of the cosmos, who directs edicts to the sky servants of the churches. Presumably we can gain some understanding of the quality of these early Christian groups from these edicts. As a matter of fact, most studies of the book of Revelation conjure up their image of the causes provoking the apocalyptic mind-set in general, and this book in particular, on the basis of information drawn from these "letters."

Now what is truly remarkable about all these "letters" is their distress over deception. As Pilch has noted:

> The diverse, intense concentration of vocabulary related to deception and
> lies suggests that the social situation in each church involved a disturbing
> degree of inauthenticity, misrepresentation, defamation, lies, deceit, de-
> nial, delusion and the like (1992: 126).

What really exists, the object of the prophet's vision, stands under an
extremely heavy overlay of appearance.

There is really no great concern about persecution, political or
otherwise. That the author of the book may have been exiled to Patmos
for practicing astral prophecy is quite plausible (see Cramer 1954:
232–83 on astrology in Roman law). But that this individual's exile was
indicative of the political persecution of Christians is simply not indicated in the work. There may have been conflict, but conflict is not
persecution, for while some poor Christians in Smyrna will be thrown
into prison (we are not told why), and a certain Antipas was killed in
Pergamum, this hardly indicates persecution. Concern about persecution in the book of Revelation seems to derive from scholars who have
read Daniel and use the lenses picked up from that astral prophet in
their "apocalyptic" reading.

If the message entrusted to John is not concerned with encouraging people in the face of political persecution and threat of death, what
is his concern? The emphatic and repeated encouragement to endure,
persevere, to overcome the situation are the expected Mediterranean
solutions to distressing situations. The typical Mediterranean mode of
dealing with distress is by enduring patiently and gracefully, so unlike
the U.S. option, which is to act energetically and forcefully in distress
(Draguns 1988: 146–47). But what triggers the distress? The vigorous
and frequent warnings against deception and misrepresentation rather
clearly indicate that our astral prophet encountered a cosmic Lord Jesus
much concerned about disloyalty and deviance among persons presently
showing allegiance to him. The endurance they are urged to practice is
endurance in the face of frequent attempts at deception by a range of
deceivers, from Satan to a coterie of their contemporaries.

Consider again each of the foregoing documents to the churches
and note the theme of deception: Ephesus was infiltrated by persons
who claimed "they are apostles and are not," evaluated by the inhabitants as "false" (2:2; see also 21:8). Smyrna was "defamed" (2:9; see also
13:1, 5, 6; 16:9, 11, 21; 17:3) by "those calling themselves Judeans while
they are not," hence by impostors, pretenders or deceivers. These fake
Judeans form a "synagogue of Satan" (2:9). Satan, of course, is the
deceiver par excellence ("that ancient Serpent . . . the deceiver of the
whole world"; 12:9; see 2:20; 13:14; 18:23; 19:20; 20:3, 8, 10).

This cosmic deceiver has his throne in Pergamum, though to their
credit the believers there did not "deny" Jesus (2:13; see 3:8); denial is
yet another form of lie or deception. Still, some persons in Pergamum

follow Balaam (2:14; see Num 25:1–5; 31:16), a proverbial "false" prophet in the biblical tradition. He taught Balak "to set a trap," by eating food offered to idols and by committing fornication, a code-word for idolatry; this is what the Nicolaitans do (2:15; previously mentioned at Ephesus in 2:6).

In Thyatira there is "the woman Jezebel who calls herself a prophetess" (1 Kgs 16:31; 2 Kgs 9:22, 30). Obviously she is no prophetess, but rather beguiles some believers (2:20) with the so-called deep things of Satan (2:24) that lead persons astray. As for Sardis, there are some whose behavior is totally deceptive, for they are labeled as living, but are truly dead (3:1); their deeds are "incomplete" (3:2); they are lacking or deficient in requisite authenticity or integrity under the scrutiny of God.

Philadelphia, too, evidences liars and impostors who really form a synagogue of Satan (3:9). Again, these are persons who claim to be Judeans but are not. They deceive, posture, and mislead others. Fortunately the believers of Philadelphia have not been deceived and thus have not denied Jesus' name (3:8) as others have. They have not lied about Jesus.

Finally, the Laodiceans are ambiguous, "lukewarm" (3:16). Such ambiguity is itself a form of deception since one cannot be sure which way persons will go. This is revealed in the fact that they claim to be one thing (rich, prosperous, satisfied) but in reality they are quite something else (wretched, pitiable, poor, blind, and naked, 3:17; see Pilch 1992: 126–27).

As the general theme of the book reveals, deception entails idolatry, the public dishonoring of God. And this dishonor requires satisfaction, should people not have a change of heart. The communities at Ephesus (2:5), Pergamum (2:16), Thyatira (2:21), Sardis, (3:3) and Laodicea (3:19) are urged to a change of heart. Perhaps such a change of heart is now possible. Yet as the author will reveal, while people can change, they invariably refuse to do so and live with their duplicity and ensuing idolatry. This in fact has been evidenced by the inhabitants of the land and the city that housed God's own temple. The call to a change of heart (9:20–21) was spurned (Sector 2). Similarly the seer finds that the ranks of antediluvians, human and non-human alike, also reject the summons to a change of heart (16:9, 11) (Sector 3). By the time John gets to see the situation of the residents of the first and most magnificent of cities on earth, it is long beyond time for a change of heart (Sector 4).

In sum, endurance in the face of the deceit and the allure of civilization, as well as the continued allegiance to God and his Messiah, is the only reasonable response for those pledging allegiance to God and his Messiah. We now turn first to a consideration of this God who demands human allegiance, then to his Messiah as presented in this book.

12.2. RADICAL MONOTHEISM

The term "theology" here means conceptual elaborations concerning God. The term is not to be identified with ideology in general or religious ideology in particular. These terms are much broader than theology. Theology, rather, deals with the articulating of conceptions of God. An astronomic approach to the book of Revelation does indeed yield some interesting theological surprises.

The image of God in the book of Revelation differs radically from the traditional picture of the tribal God of Israel. That God was Yahweh, "our" God. The traditional Israelite creed stated: "You shall love Yahweh, your God" (Deut 6:4). Such in-group language explicitly postulates the existence of other gods, "their God." In fact the Ten Commandments only prohibit denying primacy to Yahweh, the God of Israel: "You shall have no other Gods before me!"

The book of Revelation implies the existence of solely one, ultimate All, God, the "Beginning and the End," totality in a single being. This is truly a radical revelation in a world of multiple deities. Even Paul speaks of "many gods and many lords" (1 Cor 8:5) and does not deny their existence. Any cosmic beings designated as deities by John's contemporaries are regarded simply as sky beings in God's entourage. The twenty-four decans about the cosmic center are viewed as privileged elders, and the main divine constellations at the four corners of the horizon are considered four living cosmic beings in the service of God. And all the many sky winds and sky beings form part of God's entourage. The deities in charge of cosmic bodies such as the planets are subject to God's bidding. While John reads his experiences in the light of the expectations provided by Israel's story, he goes far beyond the image of the traditional tribal God of Israel, the God of Abraham, Isaac, and Jacob, for the God he experiences is the sole God of all reality, who is in charge of the cosmos. This is the God of all nations and tribes and peoples and tongues. There is no other.

God's main attributes include abiding presence (in later philosophical terms, eternity). Hence in 1:4b we read that God is entitled "He Who Is and Who Was and Who Is Coming." And in 1:8 this Ever Present One is identified as the Almighty. The Greek term for Almighty is *Pantokrator* (Παντοκράτωρ, found also at 4:8; 11:17; 15:3; 16:7; 21:22). The word literally means "Controller of Everyone and Everything." This attribute of God proclaims God to be superior in power to all the cosmic forces we are about to encounter in the course of the book. As noted previously, the culturally distinctive titles such as the Orphic "Beginning and End," or "Alpha and Omega," the first and last letters of the Greek alphabet presuppose due learning on John's part. For example, he surely knew about the process of manipulating letters of the alphabet in divination. But it is doubtful whether John's audience shared his skills. At the same time, such culturally specific titles made for relevance in the first-century Mediterranean setting. They invite the modern reader to look for equally relevant epithets to express the contemporary experience of God in a reinterpreted cosmos.

12.3. THE COSMIC JESUS

John's experience of the uniqueness of God is underscored by two other distinctive features: the role of the cosmic Jesus and the quality of the elect.

At the outset (1:5a) John gives his audience further greetings from Jesus Messiah, described here in terms of his relationship to God. Relative to God, who is the "One Who Is and Who Was and Who Is Coming," Jesus is a trustworthy witness among us. There is no need to be deceived, since Jesus can be relied on and believed in. Further, in kinship terms, he is "first born," the first born of the dead; in political terms, he is the preeminent ruler of the world. Note that until the eighteenth century, what we call "religion" was embedded in kinship and/or politics. There was domestic religion and political religion in the ancient Mediterranean, but no "religion" pure and simple (Malina 1986b). Hence the "religious" titles of Jesus will be kinship titles and/or political titles. And it is these that we find in the book of Revelation.

From the outset, in the first celestial scenario, Jesus the Messiah is presented as Lord of the pole of the universe, with the pivotal cosmic stars in his control, his "right hand." He is *polokrator* (πολοκράτωρ) of the universe already. He thus transcends the role of Messiah of Israel in incredible fashion. The role Jesus occupies, as revealed to John, far surpasses the narrowed and confining role ascribed to him by his earthly followers, for Jesus is cosmic Lord.

Furthermore, this cosmic Lord of the pole of the universe is identified with the zodiacal Lamb/Ram. This is the sky being that has preeminence and primacy over all celestial beings. The Lamb/Ram, as first of the zodiacal constellations, received this primacy before the outfitting of the earth, when the creator populated the sky with the cosmic beings presently to be found there. Furthermore, it was generally believed that when the sky returned to the position that it had at its inception with creation, the whole universe would be transformed. The exalted Jesus now occupies this cosmic center associated with the Lamb/Ram. The transformation of the universe cannot be far off.

The cosmic Jesus, by means of the edicts in chs. 2 and 3 to the sky servants, looks to the well-being of the churches. The sky servants are to deliver these edicts with their message of support, judgment, and promise with a view to allaying deception and to allow for ongoing endurance. John's role is to transmit these communications to the respective guardian beings. The description of the edict-giver, specifically his status and role, authorizes the commands. Here the edict-giver is described as the one with the seven stars in his right hand, that is, the πολοκράτωρ, *polokratōr*, the one who controls the fate of the cosmos. He walks about in the middle of the seven golden lampstands, the planets; he can disregard their controlling power at will. The edict-giver is thus described as truly all-powerful over every actual and potential source of power in the universe. In a culture that submitted to nature and its forces, relationship with this all-powerful personage would offer all sorts of options for a renewed zest for living.

At the beginning of each edict, the edict-giver provides a self-description that authorizes the edict that follows. These self-descriptions are rooted in the opening of the book (now called ch. 1). Thus:

1. "the one holding the seven stars in his right hand, the one walking about in the middle of the seven golden lampstands" (2:1) relates back to 1:16 and 1:12–13.

2. "the First and the Last, he who was dead and lives on" (2:8) is a reference from 1:18.

3. "the one who has the sharp two-edged sword" (2:12) goes back to 1:16.

4. "the son of God, the one who has eyes like flames of fire, and whose feet are like brass" (2:18) relates back to 1:14–15.

5. "the one having the seven sky winds of God and the seven stars" (3:1) refers to 1:4; but here the sky winds before God's throne are now controlled by the edict giver; the seven stars, of course, go back to 1:16 and the opening edict, 2:1.

6. "the holy one, the truthful one, the one having the key of David, who opens and no one will close, and who closes and no one will open" (3:7). The first part of this designation goes back to 1:2, but the second part is quite new, cited from Isa 22:22. In Isaiah the passage gives a promise for Eliakim the son of Hilkiah, which was never realized. Our author sees its realization in Jesus the Messiah; and in context it recalls the keys of Death and Hades in 1:18.

7. "the Amen, the trustworthy and truthful witness, the beginning of God's creation" (3:14) refer to Jesus the eminently credible witness in 1:2 and 1:5. If we stay in context, Jesus Messiah is the beginning of God's creation insofar as first-born of the dead, and now ruler above all kings of the earth, as noted in 1:5.

The cumulative effect of these designations is to mark off Jesus the Messiah as supremely eminent because of his power. Power means the ability to control others based on an implied sanction of force. Now all the designations are designations of power. Those numbered 1 through 6 have the power rooted in the constellational setting of Jesus the Messiah, while 6 in part and 7 in entirety point to his position with God.

The fundamental question that concerned the first generation of Christians was: where was Jesus now after the resurrection? What was he doing? What is he doing for us? Consequently the various descriptions of Jesus after his resurrection, since they describe him relative to those who believed in him, try to explain his present role for his followers. For example, in Acts 3:19–21, Jesus is indeed God's designated Messiah, soon to come as Messiah with power: "Repent, therefore, and turn again, that your sins may be blotted out, that times of refreshing may come from the presence of the Lord, and that he may send the Messiah appointed for you, Jesus, whom the sky must receive until the time for establishing all that God spoke by the mouth of his holy prophets from of old." John's designations for Jesus Messiah are far more radical. For our seer, Jesus is already exercising power, specifically as *polokratōr* (πολοκράτωρ) controller of the universe at the pole where God's throne is.

Other features in the work underscore the eminence of Jesus Messiah. In his visions in Sector 2, the seer recounts how Jesus Messiah, "the lion of the tribe of Judah, the root of David" is the cosmic Lamb at the head of creation. Through dying, Jesus overcame in order to open the scroll and its seven seals—which, as we saw, were directed to the land of Israel and its central city Jerusalem (5:5–6)! Now as honored, eminent, cosmic personage, he directs, supports and consoles those who trust him (7:17).

In Sector 3, John only cursorily notes the enthronement of the cosmic Child next to God. Yet it takes little astral imagination to notice the relationship of this cosmic male Child and the constellation Aries. The Semitic name for Aries, *Taleh*, means "male lamb" as well as "boy" (Gospel readers know the female version of this word in Mark 5:41 where *Talitha* is translated by Mark as "little girl"). Obviously the cosmic Child (Taleh) of ch. 12 is surely the Lamb (*Taleh*) of God of Christian tradition. Thus in the same Sector 3, John later sees the cosmic Lamb, with God since the foundation of the world, as preeminent king and lord (19:16). In that capacity, he is God's Utterance or Statement ("Word"), and he conquers the cosmic enemies of God, who deceive humankind and negatively impact God's creation (19:11–14).

Finally, in Sector 5 John informs us that for those who trust the witness of Jesus and are faithful to God, there is no separation at death. Rather, they directly live and rule with Christ "for a thousand years," that is, until all is transformed, made new.

The final line of the work invokes the Lord Jesus' favor upon all the addressees of the letter (22:21). While such a concluding wish might be a standard letter-writing device, it does call attention to Jesus as

Lord, who is coming "quickly." Favor is the benefaction provided by a patron or mediated by a broker. Jesus is expected to play one or another of these roles now for those with allegiance to him, who are not deceived because they trust in his witness.

12.4. THE QUALITY OF THOSE WHO TRUST JESUS

While John's experience in the outer reaches of the cosmos has him describing interactions with myriads of sky servants and holy ones, every so often he does refer to the human beings who trust Jesus. Perhaps the most significant statement has to do with the list in ch. 7. There the number of the persons chosen from Israel is rather limited, a countable number of 144,000. But the number of persons chosen from outside Israel is truly stupendous, uncountable. Clearly the prophet again has something distinctive to say by underscoring this feature because, while his perspective and expectations are fully within the story of Israel, and while he interprets his astral experiences in terms of Israel's story, his concerns are much wider. Much of his account deals with realms beyond his time-bound and space-bound earth and the social concerns connected with human societies. His description of reality beyond the vault of the sky removes him in space. His concerns extend far beyond Judea, Judean concerns, and Jerusalem. As a matter of fact, for him, the only true "holy city" is the new Jerusalem. And this Jerusalem, the final city of humankind, is the only place worth living, the only true "holy land."

While rooted in Israel's past activities, his concerns extend far beyond Israel's history. They move back to the time of the creation of the cosmos and its inhabitants, human and nonhuman; they move back to the time of antediluvians and of the first postdeluvian city of humankind. This movement back to cosmic prehistory is really nothing more than a learned consideration of what exists in the sky at present. Present cosmic arrangements are replete with evidence of the past as well as of the forthcoming. John's experiences simply bypass Israel's history. He is pushed to put cosmic creation and humankind as a whole on center stage, with the cosmic Lamb as the focus of the whole scenario. If anything, his initial attention in Sector 2 does focus on the destruction of "the land" and its central city in the scenarios of chs. 5–11. The cosmic Lamb, "lion of the tribe of Judah, the root of David," opens the seals of the scroll that spell disaster for Israel: the inhabitants of the land that holds the "great city where their Lord was crucified."

Those chosen by God, of course, are those who maintain allegiance to God, who do not dishonor God by idolatry. Thanks to the cosmic Lamb, they include people from every nation and tribe and people and tongue without number.

12.5. THE TRANSFORMATION OF THE COSMOS

Of course astral prophecy is essentially vertical. It is rooted in a present-oriented, up-and-down dimension. This feature implies a perception of power wielded by celestial beings and events, with consequent control of human social living. However, the up-and-down spatial perspective can be laid on its side and then translated and read in a "now and later" horizontal orientation. In this way, the prophet's cosmic journeying to explain the present becomes an ideology of future-oriented, social transformation. In other words, astral prophecy always seems to lend itself to the tendency to take the vertical astronomics of the seer and to "horizontalize" it into an ideology of future cosmic transformation, in which the world will end and another creation "out of nothing" will emerge. The ideology of social transformation is invariably the horizontal fallout of astral prophecy. This is not unlike taking a time perception such as night, and converting it into a space perception, such as frontier. Time, like space, can be occupied and is treated so by humans. Nighttime social life in U.S. urban areas resembles social life on former land frontiers (see Melbin 1978). Similarly, one may take a space percept such as the sky and its dimensions and convert it into a time percept, such as forthcoming and future.

This seems to be exactly what later readers of the book of Revelation did (for how Revelation was read over the ages, see Kretschmar 1985; Berger 1976; Landes 1988, Verbeke et al. 1988). They read the work "indoors," apart from actual astral scenarios, as a purely literary phenomenon imparting a set of ideas. In the process, the vertical qualities of the sky dimensions were selectively unattended to, while the ideas in the book yielded a horizontal "apocalyptic." And this "apocalyptic" was quite readily adaptable to linear time and "eschatological" schedules.

It seems quite certain that ancient Mediterraneans were not future-oriented at all. In other words, there is nothing in the book of Revelation that refers to the future. Even the new Jerusalem is descending right now! The reason for this is that the author of the book and his audience were concerned with their present and with those dimensions of human living immediately rooted in their present, that is, the forthcoming (see Malina 1989). Astral prophetic narratives similarly are concerned with what is present and with what is forthcoming because it is already present someplace or in some form. As a matter of fact, celestial phenomena could yield information about "the future" only because that "future" information was rooted in the present situation and course of the sky. Celestial predictions are rooted in the past, present, and forthcoming.

What then might we appropriate religiously from this book? Perhaps our fundamental religious difficulty today is one of cosmic orientation. In an uncentered cosmos people are hard put to develop the sense of cosmic well-being available to our ancestors in faith. We need to feel at home on an extremely insignificant planet in an inconceivably enormous, expanding, universe. Perhaps contemplation with the seer of Patmos focused on the God of the sky as the true center of the cosmos will offer insight into our proper place in creation. With John we might consider Jesus as in fact the true wielder of cosmic power, designated by God to restore all things in the universe as the Creator wishes. Thanks to John's astral prophecy, Christians know where Jesus is and what he does. His witness enables us to avoid deception and to develop a Christian sense of at-homeness in an expanding cosmos. Perhaps the at-one-ment that solved the set of religious problems that plagued our ancestors in faith might share center stage with the at-homeness that we need to set our own modern problem with religion on course.

APPENDIX A: ON THE DECANS:
INFORMATION FROM FIRMICUS MATERNUS

Firmicus Maternus summarizes the decans and their role:

1. Each sign is divided into three parts, and each part has one decan, so that in each sign there are three decans, each having ten degrees out of the thirty, and over those ten degrees it exercises its power and control. They have infinite power and freedom in indicating the fates of men.

2. In addition, the decans themselves are allotted to individual planets, so that if the planet should be in that decan, even though it is in a strange sign, it is considered as if it were in its own sign. Located in its own decan it accomplishes the same thing as when in its own sign.

3. The first decan of Aries belongs to Mars, the second to the sun, the third to Venus. The first decan of Taurus belongs to Mercury, the second to the moon, the third to Saturn. Of Gemini, the first decan belongs to Jupiter, the second to Mars, the third to the sun. Of Cancer the first to Venus, the second to Mercury, the third to the moon. Of Leo the first to Saturn, the second to Jupiter, the third to Venus. In Virgo the first to the sun, the second to Venus, the third to Mercury. In Libra the first decan belongs to the moon, the second to Saturn, the third to Jupiter. Of Scorpio the first to Mars, the second to the sun, the third to Venus. Of Sagittarius the first to Mercury, the second to the moon, the third to Saturn. Of Capricorn the first belongs to Jupiter, the second to Mars, the third to the sun. In Aquarius the first decan belongs to Venus, the second to Mercury, the third to the moon. In Pisces the first decan belongs to Saturn, the second to Jupiter, the third to Mars.

4. Some who wish to elaborate this in more detail add three divinities each to every decan, which they call *munifices*, that is, *liturgi*, so that for every sign, nine *munifices* can be found, and every decan is divided into three *munifices*.

5. Again the nine *munifices* which they say are allotted to every sign they divide into an infinite number of powers of divinities. By these they say are decreed sudden accidents, pains, sicknesses, chills, fevers, and everything that happens unexpectedly. Through these divinities they say defective births are produced among men.

6. But this part of the doctrine we must of necessity pass over in this book. The Greeks also, who tried to reach the secrets of that theory, stopped at the first stage and left the subject with a certain reluctance. But now we must return to the doctrine where we left it. (*Mathesis* 2.4.1–6; Rhys Bram 1975: 34–36).

1. I am now about to explain fearful secrets which the revered ancients left wrapped in obscurity so that they should not come to the ears of the profane. Give this your full attention, with a calm mind, so that you may understand easily what I am about to say.

2. We said in the book of principles that each sign has three decans. These decans have great divine power and by themselves determine all good and bad fortune. Nechepso, the most just emperor of Egypt and a truly good astrologer, by means of the decans predicted all illnesses and afflictions; he knew which decan produced which illness and which decans were stronger than others. From their different nature and power decans he discovered the cure for all illnesses, because one nature is often overcome by another, and one god by another.

3. There are 36 decans in the whole circle of the zodiac and they are divided among the twelve gods, that is the twelve signs. There are three decans to every sign, but their power does not extend to all 30 degrees of each sign. In every sign decans possess certain degrees and not others. Those they possess are called "full"; those where they have no power, "empty."

4. Those natives who have their chart the sun, moon and all five planets in full degrees will be elevated like gods with the protection of the greatest majesty. But it is never possible in human charts to have the ascendant, the sun and moon, and five planets in full degrees. Those who have one planet in full degrees will be mediocre; those who have two will approach a certain amount of good fortune; three, good fortune beyond the ordinary; with four they reach royal happiness. Beyond that it is not possible for human charts. But those who have neither the ascendant nor any planet in full degrees will be always wretched, destitute, paupers involved in every kind of ill fortune.

5. Thus you must diligently observe this possibility in all houses and all planets. If the ascendant is in full degrees, the natives will be very strong in vitality, courage, animal spirits, type of body, and power of authority. Those who have the ascendant in empty degrees are small of body, depressed in mind, weak

in bodily strength, always subservient, serving more powerful men, and lost the initiative in all business affairs.

6. In a similar way the midheavens in empty degrees predicts lack of success, but in full degrees indicates everything strong and valid which the house is accustomed to predict. The same is true of the Part of Fortune, the ruler of the chart, and the one who determines occupations. For all these, even though located in favorable houses, if not in full degrees lose their power. But if they are in full degrees they more firmly guarantee everything they promise.

7. . . . [A list of full and empty degrees and the (Egyptian) names of all decans in order now follow . . .]

. . .

20. That most true and immutable theory the ancients left wrapped in obscurity so that it should not come to the notice of everyone. The great Petosiris touched on it only lightly; not that he was not familiar with it (for he had arrived at all hidden secrets), but he did not want to divulge it lest his work should lose its divine character. Therefore, when you have collected all your data, look carefully at the individual planets and houses and note which of them are in empty degrees. For only then will you be able to explain the whole forecast (*Mathesis* 4.22.1–20; Rhys Bram 1978: 147–50).

Appendix B: An Israelite Dodekaeteris: The Treatise of Shem

The opening phrase, "If the year begins in . . . " is that of the translator. It is obviously incorrect, since a *Dodekaeteris* as this one begins: "If it is the year of Aries."

[1]If the year begins in Aries[1]: The year will be lean. Even its fourfooted (animals) will die; and many clouds will neither be visible nor appear. And grain will not reach (the necessary) height, but its rye will (reach good height) and will ripen. And the river Nile will overflow (at) a good rate. And the king of the Romans will not remain in one place. And the stars of heaven will be dispersed as sparks of fire; and the moon will be eclipsed. And the first grain will die, but the last grain will be harvested. And from Passover [until the New Year] produce will have a blight. And the year will be bad, for a great war and misery (will occur) on all the earth, and especially in the land of Egypt. And many ships will be wrecked when the sea billows. And oil will be valued in Africa; but wheat will be reduced in value in Damascus and Hauran; but in Palestine it will be valued. And (in that region there will be) various diseases, and sicknesses, even fighting will occur in it. But it will be allowed to escape from it and be delivered.

---

[1] Charlesworth further notes: "The author obviously is thinking about the houses (geoarc) of the zodiac, which change approximately every two hours as the earth daily rotates on its axis. He is not referring to the signs (heliarcs) of the zodiac, which divide the year into twelve parts as the earth revolves around the sun. Each year begins in a different house, but years begin in the same sign for intervals of approximately two thousand years. Since the beginning of recorded history years have begun in only three signs: Taurus, Aries and Pisces" (1.481, n. c). This explanation is totally off the mark; Barton 1994: 69–70, follows Charlesworth. The ancient author was obviously thinking of the sequence typical of *Dodekaeterides*.

[2]And if the year begins in Taurus: Everyone whose name contains a Beth, or Yudh, or Kaph will become ill, or be wounded by an iron (weapon). And there will be fighting. And a wind will go out from Egypt and will fill the entire earth. And in that (year) there will be wheat and abundant rains, but the nobles of the land and of the surrounding region will destroy (the crops). And the [rain] of (this) year will be withheld for three months, and afterward produce will be exceedingly expensive for thirtysix days. And many people will die from diseases of the throat, then leanness will cease. And the first grain will perish in like manner, but the last grain will be harvested. And barley and dried peas will (also) be harvested. And devils will attack men but will not harm them in any way. And two kings will oppose one another. And the large river Nile will rise above its banks. Those who are on a ship in the midst of the sea or people who are on the sea will be in severe misery. But at the close of the year there will be great blessing.

[3]And if the year begins in Gemini: The moon will be beautiful and a north wind will blow and rain will come from it. And everyone whose name has a Taw, or Heth, or Mim will have on his face leprosy or a mark. And in the beginning of the year there will be a harsh war. And there will be spring rains and grain [will be good] and beautiful, and especially the grain that has been irrigated. And mice will multiply on the earth. And the Romans [and the Parthians] will make severe wars with each other. And the Romans will proceed by ships on the sea, then they will cause a war and destroy the (Parthians). And evil people will proceed in this world, and they will do evil; then there will be anxiety and harsh misery. But at the end of the year there will be prosperity; even the river Nile will overflow exceedingly.

[4]And if the year begins in Cancer: In the beginning of the year there will be a sufficiency of produce and people will be healthy. And the Nile will overflow half its (usual) rate. And Alexandria will be afflicted, and misery from the plague will be in it. And the stars will shine magnificently for the moon will be eclipsed. And many ships will be wrecked in the sea. And in the beginning of the ye[ar wheat and barley will be expensive.] And winds will increase, then many people will be ill from sties (of the eyes) and from coughing and vomiting. And wine will be abundant, but bulls, and sheep, and small cattle will perish, even dried peas will perish. But oil will compensate (for) them. Then at the end of the year the harvest will be wearisome for nine days, but afterward there will be rain. And great blessing will be in (this year).

[5]And if the year begins in Leo: There will be spring rains, then the soil will be deprived of the north winds. And grain will be enjoyed, for indeed the food of men will be good. And wheat and rice and dried peas will be expensive, and wheat must be irrigated. And oil and dates will be expensive. And there will be disease among men. And pregnant (females) and small cattle will die. And the king will strive with a king. And the large locust(s) will come and will not subside; but somewhat [gradually] they will swirl in circles and shrink (back) together. And the river Nile will overflow its highest rate. And people will have headache(s). Then at the end of the year there will be much rain.

[6]And if the year begins in Virgo: Everyone whose name contain Yudh or Semkath, and Beth, and Nun will be diseased and robbed, and will flee from his home. And (this misfortune) will occur in the beginning of the year. And shortage of water will be in every circle. And the first grain will not prosper. And people will suffer (many) miseries in winter and summer. But the last grain will be harvested and it will be good. And produce will be expensive in Hauran and Bithynia but at the end of the year it will be inexpensive. Even wine will be less (expensive) and pleasant. And dates will be abundant. But oil will be expensive. And wheat and barley will be valued, but dried pea(s) will be reduced in value. And rain will be late and will not fall upon the earth until thirty days before the Passover [feast]. And the king will strive with a king and will slay him. And Alexandria will be lost. And [the Nil]e will not overflow well. And many ships will be wrecked. But at the end of the year there will be a sufficiency about everything.

[7]And if the year begins in Libra: There will be spring rains. And the year will be transformed. And people will be spared from the east wind. And fig trees will not produce fruit. But dates and oil will be plentiful. But wine will be expensive. And wheat will valued greatly. And the locust will appear. And a severe war will occur in Africa. And men will have severe diseases. And in the middle of the year rain will be held back (for) twenty days. And cultivated wheat will not ripen well. And all lands will be good. And everyone whose name has a Yudh or Beth will be sick, and he will have anxiety, and will go into exile from his land. And wine will be damaged. And adultery will increase, and (licentious) desires will increase. And the king will stay in one place. And power will leave the land. And the nobles will flee to the sea, and there will be between (them) [in] the [sea] severe war. And there will be in Galilee a severe earthquake. And robbers will gather in Hauran and in Damascus. And the river Nile will overflow (at) its highest rate. And a severe plague will occur in Egypt, and it will be in [Gali]lee as in Beth Bardune (the Place of Mules?). People will be troubled because of (the lack of) rain.

[8]And if the year begins in Scorpio: The north wind will blow in the beginning of the year, and there will be many spring rains. And at the end of the year everything will be expensive. And rain will diminish until people recite petition(s) and prayer(s), and beseech with alms the living God. And there will be disease among women who are pregnant. And many men on account of affliction [will migrate] from their countries. And wheat and barley will be harvested very little, but dried peas will be harvested. And there will be (sufficient) wine and oil. And ulcers will develop within the bodies of men but will not injure them. And the Nile will overflow half of its (usual) rate. And (there will be) whispers (of hope) for small cattle. And everyone whose name has a Taw or Yudh will become sick, but will recover health. And everyone born in Scorpio (will) survive (his birth), but at the end of the year he will be killed.

[9]And if the year begins in Sagittarius: Everyone whose name contains a Beth or Pe will have misery and a severe disease, and in the beginning of the year it will increase in severity. And men in many places will be troubled. And in the land of Egypt there will be sown only a (very) little. And in the middle of

the year there will be much rain. But men will gather produce into granaries because of the (following) drought. And grain will not be pleasing. Even at the end of the year it will not be good. But wine and oil will be considered good. And adultery will increase and small cattle will die.

[10]And if the year begins in Capricorn: Everyone whose name contains a Qoph will become sick and be plundered and wounded with a sword. And the east wind (will) rule the year. And everyone (should) sow (early); the last (to sow) will be unsuccessful. And in the beginning of the year [everything] will be expensive. Waves and storms will increase, (so that) they (who are on the sea) will die. And in the middle of the year produce will be expensive. And thieves will increase. And governmental officials will be cruel. Even wasps and (small) reptiles of the earth will increase, and they will harm many people. And many people (will move) from one place to another because of the existing war. And wars will increase on the earth. Then at the end of the year rain will diminish. And in (some) places grain will be harvested, but in (other) places grain will perish. And there will be a disease in Damascus and in Hauran. And there [will be] a famine along the [se]acoast. And adultery will increase. And people will recite petition(s) and prayers and (observe) a fast and (give) alm(s) (in hope for) rain. And irrigated grain will be good.

[11]And if the year begins in Pisces: Everyone whose name contains a Kaph or Mim (will) become sick and (eventually) slain. The year will be good. And the grain (will be) good and healthy. And there will be spring rains. And fishing in the sea will be [prosper]ous. And when (the sea) billows ships will be wrecked. And (people) will become sick. And wine and oil and wheat, each of them, shall be pleasing. Then grain will be good. There will be wars and much desolation in cities; and villages will be transferred and displaced from one place to another. And robbers will come from Palestine and [many will wa]ge a great war against three cities. And the Romans (sometimes will be) victorious and (sometimes) easily overcome. And there will be a great disease among men. And there will come forth a black man who seeks the kingdom. And the house of the kingdom will perish. And the king will seek to understand what men are saying, and (will) lay waste many cities. And no one will be able to stop him; and the fear of God and his mercies (will) be absent from him. Then at the end of the year there will be peace and prosperity among men, and love and harmony among all the kings who are on the entire earth.

[12][The section on] Aquarius, which (of course) is before Pisces, nevertheless because of a mistake, was copied in the (following) manner. If it is the year of Aquarius, everyone whose name contains a Lamadh or Pe (will) become sick or utterly ruined by marauders. And in the beginning of the year rain will increase. And the Nile will overflow its full rate. And Egypt (will rule) over Palestine. [Barley] will be harvested. And lamb(s) and sheep will prosper. And the west wind (will) govern the year. And the king will fight with a king. And the first grain will prosper; but dried pea(s) will not sprout (very) much although they (will) be harvested. And merchants (will) seek help from the living God (trans. Charlesworth *OTP* 1.481–86).

APPENDIX C: ON PLANTS AND THE ZODIAC: LETTER OF SOLOMON TO ROBOAM

The plant of Krios (Aries) is the water-milfoil. Its juice, mixed with rose oil, when the same zodiacal sign rules, has marvelous power, and it will restore health in three days after a mortal blow from a sword. If a person who possesses evil spirits anoints himself with the juice of the plant, he gets advantage from this possession. And he makes these spirits favorable. The root worn in an amulet on the right arm makes the wearer win favor from everyone, and all sorrow will flee far from the wearer.

The plant of Tauros (Taurus) is the clover. Pick it when the same zodiacal sign, that is Tauros, rules. It has the following powers: Place its fruit and blossoms into a sack made of the hide of an unborn calf and wear it whenever you go into the presence of kings and of rulers and princes, and you will have great honor. If one anoints himself with the leaves . . . ; the juice heals the eyes and and every ailment of the eyes. The root worn in an amulet repels demons and sadness causing agents. [In the codex there follow seven empty lines].

The plant of the Didymoi (Gemini) is the gladiola. When the same zodiacal sign rules, pick its blossoms and place them into a newly-born child's crib, and wear the blossoms and the child will be beloved by small and great alike. Its leaves worn in an amulet will heal the demon-possessed. And give its upper root to human and beast to eat and he will love you, but give the lower root and they will hate. [In the codex there follow seven empty lines].

The plant of Karkinos (Cancer) is the mandrake; pick it when the same zodiacal sign, Karkinos, rules. When you anoint the ears with its blossoms, it heals every sickness of headache. And give its root to a barren woman to eat, two pieces each the size of a grain of wheat from the first day of her purification to the fourteenth day, and she will conceive, and she is to wear some of the plant. [In the codex there follow seven empty lines].

The plant of Leo is called the black horehound; pick it on the day when its zodiacal sign rules. With its juice, anoint crushed bones and bind them; they will marvelously be hardened (to previous shape). Wear its root and you will catch very many fish. And if you mix the juice of its leaves with oil, it will work like balsam. [In the codex there follow five empty lines].

Nightshade (or thorn apple) is the plant of Parthenos (Virgo). Pick it at the hour and day when Parthenos rules. And pick its leaves and fruits and mix them with sufficient tallow and anoint those suffering from a flux and they will be healed immediately. And pick the shoots of the plant and make a wreath of them and put it on a maiden; if she smiles, she is corrupt and is not a virgin; and if she has a gloomy look or weeps, she is a virgin. And if you bind its root with the skin of a wolf and wear it, you will be unconquerable, overcoming everyone. [In the codex there follow two empty lines].

The plant of Zygos (Libra) is the needle furze (*belonike*). Pick it when Zygos rules. So you will have great powers. Its fruit, when drunk, heals those possessed by demons, and the moon-struck and those with kidney stones and those with colic. Its leaves, when eaten, heal every ache of the one eating. Its root, when inhaled as smoke, heals rapid breathing and catarrh and bewitchment. Again make its root into an amulet by wrapping it in the skin of a fox and bind it on your right arm and you will be unfearing of robbers or demons. [Six empty lines follow).

Scorpio's plant is the dog-tongue (*kynoglosson*). Pick it when Scorpio rules. It has marvelous and awful power. Pick its seed and make it into an amulet in deer skin and it will keep away every wicked thing and appear fearsome and glorious. And should you ever speak as a liar, they will believe you as God. After grinding its leaves, take the juice and mix with lily oil; then anoint any injury and it will heal marvelously. Hold its root in your hand and dogs will not annoy you. Again after grinding a perfect plant, make it into an ointment with sufficient tallow and anoint persons with a flux and they will be healed in three days. And if you will give any wild animal to eat of its root, it will be become tame. It also has other powers, which experimenting will make known. [Two vacant lines follow].

The plant of Toxotes (Sagittarius) is the mulberry (*anakardios*); pick it when the zodiacal sign Toxotes rules. Twist up a whole root together with the skin of a fox and wear it over the head; then you will overcome all teachers, juries, judges, kings and tyrants. Make its leaves, after grinding them, into an ointment and apply it to any inflammation and pain of the kidneys and it will marvelously be healed, so as to amaze everyone. Its root has still other power. Placed within the house, there will be good fortune and happiness in that house; and do not marvel at the good fortune of the plant, but at the God giving the favor. [Six vacant lines follow]

The plant of Aigokeros (Capricorn) is called the stinking tutsan (*tragion*). Pick it when this zodiacal sign rules. For should you give a woman to drink of its fruit, she will live but a few days. If you wear its leaves, all wild beasts will run away from you; however it would be best if a person wear the plant: and should a great number of wild beasts and lions encircle him, they will approach him as to God himself and will not touch him. And they will not do him injury unless he dreamt of them. Give the root to an epileptic to eat and he will be healed in three days and exceedingly so. And he will be fearless wherever he find himself night and day and in every season and in every locale. If one wear it as a phylactery, he will receive the favor of prophecy from God. [Three empty lines follow].

The plant of Hydrochoos (Aquarius) is the one called the hairy crowfoot (*batrachion*). After grinding its leaves while preserving the juice, give a dose of it if you wish that a person go into convulsions and undergo death. Pick its root and put it into a fish's skin when Hydrochoos rules and place it into a boat and it will shipwreck at the place to which it departed. Its blossoms, when worn, heal. This plant has still other powers. If you grind the leaves and mix in fine flour and place the mixture on the scabby and callused part of wounds, in three hours it will be removed.

The plant of Ichthys (Pisces) is the birthwort (*aristolochia*). When the zodiacal signs rules, pick it. It contains great favor. When its fruit is drunk with wine and honey, it chases away every sickness of the body. And when its root is burnt as fumigant and worn, it drives away every demon and every sort of trouble; and it chases out every sickness and affliction from the one eating its root. It is also an antidote for all venomous animals. For should a person be bitten by one of them and infected by any serpent or other destructive animal, having done these things and applied them on the site, he will be healed immediately.

Here are the plants of the seven planets, most conscientious Roboam. When you wish to gather them, collect them at the hour that the planet dominates having been set in motion at that hour. And having performed the invocation of names and the prayers, you will work with them in marvelous fashion; and this is not to be divulged in speech to any person outside.

The plant of Zeus (Jupiter) is the chrysankathon (unknown). Pick it at the hour that Zeus rules, and invoke the name of the sky servants and recite the prayers and one has awful and fearsome healings. If you give the root to eat at the 7th hour of the morning, it will heal the moon-struck. If you will give its root to a demon-possessed person to wear along with frankincense, the demon will flee. As for those falling down from an affliction and foaming, have them drink the root with lulakion (?) and one will be healed immediately. Grind up some leaves and take the juice and apply it to amputated places, sword gashes and wounds and you will heal it in 18 hours. If you give the head of the plant to be worn as amulet, a man will not be afraid of being affected by magicians. If there is a person that suffers from the drinking of poison, have him drink a potion made of the head of the plant and water and honey, and he will be healed.

The plant of Ares (Mars) is the pentasites. Collect it at the hour of Ares and wear its sword-shaped leaves wrapped in wolf fur and should myriads of enemies surround you, they will not be able to hurt you, but you will be saved unharmed from them. Grind up and dry out some leaves, then give it with wine to drink to either male or female having a flow of blood from the body, and it will be marvelously healed so that everyone will be amazed at the power of the plant. Wear the root in every battle and in every battle array, and you will conquer and be saved unharmed, so that you will be amazed at the divine power. A person wearing the blossom of the plant will be envied by all persons and will be admired and proficient with power.

The plant of Kronos (Saturn) is the heliotrope. Pick it at the hour when Kronos rules. Say the prayers and the invocation of names of the sky servants of the ones ruling. And the plant has these powers. If you will secretly give a person to eat of its blossoms, there will come upon that person fever and shuddering from cold. If you will give two blossoms, then the condition will bet twice as bad, three blossoms, three times as bad, four blossoms, four times as bad, and so forth. If you secretly put its leaves in someone's pillow, he will not get up until you should remove it from his pillows. If you will give it to a person to eat, there will come upon him ill health unto death during all the time of his life and he will not get up until you give him to eat of the plant of Dios (Jupiter). Wear the root on yourself as a phylactery against mockery (?).

The plant of Helios (Sol) is called the helioskopos, among the Italians *girasole*. For it inclines its head toward where Helios (sun) is, hence it is called sunflower. Gather this plant at the hour when Helios rules, with prayers, and place its blossoms and fruit in the skin of an eagle and wear them on yourself. Where there is a treasure, it will be discovered immediately, with the blinking of the eye. You will see gold or silver where they lie and immediately the earth will close up over them again. Having then marked the place with a sign, you will dig and you will find what you had seen. Having ground the leaves and mixed them with extract of rose and honey, anoint your face and go out. And every wild person and brigand will greet you and honor you like God. Wear the root wrapped in the skin of an ass; you will soften irate rulers and kings. But if one wrap the roots in the skin of a seal and wear it, he will be admired and honored by kings and princes and elites. The plant has these powers that simply cannot be stopped.

The plant of Aphrodite (Venus) is called the orchid (*satyrion*). Collect it at the hour when Aphrodite rules, with prayers and angels. And pick its blossoms and fruit and wrap them in the skin of a young gazelle and wear it on your right arm and it will be a love charm for all women. Grind up its leaves and add rose nectar with honey and anoint your face and go out. And whatever sexual relation or marriage you begin, it will be successful. And if you say anything, it will be believed. And if you should list the names and give the most tender fruit of the root to whichever woman you wish, she will love you and come to agreement just like a husband by his wife. If you give the root finely ground as sand to persons in love while reciting the list of names and at the hour of Kronos, immediately they will hate each other and will be at odds with each other.

The plant of Hermes (Mercury) is called the cinqfoil (*pentadaktylon*). Collect it at the hour when Hermes rules, with the prayers and invocation of names. And pluck its blossoms and fruit and wrap it in the heart of a dark cat (male or female) and wear it on yourself, then you will be invisible. And if you do anything, it will not be known. When its leaves are dried and prepared as powder and mixed with oil, anoint all sorts of afflictions of the eye, blinding, misting over, painful blurring, bird blindness and you will heal immediately. If you wear some of the tendrils (*daktylos*) of the root, you will cure every suffering of the hands and of the fingers/toes (*daktylos*). If you eat of the tendrils of the root, you will be a memorizer and rhetorician in words. And then if you hear something, it will not be unnoticed (by you). And again should you wrap the root with dog skin and wear it, dogs will not attack you. And again should you wrap the root with fish skin, wear it and you will catch whichever fish you want to. And again should you wrap the root with the light colored (*blantios*) and genuine calf, go and hunt wild animals and wild cattle. For this plant has these powers and many more besides that simply cannot be thwarted. And the root eaten daily repels every sort of illness of the body and supports the advancement of life. Wear the root with medicinal frankincense. Then you will be preserved from all the magic and occult arts of wicked men.

The plant of Selene (Luna) is called the peony (*glaophote*); among the Italians it is called *lunaria*. Gather this plant at its (Selene's) hour with prayers and with the names of angels, hours, month, wind and its proper zodiacal house, that is Karkinos (Cancer). It has the following favors: if you wear its head with the comb of a rooster, all the endeavors to which you apply yourself will take place most quickly and in all your tasks the way will be good for you. It gains profit in every enterprise. If you mix some of its dewy leaves while the Selene is waxing, with pieces of gold or silver and other struck money and wear these pieces in all the business you will transact, in a very short while your treasury will grow and you will become lord of much money. Again if having collected the leaves you mix them with the money of your enemy, this money will vanish. Similarly if you should give a person some of the same leaves, everything will succeed for him. If he eats them, again those dewy leaves will give him advancement. If you throw the stem of the plant and the root into any sort of metal in a foundry and melt it, you will find it pure as gold, brilliant and genuine. This plant has still many other powers and favors. Amen (CCAG VIII, 2, 159–65).

APPENDIX D: ON EARTHQUAKES: DIO CASSIUS: AN ANCIENT MEDITERRANEAN INFORMANT

While the emperor was tarrying in Antioch, a terrible earthquake occurred; many cities suffered injury, but Antioch was the most unfortunate of all. Since Trajan was passing the winter there and many soldiers and many civilians had flocked thither from all sides in connection with law-suits, embassies, business or sightseeing, there was no nation or people that went unscathed; and thus in Antioch the whole world under Roman sway suffered disaster. There had been many thunderstorms and portentous winds but no one would ever have expected so many evils to result from them. First there came, on a sudden, a great bellowing roar and this was followed by a tremendous quaking. The whole earth was upheaved, and buildings leaped into the air; some were carried aloft only to collapse and be broken in pieces, while others were tossed this way and that as if by the surge of the sea and overturned, and the wreckage spread out over a great extent even of the open country. The crash of grinding and breaking timbers together with tiles and stones was most frightful; and an inconceivable amount of dust arose, so that it was impossible for one to see anything or to speak of hear a word. As for the people, many even who were outside the houses were hurt, being snatched up and tossed violently about and then dashed to the earth as if falling from a cliff; some were maimed and others were killed. Even trees in some cases leaped into the air, roots and all. The number of those who were trapped in the houses and perished was past finding out; for multitudes were killed by the very force of the falling debris, and great numbers were suffocated in the ruins. Those who lay with a part of their body buried under the stones or timbers suffered terribly being able neither to live any longer nor to find an immediate death.

Nevertheless, many even of these were saved, as was to be expected in such a countless multitude; yet not all such escaped unscathed. Many lost legs or arms, some had their heads broken and still others vomited blood; Pedo the consul was one of these, and he died at once. In a word, there was no kind of violent experience that those people did not undergo at that time. And as heaven continued the earthquake (*seiontos tou theou*) for several days and nights, the people were in dire straits and helpless, some of them crushed and perishing under the weight of the buildings pressing upon them, and others dying of hunger, whenever it so chanced that they were left alive either in a clear space, the timbers being so inclined as to leave such a space, or in a vaulted colonnade. When at last the evil had subsided someone who ventured to mount the ruins caught sight of a woman still alive. She was not alone, but had also an infant; and she had survived by feeding both herself and her child with her milk. They dug her out and resuscitated her together with her babe, and after that they searched the other heaps, but were not able to find in them anyone still living save a child sucking at the breast of its mother, who was dead. As they drew forth the corpses they could no longer feel any pleasure even at their own escape.

So great were the calamities that had overwhelmed Antioch at this time. Trajan made his way out through a window of the room in which he was staying. Some being of greater than human stature (*meizonos tinos he kata anthropon*), had come to him and led him forth, so that he escaped with only a few slight injuries; And as the shocks extended over several days, he lived out of doors in the hippodrome. Even Mount Casius itself was so shaken that its peaks seemed to lean over and break off and to be falling upon the very city. Other hills also settled, and much water not previously in existence came to light, while many streams disappeared (Dio Cassius, *Roman History* 68, 24–25, LCL).

APPENDIX E: ON COMETS: MORE FROM NECHEPSO-PETOSIRIS

The comet Swordfish. This heavenly body is assigned to Mercury, and it produces effects not less than the preceding comet and longer lasting. If it looks to the east the grandees of Persia and Ethiopia will kill their kings with poison, and the same crime will be perpetrated in Phoenicia against the men at the top, and people everywhere will be thrown into panic by false rumors. If it rises in the south it brings similar death-dealing treachery to the Egyptians and the other Libyan peoples; the Egyptians will have a reversal of their troubles but the Libyans will be consumed in internecine wars. When it faces the west it brings like threats to the rulers there as their mutual suspicions break into open warfare. When it faces the North it indicates a mingling of northern and Libyan peoples, with a daughter of a Libyan ruler given in marriage to a northern chieftain and plotting against her father—his own child!—and betraying him in her surrender to an unholy passion for her husband.

The comet Torch. So called from its appearance, the comet Torch both belongs to Mercury and is independent. When it faces the east it prophesies hazy weather and resulting damage to the grape vine, for the haze spawns the grubs called bloodworms. The damage will be general, but worst in Upper Armenia, along the Euphrates, in Phoenicia and the Taurus region of Cilicia. Not only by day but also at night the haze will be so thick as to blot out lit torches. The darnel weed will choke standing crops, and a poisonous dampness will damage them after harvesting. Rivers will overflow their banks as violent rainstorms burst and thunderbolts crash. But the haze will continue nonetheless, and ever-flowing rivers will dry up. If it faces the south, the weather will be still drier and more pestilential, the Nile will dry up and everything will swarm with reptiles. If the North, the haze will be dispelled by the cold of that direction, but fire will unexpectedly weep the forests and the mountains to the point where even those living on summits and in hilltop forts will not be out of harm's way; there will be numerous deaths, especially in Egypt. When it rises facing the west it prophesies thunderbolts for the land and death for the cattle, and the burnings will be hard to bear.

The Comet. This is the star of Jupiter and is so prominent that all other portent-bearing stars are called comets after it. When it points a bright, silvery tail to the east and Jupiter is in Cancer or Scorpio or Pisces, it prophesies great good fortune for the Persians: they will rise and pour into Roman territory, seizing cities and forts, taking an untold multitude of captives and great wealth, and returning victorious to their own land without anyone daring to oppose them. When this comet rises with face averted, it brings failure to those from whom it is averted. If it faces the south, the Nile will bestow its gifts unstintingly. There will be peace and plenty in Egypt, concord and unalloyed ease for all. If turning its back on the east it faces the west, the Romans will enjoy boundless good fortune: they will wage successful war against the Persians, the king of the Persians himself will be killed and an abundance of all their foods will come into the possession of the Roman state; spectacles without end and lavish donatives and elaborate chariot races will be carried out for the gratification of the people; in a word, there will be general rejoicing in the state. If it faces the North turning its back on the south, the peoples of Europe will ravage Libya under the rules of war and likewise the peoples of the northeast against those of the southwest; but the very worst will be visited upon the peoples in the southeast and Egypt by the very soldiers settled there to render aid and guard the borders.

The comet Quoit. So called, it is said, from its shape, and because it is circular it is not clear in which direction it faces. Its rising bodes ill for all in common. And it depends on none of the planets but shines with the reflected light of the sun. Therefore it threatens general disturbances, wars from the North, destruction of great figures and success of the mean and ignoble, and it brings danger to the leading classes. The armies of the Romans will be defeated everywhere, coming close to total destruction. (Taken from Nechepso-Petosiris frag. 9, trans. N. Lewis 1976: 145–47.)

BIBLIOGRAPHY

There are three frequent abbreviations that recur in the course of this book: LCL, *OTP,* and CCAG. These abbreviations refer to collections of ancient writings of fundamental value for a work of this sort. The first is LCL; it refers to volumes in a large collection of Greek and Latin classical authors with English translation called the Loeb Classical Library, now published at Harvard University. The second is *OTP,* standing for *Old Testament Pseudepigrapha;* this is a two-volume collection of late Israelite writings edited by James Charlesworth and published by Doubleday in 1983 and 1985. Finally there is CCAG, which stands for the Latin equivalent of *Catalogue of Codices of Greek Astrologers,* a representative sampling of astronomic documents collected by a team of scholars formed in 1898 and closed in 1953.

Ancient Sources

Abu Ma`shar
    1968   *Albumasaris De Revolutionibus Nativitatum.* Ed. David
                         Pingree. Bibliotheca scriptorum Graecorum et Romanorum
                         Teubneriana. Leipzig: Teubner Verlag.
Ammianus Marcellinus
    1935–39   *History.* Trans. John C. Rolfe. 3 vols. Loeb Classical Library.
                         Cambridge: Harvard Univ. Press.
Apuleius
    1989   *Metamorphoses.* Trans. J. Arthur Hanson. 2 vols. Loeb
                         Classical Library. Cambridge: Harvard Univ. Press.

Aratus
1955 [1921]   In *Callimachus, Lycophron and Aratus.* Trans. G. R. Mair.
               Loeb Classical Library. Cambridge: Harvard Univ. Press.
Aristotle
1957 [1936]   *On Prophecy in Sleep.* In *Aristotle: On the Soul, The Parva
               Naturalia, On Breath.* Trans. S. W. Hett. Loeb Classical
               Library. Cambridge: Harvard Univ. Press.
Artemidorus
1975   *The Interpretation of Dreams (Oneirocritica).* Trans. Robert
               J. White. Park Ridge, N.J.: Noyes.
Aulus Gellius
1946 [1927]   *Attic Nights.* Trans. John C. Rolfe. Loeb Classical Library.
               Cambridge: Harvard Univ. Press.
Aune, David E., trans.
1983   *Potter's Oracle.* In *Prophecy in Early Christianity and the
               Ancient Mediterranean World.* Pages 76–77. Grand Rapids:
               Eerdmans.
Autolycos of Pitane
1979   *Peri kinoumenes sphairas. La sphère en mouvement; Levers
               et couchers héliaques.* Ed. and trans. Germaine Aujac,
               Jean-Pierre Brunet, and Robert Nadal. Paris: Belles Lettres.
Avienus
1981   *Les Phénomènes d'Aratos.* Ed. and trans. Jean Soubiran.
               Paris: Belles Lettres.
Betz, Hans Dieter, ed.
1986   *The Greek Magical Papyri in Translation including the
               Demotic Spells.* Chicago: Univ. of Chicago Press.
Celsus
1989   *Contro i cristiani Against the Christians.* Trans. S. Rizzo.
               Biblioteca universale Rizzoli. Milan: Rizzoli.
Charlesworth, James H., ed.
1983–85   *Old Testament Pseudepigrapha.* 2 vols. Garden City:
               Doubleday.
Cicero
1928–   *Works.* Various trans. 27 vols. Loeb Classical Library.
               Cambridge: Harvard Univ. Press.
Clement of Alexandria
1981   *Stromate V.* Ed. and trans. Alain Le Boulluec. Tome II.
               Sources Chrétiennes 279. Paris: Cerf.
Cleomedes
1891   *De motu circulari corporum caelestium.* Ed. Herman Ziegler.
               Leipzig: Teubner.
De Moor, Johannes C.
1987   *An Anthology of Religious Texts from Ugarit.* Religious
               Texts Translation Series NISABA 16. Leiden: E. J. Brill.
Dio Cassius
1914–27   *Roman History.* Trans. Earnest Cary. 9 vols. Loeb Classical
               Library. Cambridge: Harvard Univ. Press.

Diodorus of Sicily
1933–   *Library of History*. Trans. C. H. Oldfather, et al. 12 vols.
             Loeb Classical Library. Cambridge: Harvard Univ. Press.
Diogenes Laertius
1931–38   *Lives of Eminent Philosophers*. Trans. R. D. Hicks. 2 vols.
             Loeb Classical Library. Cambridge: Harvard Univ. Press.
Dorotheus Sidonius
1976   *Carmen astrologicum*. Ed. and trans. David Pingree. Leipzig:
             Teubner.
Epictetus
1925   *The Discourses*. Trans. W. A. Oldfather. Loeb Classical
             Library. Cambridge: Harvard Univ. Press.
Epiphanius
1863   *Panarion sive arcula adversus 80 haereses Bk I-II. Patrologia
             Graeca*. Ed. J. P. Migne. Vol. 41. Pages 174–1290. Paris:
             Migne.
Firmicus Maternus
1975   *Ancient Astrology, Theory and Practice Matheseos Libri
             VIII*. Trans. Jean Rhys Bram. Park Ridge, N.J.: Noyes.
García Martínez, Florentino
1994   *The Dead Sea Scrolls Translated: The Qumran Texts in
             English*. Trans. Wilfred G. E. Watson. Leiden: Brill.
Geminos
1975   *Introduction aux Phénomènes*. Ed. and trans. Germaine
             Aujac. Paris: Belles Lettres.
Hackforth, R., trans.
1952   *Plato's Phaedrus*. Cambridge: Cambridge Univ. Press.
Hennecke, Edgar, Wilhelm Schneemelcher, and R. McL. Wilson
1992   *New Testament Apocrypha*. 2 vols. Louisville:
             Westminster/John Knox.
Hermes, Wilhelm Gundel
1936b.   *Neue astrologische Texte des Hermes Trismegistos: Funde
             und Forschungen auf dem Gebiet der antiken Astronomie
             und Astrologie*. Abhandlungen der Bayerischen Akademie
             der Wissenschaft, Philosophisch-historische Abteilung,
             N.F. 12. Munich: Bayerische Akademie der
             Wissenschaften.
Herodotus
1920–21   *The Histories*. Trans. A. D. Godley. Loeb Classical Library.
             New York: G. P. Putnam's Sons.
Hippolytus
1957   *Refutation of All Heresies*. In *The Ante-Nicene Fathers*. Ed.
             Alexander Roberts and James Donaldson. Vol. 5. Grand
             Rapids: Eerdmans, repr.
Horsley, Gregory H. R.
1982   *New Documents Illustrating Early Christianity: A Review of
             the Greek Inscriptions and Papyri Published in 1977*. North
             Ryde, NSW: Macquarie Univ.

Horsley, Gregory H. R., and Stephen Llewelyn, eds.
1981–.   *New Documents Illustrating Early Christianity: A Review of*
                 the Greek Inscriptions and Papyri Published in 1976. 6 vols.
                 North Ryde, NSW: Macquarrie Univ.

Hyginus
1960   *The Myths of Hyginus.* Trans. Mary Grant. University of
                 Kansas Humanistic Studies 34. Lawrence: Univ. of Kansas
                 Press.

Hyginus
1983   *L'Astronomie.* Ed. and trans. André Le Boeuffle. Paris:
                 Belles Lettres.

Isidore of Seville
1982–83   *Libri XX etymologiarum. San Isidro de Sevilla Etimologías.*
                 Ed. and trans. Jose Oroz Reta and Manuel A. Marcos
                 Casquero. 2 vols. Madrid: Biblioteca de Autores Cristianos.

Jacoby, Felix, cited from
1958   Berossos of Babylon. *Die Fragmente der griechischen*
                 Historiker, Teil 3: Geschichte von Städten und Völkern
                 Horographie und Ethnographie, C: Autoren über einzelne
                 Länder Nr. 608a–856 Erster Band: Aegypten– Geten Nr.
                 608a–708. Pages 364–95. Leiden: Brill.

Joannes Laurentius Lydus
1897   *Liber de ostentis et calendaria graeca omnia.* Ed. Kurt
                 Wachsmuth. Leipzig: Teubner.

Joannes Laurentius Lydus
1967 [1898]   *Liber de mensibus.* Ed. Richard Wuensch. Stuttgart: Teubner.

Josephus
1926–65   *The Works.* Trans. H. St. John Thackeray. 10 vols. Loeb
                 Classical Library. Cambridge: Harvard Univ. Press.

Koenen, Ludwig
1968   *Potter's Oracle.* "Die Prophezeiungen des 'Töpfers,' "
                 Zeitschrift für Papyrologie und Epigraphik 2:178–209.

Kyranides, Louis Delatte
1942   *Textes Latins et vieux français relatifs aux Cyranides.*
                 Bibliothèque de la Faculté de Philosophie et Lettres de
                 l'Université de Liège, 93. Liège and Paris: E. Droz.

Llewelyn, S. R., with R. A. Kearsley
1992   *New Documents Illustrating Early Christianity: A Review of*
                 the Greek Inscriptions and Papyri Published in 1980–81.
                 North Ryde, NSW: Macquarrie Univ.

Lucian
1913–67.   *The Works.* Trans. A. M. Harmon. 8 vols. Loeb Classical
                 Library. New York: Macmillan

Lycophron
1955 [1921]   In *Callimachus, Lycophron and Aratus.* Trans. A. W. Mair.
                 Loeb Classical Library. Cambridge: Harvard Univ. Press.

Macrobius
1969   *The Saturnalia.* Trans. Percival Vaughn Davies. New York:
                 Columbia Univ. Press.

Malina, Bruce J., trans.
1968   *Targum Joshua. The Palestinian Manna Tradition.* Arbeiten
                zur Geschichte des späteren Judentums und des
                Urchristentums VII. Leiden: Brill.
Manilius
1977   *Astronomica.* Trans. G. P. Goold. Loeb Classical Library.
                Cambridge: Harvard Univ. Press.
Martianus Capella
1925   *Opera.* Ed. Adolfus Dick. Leipzig: Teubner.
Milik, Józef T., with Matthew Black
1976   *The Books of Enoch: Aramaic Fragments of Qumran Cave 4.*
                Oxford: Clarendon.
Neugebauer, Otto with Matthew Black
1981   *The "Astronomical" Chapters of the Ethiopic Book of Enoch
                72 to 82.* Copenhagen: Munksgaard.
Neugebauer, Otto, and H. B. Van Hoesen
1959   *Greek Horoscopes.* Transactions of the American
                Philosophical Society. Philadelphia: American Philosophical
                Society.
Nock, Arthur D., and A. J. Festugière, eds. and trans.
1946   *Corpus Hermeticum.* 4 vols. Collection des Universités de
                France. Paris: Les Belles Lettres.
Nonnos
1940–42   *Dionysiaca.* Trans. W. H. D. Rouse. 3 vols. Loeb Classical
                Library. Cambridge: Harvard Univ. Press.
Ockley, Simon, trans., and A. S. Fulton, rev. and intro.
n.d.   Ibn Tufail, Abu Bakr. *The History of Hayy Ibn Yaqzan.* New
                York: Stokes.
Ovid
1916   *Metamorphoses.* Trans. F. J. Miller. 2 vols. Loeb Classical
                Library. Cambridge: Harvard Univ. Press.
Paton, W. R., trans.
1917   *The Greek Anthology: Book IX: The Declamatory and
                Descriptive Epigram.* Vol 3. Loeb Classical Library.
                Cambridge: Harvard Univ. Press.
Petosiris-Nechepso
1976   *The Interpretation of Dreams and Portents.* Trans. Napthali
                Lewis. Sarasota: Hakkert.
Philo of Alexandria
1929–62   *The Works.* Trans. F. H. Colson and G. H. Whitaker. 10 vols.
                Loeb Classical Library. New York: Putnam.
Philo of Byblos
1981   *The Phoenician History.* Ed. and trans. Harold W. Attridge
                and Robert A. Oden Jr. Catholic Biblical Quarterly
                Monography Series 9. Washington: Catholic Biblical
                Association of America.
Plato
1917–29   *The Works.* Various trans. 10 vols. Loeb Classical Library.
                New York: G. P. Putnam's Sons.

Plotinus
1966–88   *Enneads.* Trans A. H. Armstrong. 7 vols. Loeb Classical Library. Cambridge: Harvard Univ. Press.

Plutarch
1914–26   *Plutarch's Lives.* Trans. Bernadotte Perrin. 11 vols. Loeb Classical Library. Cambridge: Harvard. Univ. Press.

Plutarch
1927–1969   *Moralia.* Various trans. 16 vols. Loeb Classical Library. Cambridge: Harvard Univ. Press.

Porphyry
1958   *Porfirio: Lettera ad Anebo (Letter to Anebo).* Ed. and trans. A. R. Sodano. Naples: L'Arte tipografica.

Ptolemy
1940   *Tetrabiblos.* Trans. F. E. Robbins. Loeb Classical Library. Cambridge: Harvard Univ. Press.

Ptolemy
1984   *Almagest.* Ed. and trans. G. J. Toomer. New York: Springer.

Seneca
1917   *Tragedies.* Trans. F. J. Miller. 2 vols. Loeb Classical Library. Cambridge: Harvard Univ. Press.

Seneca
1971   *Quaestiones Naturales.* Trans. T. H. Corcoran. 2 vols. Loeb Classical Library. Cambridge: Harvard Univ. Press.

Seutonius
1914   *Lives.* Trans. J. C. Rolfe. 2 vols. Loeb Classical Library. Cambridge: Harvard Univ. Press.

Sextus Empiricus
1933–49   *The Works.* Trans. R. G. Bury. 4 vols. Loeb Classical Library. Cambridge: Harvard Univ. Press.

Tacitus
1925   *The Histories.* and *The Annals.* Trans. Clifford H. Moore and John Jackson. 4 vols. Loeb Classical Library. Cambridge: Harvard Univ. Press.

Tertullian
1957   *Against Marcion.* In *The Ante-Nicene Fathers.* Ed. A. Roberts and J. Donaldson. Vol. 3. Grand Rapids: Wm. B. Eerdmans.

Theon of Smyrna
1878   *Expositio Rerum Mathematicarum ad Legendum Platonem Utilium.* Ed. Eduard Hiller. Leipzig: Teubner.

Theophrastus
1916   *On Weather Signs.* In *Theophrastus: Enquiry into Plants and Minor Works.* Trans. Arthur Hort. Pages 390–433. Vol 2. Loeb Classical Library. Cambridge: Harvard Univ. Press.

Various eds.
1895–1953   *Catalogus Codicum Astrologorum Graecorum.* 12 vol. Vol. 5 has 4 parts, 8 has four parts, 9 has two parts, 11 has two parts, the rest are single. Brussels: Lamertin.

Varro
1938   *On the Latin Language.* Trans. Roland G. Kent. Vol. 1. Loeb
               Classical Library. Cambridge: Harvard Univ. Press.
Vermes, Geza
1987   *The Dead Sea Scrolls in English.* 3d ed. Sheffield: JSOT Press.
Vettius Valens
1908   *Anthologiarum Libri.* Ed. Wilhelm Kroll. Berlin: Weidmann.
Virgil
1950 [1935]   *Aeneid I-VI.* In *Virgil.* Trans. H. Rustin Fairclough. 2 vols.
               Cambridge: Harvard Univ. Press.
Winter, John Garrett
1936   *Papyri in the University of Michigan Collection.* University of
               Michigan Studies. Humanistic Series 40. Ann Arbor: Univ.
               of Michigan Press.

Modern Studies

Abry, Josèphe-Henriette
1983   "L'astrologie à Rome: les Astronomiques de Manilius."
               Pallas 30: 49–62.
Allen, Richard Hinckley.
1963 [1899]   *Star Names: Their Lore and Meaning.* New York: Dover.
Aujac, Germaine
1966   *Strabon et la science de son temps.* Paris: Belles Lettres.
1980   "Le zodiaque dans l'astronomie grecque." *Revue d'histoire
               des sciences* 33: 3–32.
1981   "Les Représentations de l'éspace géographique ou
               cosmologique dans l'antiquité." *Pallas* 28: 3–14.
Aulén, Gustaf
1969   *Christus Victor: An Historical Study of the Three Main Types
               of the Idea of Atonement.* Trans. by A. G. Herbert. New
               York: Macmillan.
Balfour, Edward
1976   "Graha." *Encyclopaedia Asiatica.* 3: 1243. New Delhi: Cosmo.
Barrett, C. K.
1961   *The New Testament Background: Selected Documents.* New
               York: Harper Torchbooks.
Barrett, C. K., A. H. B. Logan, and A. J. M. Wedderburn, eds.
1983   "Gnosis and the Apocalypse of John." *The New Testament
               and Gnosis: Essays in Honour of Robert McL. Wilson.* Pages
               125–37. Edinburgh: T. & T. Clark.
Barton, Tamsyn
1994   *Ancient Astrology.* London: Routledge.
Battisti, Eugenio, et al.
1960   "Astronomy and Astrology." *Encyclopedia of World Art.* 2:
               29–88. New York: McGraw-Hill.

Beck, Roger
1987   "The Anabibazontes in the Manichaean Kephalaia."
              Zeitschrift für Papyrologie und Epigraphik 69: 193–96.
Beck, Roger
1988   *Planetary Gods and Planetary Orders in the Mysteries of
              Mithras.* Etudes preliminaires aux religions orientales dans
              l'Empire romain 109. New York: Brill.
Berger, Klaus
1976   *Die griechische Daniel-Diegese: Eine altkirchliche
              Apokalypse.* Studia Post-Biblica 27. Leiden: Brill.
Berthier, André, and René Charlier
1955   *Le Sanctuaire punique d'el-Hofra à Constantine.* Paris: Arts
              et Métiers Graphiques.
Bezold, Carl, and Franz Boll
1911   *Reflexe astrologischer Keilinschriften bei griechischen
              Schriftstellern.* Sitzungsberichte der Heidelberger Akademie
              der Wissenschaft, Philosophisch-historische Klasse 7.
              Heidelberg: Carl Winter.
Bezold, Carl, with August Kopff and Franz Boll
1913   *Zenit- und Aequatorialgestirne zum babylonischen
              Fixsternhimmel.* Sitzungsberichte der Heidelberger
              Akademie der Wissenschaft, Philosophisch-historische Klasse
              11. Heidelberg: Carl Winter.
Black, Jeremy, and Anthony Green
1992   *Gods, Demons and Symbols of Ancient Mesopotamia: An
              Illustrated Dictionary.* Illus. Tessa Richards. Austin: Univ. of
              Texas Press.
Boismard, M. E., A. Robert, and A. Feuillet, eds. trans. P. W. Skehan et al.
1965   "The Apocalypse." *Introduction to the New Testament.* Pages
              691–722. New York: Desclee.
Boll, Franz
1967 [1903]
              *Sphaera: Neue griechische Texte und Untersuchungen zur
              Geschichte der Sternbilder.* Hildesheim: Georg Olms.
1967 [1914]   *Aus der Offenbarung Johannis: Hellenistische Studien zum
              Weltbild der Apokalypse.* Amsterdam: Hakkert.
1916   "Das Eingangsstück der Ps.-Klementinen." *Zeitschrift für der
              neutestamentlichen Wissenschaft* 17: 139–48.
(1917/18)   "Der Stern der Weisen." *Zeitschrift für der
              neutestamentlichen Wissenschaft* 18: 40–48.
1919   *Sternglaube und Sterndeutung: Die Geschichte und das Wesen
              der Astrologie.* 2nd ed. Leipzig/Berlin: Teubner.
1977 [n.d.]   *Storia del Astrologia.* Bari: Laterze.
Bouché-Leclerq, August
1979   *L'Astrologie grecque.* Aalen: Scientia Verlag.
Bourguignon, Erika
1979   *Psychological Anthropology: An Introduction to Human
              Nature and Cultural Differences.* New York: Holt, Reinhart
              & Winston.

Bousset, Wilhelm
1970   *Kyrios Christos: A History of the Belief in Christ from the*
            Beginning of Christianity to Irenaeus. Trans. John E. Steely.
            Nashville: Abingdon.
Brown, Robert, Jr.
1899–1900   *Researches into the Origin of the Primitive Constellations of*
            the Greeks, Phoenicians and Babylonians. 2 Vols. Oxford:
            Williams and Norgate.
Buxton, Richard
1992   "Imaginary Greek Mountains." *Journal of Hellenic Studies*
            112: 1–15.
Carmignac, Jean
1965   "Les Horoscopes de Qumrân." *Revue de Qumran* 5: 199–217.
1979   *Le Mirage de l'Eschatologie: Royauté, Règne et Royaume de*
            Dieu sans Eschatologie. Paris: Letouzey et Ané.
Carroll, Scott
1989   "A Preliminary Analysis of the *Epistle of Rehoboam.*"
            Journal for the Study of the Pseudepigrapha 4: 91–103.
Chapman, Dean W.
1995   "Locating the Gospel of Mark: A Model of Agrarian
            Geography." *Biblical Theology Bulletin* 25: 24–36.
Charles, R. H.
1920   *An Exegetical and Criticial Commentary on the Book of*
            Revelation. 2 vols. Edinburgh: Clark.
Charlesworth, James H.
1987   "Jewish Interest in Astrology during the Hellenistic and
            Roman Period." *Aufstieg und Niedergang der römischen Welt*
            II,20.2, 926–50.
Collins, John J., ed.
1979   *Apocalypse: The Morphology of a Genre. Semeia 14.*
            Missoula: Society of Biblical Literature.
1984   *Daniel: With an Introduction to Apocalyptic Literature.* The
            Forms of the Old Testament Literature 20. Grand Rapids:
            Eerdmans.
Collon, Dominique
1987   *First Impressions: Cylinder Seals in the Ancient Near East.*
            Chicago: Univ. of Chicago Press.
Cramer, Frederic H.
1954   *Astrology in Roman Law and Politics.* Memoirs of the
            American Philosophical Society 37. Philadelphia: American
            Philosophical Society.
Critchlow, Keith
1976   *Islamic Patterns: An Analytical and Cosmological Approach.*
            New York: Thames & Hudson.
Culianu, I. P.
1979   "Démonisation du Cosmos et dualisme gnostique." *Revue*
            Historique des Religions 196: 3–40.
1981   "Ordine et disordine delle sfere: Macrobius. In S. Scip.
            1,12,12–13." *Aevum* 55: 96–110.

1982   "L'Ascension de l'âme' dans les mystères et hors des mystères."
                 *Soteriologia dei Culti orientali nell'imperio Romano: Atti del
                 Colloquio internazionale . . . Roma 24–28 sett. 1979.* Ed. U. Bi-
                 anchi and M. J. Vermaseren. Pages 276–302. Leiden: Brill.

Cumont, Franz
1960 [1912]   *Astrology and Religion Among the Greeks and the Romans.*
                 New York: Dover Publications.
1919   "Zodiacus." In *Dictionnaire des antiquités grecques et
                 romaines V.* Ed. C. Darembert and E. Saglio. Pages 1046–62.
                 Paris: Hachette.

Dahl, Nils A.
1975   "Cosmic Dimensions and Religion Knowledge (Eph 3: 18)."
                 Jesus und Paulus: Festschrift Werner G. Kümmel. Ed. E. E.
                 Ellis and E. Grässer. Pages 57–75. Gottingen: Vandenhoeck
                 & Ruprecht.

Daniélou, Jean
1964   *The Theology of Jewish Christianity.* Chicago: Regnery.

Davidson, Maxwell J.
1992   *Angels at Qumran: A Comparative Study of 1 Enoch 1–36,
                 72–108 and Sectarian Writings from Qumran.* Journal for the
                 Study of the Pseudepigrapha, Supplement Series 11.
                 Sheffield: Academic.

De Mailly Nesle, Solange
1987   *Die Astrologie: Von der Sterndeutung zum Horoskop.* Trans.
                 Antoinette Gittinger. Munich: Calwey.

De Martino, Ernesto
1977   *La fine del mondo: contributo all'analisi delle apocalissi
                 culturali.* Ed. Clara Gallini. Turin: G. Enaudi.

De Saussure, Léopold
1924   "La Série septénaire, cosmologique et planétaire." *Journal
                 Asiatique* 204: 333–70.

Delcor, M.
1966   "Recherches sur un horoscope en langue hébraique
                 provenant de Qumrân." *Revue de Qumran* 5: 521–42.

Del Corno, D.
1978   "I sogni e la loro interpretaztione nell'età dell'imperio."
                 Aufstieg und Niedergang der römischen Welt II, 16.2, 1605–18.

Derrett, J. Duncan M.
1988   "The Son of Man Standing." *Bibbia e Oriente* 30: 71–84.

Dilke, A. O. W.
1987   "Cartography in the Ancient World: A Conclusion." *The
                 History of Cartography. Vol. One: Cartography in
                 Prehistoric, Ancient and Medieval Europe and the
                 Mediterranean.* Ed. J. B. Harley and David Woodward.
                 Pages 276–79. Chicago: Univ. of Chicago Press.

Dodd, Charles H.
1957   "The Appearances of the Risen Christ: An Essay in
                 Form-Criticism of the Gospels." *Studies in the Gospels.* Ed.
                 D. E. Nineham. Oxford: Oxford Univ. Press.

Draguns, Juris G.
1988   "Personality and Culture: Are They Relevant for the
               Enhancement of Quality of Mental Life?" *Health and*
               Cross-Cultural Psychology: Toward Applications. Ed. P. R.
               Dasen, J. W. Berry, and N. Sartorius. Pages 141–61.
               Newbury Park *et alibi*: Sage Publications.
Dupuis, Charles F.
1984 [1872]   *The Origin of All Religious Worship.* Intro. R. D.
               Richardson. New York: Garland [Trans. of *Origine de tous*
               les cultes. 1798, New Orleans].
Edgeworth, Robert J.
1992   *The Colors of the Aeneid.* American Univ. Studies Series
               XVII Classical Languages and Literature 12. New York:
               Peter Lang.
Eggermont, P. H. L.
1973   "The Proportions of Anaximander's Celestial Globe and the
               Gold-Silver Ratio of Croesus' Coinage." *Symbolae Biblicae*
               et Mesopotamicae Francisco Mario Theodoro de Liagre Böhl
               Dedicatae. Studia Francisci Scholten memoriae dicta. Vol. 4.
               Ed. M. A. Beek, A. A. Kaapman, C. Nijland and J.
               Ryckmans. Pages 118–28. Leiden: Brill.
Elliott, John H.
1991   *A Home for the Homeless: A Sociological Exegesis of I Peter,*
               Its Situation and Strategy. 2nd rev. ed. Minneapolis:
               Augsburg/Fortress.
1993   "Sorcery and Magic in the Revelation of John." *Listening* 28:
               261–76.
Fox, Robin Lane
1987   *Pagans and Christians.* New York: Knopf.
Festugière, André-J.
1939   "L'Expérience due médecin Thessalos." *Revue Biblique* 48:
               45–77.
1950   *La Révélation d'Hermès Trismégiste: Vol. I. L'Astrologie de*
               les sciences occultes. Paris: Gabalda.
Flamant, Jacques
1983   "Sont-ils bons? Sont-ils mauvais?" *Pallas* 30: 95–106.
Florisoone, A.
1950   "Les origines chaldéennes du zodiaque." *Ciel et Terre* 66:
               256–68.
1951   "Astres et constellations des Babyloniens." *Ciel et Terre* 67:
               153–69.
Ford, Josephine Massyngberde
1975   *Revelation.* The Anchor Bible. Garden City: Doubleday.
Freundorfer, Joseph
1929   *Die Apokalypse des Apostels Johannes und die hellenistische*
               Kosmologie und Astrologie. Freiburg im Breisgau: Herder.
Gamson, William A.
1992   "The Social Psychology of Collective Action." In *Frontiers in*
               Social Movement Theory. Ed. Aldon D. Morris and Carol

McClurg Mueller. Pages 53–76. New Haven and London: Yale Univ. Press.

García Martínez, Florentino, and E. J. C. Tigchelaar
1989   "1 Enoch and the Figure of Enoch: A Bibliography of Studies 1970–88." *Revue de Qumran* 14: 149–74.

Goodenough, Erwin R.
1958   *Jewish Symbols in the Greco-Roman Period.* Vol. 8. New York: Pantheon.

Goodman, Felicitas
1990   *Where the Spirits Ride the Wind: Trance Journeys and Other Ecstatic Experiences.* Bloomington: Indiana Univ. Press.

Grabbe, Lester L.
1989   "The Social Setting of Early Jewish Apocalypticism." *Journal for the Study of the Pseudepigrapha* 4: 27–47.

Grelot, Pierre
1958   "La Géographie mythique d'Hénoch et ses sources orientales." *Revue Biblique* 65: 33–69.

Grössing, Helmuth
1990   "Weltmodell im antiken Griechenland." In *Mensch und Kosmos: Oberösterreichische Landesausstellung 1990.* Ed. Wilfried Seipel. Pages 61–66. Band I. Linz: Oberösterreichisches Landesmuseum.

Gry, Leon
1939   "La Date de la fin des temps selons les révélations ou calculs de Pseudo-Philon et de Baruch apocalypse syriaque." *Revue Biblique* 48: 337–56.

Gundel, Wilhelm
1933   *Sternglaube, Sternreligion und Sternorakel.* Leipzig: Quelle & Meyer.
1936a   *Dekane und Dekansternbilder: Ein Beitrag zur Geschichte der Sternbilder der Kulturvölker, mit einer Üntersuchung über die Ägyptischen Sternbilder und Gottheiten der Dekane von S. Schott.* Studien der Bibliothek Warburg, XIX Gluckstadt and Hamburg: J. J. Augustin.
1950   "Astrologie." In *Reallexikon für Antike und Christentum* I. Pages 817–31. Stuttgart: Hiersmann.
            "Astronomie." In *Reallexikon für Antike und Christentum* I. Pages 831–36. Stuttgart: Hiersmann.

Hachlili, Rachel
1977   "The Zodiac in Ancient Jewish Art: Representation and Significance." *Bulletin of the American Schools of Oriental Research* 288: 61–77.

Handy, Lowell K.
1994   *Among the Host of Heaven: The Syro-Palestinian Pantheon as Bureacracy.* Winona Lake, Ind.: Eisenbrauns.

Hanson, John S.
1980   "Dreams and Visions in the Graeco-Roman World and Early Christianity." *Aufstieg und Niedergang der römischen Welt* II,23.2, 1395–427.

Hanson, K. C.
1993   "Blood and Purity in Leviticus and Revelation." *Listening*
                28: 215–30.
Harley, J. B., and David Woodward, eds.
1987   "Greek Cartography in the Early Roman World. *The History
                of Cartography. Vol. One: Cartography in Prehistoric,
                Ancient and Medieval Europe and the Mediterranean.*
                Chicago: Univ. of Chicago Press. Pages 161–76.
                "The Growth of Empirical Cartography in Hellenistic
                Greece." *The History of Cartography. Vol. One: Cartography
                in Prehistoric, Ancient and Medieval Europe and the
                Mediterranean.* Pages 148–60. Chicago: Univ. of Chicago
                Press.
Hengel, Martin
1974   *Judaism and Hellenism: Studies in Their Encounter in
                Palestine during the Early Hellenistic Period.* 2 vols. Trans.
                John Bowden. Philadelphia: Fortress.
Hill, Charles E.
1992   *Regnum Caelorum: Patterns of Future Hope in Early
                Christianity.* Oxford: Clarendon.
Hill, D. E.
1973   "The Thessalian Trick." *Rheinisches Museum für Philologie*
                116: 221–38.
Hübner, Wolfgang
1983   "L'Astrologie dans l'Antiquité." *Pallas* 30: 1–24.
1989   *Die Begriffe "Astrologie" und "Astronomie" in der Antike:
                Wortgeschichte und Wissenschaftssystematik mit einer
                Hypothese zum Terminus "Quadrivium."* Akademie der
                Wissenschaften und der Literatur, Mainz. Stuttgart: Steiner
                Verlag.
Hyland, Ann
1990   *Equus: The Horse in the Roman World.* New Haven: Yale
                Univ. Press.
Jacobsen, Thorkild
1976   *The Treasures of Darkness: A History of Mesopotamian
                Religion.* New Haven: Yale Univ. Press.
Jastrow, Morris
1971   *The Civilization of Babylonia and Assyria: Its Remains,
                Language, History, Religion, Commerce, Law, Art, and
                Literature.* New York: B. Blom.
Jeremias, Joachim
1969   *Jerusalem in the Time of Jesus.* Trans. by F. H. and C. H.
                Cave. Philadelphia: Fortress.
Johnston, Sarah Iles
1992   "Riders in the Sky: Cavalier Gods and Theurgic Salvation in
                the Second Century A.D." *Classical Philology* 87: 303–21.
Jones, C. P.
1987   "Stigma: Tattooing and Branding in Graeco-Roman
                Antiquity." *Journal of Roman Studies* 77: 139–55.

Kahn, Charles H.
1960   *Anaximander and the Origins of Greek Cosmology.* New
            York: Columbia Univ. Press.
1979   *The Art and Thought of Heraclitus: An Edition of the
            Fragments with Translation and Commentary.* Cambridge:
            Cambridge Univ. Press.
Kant, Laurence H.
1987   "Jewish Inscriptions in Greek and Latin." *Aufstieg und
            Niedergang der römischen Welt* II, 20, 2, 617–713.
Krafft, Fritz
1990   "Des Menschen Stellung im Universum." In *Mensch und
            Kosmos: Oberösterreichische Landesausstellung 1990.* Ed.
            Wilfried Seipel. Pages 361–76. Band I. Linz:
            Oberösterreichisches Landesmuseum.
Kretschmar, Georg
1985   *Die Offenbarung des Johannes: Die Geschichte ihrer
            Auslegung im 1. Jahrtausend.* Calwer Theologische
            Monographien 9. Stuttgart: Calwer.
Kunitzsch, Paul
1989   *The Arabs and the Stars: Texts and Traditions on the Fixed
            Stars and their Influence in Medieval Europe.* Northampton:
            Variorum.
Kvanvig, Helge S.
1988   *Roots of Apocalyptic: The Mesopotamian Background of the
            Enoch Figure and of the Son of Man.* Wissenschafliche
            Monographien zum alten und neuen Testament 61.
            Neukirchen-Vluyn: Neukirchen.
1989   "The Relevance of the Biblical Visions of the End Time:
            Hermeneutical Guidelines to the Apocalyptic Literature."
            Horizons of Biblical Theology 11: 35–58.
Landes, Richard
1988   "Lest the Millenium Be Fulfilled: Apocalyptic Expectations
            and the Pattern of Western Chronography 100–800 CE." In
            The Use and Abuse of Eschatology in the Middle Ages. Ed.
            Werner Verbeke, Daniel Verhelst and Andries
            Welkenhuysen. Pages 137–211. Mediaevalia Lovaniensia
            I/15. Leuven: Leuven Univ. Press.
Lawlor, Robert and Deborah, trans.
1979   *Mathematics Useful for Understanding Plato.* San Diego:
            Wizard Bookshelf.
Le Boeuffle, André
1969   "Une vierge au caducée dans les illustrations de certain
            manuscrits latins astronomiques et astrologiques." *Revue de
            Philologie* 43: 254–57.
1977   *Les noms latins d'astres et de constellations.* Paris: Belles
            Lettres.
1987   *Astronomie, astrologie: Lexique latin.* Paris: Picard.
1989   "Le séjour celeste promis à Neron par Lucain *Bellum Civile*
            I, 53–59." *Bulletin de l'Association George Budé,* 165–71.

Le Déaut, Roger
    1963   *La Nuit Pascale: Essai sur la signification de la Pâque juive à
                    partir du Targum d'Exode XII 42.* Analecta Biblica 22.
                    Rome: Pontifical Biblical Institute.
Leclercq, Henri
    1924   "Agneau." *Dictionnaire d'archéologie chrétienne et de
                    liturgie,* I/1: 877–905. Ed. Fernand Cabrol and Henri
                    Leclercq. Paris: Letouzey et Ané.
Lehmann-Nitsche, Robert
    1934   "Der apokalyptische Drache: Eine astral-mythologische
                    Untersuchung über Apoc. John. 12." *Zeitschrift für
                    Ethnologie* 65: 193–230.
Lieberman, Saul
    1965   *Greek in Jewish Palestine.* 2nd ed. New York: Philipp Feldheim.
L'Orange, Hans Peter
    1982 [1947]
                    Apotheosis in Ancient Portraiture. New Rochelle: Caratzas
                    Brothers.
    1982 [1953]   *Studies on the Iconography of Cosmic Kingship in the
                    Ancient World.* New Rochelle: Caratzas Brothers.
MacMullen, Ramsey
    1971   "Social History in Astrology." *Ancient Society* 2: 105–16.
Malina, Bruce J.
    1986a   "The Received View and What It Cannot Do: III John and
                    Hospitality." In *Social-scientific Criticism of the New
                    Testament and Its Social World.* Ed. John H. Elliott. Semeia
                    35, 171–94.
    1986b   "Religion in the World of Paul: A Preliminary Sketch."
                    Biblical Theology Bulletin 16: 92–101.
    1989   "Christ and Time: Swiss or Mediterranean." *Catholic Biblical
                    Quarterly* 51: 1–31.
    1991   "Reading Theory Perspective: Reading Luke–Acts." *The
                    Social World of Luke–Acts: Models for Interpretation.* Ed.
                    Bruce J. Malina, and Jerome H. Neyrey. Pages 3–23.
                    Peabody, Mass.: Hendrickson.
    1993   "Apocalyptic and Territoriality." In *Early Christianity in
                    Context: Monuments and Documents. Essays in Honour of
                    Emmanuel Testa.* Ed. Frederic Manns and Eugenio Alliata.
                    Pages 369–80. Jerusalem: Franciscan Printing Press.
Martin, Jean-Pierre
    1983   "Néron et le pouvoir des astres." *Pallas* 30: 63–74.
McKay, John
    1973   *Religion in Judah under the Assyrians.* Studies in Biblical
                    Theology. 2nd Series 26. Naperville: Allenson.
Melbin, Murray
    1978   "Night as Frontier." *American Sociological Review* 43: 3–22.
Menninger, Karl
    1969   *Number Words and Number Symbols: A Cultural History of
                    Numbers.* Trans. Paul Broneer. Cambridge: M.I.T.

Merkelbach, R.
1991   "Zwei Beiträge zum Neuen Testament." *Rheinisches
            Museum für Philologie* 134: 346–51.
Meslin, Michel
1981   *L'uomo romano: uno studio di antropologia.* Milano: Oscar
            Studio Mondadori.
Milik, Józef T.
1958   "Hénoch au pays des aromates ch. xxvii à xxxii: Fragments
            araméens de la grotte 4 de Qumrân." *Revue Biblique* 65:
            70–77.
1959   *Ten Years of Discovery in the Wilderness of Judaea.* Studies
            in Biblical Theology. 1st Series 26. Naperville: Allenson.
Moore, Michael S.
1982   "Jesus Christ: 'Superstar' Revelation xxii 16b." *Novum
            Testamentum* 24: 82–91.
Neugebauer, Otto
1955   "The Egyptian Decans." In *Astronomy and History: Selected
            Essays.* Pages 205–9. New York: Springer [Vistas in
            Astronomy Vol. I. Ed. A. Beer. Pages 47–51. London:
            Pergamon.].
1975   "A Greek World Map." In *Astronomy and History: Selected
            Essays.* Pages 372–78. New York: Springer [*Hommages à
            Claire Préaux.* Pages 312–17. Brussels: Univ. of Bruselles.].
Nock, Arthur D.
1972   "Astrology and Cultural History." In *Essays on Religion and
            the Ancient World.* Vol. 1. Ed. Zeph Stewart. Pages 493–502.
            Cambridge: Harvard Univ. Press.
Noll, Rudolf
1980   *Das Inventar des Dolichenusheiligtums von Mauer an der Url
            Noricum.* 2 Teilen. Der römische Limes in Österreich XXX.
            Vienna: Österreichischen Akademie der Wissenschaft.
Oppenheim, A. Leo
1956   *The Interpretation of Dreams in the Ancient Near East.*
            Transactions of the American Philosophical Society 46/3.
            Philadelphia: The American Philosophical Society.
Oster, Richard
1982   "Numismatic Windows into the Social World of Early
            Christianity: A Methodological Inquiry." *Journal of Biblical
            Literature* 101: 195–223.
Pagels, Elaine H.
1978   "Visions, Appearances, and Apostolic Authority: Gnostic
            and Orthodox Traditions." In *Gnosis: Festschrift für Hans
            Jonas.* Ed. Barbara Aland. Pages 415–30. Goetttingen:
            Vandenhoeck & Ruprecht.
Parpola, Simo
1993   "The Assyrian Tree of Life: Tracing the Origins of Jewish
            Monotheism and Greek Philosophy." *Journal of Near
            Eastern Studies* 52: 161–208.

Pauly, A., G. Wissowa, and W. Kroll, eds.
1914   "Dekane." *Real-Encyclopädie der klassischen
            Altertums-wissenschaft.* Supplement Vol. VII, 116–24.

Pétrement, Simone
1990   *A Separate God: The Christian Origins of Gnosticism.* Trans.
            Carol Harrison. San Francisco: Harper.

Piaget, Jean
1979   *The Child's Conception of the World.* Trans. Joan and
            Andrew Tomlinson. Totowa, N. J.: Littlefield, Adams.

Piaget, Jean, and Barbel Inhelder
1967   *The Child's Conception of Space.* Trans. F. J. Langdon and
            J. L. Lunzer. New York: Norton.

Piaget, Jean, Barbel Inhelder, and Alina Szeminska
1960   *The Child's Conception of Geometry.* Trans. E. A. Lunzer.
            New York: Norton.

Pilch, John J.
1978   *What Are They Saying About the Book of Revelation.* New
            York: Paulist.
1992   "Lying and Deceit in the Letters to the Seven Churches:
            Perspectives from Cultural Anthropology." *Biblical Theology
            Bulletin* 22: 126–35.
1993   "Visions in Revelation and Alternate Consciousness: A Per-
            spective from Cultural Anthropology." *Listening* 28: 231–44.

Pingree, David et al.
1979   "Astrologie." *Theologische Realenzyklopädie.* 4:275–315.
            Eds. Gerhard Krause and Gerhard Müller. Berlin/New York:
            Walter de Gruyter.

Placanica, Augusto
1990   *Segni dei tempi: il modello apocalittico nella tradizione
            occidentale.* Venezia: Marsilio.

Prigent, Pierre
1990   *Le Judaisme et l'image.* Texte und Studien zum Antiken
            Judentum 24. Tübingen: Mohr.

Quispel, Gilles
1979   *The Secret Book of Revelation: The Last Book of the Bible.*
            New York: McGraw-Hill.

Reitzenstein, Richard
1978   *Hellenistic Mystery-Religions: Their Basic Ideas and
            Significance.* Trans. John E. Steely. Pittsburgh: Pickwick.

Riddle, John M.
1992   *Contraception and Abortion from the Ancient World to the
            Renaissance.* Cambridge: Harvard Univ. Press.

Riley, Mark
1987   "Theoretical and Practical Astrology: Ptolemy and His
            Colleagues." *Transactions of the American Philological
            Association* 117: 235–56.

Rinaldi, Giancarlo
1987   "Sognatori e visionari 'biblici' nei polemisti antichristiani."
            Augustianum 29: 7–30 (congress papers on the subject of

Sogni, visioni e profezie nell'antico cristianesimo. XVII
Incontro di studiosi dell' antichitá cristiana, Rome 1987).

Rivaud, Albert
1970   *Platon: Oeuvres Complètes.* Tome X: Timée — Critias. Paris:
            Belles Lettres.

Robin, Léon
1933   *Platon: Oeuvres Complètes.* Tome IV — 3e Partie: Phèdre.
            Paris: Belles Lettres.

Rochberg-Halton, Francesca
1987   "The Assumed 29th AHU Tablet of ENUMA ANU
            ENLIL." In *Language, Literature and History: Philological
            and Historial Studies presented to Erica Reiner.* Ed.
            Francesca Rochberg-Halton. Pages 327–50. New Haven:
            American Oriental Society.
1989   "Babylonian Horoscopes and their Sources." *Orientalia* 58:
            102–23.

Rohde, Erwin
1925   *Psyche: The Cult of Souls and Belief in Immortality among the
            Greeks.* Trans. by W. B. Hillis. New York: Harcourt, Brace.

Russell, Jeffrey B.
1991   *Inventing the Flat Earth: Columbus and Modern Historians.*
            New York: Praeger.

Sack, Robert D.
1986   *Human Territorialiaty: Its Theory and History.* Cambridge
            Studies in Historical Geography 7. Cambridge: Cambridge
            Univ. Press.

Saler, Benson
1977   "Supernatural as a Western Concept." *Ethos* 5: 31–53.

Saulnier, Christiane
1989   "Flavius Josèphe et la propagande flavienne." *Revue
            Biblique* 96: 545–62.

Savage-Smith, Emilie
1985   *Islamicate Celestial Globes: Their History, Construction, and
            Use, with a Chapter on Iconography by Andrea P. A. Belloli.*
            Smithsonian Studies in History and Technology 46.
            Washington: Smithsonian Institution.

Schilling, Robert
1979   "Genius et ange." In *Rites, cultes, dieux de Rome.* Pages
            415–43. Paris: Klincksieck.

Scott, Alan
1991   *Origen and the Life of the Stars: A History of an Idea.*
            Oxford: Clarendon.

Segal, Alan F.
1980   "Heavenly Ascent in Hellenistic Judaism, Early Christianity
            and their Environment." *Aufstieg und Niedergang der
            römischen Welt* II,23.2, 1334–94.

Seipel, Wilfried, ed.
1990   *Mensch und Kosmos: Oberösterreichische Landesausstellung
            1990.* 2 vols. Linz: Oberösterreichisches Landesmuseum.

Shulman, Sandra
    1978   *Geschichte der Astrologie von der Antike bis zur Gegenwart.*
                    Eltville am Rhein: Rheingauer Verlagsgesellschaft.
Smith, Jonathan Z.
    1977   "The Temple and the Magician." In *God's Christ and His
                    People: Studies in Honour of Nils Alstrup Dahl.* Ed. Jacob
                    Jervell and Wayne A. Meeks. Pages 233–47. Oslo:
                    Universitetsforlaget.
Smith, Morton
    1983   "On the History of Apokalypto and Apokalypsis." In
                    *Apocalypticism in the Mediterranean World and the Near
                    East.* Ed. David Hellholm. Pages 9–20. Tubingen: Mohr.
Stander, H. F.
    1989   "The Starhymn in the Epistle of Ignatius to the Ephesians
                    19: 2–3." *Vigiliae Christianae* 43: 209–14.
Stegemann, Victor
    1938   "Zu Kapitel 69 der Kephalaia des Mani." *Zeitschrift für die
                    neutestamentliche Wissenschaft* 37: 214–23.
    1989   "Fatum und Freiheit im Hellenismus und in der Spätantike."
                    Gymnasium 50: 165–91.
Stern, Henri
    1981   "Les calendriers romains illustré." *Aufstieg und Niedergang
                    der römischen Welt* II,12.2, 431–75.
Strobel, August
    1987   "Weltenjahr, grosse Konjunktion und Messiasstern. Ein
                    themageschichtlicher Überblick." *Aufstieg und Niedergang
                    der römischen Welt* II,20.2, 988–1188.
Suter, David
    1980   "Fallen Angel, Fallen Priest: The Problem of Family Purity
                    in I Enoch 6–16." *Hebrew Union College Annual* 50: 115–35.
Swerdlow, N. M.
    1991   "Review Article: On the Cosmical Mysteries of Mithras."
                    Classical Philology 86: 48–63.
Talmon, Y.
    1966   "Millenarian Movements." *Archives europeéns de sociologie*
                    7: 159–200.
Sills, David L., ed.
    1968   "Millenarism." *International Encyclopedia of the Social
                    Sciences.* Pages 349–62. New York: Macmillan.
Taub, Liba Chaia
    1993   *Ptolemy's Universe: The Natural Philosophical and Ethical
                    Foundations of Ptolemy's Astronomy.* Chicago: Open Court.
Thiele, Georg
    1898   *Antike Himmelsbilder: Mit Forschungen zu Hipparchos,
                    Aratos und seinen Fortsetzern und Beiträgen zur
                    Kunstgeschichte des Sternhimmels.* Berlin: Weidmann.
Thomas, Jöel
    1983   "Astrologie, Alchemie et Structures Ontologiques dans les
                    mystères de Mithra." *Pallas* 30: 75–94.

Trevett, Christine
    1989   "Apocalypse, Ignatius, Montanism: Seeking the Seeds."
                    Vigiliae Christianae 43: 313–38.
Ulansey, David
    1986   "Mithras and Perseus." *Helios* 13: 33–62.
    1987   "Mithraic Studies: A Paradigm Shift?" *Religious Studies
                    Review* 13: 104–10.
    1989   *The Origins of the Mithraic Mysteries: Cosmology and
                    Salvation in the Ancient World.* New York: Oxford Univ.
                    Press.
    Dec. 1989   "The Mithraic Mysteries." *Scientific American* 261: 130–35.
    1991   "The Heavenly Veil Torn: Mark's Cosmic *Inclusio.*" *Journal
                    of Biblical Literature* 110: 123–5.
Verbeke, Werner, Daniel Verhelst, and Andries Welkenhuysen, eds.
    1988   *The Use and Abuse of Eschatology in the Middle Ages.*
                    Mediaevalia Lovaniensia I/15. Leuven: Leuven Univ. Press.
Walker, Norman
    1960   "The Reckoning of Hours in the Fourth Gospel." *Novum
                    Testamentum* 4: 69–73.

Index of Modern Authors

INDEX OF ANCIENT SOURCES

Ancient Authors

Barnabas
12:10–11 82

Berossos of Babylon

Babyloniaka
6 181

Book of Decans
18

Book of Hermes
  Trismegistus
41, 10–11 239
60, 1 239

CCAG
II, 144 120
II, 145 120
II, 148 124
II, 151 125
III, 30 125
III, 31 123
V, 1, 176 123
V, 1, 177 124
V, 1, 242 125
V, 3, 97 122
VII, 87 43
VII, 104–105 128
VII, 132 124
VII, 136–137 122
VII, 140 145
VII, 165 125
VII, 166 124
VII, 167 38
VII, 169 122
VII, 170 122, 125
VII, 176 42
VII, 177–180 121
VII, 179 41, 136
VII, 183 123
VII, 183, 6 119
VII, 185 125
VII, 205 124
VII, 206 125
VII, 226 38
VII, 229 125
VIII, 2, 143ff. 141

VIII, 2, 157–158 224
VIII, 2, 159–165
  276–80
VIII, 3, 125 123
VIII, 3, 135 31
VIII, 3, 136 34
VIII, 3, 137 140
VIII, 4, 119 239

Celsus

Against the Christians
  33–34

Cicero

*On the Nature of the
  Gods*
2.13–15 116
2.53 250

The Republic
6.16, 29 130
6.17 118
6.18–19 104
6.24 100, 240–41

Clement of Alexandria

Protreptikos
5.65 209

Stromata
5.6.35, 5 92

Cleomedes

*On the Circular Motion
  of Celestial Bodies*
1.1, 3–4 83

Corpus Hermeticum

IX, 3 8

XXIV, 3 39

Asclepius
33 7

Poimandres
IV, 5 83

X, 25 83
XI, 19 83

Dio Cassius

Roman History
45.7, 1–2 115
53.27, 2–3 80
68.24–25 281–82
68.30, 1 208

Diodorus of Sicily

Library of History
1.27, 4–5 35
1.73, 4–5 43
2.29, 4 42
2.31, 4 93–94
5.46, 3 35
6.1, 6–7 34

Diogenes Laertius
6.102 241

Dorotheos of Sidon
  190
V, 43 230

Epictetus

Discourses
4.13.1 171

Epiphanius

Adversus haereses
1.1.16 242

Panarion
16.2.1 74, 101

Firmicus Maternus

Mathesis
3.1.17–18 102
4.22.1–20 269–71
6.2.1 99
6.2.3 99